CATALOGUE OF

SILVER

IN THE

GROSVENOR MUSEUM, CHESTER

CATALOGUE OF
SILVER
IN THE
GROSVENOR MUSEUM, CHESTER

PETER BOUGHTON

Published by Phillimore for Chester Museums
Supported by
The Pilgrim Trust
The Museums and Galleries Commission
The Jerwood Foundation
The Department for Culture, Media and Sport
Chester City Council
The Grosvenor Museum Society
The Monument Trust
The Goldsmiths' Company Charities

PHILLIMORE

2000

Published by
PHILLIMORE & CO. LTD.,
Shopwyke Manor Barn, Chichester, West Sussex

ISBN 1 86077 153 X

This book is dedicated with gratitude and respect to
CANON MAURICE RIDGWAY
the paramount scholar of Chester silver

Printed and bound in Great Britain by
BUTLER AND TANNER LTD.
London and Frome

CONTENTS

LIVERPOOL GOLDSMITHS

CHESHIRE CHURCH PLATE

APPENDIX

FOREWORD
by Sir Nicholas Goodison
Chairman of the National Art Collections Fund

One of the delights of travelling in the United Kingdom is discovering the many remarkable local museum collections throughout the regions. Many of them concentrate on showing local artefacts in the context of local history. Others are of truly national importance. Some hold suprising collections of works of art unconnected with their locality, the result often of an enlightened gift or bequest, often strengthened in later years by the collecting policies of committed curators. Best of all are those collections which have not only been carefully built up but have also been thoroughly researched and published so that we can all benefit from the museum's scholarship. The purpose of a museum is not only to preserve objects and to display them; it is also to teach. The visitor should leave excited by the discovery, pleased with the display, fired with the learning experience, and wanting to come back.

The collection of silver at the Grosvenor Museum in Chester has been carefully built up to illustrate the importance of a locally established industry. It also contains some fine examples of local church plate and of trophies for the Chester race meetings. The collection is of far more than local interest, including several objects of national importance. There are no less than 92 pieces assayed at the Chester Assay Office and many fine related objects from London and elsewhere. Almost the entire collection is on permanent display.

I am delighted to be asked to write a foreword to this catalogue of the collection because the National Art Collections Fund, of which I am the Chairman, has helped the museum to buy several of the finest pieces in the collection. The Fund is a privately financed charity, with over 120,000 subscribing members, dedicated to helping museums throughout the United Kingdom to acquire objects of quality and local interest and so to enrich their collections and delight their visitors. We do this by providing cash grants when we are satisfied that the object is of high enough quality. We also encourage gifts and bequests, many of them channelled through the Fund and protected by the conditions which the Fund attaches to its gifts. We have helped the Grosvenor Museum to buy eighteen of the pieces of silver in its collection and have acted as the channel for three more. It was particularly pleasing that we were able to help with the acquisition of the collection's first piece of Chester-assayed silver, the serving spoon by Thomas Robinson of 1709-10, which we presented to the museum in 1952. Other purchases include the five race trophies, the two flagons from St Michael's with their very fine armorial engraving, the pair of parcel-gilt tumbler cups by Richard Richardson and the rare Chester Palatinate seal matrices of 1706. It is no exaggeration to say that the Fund has played a crucial role in the building up of the collection, as it has for many collections across the United Kingdom.

A good collection needs a good catalogue. Without a catalogue it is not easy for the museum to fulfil its educational role. Display placards are small and cannot possibly record the extent of the museum's research or the details of the object's history. So it is with great enthusiasm that I welcome Peter Boughton's catalogue of this collection of silver. The museum attracts over 100,000 visitors each year. They will find this catalogue of immense help in the interpretation of one of the best local collections in the country.

ACKNOWLEDGEMENTS

It is a great pleasure to record my profound thanks to Canon Maurice Ridgway and Nicholas Moore. Canon Ridgway's three-volume history of Chester silver, together with his many other publications, forms a monumental body of scholarship. His work has fundamentally informed both the development of the collection and the writing of this catalogue, and my debt is clear throughout the entries for Chester-related silver. Nicholas Moore, Curator of the Grosvenor Museum from 1975-90, pursued the creation of the collection with vision and determination. Of the 123 full catalogue entries, he inherited just eight and acquired a further 103—a truly remarkable achievement. The fruits of Canon Ridgway's writing and Nicholas Moore's collecting enable us all to appreciate one of the most distinctive features of Chester's cultural heritage.

I am immensely grateful to James Lomax, who very kindly read the entire text and has been unfailingly generous in his encouragement. I would like to thank Sir Nicholas Goodison for so kindly agreeing to write the foreword. I also owe a particular debt of gratitute to Gale Glynn who researched the armorials; to Dr. Howard Coutts who read the section on the Ormonde silver; to Robin Emmerson who read the entries for the church plate; to Gerrard Barnes for biographical and bibliographical research; to Graham Usher who identified the wooden mounts; and to Captain Sir Thomas Barlow, Bt., who read the entries for the bottle tickets.

Many people have helped in many ways, and I would like to record my thanks to: The Most Hon. The Marchioness of Anglesey, The Rt. Hon. The Earl of Annandale and Hartfell, Mr. M.Y. Ashcroft, Graham Baker, Michael Ball, Andrew Barber, David Beasley, Stella Beddoe, David Beech, Simon Beer, Phyllis Benedikz, Stephen Benham, Victoria Bolton, Paul Booth, Sir Richard Brooke, Bt., Ian Bruce, Alexis Butcher, Anthony Carr, John Cherry, John Clark, Pamela Clark, Mrs. Georgina Clayton, Dr. Barry Cook, Julia Cook, The Rt. Hon. The Earl of Cromer, Nicholas Cummings, Susanna Davies-Lloyd, Hazel Davison, Mark Dennis, Graham Dyer, Ann Eatwell, Dr. Richard Edgcumbe, Julie Edwards, Sir John Grey Egerton, Bt., Judy Egerton, Mr. P.R. Evans, Oliver Fairclough, Diane Faulks, Dr. Jane Fenlon, Captain Gordon Fergusson, Audrey Fisk, Dr. Margaret Gill, Philippa Glanville, Alexis Goodin, Janet Goose, Ruth Gordon, Robert Gowland, Simon Harrison, The Ven. Christopher Hewetson, Melissa Ho, Paul Johnson, Grahame Jones, Timothy Kent, Antonia Leak, Miss Joyce Lowe, Peter & Janet Lowe, Jonathan Marsden, Maggie McKean, Douglas Muir, Molly Pearce, Jonathan Pepler, Elizabeth Pergam, Elizabeth Pettitt, Ian Pickford, Julia Poole, Rosemary Price, Philip Priestley, Roger Pringle, Dr. Mark Redknap, Dr. Paul Roberts, Richard Sabin, Timothy Schroder, Thomas Seaman, Peter Sedgley, Dr. John Simmons, Eileen Simpson, Graham Snelling, Karen Snowden, Edmund Southworth, Jill Springall, Michael Stammers, The Revd. Brian Statham, Andrew Taylor, Dr. Ian Wallace, Edward Walton, Rachel Walton, Mr. A.G. Ward, Simon Ward, Rachel Warley, His Grace The Duke of Westminster OBE TD DL, Natalia Wieczorek, Dr. Dan Weinbren, Harry Williams-Bulkeley, Eileen Willshaw, Heather Wilson, Timothy Wilson, Pamela Wood, Linda Woolley and David Wootton. I am also indebted to the staff of the British Library, Cheshire Record Office, Chester Library, Chester Record Office, Liverpool Record Office, Manchester Central Library, the National Art Library and the National Library of Ireland.

I would like to thank Noel Osborne and Nicola Willmot at Phillimore for all their kindness and help. I am grateful to many people at the Grosvenor Museum, and especially to Simon Warburton, who took all the photographs; to Ruth Marshall and Sue Rogers for secretarial and administrative assistance; to my curatorial colleagues Dan Robinson, Steve Woolfall, Sophie Fowler and Moya O'Mullane for their encouragement; to Fiona Salvesen, who undertook the duties of my keepership for a year while I completed the majority of the research and writing; and to Sharn Matthews, Museums Officer, for her wholehearted support for this project since its inception.

The research and publication of this catalogue were made possible by a number of exceptionally generous grants, and I am delighted to acknowledge the support of the Pilgrim Trust, the Jerwood/MGC Cataloguing Grants Scheme (jointly funded by the Museums and Galleries Commission, the Jerwood Foundation and the Department for Culture, Media and

Sport), the Grosvenor Museum Society, the Monument Trust and the (London) Goldsmiths' Company Charities.

The collection has benefited enormously from the generosity of many donors, including H.M. Treasury, Miss M.C. Singlehurst, Miss L.L. Drumm, Miss M. Marshall, Miss E.M. Sutcliffe, the National Art Collections Fund, Mr. B.S. James, Dr. S. Lang, Lowe & Sons, Mrs. E.D. Norman, and Sir Stanley and Lady Unwin. However, most acquisitions would have been impossible without grant aid, and the museum gratefully acknowledges the invaluable support of the MGC/V&A Purchase Grant Fund, the Heritage Lottery Fund, the National Art Collections Fund, the Grosvenor Museum Society, the Pilgrim Trust, the Beecroft Bequest, the National Heritage Memorial Fund, His Grace The Duke of Westminster OBE TD DL, the London Goldsmiths' Company, a bequest from Miss Mary Newboult, the Marc Fitch Fund, Mr. G.D. Lockett, Lloyd's Bank, Cheshire County Council, Lowe & Sons, Viscount Leverhulme, Boodle & Dunthorne, Marks & Spencer, Richard Green, Mappin & Webb, Mr. D.M. Beaton, the Silver Society, James Walker Ltd. and Mrs. E.M. Bell. Almost all the collection is permanently displayed in the Ridgway Gallery, opened by H.R.H. The Prince of Wales and substantially grant-aided by the European Regional Development Fund and the Museums and Galleries Improvement Fund (jointly funded by the Wolfson Foundation and Family Charitable Trust and the Department of National Heritage).

INTRODUCTION

The Grosvenor Museum's silver collection developed within the historical context of the publication and exhibition of Chester-related silver. The study of marks on English silver began a century before the museum's first acquisition, with the publication of Octavius Morgan's article 'On the Assay Marks on Gold and Silver Plate' in 1852, but Chester was only mentioned in passing, and his 1853 'Table of the Annual Assay Office Date Letters' was limited to London. His work was followed by the earliest book on the subject, *Hall Marks on Gold and Silver Plate* by William Chaffers, first published in 1863, which likewise made only fleeting reference to Chester. This was succeeded by *Old English Plate* by Wilfred Cripps, first published in 1878, whose eight pages on Chester included tables of date letters but no makers' marks.

A new standard of scholarship was set in the new century with the publication in 1905 of Charles Jackson's *English Goldsmiths and their Marks*, whose 30-page chapter on Chester included the names and dates of the city's goldsmiths from 1225, makers' marks from 1668 and date letters from 1687. A greatly expanded and corrected second edition appeared in 1921. The Bolton antiquary Thomas Stanley Ball published an article on 'Ancient Chester Goldsmiths and their Work' in 1914, which was republished in a slightly revised version in 1932: this presented a concise history of Chester silver, drawing upon records for biographical information and surviving pieces for the marks.

One of the historic collections of Chester-made silver is that belonging to the Trustees of the Chester Municipal Charities, comprising the seal matrix of the Hospital of St John the Baptist and the 35 badges of the gownsmen or pensioners. The 1875 *History of the Municipal Charities of Chester* by William Brown, a trustee, included illustrations of these pieces and details of the benefactions which they commemorate.

A far grander collection is that at Chester Town Hall, which now numbers 23 items of regalia and 114 pieces of civic plate, including 29 objects by Chester goldsmiths. *The Corporation Plate of England and Wales* by L. Jewitt and W. Hope, published in 1895, gave detailed information on five items from Chester's regalia and concise entries for 18 other pieces. T. Stanley Ball published a series of 15 articles in 1905, providing a highly detailed history and catalogue of the 'Chester Civic Plate and Regalia'. A summary treatment was included in two later booklets, Hugh Dutton's 1928 *Chester Town Hall and its Treasures* and Margaret Groombridge's 1950 *Guide to the Charters, Plate and Insignia of the City of Chester*.

The other historic holdings of silver in Chester are those of the cathedral and the Anglican churches, described and discussed in T. Stanley Ball's 1907 complete catalogue of the *Church Plate of the City of Chester*. Frank Simpson's 1909 *History of the Church of St Peter in Chester* provided a similar treatment of that church's silver.

The first exhibition of silver in Chester was organised by the Cheshire Joint Standing Committee to celebrate the Festival of Britain in 1951. Held at County Hall, this comprised ecclesiastical and secular silver from Cheshire and its borders. The 148-entry catalogue, including 26 pieces by Chester goldsmiths, was written by Charles Brocklehurst, a resident of Macclesfield and former head of silver at Christie's.

The Grosvenor Museum had been built in 1885-6 to house the collections of the Chester Archaeological Society and the Chester Society of Natural Science, Literature and Art, together with Schools of Science and Art. The costs were met by Hugh Lupus Grosvenor, 1st Duke of Westminster, and a public appeal. Chester City Council took over the administration of the museum in 1915, assumed full control of the collections and displays in 1938, and ten years later appointed Graham Webster as the first professional curator.

In 1951 the Trustees of the Chester Municipal Charities placed their silver on long-term loan to the museum, and the following year the first piece of silver was acquired for the permanent collection. This was a serving spoon by Thomas Robinson, hallmarked at Chester in 1709 (no.6). It was presented by the National Art Collections Fund, Britain's largest independent art charity, whose grants and gifts have played a vital role in securing the pieces for 21 of the catalogue entries. Also in 1952 six pieces of London-made silver from the civic plate, and the Water Bailiff's Oar by Richard Richardson I of Chester, were shown in London at the Goldsmiths' Hall exhibition of *Corporation Plate.*

The Chester Assay Office closed in 1962, an event commemorated by Judith Banister's article on the 'Last of the Chester Silver'. On a happier note the museum, under the curatorship of Hugh Thompson, purchased the first of its Chester race trophies, a London-made punch bowl by Hester Bateman (no.94). Some 19th century silver from London and Edinburgh (nos.132, 135, 148) was presented by Miss E.M. Sutcliffe in 1962 and the following year the Joseph Rayner Stephens Cup (no.110), commemorating the imprisonment of a Chartist in Chester Castle, was presented by Sir Stanley and Lady Unwin through the National Art Collections Fund. In 1966 the Water Bailiff's Oar from the civic plate was shown in London at the National Maritime Museum's exhibition of *Oar Maces of Admiralty.*

The scholarship of Chester silver took a huge leap foreward in 1968 with the publication of *Chester Goldsmiths from early times to 1726* by Canon Maurice Ridgway, Vicar of Bowdon. This meticulously-researched history elucidated all the marks, and presented the biography of each goldsmith along with a descriptive catalogue of every known piece of his silver.

In 1970 some 19th- and 20th-century silver from London, Birmingham and Sheffield (nos.130, 133, 140-1, 144-5) was transferred from Chester Record Office to the museum, and a bequest of 18th- and 19th-century silver from London, Birmingham, Sheffield and New-castle (nos.124-5, 127-9, 137-8, 143, 146-7) was received from Miss M.C. Singlehurst. Nineteenth- and 20th-century London and Birmingham pieces (nos.136, 139, 142) were presented the following year by Miss M. Marshall.

An active collecting policy began in 1972, under the curatorship of Dennis Petch, with the purchase of a jug by Ralph Walley (no.8). Acquired after the temporary refusal of an export licence, its funding established a pattern for the future, with the first of 67 grants from the V&A Purchase Grant Fund (later the MGC/V&A Purchase Grant Fund), the first of 26 grants from the London Goldsmiths' Company and the first of 14 grants from the Pilgrim Trust. Two pieces of 18th-century London-made silver were placed on loan from Tarvin church the same year.

For the Chester Festival in 1973 the local goldsmiths Lowe & Sons put on an *Exhibition of Antique Silver*, to which the museum lent the Hester Bateman punch bowl. The museum mounted its first exhibition of silver, with a 147-entry catalogue by Margaret Buchanan, assistant curator, covering predominantly Chester-hallmarked civic, church and domestic plate. The exhibitions were publicised in an article by Judith Banister, and the year also saw the publication of Canon Ridgway's booklet on *Some Chester Goldsmiths and their marks*, which acted as an interim report on the period 1727-1962.

A tea canister by Richard Richardson II & William Richardson II (no.33) was purchased in 1973, the first of 17 acquisitions grant-aided by the Beecroft Bequest. Christopher Lever's article on '400 Years of Chester Goldsmiths' was published in 1974, and the same year the museum purchased its second Chester race trophy, a London-made punch bowl by Fuller White (no.93), and a skewer by Mary Huntingdon (no.65). The first pieces from a large private collection, now numbering 59 items of Chester silver, were placed on loan in 1974, and Dennis Petch's last acquisition, a Chester-hallmarked badge by Thomas Armitt of Manchester (no.85), was purchased in 1975.

Nicholas Moore was appointed curator in 1975, inheriting eight significant pieces of silver: with limited resources but unlimited determination he transformed the collection out of all recognition. In 1976 he purchased a tankard by Ralph Walley (no.7), the first of 15 acquisitions grant-aided by His Grace The Duke of Westminster (then Earl Grosvenor), a consistently generous benefactor of the museum. Canon Ridgway's 1976 article on 'Chester Silver' gave an overview of the changing sequence of marks, and Graham Thomas's handlist of the silver then housed in the museum (including much of the civic plate) appeared in 1977, in which year Mrs. E.D. Norman presented a silver-cased London work box of 1889 (no.134). In 1977 and '78 Canon Ridgway published the first two articles in a projected series cataloguing the 'Church Plate of the Diocese of Chester', covering Acton to Chelford: a book of this title is now approaching publication.

In 1978 a saucepan by Benjamin Pemberton I (no.15) was presented by the National Art Collections Fund; the Chester Gold Cup for 1766 (no.95) was purchased with the help of a public appeal; and the Ralph Walley jug was lent to an exhibition celebrating 500 years of hallmarking at Goldsmiths' Hall. Chester celebrated its 1900th anniversary in 1979, and an exhibition at the museum showed 18 items of silver (including five loans) alongside pictures and ceramics, catalogued by Janet Goose, keeper of art and recent history. The museum lent the 1766 Gold Cup to an exhibition of regalia and civic plate in the Town Hall, which was accompanied by Nicholas Moore's booklet *Silver of the City of Chester*. Also in 1979 the museum purchased two pairs of table spoons and a chamber candlestick by three generations of the Richardson family (nos.10, 24, 47).

The pace of acquisitions quickened in 1980, with the transfer from the City Treasurer of a pair of tea spoons by Joseph Duke I and some 19th century London silver (nos.35, 126, 131), and the purchase of a pair of tumbler cups by Richard Richardson II (no.29) and pieces by Richard Richardson IV, John Lowe I and John Coakley of Liverpool (nos.22, 49, 67, 79). Also in 1980 the museum lent 18 items for an exhibition of *Chester Assayed Silver* at Lowe & Sons, and Canon Ridgway published 'The Early Plate of Chester Cathedral', thoroughly updating a chapter in T. Stanley Ball's 1907 book. 1981 began with the purchase of the Chester Gold Cups for 1814 and 1815 (nos.96-7), the first of 57 acquisitions grant-aided by the Grosvenor Museum Society, the museum's outstandingly supportive friends' group. The museum also purchased pieces by Benjamin Pemberton I, George Lowe I, John Twemlow, John Lowe I and Joseph Walley of Liverpool (nos.18, 57, 62, 66, 70, 75).

In 1982 Nicholas Moore published a concise history of 'The Chester Race Trophies', and the museum lent nine items for an exhibition of *Richard Richardson Silver* at Mappin & Webb, whose premises had been the Richardson shop. The museum purchased a hot water jug by George Lowe I (no.63) and pieces by Richard Richardson II, George Walker I, Robert Bowers I and John Helsby of Liverpool (nos.28, 38, 54, 64, 83). 1982 also saw the museum's largest acquisition, when 62 items from the Marquess of Ormonde's collection were allocated after acceptance in lieu of estate duty. This 18th- and 19th-century aristocratic silver from London, Dublin and Sheffield, including pieces by Paul Storr, added a major new dimension to the collection, with dining and presentation plate, tea silver and candlesticks (nos.111-23).

Six pieces of Chester silver and four race trophies were lent to an exhibition at Manchester City Art Gallery, celebrating the 80th anniversary of the National Art Collections Fund in 1983. That year the museum purchased the Delamere Horn (no.106) and pieces by Richard Richardson II or III, George Walker I, George Lowe I, John Coakley of Liverpool and the Keswick School of Industrial Arts (nos.34, 41, 60, 80, 91), and Dr. S. Lang presented a Chester-hallmarked photograph frame by James Deakin & Sons of Sheffield (no.89).

Five pieces of Chester silver, two race trophies and the Joseph Rayner Stephens Cup were displayed by the National Art Collections Fund in London at the 1984 Fine Art and Antiques Fair, Olympia. The same year saw the largest and most comprehensive exhibition of *Chester Silver* ever mounted. Organised jointly by Sotheby's Chester (where it was held) and the Grosvenor Museum, the 236-entry catalogue by Nicholas Moore included 163 pieces by Chester goldsmiths, together with work from Liverpool, Manchester and Birmingham. Also in 1984 the museum purchased a two-handled cup by Thomas Robinson (no.5), the last piece of Chester-hallmarked silver (no.73), the Tom Rance Tea Pot (no.109) and pieces by William Richardson I, Daniel Kirkes, Robert Pyke, Richard Richardson II, William Twemlow, George Lowe I, John Sutter of Liverpool and Charles Lewis of Wincanton (nos.14, 19, 20, 32, 51, 58, 81, 149).

Canon Ridgway's *Chester Silver 1727-1837*, published in 1985, was a worthy sequel to his 1968 volume and another huge contribution to scholarship. That year the museum purchased a double beaker by Richard Richardson II (no.31) and pieces by Joseph Duke I, George Walker I and the Keswick School of Industrial Arts (nos. 21, 36, 39, 90, 92); Mr. B.S. James presented a Chester-hallmarked shoe horn by Jones & Crompton of Birmingham (no.88); and a private collector lent a tankard by Ralph Walley and a pair of mugs by Richard Richardson III. Nicholas Moore's articles on 'Chester Silver of the Georgian Period' (1985) and 'Silver from the City of Chester' (1986) provided concise overviews. Combining major and minor acquisitions, the museum purchased a spoon by William Mutton (no.3), the St Martin Cup by Richard Richardson II (no.27), a badge by John Sutter of Liverpool (no.82) and the Arderne Tankard (no.107) in 1986, followed in 1987 by a tumbler cup by Richard Richardson II (no.25) and a silver-mounted coconut cup by George Lowe I (no.59).

1988 saw the collection's second largest expansion, with the acquisition of two major groups of silver. Plate from the redundant Chester churches of St Michael, St Olave, St Bridget and St Martin was purchased with the help of grants from the National Heritage Memorial Fund and a bequest from Miss Mary Newboult. This included pieces by the Chester goldsmiths William Mutton and Richard Richardson I (nos.1, 11-13), a pair of flagons by Seth Lofthouse (no.99) and other 17th–19th-century London silver (nos.98, 100-3). The museum also purchased much of the Lowe family collection, acquiring pieces by Benjamin Pemberton I, Richard Richardson II, George Walker I, James Dixon, Richard Richardson IV, the unknown maker ST, George Lowe I, John Lowe I, John Foulkes Lowe, George Bennett Lowe, Joseph Walley and Joseph Hewitt of Liverpool, and William Hardwick of Manchester (nos. 16-17, 23, 30, 37, 40, 42-5, 50, 52, 55-6, 61, 68-9, 71-2, 76-7, 84).

The museum's only purchase in 1989 was a cruet frame by Richard Richardson II (no.26), but two collections were placed on loan: 19 items of 18th- to 20th-century Chester-hallmarked silver from the Chester Goldsmiths' Company, and four pieces of 18th-century London silver from the Trustees of Matthew Henry's Chapel, Chester. The Delamere Horn was shown at the British Museum in an exhibition marking the publication of the 200th volume of the *Victoria County History*, and four pieces of church plate and five items from the Lowe collection were displayed at the Victoria and Albert Museum to highlight the support of the MGC/V&A Purchase Grant Fund. 1989 also saw the publication of an extensively updated and enlarged edition of *Jackson's Silver & Gold Marks of England, Scotland & Ireland*, with the chapter on Chester re-written by Canon Ridgway.

Nicholas Moore's last acquisition before leaving the museum in 1990 was a pair of bottle tickets by George Lowe I (no.53). The following year the museum purchased a beaker by Richard Richardson III (no.48) and Chester-hallmarked Birmingham silver by Nathan & Hayes and Stokes & Ireland (nos.86-7), and was lent a Richard Richardson I flagon from Coddington church.

1992 witnessed another milestone in the development of the collection, with the opening of the Ridgway Gallery at the Grosvenor Museum by H.R.H. The Prince of Wales. Named after Canon Ridgway in recognition of his outstanding contribution to the study of Chester silver, the gallery displays almost all the permanent collection together with a large number of loans. The Spirit of Chester Bowl (no.74) was presented by Lowe & Sons to mark the opening of the gallery, and the Chester Cup for 1939 was lent from a private collection. The gallery was publicised in articles by Timothy Schroder and Sarah Callaghan, and in 1993 Canon Ridgway published articles on Chester spoons and coffin plates.

In 1994 the museum purchased a mug by Alexander Pulford (no.9) and a silver-mounted cowrie shell snuff box by Nicholas Cunliffe of Liverpool (no.78), while the churches of Over and Little Budworth lent seven pieces of 17th- and 18th-century London plate. In 1995 the museum purchased a pair of table candlesticks by James Dixon (no.46) and silver from St Lawrence's Church at Stoak, comprising pieces by William Mutton (no.2) and 18th-century London goldsmiths (nos.104-5). 1996 saw the publication of *Chester Silver 1837-1962*, completing Canon Ridgway's great trilogy and including a wealth of information from the Chester Plate Duty Books of 1784-1840, which had been rediscovered by Philip Priestley. In 1996 the museum purchased a tobacco box with a lid by Peter Edwardes II (no.4), and the following year acquired the Chester Palatinate Seal Matrices (no.108) with the help of a grant from the Heritage Lottery Fund.

The Grosvenor Museum has built the largest and most comprehensive collection of Chester-hallmarked silver, complemented by distinct groups of other locally-related pieces. The only significant Chester goldsmiths unrepresented in the collection are John Lingley, Peter Pemberton I, Nathaniel Bullen, Thomas Maddock, John Walker I and Margaret Joyce Lowe & John ffoulkes Lowe. Unrepresented object types by Chester goldsmiths form a somewhat longer list, but the most notable omission is an example of the Chester-hallmarked Neo-Classical silver by Boulton & Fothergill of Birmingham. It is hoped that the collection will continue to develop, in order to provide ever greater aesthetic delight and intellectual stimulation for the museum's many visitors.

A NOTE ON THE TEXT

This catalogue is devoted to the permanent collection of silver in the Grosvenor Museum, Chester, as at 1 April 2000. It excludes all loans, silver-plated wares, pewter, jewellery, watch-cases, medals and archaeological material.

The catalogue is divided into six sections, most of which are further subdivided: Chester Hallmarked Silver from Chester, Liverpool, Manchester, Birmingham, Sheffield and Keswick; Chester Race Trophies, comprising the City Plate and the Gold Cup; Cheshire Church Plate from four Chester churches and from Stoak; Cheshire Silver; the Ormonde Silver; and an Appendix of pieces from London, Birmingham, Sheffield, Newcastle, Edinburgh and Wincanton. The entries are arranged chronologically within each subdivision.

The Chester goldsmiths are arranged according to the date they joined the Chester Gold-smiths' Company or, for those who were not members, the date their career began. The makers of Chester hallmarked silver from elsewhere are arranged in date order according to their earliest piece in the collection.

Under old style dating, the year began officially on 25 March, but this was changed to new style dating in 1752, since when the year has begun on 1 January. For the sake of simplicity, all date references follow the new style.

Most pieces of silver are stamped with a date letter, whose use generally overlapped two calendar years. Dates are therefore cited in the form 1752-3 at the start of an entry, but for simplicity subsequent references are abbreviated to the form 1752.

The identification of the Chester date letters follows Ridgway 1985, pp.36-48 for 1687-1839, and Ridgway 1996, pp.172-4 for 1839-1962. Date letters from the other assay offices follow Jackson.

The number of marks on each piece is stated. Only where this is less than the full number of marks used at this date at this assay office are those marks present fully identified.

The 'maker's mark' signifies the master of the workshop or retailer of the piece, rather than necessarily identifying the actual maker. The precise form of each maker's mark is referenced to its illustration in a volume in the Bibliography.

The terminology for the styles of engraved lettering is taken from Fairbairn, pl.131. Unless otherwise stated, all engraved armorials and inscriptions are believed to date from around the time the piece was made.

A discussion about the function and evolution of a particular type of object usually takes place in the first entry of its type. Likewise, a brief biography of each goldsmith accompanies the first entry for his work—either preceding a group of pieces for Chester Hallmarked Silver, or contained within the entry under subsequent sections.

Each Provenance concludes with the Museum's accession number, whose date gives the year of acquisition unless otherwise stated. The exhibition and publication history of each piece refer to the Bibliography and the list of Exhibitions which follows it.

CHESTER HALLMARKED SILVER

CHESTER GOLDSMITHS

Chester was founded in A.D. 79 as the Roman fortress of Deva, which became the headquarters of the 20th legion. A civilian settlement grew up outside the fortress, whose original defences were rebuilt in stone. Parts of the Roman masonry remain visible to this day, and the principal axes of the city's street pattern still follow the layout of the fortress, which the Romans abandoned *c*.380. In the 5th and 6th centuries Chester formed part of the Welsh kingdom of Powys, and in the early 7th century it was absorbed into the English kingdom of Mercia. In 907 the relics of the Mercian princess St Werburgh were brought to Chester and enshrined in an existing church on the site of the present cathedral. Also in 907 Chester became a burh or fortified town, and the defences were refurbished. Chester grew into a prosperous port with a wide-ranging trade in the 10th century, and during the reign of Athelstan (924-39) it contained the most prolific mint in England. In 1070 William the Conqueror estabished the castle and the administrative structure which became the County Palatine of Chester, and the Normans later extended the city walls. St John's Church served as the cathedral of the diocese of Lichfield from 1075-95, and in 1092 St Werburgh's Church was refounded as a Benedictine abbey. Thus was created a prosperous city in which goldsmithing could flourish.[1]

A charter of *c*.1200 from Earl Ranulph III of Chester confirmed the establishment of the Guild Merchant in the city. This probably gave official approval to an already long established practice, enabling the leading citizens to regulate all the trade within Chester. The Guild Merchant would have included the goldsmiths, and records of individual goldsmiths survive from *c*.1225. The city guilds, eventually numbering 26, emerged during the later Middle Ages from the trade situation created by the Guild Merchant. Among them was the Chester Goldsmiths' Company, first recorded in 1531, whose earliest minute book was begun *c*.1554-8.

The Chester Goldsmiths' Company controlled the work of the city's goldsmiths. It laid down rules governing apprenticeship, standards of craftsmanship, and the assaying and marking of finished goods. It was also a social organisation, taking part in the mystery plays, the horse races and the Midsummer games.

When the Chester goldsmiths began to put identity marks on their wares in the mid-16th century, they used a single punch to indicate the maker. The earliest Chester goldsmith to do so was probably William Mutton, who used a rebus (visual pun) on his name, a sheep's head within an ornamental shield. Other Chester goldsmiths used their initials.

The early 17th century saw the decline of the Chester goldsmiths, due to competition from London and later to the devastating effects of the Civil War. After the Civil War the Chester Goldsmiths' Company was revived, and an attempt was made by Peter Pemberton I to introduce a mark which would identify the silver with the city, in the form of an ornamental shield with a single wheatsheaf taken from part of the city arms. He seems to have been alone in adopting this symbol, although he and others were at this time using a variety of marks with the word 'sterling'.

The company's minute books record a determined effort to institute a more disciplined assay, when on 1 February 1687 a statement of intent was drawn up and signed by the Chester goldsmiths. This laid down that all silver from this date onward was to bear four marks: the maker's mark, the city arms (an upturned sword between three wheatsheaves), the city crest (a sheathed sword and belt) and a date letter. The date letter altered only when there was a change of warden. During the 1680s and '90s the Chester goldsmiths established a tradition of producing good, heavy-gauge silver, often of very simple design, and this continued throughout the 18th century.

An Act of Parliament closing all provincial assay offices brought the first series of Chester date letters to an end on 25 March 1697, and for the next few years the Chester goldsmiths must have wondered how to proceed. Some would undoubtedly have claimed the right to continue working, since the city was part of the County Palatine of Chester, which had enjoyed a degree of independence from Parliament and was excluded from earlier statutes governing goldsmithing. During this period without town marks or date letters, several Chester goldsmiths struck their work with repeated maker's marks.

The Act which closed the provincial assay offices in 1697 also introduced the Britannia standard for silver, marked with the seated figure of Britannia. Henceforth, silver plate was to be made from purer silver (an alloy containing 95.84 per cent silver) than the sterling silver standard of coinage (which was 92.5 per cent). One of the main purposes of this move was to stop the practice of clipping coins. In time, the compulsory enforcement of the double standard became unnecessary, and the Act was repealed in 1720.

It proved impossible to ensure that all English silver was assayed in London, so another Act in 1701 created assay offices in the five provincial cities, including

Chester, where temporary mints had been set up for the Great Recoinage of 1696-8. Although some Chester goldsmiths declined to work under this new system and passed from the scene, others were content to allow the Chester Goldsmiths' Company to be responsible for running the new assay office. They changed their marks to the first two letters of their surnames as the Act directed, and registered them on a copper plate. Twelve series of alphabets were used for the annual date letter at Chester between 29 September 1701 and 1962. Britannia silver from Chester bears five marks: the maker's mark, the Chester city arms, the figure of Britannia, the lion's head erased and a date letter.

The Chester Goldsmiths' Company had been in decline at the end of the 17th century, but its fortunes rose again in the 18th century along with those of the Richardson family. Richard Richardson I was admitted to the company in 1708 and founded a goldsmithing dynasty which spanned the century. The Richardsons served as wardens and assay masters in the company and were also active in civic life. In 1791 Richard Richardson IV quarrelled with other members of the company and resigned as assay master, and a further quarrel in 1800 severed relations between the family and the company after a century of fruitful co-operation.

The use of the sterling standard was authorised again from 1 June 1720, and Chester silver after this date bears five marks: the maker's mark, the lion passant guardant, the leopard's head crowned, the Chester city arms and a date letter. From 1701 to 1778 the Chester mark was the coat of arms which had been granted to the city in 1580—the three lions of England dimidiating the three wheatsheaves of Chester. From 1778 this was replaced by the ancient Chester coat of an upturned sword between three wheatsheaves, which continued until 1962. The duty mark, depicting the sovereign's head, was used between 1784 and 1890 to denote that excise duty had been paid.

The Georgian age was one of increasing prosperity for both the city and the company. Chester's role as a county town, its position on the canal system and its flourishing trade with Ireland created wealth which could be spent on silver plate, and by the early 19th century the city was also a tourist attraction for wealthy visitors. The 18th century was the heyday of Chester silver and, as well as the Richardson family, many other goldsmiths were active in the city. In addition, the assay office was hallmarking goods from other cities such as Liverpool and Manchester, and goldsmiths who were not members of the company were charged a fee for having their work assayed. These fees enabled the company to pay its officers a small wage, and the management of the assay office gradually became more professional. Silver was hallmarked in the assay master's own workshop until 1846, when premises in Goss Street were acquired.

The Lowe family, like the Richardsons before them, dominated the silver trade in Chester for over a century. George Lowe I was admitted to the company in 1791 and was elected warden three years later. In 1804 he moved his business to premises in Bridge Street Row East, which the shop still occupies. Members of the Lowe family continued to work at the assay office until its closure, and they remain leading members of the Chester Goldsmiths' Company to this day.

After 1884, Chester was one of only four assay offices in England, along with London, Birmingham and Sheffield. Between the late 19th century and the Second World War vast quantities of silver were sent from Birmingham, Sheffield and elsewhere to the Chester Assay Office in Goss Street, which was popular because of its fast and efficient service, but it was closed by Act of Parliament on 24 August 1962. Since 1988 the punch of a single wheatsheaf has been used, under the control of the Chester Goldsmiths' Company, as the city of origin mark on silver made or finished in Chester.[2]

NOTES:

1. Boughton 1997, p.8.
2. Ridgway 1973, pp.5-8; Ridgway 1976; Moore 1986; Ridgway 1996, p.23.

William Mutton

William Mutton became a freeman in 1555 and was a member of the Chester Goldsmiths' Company. He lived in Bridge Street and was probably the earliest Chester goldsmith to use a maker's mark. He was sheriff of Chester in 1583-4 and died in 1584.[1]

The silver-gilt mouthpiece of the Delamere Horn (no.106) may also be by him.

NOTE:

1. Ridgway 1968, pp.51-4; Ridgway 1973, p.5.

1 PARCEL-GILT COMMUNION CUP

William Mutton of Chester, c.1570

Maker's mark only below rim (Ridgway 1968, p.51)

Height 19.6 cm. (7.7 in.)

Weight 420 g. (14.8 oz.)

See Colour Plate I

Silver, with rubbed bands of gilding on the foot-ring, knop, three bands of egg-and-dart ornament and both sides of the lip. The angled foot-ring is soldered to the raised, low domed foot. The double-spool stem is raised in two sections, joined by a compressed spherical knop, which is cast and turned. Seamed bands of die-struck egg-and-dart ornament are applied to the foot-ring and

1

at either end of the stem. The bowl is raised, with a slightly rounded base and flaring sides. It is engraved with six strapwork panels containing diagonally-hatched scrolling arabesques, with arabesque pendants alternately above and below the interlacing of the panels. One side is engraved in script above the strapwork: 'The communion cup / of St Michaells / In Chester'.

The inscription was added in the late 17th or early 18th century, since the style of the script is very close to that on the 1697 patens from St Bridget's (no.102) and the 1702 flagons from St Michael's (no.99).

As Timothy Schroder has explained, the form of the Elizabethan communion cup 'is due entirely to the liturgical consequences of the Reformation in England. In the Roman liturgy the chalice was restricted to the celebrant priest, only the bread being taken by the congegation. Therefore, in most cases, the bowl of the chalice was small. In 1548, after the death of Henry VIII, the cup was made available to the laity. Although this practice was halted during the reign of Mary (r.1553-58), when the country returned to Roman Catholicism, it was restored in 1559 following the accession of Queen Elizabeth I. Steps were taken after 1548 and again after 1559 to convert the chalices into vessels of larger capacity. The intention seems to have been less theological than practical and political: to produce a cup not only better suited to the new liturgy but also quite distinct in form from those of the old order.'[1]

Charles Oman lists 18 Edwardian communion cups,[2] and the St Michael's cup is close to one of these, made in London in 1551.[3] More than 2,000 Elizabethan communion cups survive, most of them dating from the late 1560s until 1577, and divided fairly evenly between London and provincial manufacture. Most Elizabethan communion cups were formed from the metal of old chalices, and the St Michael's cup is typical of the most popular type. The comparative simplicity of the design was conditioned chiefly by the need to minimise the cost of labour while producing a bowl of maximum capacity. This militated against elaborate decoration and cast parts, both of which would have added to the cost.[4]

Engraved strapwork panels containing scrolling arabesques are seen on the earliest Elizabethan communion cup, made in London in 1558,[5] and occur regularly thereafter on London-made cups. Arabesque pendants outside the junction of the panels are frequently found, occuring for example on a London-made cup of 1562,[6] which also exhibits another common feature, die-struck egg-and-dart ornament on the foot-ring. There was nothing ecclesiastical about this engraved ornament, which is also found on domestic pieces. The designs were not very demanding, and could be carried out in the workshops of goldsmiths who did not employ specialist engravers. Elizabethan secular silver was often fully gilded, as was much cathedral plate,[7] but parcel-gilding was less common and, although there are surviving examples on pre-Reformation English church plate,[8] parcel-gilding is rarely found on Elizabethan ecclesiastical silver. In both design and execution, William Mutton's cup is as good as much of what was being produced in London at this time.

William Mutton was an enthusiastic Protestant. He was a churchwarden of St Michael's from 1568, when he sold the timber from the rood loft, and ten years later he sold the lead from the cross. His zeal for the Reformation helped him become sheriff of Chester in 1583. He died in office the following year, reputedly poisoned after having demolished three of Chester's public crosses. Mutton must have taken great delight in converting Catholic chalices into Protestant communion cups, since it suited his religious views and was also very good for trade.[9]

William Mutton's first datable church plate is the communion cup and plate paten for Holy Trinity, Chester, recorded in the churchwardens' accounts for 1570.[10] The St Michael's cup is sufficiently close in shape and construction to suggest a very similar date.[11] As Canon Ridgway says, 'no reference is made to it in the churchwardens' accounts, and one must presume he gave it in exchange for the older plate' some two years after becoming a warden.[12]

Fifteen communion cups bearing William Mutton's mark have survived, five of them firmly datable between 1570 and 1578, and all of them variations of the same basic type.[13] The 1570 cup from Holy Trinity, Chester, is parcel-gilt, and the cup of c.1570 at Great Budworth has traces of gilding.[14] The other decorative features of the St Michael's cup recur more frequently, with die-struck egg-and-dart ornament appearing on ten cups and strapwork panels with scrolling arabesques engraved on eleven: the engraving on the Great Budworth cup is almost identical.[15]

The only other surviving Elizabethan communion cups marked by a Chester goldsmith are the eight by John Lingley I, and they are very similar to Mutton's.[16] Parcel-gilding is found on two unmarked Elizabethan cups in the Chester area: one at St Mary's, Denbigh, which was almost certainly the work of a Chester goldsmith; and another at Gawsworth, Cheshire, which may have been made in Chester.[17]

Only four of William Mutton's communion cups lack matching patens, whereas seven have paten covers and three have plate patens. There is a slight possibility that St Michael's retained its medieval silver-gilt paten,[18] and the parcel-gilding on Mutton's cup would have complemented this. However, it is far more likely, not least because of his zealous Protestantism, that Mutton made a new paten. This would have been a plate paten, probably very similar to his 1570 one for Holy Trinity, since the splay of the gilded lip would not comfortably fit a paten cover. Whether medieval or Elizabethan, the paten was

presumably superseded by one presented in 1639 (no.13).

PROVENANCE: St Michael's Church, Chester (probably presented by William Mutton, c.1570); Transferred to Chester Team Parish, 1972; Purchased with grant aid from the MGC/V&A Purchase Grant Fund, National Heritage Memorial Fund, National Art Collections Fund, Pilgrim Trust, Duke of Westminster, Mary Newboult Bequest, Grosvenor Museum Society 1988.35

EXHIBITED: Chester 1951, no.5, pl.II; Chester 1973 II, p.30 no.12; London V&A 1989.

PUBLISHED: Ball 1907, pp.68-9 no.I; Ridgway 1968, p.56 no.3, pl.12; Pevsner & Hubbard, p.152; Richards, p.120 (a); Ridgway 1973, illustrated; The *Independent*, 15 December 1987, illustrated; NACF Review 1989, no. 3432 (8); Boughton 1992 I; Schroder 1992, p.36; Callaghan, illustrated p.30.

NOTES:

1. Schroder 1988 I, p.54.
2. Oman 1957, p.310.
3. Maker's mark a bird's head erased; at St Michael, Southampton (Oman 1957, pl.52a).
4. Oman 1957, p.193; Schroder 1988 I, p.56.
5. At St Michael-le-Belfry, York (Oman 1957, pl.54).
6. Maker's mark GK in a heart; at Ashby-de-la-Zouch, Leicestershire (Oman 1957, pl.57a).
7. Oman 1978, p.36; Oman 1957, p.156.
8. e.g., a late 15th-century chalice and paten, and a chalice and paten of 1527 (Glanville 1990, nos.134-5). Vast amounts of pre-Reformation church plate had been parcel-gilt (James Lomax, note, 22 October 1999).
9. Ridgway 1968, pp.52-3.
10. Ridgway 1968, p.55, pl.13.
11. Both Ball 1907, p.68, and Richards, p.120, say that it was probably made c.1560-70, but this seems less likely.
12. Ridgway 1968, p.53.
13. Another two unmarked cups are almost certainly by him (Ridgway 1968, p.57).
14. Ridgway 1968, pp.55, 58.
15. Ridgway 1968, pp.xv-xvi, 58-64; for the Great Budworth cup see pl.16.
16. Ridgway 1968, pp.44-51.
17. Ridgway 1968, pp.73-4, 78.
18. Ball 1907, p.66.

2 COMMUNION CUP AND PATEN COVER

Cup: William Mutton of Chester, c.1570-8
Cover: remade 1804-5

Cup: maker's mark only below rim (Ridgway 1968, p.51)
Cover: fragment of single mark inside shoulder

2

Height: cup 15.7 cm. (6.2 in.), cover 3 cm. (1.2 in.)

Diameter of cover 8.5 cm. (3.35 in.)

Weight: cup 178 g. (6.3 oz.), cover 69 g. (2.4 oz.)

Silver. The cup's horizontal foot-ring is die-struck with egg-and-dart ornament and is soldered to the raised, low domed foot. The double-spool stem is raised in two sections, terminating in die-struck bands and joined by a compressed spherical knop, which is cast and turned. The flat-bottomed bowl is raised, with flaring sides rising to an almost vertical rim. The bowl is engraved with a band of diagonally-hatched scrolling arabesques within two diagonally-hatched strapwork panels. The side of the bowl is engraved beneath the strapwork with the sacred monogram, cross and nails within a glory.

The cover is flat with a raised convex shoulder and an applied vertical bezel which fits over the rim of the cup. The cover stands on a spool-shaped stem with an applied flat button-foot.

The engraving of the sacred monogram was almost certainly added in 1772, when a waiter/paten (no.104) and ewer/flagon (no.105) were presented to Stoak church by John Grace of Whitby Hall. The engraving on all three pieces appears to be by the same hand. The wardens' accounts for 1772-3 record 'For mending the Cup 2s. 6d.'[1] but do not mention the engraving, which was presumably paid for by John Grace to render the old cup stylistically consistent with his donation.

IHS is an abbreviation of the name Jesus in Greek and, with a cross above the H, is seen in the decoration of religious objects of many kinds.[2] The form as seen on the Stoak silver, with the three nails of the Passion beneath the sacred monogram and the whole encircled by flames and rays, was virtually the only sacred symbol used by the Church of England in the Georgian period.

The cup is undated, but since William Mutton's five firmly datable communion cups span the period 1570-8, it seems reasonable to suggest this date range for the Stoak cup. It was acquired by the church during the long incumbency of Hugh Denson from 1563 to 1601.[3]

As Canon Ridgway has explained, the cover 'has undergone numerous changes and repairs, and may not contain any part of the original cover paten. The churchwardens' accounts contain a number of references to these changes:

3

1688-9 Paid ye Goldsmith for mending ye Communion Chalice Lid 1s.
1783-4 For sodering the callis cover 1s.6d.
1790-1 Repairing ye Cup Cover 1s.
1804-5 A Cover for the Sacrament Cup 14s.

The existing cover is evidently the one here referred to in the last item. It is unmarked except for a fragment of a single mark much mutilated upon what is now the shoulder, and although it cannot be matched with any part of the known mark of William Mutton, it is possible that a cover earlier than 1804-5 has been made use of, and if this is so, part of the William Mutton cover may have survived.'[4]

The use of household bread was permitted from 1552 with the publication of the Second Book of Common Prayer, but wafers certainly remained in use in many churches at least until the early 17th century, and the small Elizabethan paten covers were clearly suitable only for them. In 1571 Archbishop Parker wrote about the choice between wafers and bread for communion: 'most part of Protestants think it most meet to be in wafer bread … a matter not greatly material, but only obeying the Queen's Highness, and for that the most part of her subjects dislike the common bread for the sacrament.'[5]

The eight known paten covers by William Mutton are all slightly domed,[6] in contrast to the convex shoulder of the Stoak cover, which they otherwise resemble. By the time the one at Stoak came to be remade it was not required to serve as a paten, since

a waiter had been acquired for this purpose, so it was now intended to function solely as a cover.

PROVENANCE: St Lawrence's Church, Stoak, c.1570-8; Purchased with grant aid from the MGC/V&A Purchase Grant Fund, Pilgrim Trust 1995.86.1,2

EXHIBITED: Chester 1979 I, Silver no.7; Chester 1984, no.4, illustrated.

PUBLISHED: Ridgway 1968, p.59 no.8; Richards, p.307; Pevsner & Hubbard, p.338; Thomas, p.19; Boughton 1992 I.

NOTES:

1. Cheshire Record Office, P31/3/2.
2. Hall, pp.6, 160.
3. Richards, p.308.
4. Ridgway 1968, p.59.
5. Glanville 1990, p.380.
6. Ridgway 1968, pp.58, 60-3.

3 PARCEL-GILT SPOON

William Mutton of Chester, c.1580-4
Maker's mark only on bowl (Ridgway 1968, p.51)
Length 16 cm. (6.3 in.)
Weight 36 g. (1.25 oz.)

Silver, with rubbed gilding on the finial and the interior of the bowl. The bowl and stem are formed from a single piece of silver. The raised bowl is fig-shaped and up-curved. The flattened hexagonal stem is straight and tapers from the bowl to the finial, which is cast separately and soldered into place with a lap-joint. The finial comprises an elongated acanthus baluster surmounted by a gadrooned knop with a flat circular top. The interior of the bowl is engraved with a shield of arms within a cartouche.

Silver spoons are the most basic and the most personal of silver items. In medieval England they were confined to rich households, but by the 1570s yeomen farmers were acquiring them. In the 16th and 17th centuries silver spoons were regarded as a status symbol, being given at christenings, passed on as dowries, and specifically left in wills.[1]

The 'seal-top' spoon, so-called from the resemblance of its finial to a seal, is the most common type of early English spoon. Made from the mid-15th century, the earliest extant hallmarked example dates from 1525. The majority of surviving examples are 17th century but, apart from replacements made to order, seal-top spoons had fallen from fashion by 1680.[2]

After c.1575 these spoons generally have a circular end, and William Mutton's spoon belongs to the commonest type of seal-top between the late 16th and late 17th centuries.[3] The finials of these spoons were usually gilded, with the remainder left plain.[4] Mutton's spoon is typical of provincial examples in having a lap-jointed finial and the maker's mark struck in the bowl near the stem.[5]

The spoon was dated *c.*1580 in the 1935 auction catalogue (see Provenance), and this was accepted by Canon Ridgway in 1993. Given that this type of seal-top was introduced *c.*1575, the spoon clearly dates from very late in Mutton's career, and it seems prudent to extend the date-range to the year of his death.

This spoon is William Mutton's only surviving marked piece of secular silver. However, given the quality of the craftsmanship, which is as good as many London examples, it cannot have been the only one he made. A seal-top spoon of *c.*1580 by John Lingley I,[6] with a simpler finial, is the only other known Elizabethan Chester spoon. Indeed, these two spoons are the only surviving examples of pre-Civil War Chester domestic silver.

While the gilding on the finial is presumably original, that on the interior of the bowl was added in the mid-19th century along with the engraving. Despite the medieval heraldic vocabulary of a cross, crescents, chevrons and martlets, the arms are a fabrication,[7] and the cartouche bears only a vestigial resemblance to the 'English Renaissance' style, as the Elizabethan and Jacobean revival was called.[8] These alterations were made to increase the spoon's appeal to the mid-19th-century market for antique silver.

From at least the 1750s a market had emerged which valued old English silver for its antiquity and historical interest and for its contribution to period interiors. This continued in the 19th century, with public auctions of major collections from *c.*1800 and the arrival of dealers in antique silver by the 1820s. Early Victorian collectors tended to add their heraldry wherever possible and to gild their silver. A series of public exhibitions in the 1850s and '60s, dominated by ornamental plate of the late 16th to late 17th centuries, introduced historic silver to a wider public. The demands of the collector's market were met by a combination of genuine pieces, fakes, alterations and additions, and Mutton's spoon is a modest example of the latter.[9]

PROVENANCE: H.D. Ellis; Lieutenant-Colonel J. Benett-Stanford, Tisbury, Wiltshire; Sotheby's, London, 13 November 1935, lot 39; Purchased by McDonald; Phillips, London, 27 June 1980, lot 108; Sotheby's, London, 24 April 1986, lot 22; Purchased with grant aid from the MGC/V&A Purchase Grant Fund, Beecroft Bequest, Grosvenor Museum Society 1986.113

PUBLISHED: Ridgway 1968, p.64 no.26; Moore 1986, p.1292; Ridgway 1993 I, illustrated p.22; Ridgway 1996, p.179.

NOTES:

1. Mathew Shuter in NACF Review 1995, p.86; Snodin 1974, p.12.
2. Snodin 1974, pp.11, 26; Davis, p.165 n.1; Clayton 1985 I, p.381.
3. Snodin 1974, p.26. Mutton's spoon is very close to London examples of 1604 (Davis, no.172) and 1655 (Snodin 1974, pl.11).
4. Davis, p.165. For a colour illustration see Snodin 1974, pl.11.
5. Davis, p.165; Clayton 1985 I, p.371.
6. Ridgway 1996, p.179, pl.50.
7. Gale Glynn, report, 22 March 1991.
8. Jervis 1983, p.123, pl.86.
9. Glanville 1987, pp.267, 274, 279, 289, 291, 293.

Peter Edwardes II

Peter Edwardes II, the fourth generation of a family of Chester goldsmiths, was the eldest surviving son of Peter Edwardes I, to whom he was apprenticed. He became a freeman in 1680 and a member of the Chester Goldsmiths' Company in 1681. He served the company as warden 1687-92 and master 1693 or '94-1701. Alexander Pulford (see no.9) was apprenticed to him. On his father's death in 1696 he inherited the family home in Bridge Street, and he served as sheriff of Chester 1697-8. He disappeared from the company records after 1701 and had died by 1721.[1]

NOTE:

1. Ridgway 1968, pp.119, 135-6; Ridgway 1985, p.36.

4 TOBACCO BOX

Lid: Peter Edwardes II, Chester, 1687-90
Base: Edward Cornock, London, 1712-13

Lid: four marks on underside (maker's mark Ridgway 1968, p.135)
Base: four marks on side (maker's mark Grimwade no.390a)
Length: 10 cm. (3.9 in.), width 8 cm. (3.1 in.), height 2.5 cm. (1 in.)
Weight: 130 g. (4.6 oz.)

4

Lid of sterling silver and base of Britannia silver. The low domed oval lid is raised from a single sheet of silver, its rounded edge curving in toward a narrow plain rim. There is a corresponding moulding at the lower edge of the oval base, which is also raised from a single sheet. This rises to straight, vertical sides, which fit inside the rim of the detached lid.

The lid is engraved with an armorial within Baroque mantling, a saracen's head erased at the neck and wreathed about the temples, for the Wynne family, with the cadence of a second son. The underside of the base is engraved with the script initials RW, for a member of the Wynne family.

These arms are borne by all families claiming descent from Marchudd ap Cynan, 9th century Founder of the Eighth Noble Tribe of North Wales. Surnames were not generally adopted in Wales until the Tudor era, at which time Wynn(e) was a popular choice. The only Wynne family with the saracen's head crest was Wynne of Coed Coch and Trofarth, Denbighshire, who were descended from Marchudd in the senior male line.[1]

The lid of the box was presumably made for Robert Wynne, the only recorded younger son of Thomas Wynne of Trofarth, who was living in 1687.[2] Since his parents married in 1587, Robert Wynne is unlikely to have lived long enough to be the RW whose initials appear on the base of 1712-3. His elder brother was Richard Wynne of Trofarth, whose grandson, another Richard Wynne of Trofarth, married in 1735 Gaynor, sole heiress of John Wynne of Coed Coch, thereby uniting these two branches of the family. It is therefore probable that Major-General Edward William Wynne of Coed Coch and Trofarth, great-great-grandson of Richard and Gaynor Wynne, who died in 1893, was the 'General Wynne' in whose possession Sir Charles Jackson noted the box.[3]

The original base was presumably lost or damaged, and the owner had it replaced while in London in 1712-13 by a specialist tobacco box maker. The work was accomplished with remarkable sensitivity, the moulding around the edge of the base being a mirror image of that on the lid.

Tobacco was introduced into England during the late 16th century, and a large number of pocket tobacco boxes survive from 1660 to 1730. They are usually oval, 10 cm. long and, being a highly personal accessory, they are often finely and elaborately engraved with the arms of the owner or his cypher. A pipe-smoker could rest the box and its detachable fitted cover on a table while using both hands to fill his pipe.[4]

This tobacco box lid is one of only five known pieces by Peter Edwardes II. The others are a monteith of 1687-90 described by Canon Ridgway as 'among the finest pieces of plate ever made in Chester', a tankard of 1687-90 and a communion cup and paten cover of 1696.[5] Only two other 17th-century Chester tobacco boxes are known, both oval and with armorial engravings, one of c.1687-97 by Thomas Robinson and the other of c.1697-1701 by Nathaniel Bullen.[6] A slightly later Chester example, also oval and engraved but with four feet, is the table tobacco box of 1704 by Richard Richardson I.[7]

5

The armorial engraving on the lid of this box is contemporary and of high quality. It is quite different in style to the armorial on the same maker's monteith,[8] but it is remarkably close in both style and execution to the superb armorials on a pair of London-assayed flagons by Seth Lofthouse (no.99). Elements of the armorials on these flagons relate closely to illustrations in *The Academy of Armory* by Randle Holme III, published in 1688, some of whose plates had been engraved by Peter Edwardes II. The flagons were purchased in 1702 for St Michael's Church, Chester, with a bequest from Samuel Edwardes, the younger brother of Peter Edwardes II, and the engraving incorporates the arms used by the Edwardes family and an inscription recording the bequest. Since Peter Edwardes II was an accomplished engraver, although by 1702 no longer active as a goldsmith, it would be natural for him to undertake this family-related commission, and it therefore seems highly likely, on both stylistic and circumstantial evidence, that he engraved both the flagons and the box lid.

Edward Cornock, the London goldsmith who made the base of this box, was apprenticed to Henry Grant in 1698 and became free in 1708. He entered his first mark as a largeworker in 1707 and his second (sterling) mark in 1723. He is recorded in business between 1707 and 1731 and, from surviving examples, was apparently a specialist in tobacco boxes.[9]

PROVENANCE: Wynne family of Coed Coch and Trofarth, Denbighshire (lid presumably made for Robert Wynne, base probably made for later member of family); 'General Wynne' (probably Major-General Edward William Wynne of Coed Coch and Trofarth, Denbighshire); Private collection, Colwyn Bay, by 1959; Brian Beet, 1996; Purchased with the assistance of the MGC/V&A Purchase Grant Fund, Brian Beet, National Art Collections Fund, Grosvenor Museum Society 1996.550.1,2

PUBLISHED: Jackson 1905, p.369 [does not mention different maker for base]; Ridgway 1968, p.137 no.4; NACF Review 1996, no.4277, illustrated; Ridgway 1996, p.183.

NOTES:

1. *Burke's General Armoury*, p.1145; *Burke's Landed Gentry*, p.2288.
2. Pedigree in Coed Coch Deeds 3378, National Library of Wales (Stephen Benham, letter, 6 August 1997).
3. *Burke's Landed Gentry*, p.2288; Lloyd, p.322-3; Jackson 1905, p.369.
4. Newman, p.327; Clayton 1985 I, pp.431, 433; Davis, p.208.
5. Ridgway 1968, pp.136-7; Ridgway 1985, p.220; Ridgway 1996, p.183.
6. Ridgway 1968, pp.129, 177; Bullen box illustrated Lever, pl.2.
7. Ridgway 1968, p.165, pl.78.
8. Ridgway 1968, pl.35.
9. Grimwade, p.473. There are nine tobacco boxes of 1707-14

by Edward Cornock in the Assheton Bennett collection at Manchester City Art Gallery (Parkinson, pp.44-5). For tobacco boxes of 1718 and 1723 by Edward Cornock see Davis, nos.229, 231.

Thomas Robinson

Thomas Robinson became free in 1681-2. He was admitted to the Chester Goldsmiths' Company in 1682, serving as steward 1683-5, 1699-1701 and warden 1701-23. He lived in Goss Lane and died in 1723.[1]

NOTE:

1. Ridgway 1968, pp.175-7.

5 TWO-HANDLED CUP

Thomas Robinson, Chester, 1690-2

Four marks on base (maker's mark Ridgway 1968, p.175 type 1; sterling mark Ridgway 1968, p.106 type B, overstruck with the city arms)
Height 11.1 cm. (4.4 in.), width across handles 19.7 cm. (7.75 in.)
Weight 345 g. (12.15 oz.)

See Colour Plate II

Sterling silver. The cup is raised from a single sheet, with a setting-out point on its base. The low, slightly flared foot-ring is moulded and applied. The lower half of the body, inturned toward the base, is chased with alternate spiral fluting and gadrooning. The plain upper part of the body is cylindrical, tapering outward to the slightly flared moulding at the rim. The two ornate S-scroll handles are cast and applied.

The earliest known two-handled cup dates from 1523 and, with or without a cover, the form evolved into one of the most typical vessels of the second half of the 17th century, before being superseded during the first two decades of the 18th century by the taller two-handled cup and cover.[1] In contemporary usage, as Timothy Schroder has explained, 'terms such as "caudle cup", "posset cup" and "porringer" were used almost interchangeably, depending perhaps more on the use to which it was put rather than on its form'.[2]

Two-handled cups were used for caudle, a spiced alcohol-and-gruel concoction, more or less liquid according to the recipe followed. The alcohol could be red or white wine, ale or brandy and, in addition to the staple ingredients of spices and oatmeal or bread, could contain tea, eggs and sugar. Caudle was usually served to invalids and to women before and after childbirth. Posset was more conveniently drunk from a cup with an upcurved spout, and porridge was more easily eaten from a shallow bowl with one side handle.[3]

The marks on Thomas Robinson's two-handled cup include an over-struck sterling mark.[4] Sterling marks were used by some Chester goldsmiths for a few years before 1687, and the type seen on Robinson's cup—the word sterling on two lines within a shaped shield—is otherwise found only on silver by Peter Pemberton I.[5] Robinson presumably made his cup, and struck the maker's and sterling marks, some time between his admittance to the Goldsmiths' Company in 1682 and the institution of date and town marks in 1687. The cup could well have been in stock for some years before Robinson submitted it for assay, between 1690 and 1692, when the date letter and two town marks were struck, the city arms almost obliterating the sterling mark which it effectively superseded.[6]

The cup is probably the earliest of the 55 surviving pieces of silver by Thomas Robinson, whose securely dated work runs from 1690-1721.[7] It is Robinson's only known two-handled cup, although the alternate spiral fluting and gadrooning is also found on a mug of 1690-2.[8] A very similar mug (no.9) was made by Alexander Pulford c.1697-1701.

Peter Pemberton I is the only other Chester goldsmith whose comparable two-handled cups survive from this period. He made a 'fluted porringer' in 1690-2 and a miniature one with spiral fluting and punched decoration in c.1697-1701.[9] His two-handled cup of 1702 has alternate spiral fluting and gadrooning like Thomas Robinson's, but is additionally ornamented with chased ropework around the body and higher foot plus three bands of punched decoration, and he made a similar cup in 1706.[10] Richard Richardson I made a gadrooned and decorated miniature porringer in c.1713-19.[11] All the other low two-handled cups by 18th-century Chester goldsmiths have plain bodies except for five made by George Walker I in 1769-76: these revive the fluting, gadrooning and ropework, plus the punched decoration, but replace the cast handles with ribbed straps and add a chased Rococo cartouche.[12]

Two-handled cups with chased alternate spiral fluting and gadrooning and cast S-scroll handles were made in large numbers by London goldsmiths between the 1690s and the 1720s. The majority of these have bands of punched decoration,[13] as followed in Chester by Peter Pemberton I. The plainer form is less common,[14] but Thomas Robinson used it to create one of the most aesthetically satisfying pieces of 17th-century Chester silver.

PROVENANCE: Gerald S. Sanders, London; Lowe & Sons, Chester, 1983; Purchased with grant aid from the V&A Purchase Grant Fund, National Art Collections Fund, Grosvenor Museum Society 1984.23

EXHIBITED: Chester 1984, no.15, illustrated.

PUBLISHED: Banister 1962, illustrated p.39; Ridgway 1968, pp.104, 178 no.5, marks pl.53; NACF Review 1985, no.3110, illustrated; Glanville 1987, fig.63; Callaghan, illustrated p.33.

NOTES:

1. Schroder 1988 II, p.102; Clayton 1985 I, pp.133, 281; Schroder 1988 I, p.131.
2. Schroder 1988 II, p.105. A list of plate plundered from Utkinton Hall, Cheshire, in 1644 includes 'a caudle cup & A porringer' (Cheshire Record Office, DAR/E/26).
3. Wees, p.43; Clayton 1985 I, pp.78, 119; Newman, pp.65, 247.
4. Illustrated Ridgway 1968, pl.53; Glanville 1987, fig.63.
5. Ridgway 1968, pp.105-6.
6. Ridgway 1968, p.104; Philippa Glanville, letter, 12 April 1984.
7. Ridgway 1968, pp.177-80; Ridgway 1985, p.221; Ridgway 1996, pp.190-1.
8. Ridgway 1968, p.178, pl.52.
9. Ridgway 1968, pp.151, 154, the miniature one illustrated p.153 fig.5.
10. Ridgway 1968, p.156; the 1702 cup illustrated Moore 1984 I, no.25.
11. Ridgway 1996, p.187. John Bingley's covered porringer of c.1702-5, which is of a wholly different form, is the only Chester two-handled cup of this period to possess a cover (Ridgway 1996, p.180, pl.52).
12. Ridgway 1985, pp.200-1; the 1771 cup illustrated Moore 1984 I, no.108.
13. Examples include covered cups by Benjamin Rhodes, 1685 (Oman 1978, pl.98) and Robert Timbrell, 1696 (Wees, no.25); and cups by John Sutton, 1705 (Oman 1965, pl.105) and Timothy Ley, 1717 (Lomax, no.43), both with a chased rope moulding beneath an everted lip.
14. Examples include a silver-gilt covered cup of 1690 by Francis Garthorne (Brett, no.510) and a cup of 1692 with an everted lip by Robert Cooper? (Wark, no.27).

6 SERVING SPOON

Thomas Robinson, Chester, 1709-10

Five marks on back of stem near bowl (maker's mark Ridgway 1968, p.175 type 2)
Length 38.5 cm. (15.15 in.)
Weight 169 g. (5.95 oz.)

Britannia standard silver. The bowl and stem are formed from a single piece of silver. The raised bowl is a deep ovalised oblong. There is a single drop at its junction with the stem, below which a plain rat-tail extends almost halfway down the back of the bowl. There is a ridge along the upper third of the Hanoverian pattern stem, which turns sharply upward at the end.

The back of the stem is engraved with the crest of a talbot's head couped and collared dancetty. The crest looks to be early 18th century, but its use with this particular collar has not been traced.[1]

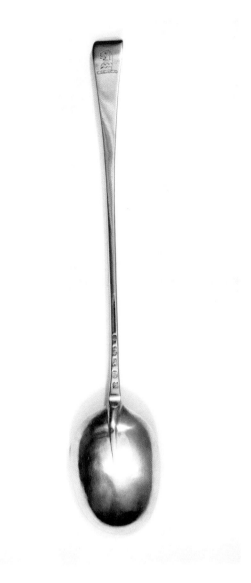

6

Large silver spoons were probably made from early times, and one of the earliest surviving examples dates from *c.*1600. Some from the late 17th and early 18th centuries have tubular silver or turned wood handles, but after *c.*1715 they are usually greatly enlarged versions of the standard tablespoon of the day.[2] Several terms have been used for these large spoons and, according to one recent definition, a serving spoon is 33-8 cm. long, a stuffing spoon is 39-45 cm. and a basting spoon measures 46-60 cm.[3] In the 18th century they were most frequently called ragout spoons, sometimes turkey spoons (when used for serving the stuffing from a roasted fowl), and were known as hash spoons in Scotland and Ireland. The term basting spoon is generally used today but it seems unlikely that, except in the grandest homes, a silver spoon engraved with the family crest would be confined to the kitchen, and it seems preferable to use the more general term serving spoon.[4]

The motif of the rat-tail appeared on London spoons in the 1660s and lasted until *c.*1730. A slender raised ridge, suggesting the shape of a rat's tail, runs down the back of the bowl. Originally intended to strengthen the bowl's junction with the stem, it soon became a decorative feature.[5]

The term 'Hanoverian' was invented for this form of stem by the 19th-century antiquary Octavius Morgan. It is named after the first two Hanoverian kings, George I and II, and was the standard spoon type during their reigns. The pattern was introduced to London in the first decade of the 18th century, reached its greatest popularity between 1715 and 1760, and continued to be made into the 1780s. The rounded end of the stem turns up, and the engraving on the smooth back of the stem was shown when the spoon was laid face down on the table in the French manner.[6]

A particularly early Hanoverian serving spoon was made in 1708 by the London goldsmith Lewis Mettayer.[7] According to Nicholas Moore, Thomas Robinson's serving spoon is 'the earliest example of a Hanoverian pattern terminal on a provincial spoon',[8] but it is equalled by a Hanoverian table spoon by Samuel Blachford of Plymouth, assayed at Exeter in 1709.[9]

The example in the Grosvenor Museum is the earliest of Thomas Robinson's four known serving spoons, all of them Hanoverian rat-tails: two of the others date from 1711 and one from 1716.[10] Twenty rat-tail table spoons by Robinson have been recorded, those of 1703-7 with dog-nose terminals but the fifteen spoons from 1711-19 having Hanoverian stems.[11]

Serving spoons by three of Robinson's contemporaries at Chester also survive. Peter Pemberton I made one with a tubular silver handle in 1705;[12] Richard Richardson I made one with a wooden handle in 1713 and with Hanoverian stems in 1715 and 1727;[13] and William Richardson I made a wooden handled serving spoon in 1722 and three Hanoverian ones in 1723 and '25.[14]

PROVENANCE: T.H. Clarke, Chester; Presented by the National Art Collections Fund 1952.103

EXHIBITED: Chester 1973 II, p.48 no.3; Chester 1979 I, silver no.19; Chester 1980; Manchester 1983, no.66; Chester 1984, no.33.

PUBLISHED: NACF Report 1952, no.1659; Ridgway 1968, p.178 no.3, marks pl.55; Thomas, p.13; Ridgway 1996, no.41.

NOTES:
1. Gale Glynn, report, 22 March 1991. The crest does not appear in Ormerod.
2. Snodin 1974, pp.34-5; Clayton 1985 I, p.375.
3. Newman, pp.34, 280, 305.
4. Snodin 1974, p.38; Newman, p.305. The Chester Plate Duty Books record a 'dole spoon' submitted by John Sutter of Liverpool in 1837 (Ridgway 1996, p.104).

7

5. Clayton 1985 I, pp.382, 378; Newman, p.258.

6. Newman, p.162; Snodin 1974, pp.12, 14, 38-9; Clayton 1985 I, p.378.

7. Snodin 1974, p.38.

8. Moore 1984 I, p.37.

9. Private collection, Norwich (letter from owner, February 1985).

10. Sotheby's, London, 12 March 1984, lot 522; J.H. Bourdon-Smith Ltd., Catalogue No.40, Autumn 1998, p.12; Ridgway 1996, p.190.

11. Ridgway 1968, pp.178-80; Ridgway 1996, p.190. Moore 1984 I illustrates several of the Hanoverian rat-tail tablespoons: five of 1711 (no.34), two of 1716 (no.36) and six of 1719 (no.37).

12. Ridgway 1968, p.155.

13. Ridgway 1968, p.171; Ridgway 1996, pp.185, 188.

14. Ridgway 1968, pp.173-4; Ridgway 1996, p.190.

Ralph Walley

Ralph Walley was baptised in 1661 and became free in 1682. He was admitted to the Chester Goldsmiths' Company in 1682, serving as steward 1685-7 and warden 1687-90. Richard Richardson I (see no.10) probably worked in partnership with him from at least 1699, but Walley did not register a new mark when the official assay office was established in 1701. He had a house and shop in Eastgate Street and died in 1703.[1]

NOTE:

1. Ridgway 1968, pp.180-2.

7 TANKARD

Ralph Walley, Chester, 1687-90

Four marks below rim and on lid (maker's mark Ridgway 1968, p.180 type 2). Maker's mark only on handle
Height to thumbpiece 19.2 cm. (7.55 in.),
diameter of base 14.2 cm. (5.6 in.)
Weight 1,008 g. (35.55 oz.)

See Colour Plate II

Silver. The plain, slightly tapering cylindrical body is raised, with an inset circular base. The applied foot-ring is moulded and reeded, and a narrower flared moulding is applied to the rim. The S-scroll handle is of D-section, with a rounded underside soldered to a straight outer edge. The handle tapers to its lower junction with the body before widening to a five-sided heel, beneath which is a large oval air hole.[1] The five-part hinge, with ribbed hinge plates and a cast ram's-horn thumbpiece,[2] joins the handle to the cover. The flat double-stepped cover has a setting-out point and is raised. Its broad rim, serrated and pointed at the front, is engraved with two pairs of thin lines. A narrow bezel is applied inside the cover.

The body is engraved opposite the handle with a shield surrounded by ostrich plumes, the commonest heraldic arrangement during the later 17th century. The style of the engraving is correct for the date of the tankard but has been re-cut. The arms are those of Radell or Betton: it is not known where the Radells lived, but the Bettons lived at Great Berwick near Shrewsbury, Shropshire, and are therefore much more likely to have owned this tankard. The original owner was probably Richard Betton VII (1649-1725), who built the present house at Great Berwick *c*.1690 on a site owned by his family from the 14th to the 19th centuries.[3]

Tankards were used for drinking beer, the alcoholic liquor brewed from barley malt and hops. Tankards are referred to from the 14th century, but the earliest surviving one made entirely from silver dates from 1556 and is pear-shaped. This was superseded by the tapering cylindrical form, probably derived from vessels of mounted horn or banded wooden staves, and the earliest silver example of this type dates from 1573. The plain tapering tankard with a flat cover was one of the standard forms during the first half of the 17th century, and became even more popular after 1660.[4]

This tankard by Ralph Walley is the second largest of the nine known Chester tankards.[5] It is one of five surviving tankards by Walley, along with two others dating from 1687-90 (one of which, at 8.75 in. high, is the largest) and two of 1690-2.[6] In addition, one tankard of 1687-90 by Peter Edwardes II is known,[7] and by Peter Pemberton I there are two of 1703 and

one from the following year.[8] All nine Chester tankards have a tapering cylindrical body moulded at the foot and rim, with an S-scroll handle, and, in the six examples where this detail is known, the rim of the cover is serrated and pointed at the front. Of the five tankards by Walley, all have a flat double-stepped cover, three have a ram's-horn thumbpiece while two have the corkscrew form, and at least two have ribbed hinge plates where one has a cut-card border. The tankard by Edwardes shares a flat double-stepped cover with those by Walley, and has a corkscrew thumbpiece. Pemberton's tankards differ most notably from Walley's in having an octagonal heel, a cast pendant drop to the hinge, a triple-stepped cover, corkscrew thumbpieces to the 1703 tankards with a bifurcated scroll thumbpiece to that of 1704 and, most distinctively, a cut-card openwork clover at the handle's lower junction with the body.

The Grosvenor Museum's tankard is remarkably close to a London-made vessel of 1635,[9] which is perhaps the finest surviving Charles I tankard, and to some London examples of the 1680s.[10] This form also appeared in the provinces in the mid-1670s,[11] and an example similar to Walley's is a Dublin tankard of 1680.[12] The possibility that some Dublin silver may have influenced Chester goldsmiths cannot be discounted, since there was a flourishing trade between the two cities at this time.[13]

Ralph Walley's five tankards comprise half his surviving work, along with a paten or alms dish of 1683, a jug of 1690-2 (no.8) and three spoons, one undated and two of 1687-90.[14]

PROVENANCE: Probably Richard Betton of Great Berwick, Shropshire, *c*.1687-90; Lloyd Tyrell-Kenyon, 5th Baron Kenyon of Gredington, by 1951; Sotheby's, London, 19 June 1969, lot 209; Mrs. Marian Close-Brooks, Milford-on-Sea, Lymington, Hampshire; Purchased in 1976 with grant aid from the V&A Purchase Grant Fund, National Art Collections Fund, Cheshire County Council, Earl Grosvenor (later Duke of Westminster) 1977.15

EXHIBITED: Chester 1951, no.126, pl.XXIII; Manchester 1983, no.64; London 1984, S.1; Chester 1984, no.17, illustrated.

PUBLISHED: Ridgway 1968, p.183 no.5, pl.39; Ridgway 1973, illustrated; NACF Report 1976, no.2612; *The Cheshire Sheaf*, 5th Series, no.46, February 1977, illustrated; Thomas, p.17; Moore 1985 II, fig.4; Moore 1986, fig.3; Callaghan, illustrated p.33.

NOTES:

1. This hole is essential to allow the hot air to escape when the handle is soldered to the body, thus avoiding the danger of an explosion (Clayton 1985 II, p.80).

2. This form, incorrectly (if compared with the illustration in Newman, p.87) termed a corkscrew thumbpiece by some writers, is called a ram's-horn thumbpiece by Gilchrist & Inglis (no.66) or a volute thumbpiece in Moore 1984 I (nos.17-18).

3. Oman 1978, p.57; Gale Glynn, report, 22 March 1991; Forrest, pp.101, 103.

4. Clayton 1985 I, p.396; Schroder 1988 I, p.76; Schroder 1988 II, pp.102, 130.

5. According to Moore 1985 II (p.36), there are 11 Chester tankards, but Canon Ridgway only records nine.

6. Ridgway 1968, pp.183-4; Ridgway 1985, pp.221-2; Ridgway 1996, p.191. Illustrated: one of 1687-90 in Moore 1984 I, no.18; one of 1690-2 in Ridgway 1968, pl.39. According to Moore 1986 (p.1293), the finely engraved armorials on Walley's tankards could be the work of Nathaniel Bullen, who is known to have specialised in engraving, but their stylistic differences seem too great to be the work of a single hand over just five years.

7. Ridgway 1985, p.220; Ridgway 1996, p.183.

8. Ridgway 1968, pp.155-6; Ridgway 1996, p.182. Illustrated in Moore 1984 I, nos.27-9.

9. Maker's mark an orb and star (Clayton 1985 I, fig.597).

10. e.g.: 1680, maker's mark a goose in a dotted circle (Brett, no.490), where the only difference is a single point to the rim; 1683, same maker (Gilchrist & Inglis, no.66, illustrated p.47); 1688, John Sutton (Brett, no.481), which has a corkscrew thumbpiece.

11. Moore 1985 II, p.34.

12. Davis, no.52.

13. Kennett, p.9. James Lomax (telephone conversation, 11 November 1999) has suggested that some Chester silver may also have influenced Dublin goldsmiths.

14. Ridgway 1968, pp.182-3; Ridgway 1985, p.222.

8 JUG

Ralph Walley, Chester, 1690-2

Four marks on base (maker's mark Ridgway 1968, p.180 type 2)
Height 18 cm. (7.1 in.)
Weight 678 g. (23.9 oz.)

See Colour Plate II

Silver with handle of stained holly (*Ilex aquifolium*).[1] The pear-shaped body is raised from a single sheet, with a setting-out point on the rounded base. The deep, moulded circular foot-ring is seamed once and soldered to the base. The neck is boldly everted and has a beak-shaped pouring lip. A narrow moulding is applied around the rim, and 17 graded beads are applied to the lip. The wooden S-scroll handle, with a thumbpiece, is positioned at 110 degrees to the lip. The handle is set in silver ferrules with serrated and engraved outer edges, and is secured by two pins at the top and by one pin at the bottom.

The body is engraved opposite the handle with a crest within a cartouche of crossed plumes. The crest, a cubit arm vested holding in the hand an arrow in bend sinister, is that of Harrison.[2]

The earliest surviving jugs are the ewers associated with basins and, becoming more varied in their use, late 17th-century jugs are pear- or helmet-shaped, with or without a cover.[3] The wooden handle of Ralph Walley's jug suggests that it was intended for a hot liquid, but the absence of a cover would not have kept it hot for long. It was described as a mead jug by Sotheby's in 1963 (see Provenance), and this romantic association with the old English drink of fermented honey has been repeated frequently since. Nicholas Moore has suggested that it was more probably used for adding hot milk to chocolate or posset (hot milk curdled by an infusion of beer or wine, with bread-crumbs, sugar and spices) or for serving mulled drinks (wine or beer heated with sugar, spices and egg yolk).[4]

Ralph Walley's jug is a unique piece of English silver. The only remotely comparable piece of Chester silver from this period is Peter Pemberton I's chocolate pot of 1703,[5] whose inverted pear-shaped body on a moulded foot-ring has a D-shaped wooden handle at an angle to its spout, and no other Chester jugs are known before the 1720s.[6]

Wooden handles on London silver are found on tea pots from 1670, on coffee pots from 1681 and on chocolate pots from 1685.[7] On some early tea pots, and on almost all coffee and chocolate pots, the handle is set at 90 degrees to the spout, but the 110 degree angle on Walley's jug appears to be unprecedented. The great majority of wooden handles on coffee and chocolate pots before 1710 are D-shaped, but a few are S-scrolled like the Chester jug, and the double-scroll handle emerges after 1700. The ferrules almost always have straight outer edges, while serrated and engraved ones are very rare: those on a slightly later London chocolate pot of 1697 by Benjamin Bradford are closely comparable to the ones on Walley's jug.[8]

The motif of graduated beading is found on a number of London pieces from the decade before the Chester jug, usually on the handle,[9] and more rarely on the spout.[10] The only other examples on Chester silver, post-dating Ralph Walley's jug, are on spoons by Peter Pemberton I, two of 1695-6 and one of *c.*1697-1701.[11]

PROVENANCE: Sotheby's, London, 14 November 1963, lot 109; A.C.D. Pain, Exeter; Christie's, London, 15 March 1972, lot 105; De Havilland (Antiques) Ltd., London; Purchased, after the temporary refusal of an export licence, with grant aid from the V&A Purchase Grant Fund, National Art Collections Fund, Pilgrim Trust, Marc Fitch Fund, London Goldsmiths' Company 1972.163

8

EXHIBITED: Chester 1973 II, p.40 no.6, illustrated p.41; London 1978, no.70, illustrated; Manchester 1983, no.65; London 1984, S.2; Chester 1984, no.19, illustrated.

PUBLISHED: Ridgway 1968, pp.182-3 no.2, pl.38; *Country Life*, 24 February 1972, illustrated p.467; Bennett 1972 II, p.30, illustrated p.35; NACF Report 1972, no.2461; *The Pilgrim Trust Annual Report* 1973, p.49; Banister 1973, pp.1876-7, fig.5; Lever, p.40, fig.4; Thomas, p.16; Clayton 1985 I, p.246, fig.329; Clayton 1985 II, pp.85, 89 fig.7; Moore 1986, p.1293, fig.2; Schroder 1992, p.36; Callaghan, illustrated p.33; Fothringham, p.309.

NOTES:

1. Wood identified by Graham Usher, 13 November 1999.

2. Gale Glynn, report, 22 March 1991.

3. Clayton 1985 I, pp.226-8.

4. Manchester 1983 exhibition catalogue, no.65; Moore 1986, p.1293. According to Christopher Lever (p.41) 'It was most probably used for punch.' Timothy Schroder (1992, p.36) suggested that it may have been made for beer, but Nicholas Moore (undated note) thought it too small and too early to be a beer jug.

5. Ridgway 1968, p.154, pl.48.

6. Jug 2.75 in. high, Thomas Robinson, *c.*1720; jug 5 in. high, Benjamin Pemberton, 1725 (Ridgway 1968, pp.147, 177-8).

7. Clayton 1985 I, pp.413, 96, 90.

8. Hackenbroch, pl.76. Shaped ferrules, without engraving, are found slightly later, as on these examples of 1701: coffee pot by Anthony Nelme and chocolate pot by Joseph Ward (Wees, nos.181, 209); chocolate pot by William Lukin (Clayton 1985 I, fig.126); coffee pot by Joseph Ward (Lomax, no.121).

9. e.g.: pair of tankards, maker's mark a goose in a dotted circle, 1681 (Brett, no.492); ewer, Ralph Leake, 1683 (Schroder 1988 I, fig.33A); tankard, maker's mark IA, 1684, and ewer, maker's mark HR, 1685 (Clayton 1985 II, p.80 fig.8, p.77 fig.14); covered porringer, Francis Garthorne, 1690 (Brett, no.510); tankard, maker's mark GC, c.1690 (Wills, fig.5).

10. e.g.: tea pot, maker's mark BB, 1689 (Brett, no.505); cordial pot, maker's mark FSS, c.1690 (Clayton 1985 II, p.84 fig.2).

11. Ridgway 1968, pp.152-3, pl.44.

Alexander Pulford

Alexander Pulford was apprenticed to Peter Edwardes II (see no.4) and became free in 1690. He was admitted to the Chester Goldsmiths' Company in 1690, serving as warden 1692-9. He did not register a new mark when the official assay office was established in 1701, but remained a member of the company, an apprentice of his becoming free in 1714. He had died by 1722.[1]

NOTE:

1. Ridgway 1968, pp.158-9.

9 MUG

Alexander Pulford of Chester, c.1697-1701

Two maker's marks only on base (Ridgway 1968, p.158 type 1, and Ridgway 1985, p.220 type 2)
Height to top of handle 7.9 cm. (3.1 in.), width across handle 9.7 cm. (3.8 in.)
Weight 131 g. (4.6 oz.)

Silver. The mug is raised from a single sheet, with a setting-out point on its slightly rounded base. The low, slightly flared foot-ring is moulded and applied. The lower half of the body, inturned toward the base, is chased with alternate spiral fluting and gadrooning beneath an applied moulded band. The plain upper part of the body has an everted rim, and the S-scroll, ribbed strap handle is applied.

The mug probably dates between the closure of Chester's unofficial assay office in 1697 and the establishment of the city's official assay office in 1701. Several of Pulford's contemporaries also struck pieces with repeated maker's marks during this period without town marks or date letters. For example, a communion cup by Richard Richardson I, dated 1699, is struck twice with the maker's mark, and three spoons by Nathaniel Bullen are each struck twice with two versions of his maker's mark.[1]

Only three other pieces by Pulford survive, a spoon of 1687-90 and an undated cupping bowl and taper stick.[2] This mug is the only known example to bear his type 2 maker's mark. The use of chased alternate spiral fluting and gadrooning on Chester silver is discussed in the entry on Thomas Robinson's two-handled cup of 1690-2 (no.5).

Only two other 17th-century Chester mugs are known, both made in 1690-2 by Thomas Robinson,[3] one of which is chased with alternate spiral fluting and gadrooning like Pulford's mug. Starting with Richard Richardson I in the 1720s, mugs of various forms were made by a number of 18th-century Chester goldsmiths (see nos.32 and 38).

Mugs first appeared in the 1670s, and *Bailey's Dictionary* of 1728 defines a mug as 'a Cup for warming drink etc.' The bell-shaped variety, with a small C-shaped handle and a moulded rib around the body, was common to both Scotland and England.[4] The 17th-century Chester mugs share this bell-shaped form with Scottish 'thistle' cups, but have chased decoration rather than applied lobed fluting.

PROVENANCE: Silver Lyon Ltd. (Henry Steuart Fothringham), Edinburgh; Michael Clayton, Edinburgh, 1973; His widow, Mrs. Georgina Clayton, 1991, by whom offered to the Museum at a specially reduced price in accordance with the wishes of her late husband; Purchased with grant aid from the MGC/V&A Purchase Grant Fund, the Dorothy Tunstall Bequest through the Grosvenor Museum Society, Beecroft Bequest 1994.19

EXHIBITED: Chester 1973 I; Chester 1984, no.22, illustrated.

PUBLISHED: Ridgway 1985, p.220; Ridgway 1996, p.184.

9

NOTES:

1. Ridgway 1968, pp.128-9, 163.
2. Ridgway 1968, p.159.
3. Moore 1984 I, nos.13-14.
4. Clayton 1985 I, pp.258, 260.

Richard Richardson I

Richard Richardson I founded a dynasty whose three generations dominated goldsmithing in 18th-century Chester. Born in 1674, he was apprenticed in 1688 to his father John Richardson, goldsmith of Worcester and London. He became a freeman of Worcester in 1697 but had moved to Chester by 1699, where he probably worked in partnership with Ralph Walley (see no.7). He became a freeman of Chester in 1703 and was admitted to the Goldsmiths' Company in 1708, serving as warden 1711-13 and assay master 1713-30. His younger brother William Richardson I (see no.14) and his son Richard Richardson II (see no.21) were apprenticed to him. His shop was in Eastgate Row and he died in 1730.[1]

NOTE:

1. Ridgway 1968, pp.160-3; Ridgway 1985, pp.130-4.

10 PAIR OF TABLE SPOONS

Richard Richardson I, Chester, 1713-4

Five marks on back of stem near bowl (maker's mark Ridgway 1968, p.160 type 3)
Length: both 19.9 cm. (7.8 in.)
Weight: (1) 61 g. (2.15 oz.), (2) 66 g. (2.3 oz.)

Britannia standard silver. Each spoon is formed from a single piece of silver, with a deep and narrow raised bowl. There is a single drop at its junction with the stem, below which a plain rat-tail extends two-thirds of the way down the back of the bowl. There is a pronounced ridge, forming hollows to either side, along the upper half of the Hanoverian pattern stem, which turns upward at the end.

The back of each stem is engraved with the crest of a sphinx sejant with wings adorsed. A sphinx usually has a lion's tail, but this one has the tail of a dragon or wyvern, creating a monster unknown to either nature or heraldry. The engraving looks early 19th-century and the crest is unidentified.[1]

Spoons and knives had been personal objects carried by an individual to a meal. Following the court's return from exile in 1660, a change in etiquette took place during the late 17th and early 18th centuries. This required a table to be set with the necessary knives, forks and spoons, hence the term 'table spoon', which has been used since at least the first half of the 18th century. With the introduction of tea and coffee,

10

condiments and desserts, spoons began to be made in a much greater variety of sizes. The table spoon, which normally has a capacity three times that of a dessert spoon, was used for soup.[2]

The earliest known spoon by Richard Richardson I dates from 1709 and has a rounded end but no ridge along the stem.[3] Eleven of his Hanoverian rat-tail table spoons survive, dating between 1712 and 1718 and comprising a single spoon, three pairs and a set of four.[4] Surviving examples show that Hanoverian rat-tail table spoons were also made in early 18th-century Chester by Thomas Robinson from 1711-19, by Thomas Maddock from 1716-20, by William Richardson I in 1719 and by Benjamin Pemberton I in 1725.[5]

PROVENANCE: Mr. K. Snowden, Barrowford, Lancashire; Purchased with grant aid from the Beecroft Bequest 1979.96.1,2

EXHIBITED: Chester 1980; Chester 1982; Chester 1984, no.44.

PUBLISHED: Moore 1985 III, one illustrated p.73; Ridgway 1996, p.185 nos.30-1.

NOTES:

1. Gale Glynn, report, 22 March 1991.
2. Pickford, pp.13-15; Newman, p.314.
3. Ridgway 1996, p.186.
4. Ridgway 1968, pp.169, 171; Ridgway 1996, pp.186-7.
5. Ridgway 1968, pp.145, 147, 179-80; Ridgway 1996, pp.189-90.

11 COMMUNION CUP

Richard Richardson I, Chester, 1718-19

Five marks below rim (maker's mark Ridgway
1968, p.160 type 3)
Height 17 cm. (6.7 in.)
Weight 310 g. (10.9 oz.), scratch weight 10=1=0

Britannia standard silver. The low domed foot is raised, with an applied moulding set back from the edge of the foot-ring. The double-spool stem is raised in two sections, which are joined with an applied moulding. The inverted bell-shaped bowl, with a setting-out point on its underside, is raised and has a thickened rim, everted externally but cylindrical within. The side of the bowl is engraved in script below the rim: 'Thomas: Bolland. / James: Johnson. / Church:Wardens. 1720.'

Although hallmarked in 1718-19, it was acquired by the church in 1720, and was therefore presumably purchased from stock rather than specially commissioned.[1]

Twenty communion cups, and five small ones for administering communion to the sick, are known to have been made by Richard Richardson I between 1699 and 1728.[2] All are variations of the same basic type and, in common with most Anglican communion cups of the 18th century, show little development from late 17th-century models.[3]

Richard Richardson I is thought to have made more ecclesiastical plate than any other provincial goldsmiths since the 16th century.[4] He appears to have enjoyed a near monopoly in Chester, where only five other communion cups are known to have been made during his career: by Timothy Gardner c.1697-1701, by John Bingley and by Peter Pemberton I in 1704, by Nathaniel Bullen in 1711, and by his younger brother William Richardson I in 1724.[5] Indeed, all the surviving Chester-made communion cups between 1713 and 1779 are by members of the Richardson family.[6] In addition to his patens, which are discussed in the next two entries, Richard Richardson I also made three flagons for church use between 1712 and 1727.[7]

PROVENANCE: St Bridget's Church, Chester, 1720; Transferred to St Mary-on-the-Hill, Chester, 1891; Transferred to Chester Team Parish, 1972; Purchased with grant aid from the MGC/V&A Purchase Grant Fund, National Heritage Memorial Fund, Pilgrim Trust, Duke of Westminster, Mary Newboult Bequest, Grosvenor Museum Society 1988.31

11

EXHIBITED: London V&A 1989.

PUBLISHED: Earwaker, p.23; Ball 1907, p.82 no.IV, illustrated opposite p.82; Ridgway 1968, p.167 no.9; Richards, p.116 (b); Pevsner & Hubbard, p.151; Boughton 1992 I.

NOTES:

1. The churchwardens' accounts before 1763 unfortunately do not survive, but the inscription strongly suggests that it was purchased by the wardens. The warden Thomas Bolland, a barber surgeon, became free in 1703, sheriff in 1713-14 and mayor in 1725-6. His fellow warden James Johnson, a brewer, became free in 1673. (Bennett 1908, p.212; Hanshall, p.178; Bennett 1906, p.162.)
2. Ridgway 1968, pp.163-70; Ridgway 1985, pp.135-8; Ridgway 1996, pp.187-9.
3. Of the examples illustrated in Oman 1957, it is closest to a London-made covered communion cup of 1695, maker's mark IH crowned, at Wapping (pl.92b).
4. Lever, p.41.
5. Ridgway 1968, pp.122, 130, 140, 154-5, 174.

12

6. The 1779 communion cup is by Richard Richardson III (Ridgway 1985, p.174). The Chester Plate Duty Books also record a communion cup by Richard Richardson IV in 1786 (Ridgway 1996, p.96).

7. Ridgway 1968, p.166; Ridgway 1985, p.136; Ridgway 1996, p.186.

12 COMMUNION CUP AND STANDING PATEN

Richard Richardson I, Chester, 1723-4

Five marks below rim of cup and near border of paten (maker's mark Ridgway 1968, p.160 type 4)

Height of cup 18.1 cm. (7.1 in.), diameter of paten 16.8 cm. (6.6 in.)

Weight: cup 288 g. (10.15 oz.), paten 243 g. (8.6 oz.)

See Colour Plate I

Sterling silver. The cup's low domed and stepped foot is raised, with an incised line around the foot-ring. The double-spool stem is raised in two sections, joined with a compressed spherical knop, which is raised and has applied wires around its centre and either edge. 'S M' is scratched inside the lower stem, and there is an incised line around the upper stem below its junction with the bowl. The bowl is raised, with a setting-out point on the underside of its rounded base. The tapering sides rise to a thickened rim, everted externally above an incised line but cylindrical within. The side of the bowl is inscribed below the rim.

The paten's low domed foot is raised, with an applied horizontal foot-ring, and is soldered to the raised spool stem. The circular paten is raised from a single sheet, having a shallow well with a setting-out point and an angled border with a moulded rim. The upper surface of the paten is inscribed.

Both cup and paten are engraved in script: 'Ex Dono Robti Pigot Arm. Tempore Majoratus Annoq Dom. 1723' (The gift of Robert Pigot, gentleman, during the time of his mayoralty in the year of our Lord 1723). Another example of Pigot's patronage is a silver punch ladle by the same maker, Richard Richardson I, likewise assayed in 1723-4, and engraved with the city arms and the inscription 'Robt. Pigot, Esqr., Mayor, 1724'.[1] Robert Pigot was steward at Eaton from *c.*1695 until his death, serving four successive baronets from Sir Thomas Grosvenor, 3rd Baronet to Sir Robert Grosvenor, 6th Baronet. He became a freeman of Chester in 1698, and was elected a councilman in 1715 and an alderman in 1720. He served as mayor in 1723-4 and died in 1750.[2]

The use of household bread for communion was authorised by the Second Prayer Book in 1552, and wafers were gradually replaced by the Protestant practice of breaking up 'the common loaf' as a visible expression of their belief that it was a common meal to be shared by all rather than a mystical experience. The paten covers of Elizabethan communion cups were designed for wafers but were inconvenient with household bread, which required larger patens.[3] Five of these larger Elizabethan patens survive, and take the form of a flat dish on a trumpet-shaped foot.[4] Household bread superseded wafers in most churches quite early in the 17th century, and the popularity of this form of paten therefore grew. The flat dish on a trumpet-shaped foot was the usual form for secular salvers throughout the 17th century, and came into general use for patens after 1660. Although it fell from secular fashion after 1715, it remained the most popular type for patens until 1830.[5]

Seven standing patens by Richard Richardson I are known, dating between 1710 and this example of 1723.[6] They are variations on the standard form of the period, and that of 1723 is little different from contemporary examples by Paul de Lamerie.[7] Only three other standing patens, made by Peter Pemberton I in 1703,[8] survive from this period of Chester silver.

PROVENANCE: Presented by Robert Pigot to St Michael's Church, Chester, 1723; Transferred to Chester Team Parish, 1972; Purchased with grant aid from the MGC/V&A Purchase Grant Fund, National Heritage Memorial Fund, Pilgrim Trust, Duke of Westminster, Mary Newboult Bequest, Grosvenor Museum Society 1988.38.1,2

PUBLISHED: Jackson 1905, paten p.370; Ball 1907, pp.71-2, cup no.IV, paten no.V; Ridgway 1968, p.167, cup no.10, paten no.12; Pevsner & Hubbard, p.152; Richards, p.120, cup (d), paten (e); Boughton 1992 I; Ridgway 1996, p.186, paten no.11, cup no.12.

NOTES:

1. Ridgway 1996, p.188. Chester 1951 exhibition catalogue, pl.XVII.
2. Eileen Simpson, letter, 15 June 1999; Bennett 1906, p.201; Hanshall, p.178; Chester Record Office, A/B/3/227v,258v, A/B/4/136.
3. Glanville 1990, p.380; Oman 1957, p.130 n.3, p.151.
4. The earliest, at All Hallows, Lombard Street, dates from 1560 (Oman 1957, p.216 n.6).
5. Oman 1957, pp.216-17, 253; Clayton 1985 I, p.317. The term 'standing paten' is a comparatively recent one, and 'footed paten' is a variant. Ridgway 1968 calls it a 'stand paten', Oman 1957 refers to 'patens shaped like salvers' (p.151), while Ball 1907 calls it a 'credence paten'.
6. Ridgway 1968, pp.164-5, 169; Ridgway 1996, p.187.
7. For examples of 1717 and 1727 see Hare 1990, nos.28-9.
8. Ridgway 1968, p.155; Ridgway 1996, p.182.

13 PLATE PATEN

Richard Richardson I, Chester, 1724-5

Five marks on rim (maker's mark Ridgway 1968, p.160 type 3)
Diameter 22.7 cm. (8.9 in.)
Weight 383 g. (13.5 oz.)

Sterling silver. The circular paten is raised from a shallow well with a setting-out point. The broad flat rim, with a simple outer moulding, is applied. It is engraved in script around the rim: 'The gift of Mrs. Alice Whitley to ye Parish-Church of St. Michl. 1639 wch. was inlarged and improved by the same Parish 1725'.

The engraver in 1725 mis-transcribed the donor's name as Whitley instead of Whitby or Whitbie, since the churchwardens' accounts, under a heading 'Gifts given by good benefactors' in 1639, include 'A silver plate given by Mrs Alis Whitbie wydow and parishioner to carry bread in at Sacraments for use at the Church for ever'. This Mrs. Alice Whitby was almost certainly the widow of Robert Whitby, who was town clerk of Chester 1602-9, sheriff 1607-8, mayor 1612-13, and was buried at St Michael's in 1631. She probably died between 1644 and 1651. Robert Whitby's son (by an earlier marriage) was Edward Whitby of the Bache, recorder 1613-39 and M.P. for Chester 1614-28, who was buried at St Mary-on-the-Hill in 1639. His widow, another Mrs. Alice Whitby (who died in 1640), presented a standing paten to St Mary's in 1639, and this may well have inspired her mother-in-law's gift of a plate paten to St Michael's the same year.[1]

The inscription describes the paten as being 'inlarged and improved' in 1725, and Richard Richardson I refashioned the old one into a flat dish with a shallow well and then applied the broad rim. The churchwardens' accounts for 1725 record 'pd Mr Richardson for a Silver plate' £1 7s. 6d.[2]

Patens of dish form had been produced in both London and the provinces throughout the reign of Elizabeth I. Patens resembling contemporary dinner plates appeared before the middle of the 17th century, and became increasingly popular during the 18th century.[3]

Four plate patens by Richard Richardson I are known, dating between 1716 and 1728.[4] A plate paten of 1706 by Nathaniel Bullen is the only other Chester example to survive from this period.[5]

PROVENANCE: Originally presented by Mrs. Alice Whitby to St Michael's Church, Chester, 1639; Re-made 1725; Transferred to Chester Team Parish, 1972; Purchased with grant aid from the MGC/V&A Purchase Grant Fund, National Heritage Memorial Fund, Pilgrim Trust, Duke of Westminster, Mary Newboult Bequest, Grosvenor Museum Society 1988.39

Exhibited: London V&A 1989.

Published: Jackson 1905, p.370; Ball 1907, p.72 no.VI; Ridgway 1968, p.168 no.22; Pevsner & Hubbard, p.152; Richards, p.120 (f); Boughton 1992 I.

NOTES:

1. Gerrard Barnes, report, August 1999; Hanshall, pp.176-7, 191-2. The original paten at St Michael's is one of two recorded in the lists of plate handed over to new churchwardens, e.g. 'one dish for Bread and Another small dish' in 1683 and 'two dishes for Bread' in 1696 (Cheshire Record Office, P65/8/2).

2. Cheshire Record Office, P65/8/3.

3. Oman 1957, pp.199, 219.

4. Ridgway 1968, p.170; Ridgway 1985, pp.135, 138.

5. Ridgway 1968, p.130.

William Richardson I

William Richardson I was born in 1690, the fourth son of John Richardson, goldsmith of Worcester and London, and was apprenticed to his elder brother Richard Richardson I (see no.10). He became free in 1720 and was admitted to the Chester Goldsmiths' Company the same year, serving as warden 1724-7 and 1735-6. His sons were William Richardson II (see no.33), who was apprenticed to him, and Richard Richardson III (see no.47). He died in 1750.[1]

NOTE:

1. Ridgway 1968, pp.172-3; Ridgway 1985, pp.130-4, 173, 185.

14 DESSERT SPOON

William Richardson I of Chester, c.1720-5

Three marks on back of stem near bowl: maker's mark (Ridgway 1968, p.172 type 1), lion passant, leopard's head

Length 16.9 cm. (6.65 in.)

Weight 41 g. (1.45 oz.)

Sterling silver. The spoon is formed from a single piece of silver. The raised bowl is deep and narrow, with a plain rat-tail extending almost the whole length of its back. There is a ridge along the upper half of the Hanoverian pattern stem, which turns upward at the end.

As Ian Pickford has explained, 'maker's marks were always the first to be struck on any piece of flatware. For this reason it is the maker's mark which is found at the very base of the stem when bottom marked.'[1] The spoon lacks the Chester mark or the date letter. However, it is firmly datable to the period 1720-5 because William Richardson I was admitted to the Chester Goldsmiths' Company in 1720 and no examples of his type 1 mark have been found on silver after 1725. In addition, the lion passant mark is the

14

and one of 1788 by Richard Richardson IV (no.50). The Plate Duty Books, however, record 102 dessert spoons by 18th-century Chester goldsmiths: 72 by Richard Richardson IV in 1785-90, one by Thomas Hill in 1789, 23 by George Walker I in 1791-6 and six by George Lowe I in 1795.[10]

PROVENANCE: Sotheby's, Chester, 2 May 1984, lot 1159 (part); Purchased 1984.27

EXHIBITED: Chester 1984, no.50.

PUBLISHED: Moore 1985 III, p.72.

NOTES:
1. Pickford, p.43.
2. Ridgway 1985, pp.27-8, 185.
3. Newman, p.258.
4. Glanville 1987, pp.54, 64; Wees, pp.120-1; Clayton 1985 I, p.377; Snodin 1974, p.12.
5. Ridgway 1968, pp.xvi, 173-5; Ridgway 1985, pp.185-7, 221; Ridgway 1996, pp.189-90.
6. Ridgway 1968, pp.173-4; Ridgway 1985, p.187; Ridgway 1996, pp.189-90.
7. Ridgway 1996, p.182.
8. Moore 1985 III, p.72.
9. Ridgway 1985, p.76.
10. Ridgway 1996, pp.86, 90, 96, 101.

form used at Chester from 1720-5, and the leopard's head is that used from 1720-31.[2] The length of the rat-tail is typical of the later examples of this motif.[3]

The French term 'dessert' was used from the 17th century for the last course of the main meal. This was served at the dining table and included flavoured jellies, custards, syllabubs, creams and fresh and candied fruits. Spoons varied in size during the 17th century, but by 1690 there was a definite distinction between table and dessert spoons. In general, they were identical in style, but the dessert spoon was smaller and remained relatively rare until the later 18th century.[4]

Twenty-five other pieces of silver by William Richardson I have been recorded, mostly flatware, but including communion cups, a paten cover, a pap boat, a coconut cup and a chocolate or coffee pot stand.[5] This is his only known dessert spoon, but he also made four other Hanoverian rat-tail spoons (a table spoon and three serving spoons) in the period 1720-5, and three Hanoverian spoons without rat-tails (a mustard spoon and two serving spoons) after 1725.[6]

Chester-made dessert spoons are comparatively rare. A spoon of c.1701-6 by Peter Pemberton I, 7.5 in. long with a bowl measuring 2.5 by 1.4 in., has been described by Canon Ridgway as a dessert spoon,[7] although Nicholas Moore has called William Richardson's example the earliest known provincial dessert spoon.[8] The only other surviving 18th-century Chester dessert spoons are six of 1772 by James Dixon,[9]

Benjamin Pemberton I

Benjamin Pemberton I was a younger son of Peter Pemberton I, to whom he was apprenticed in 1711. He became free in 1721 and was admitted to the Chester Goldsmiths' Company in 1723, serving as warden 1733-4, 1735 and 1738-54. He lived in Eastgate Street and died in 1754.[1]

NOTE:
1. Ridgway 1968, p.146; Ridgway 1985, pp.39-41, 120-2.

15 SAUCEPAN

Benjamin Pemberton I, Chester, 1726-7

Five marks on base (maker's mark Ridgway 1968, p.146 type 1)
Length across handle 17.8 cm. (7 in.), diameter 8.4 cm. (3.3 in.), height of bowl 5.7 cm. (2.25 in.)
Weight 102 g. (3.6 oz.)

Sterling silver with handle of boxwood (*Buxus sempervirens*).[1] The bulbous body is raised, with a setting-out point on its flat, circular base and a narrow double moulding around the everted rim. The beak-shaped pouring lip, ending in a flattened bead, is cast and

applied. At a right angle to the lip is an uplifted baluster handle of turned wood, attached with two pins to a long, tapering silver ferrule soldered to the body. The base is engraved with the initials A*W in Roman lettering, and is scratched with the numbers 672 over 3 30.

Pans of brass or copper involved health risks and impaired flavours, so from the 16th century silver vessels were favoured for preparing both herbal remedies and food. Chamber-cooking, which in non-noble families was the responsibility of the lady of the house rather than a servant, also called for silver as an expression of status. The skillet (a vessel with feet) was replaced by the silver saucepan and, although an example is known from the Commonwealth, the vast majority of the many surviving examples date from the 18th century, when they were sometimes called pannikans. There were two varieties of 18th-century silver saucepan and the bulbous form, illustrated by Pemberton's example, varied considerably in size and was more common than those having a cylindrical body with a flared rim and a moulded foot. The essential form of Pemberton's saucepan is found in London examples by such eminent goldsmiths as Paul de Lamerie and David Willaume II,[2] and survived into the 19th century (e.g. no.115). Small saucepans like this, with a wooden handle and a pouring lip, were clearly intended for heating liquids such as brandy or mulled wine. The drink could be warmed at the dinner table over a spirit lamp or a mortar light made of beeswax with a flax wick.[3]

Twenty-one pieces of silver by Benjamin Pemberton I have been recorded, including flatware, a mug, a jug and tumbler cups.[4] One other saucepan of his is known, very similar in form but slightly smaller and missing its date letter.[5]

Silver saucepans continued to be made in Chester for a century. Eight other bulbous-bodied ones survive: by Richard Richardson I from 1721-2, by Richard Richardson II from 1731-65 (e.g., no.22), and by George Walker I from 1768 and 1790.[6] Cylindrical saucepans were also made by Richard Richardson II in 1732 and 1747, and by George Lowe I in 1827.[7] The Chester Plate Duty Books record further saucepans and the variously spelled panakin/panikin/pannikin: six by Richard Richardson IV in 1785-9, one by George Walker I in 1792, four by George Lowe I in 1797-1826, six by William Twemlow in 1800-9 and two by Robert Bowers I in 1804-5.[8]

PROVENANCE: Private collection, Cheshire, by 1966; Spink & Son Ltd., London; Presented by the National Art Collections Fund 1978.91

EXHIBITED: Chester 1979 I, Silver no.2; Chester 1980; Manchester 1983, no.67; London 1984, S.3; Chester 1984, no.58, illustrated.

PUBLISHED: Ridgway 1968, p.148; NACF Report 1978, no.2723; Ridgway 1985, p.123 Brandy Saucepans no.2, pl.35; Moore 1985 III, illustrated p.72.

NOTES:

1. Wood identified by Graham Usher, 13 November 1999.
2. De Lamerie, 1723 (Wark, no.196); Willaume, 1740 (Newman, p.48).

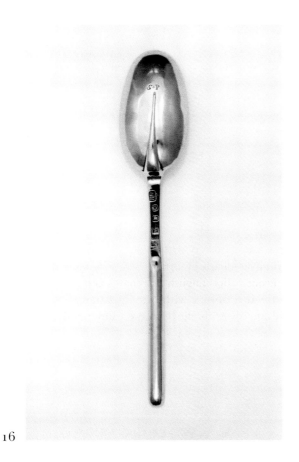

16   17

3. Newman, pp.48, 274; Glanville 1987, p.46; Wills, p.120; Taylor 1956, p.149; Clayton 1985 I, p.329; Wark, p.78.
4. Ridgway 1968, pp.147-8; Ridgway 1985, pp.123-5; Ridgway 1996, p.183; Moore 1984 I, no.59.
5. Ridgway 1985, p.123.
6. Ridgway 1968, p.186; Ridgway 1985, pp.145, 153, 164, 199; Ridgway 1996, p.186.
7. Ridgway 1985, pp.107, 148, 153.
8. Ridgway 1996, pp.78, 90-2, 96, 99, 101.

16 MARROW SPOON

Benjamin Pemberton I, Chester, 1726-7

Five marks on back of stem (maker's mark Ridgway 1985, p.122 type 1)
Length 21 cm. (8.25 in.)
Weight 60 g. (2.1 oz.)

Sterling silver. The spoon is formed from a single piece of silver. The raised bowl is deep and narrow, with a plain rat-tail extending three-fifths of the way down its back. The base of the stem is rounded on the top but flat on its underside. The upper two-thirds of the stem form a narrow, slightly tapering scoop. The initials S+P are engraved in Roman lettering beneath the rat-tail, a location which provides a more convenient surface for engraving than the rounded back of the narrow scoop.

A marrow spoon has a conventional bowl but its stem is formed as a scoop. The scoop was used to extract marrow, the soft fatty tissue in the cavities of bones, which was considered a delicacy. A marrow fork of *c.*1670 is recorded, but the earliest known marrow spoon dates from 1692. There are many 18th-century examples, but they become scarcer towards 1800 and there are few from the 19th or 20th centuries. The size of marrow spoons varies from tea spoons to serving spoons, although the majority of examples—like Pemberton's—are of table spoon size.[1]

This is one of two marrow spoons by Benjamin Pemberton I, the other being no.17. He also made six marrow scoops (an object type discussed at no.19) between 1723 and 1740.[2] The other surviving Chester marrow spoons comprise one of 1707 by Thomas Robinson, five of 1728-35 by William Richardson I, and one of 1772 by James Dixon.[3]

PROVENANCE: John ffoulkes Lowe, Chester; His sister, Miss Joyce Lowe, 1973; Purchased with grant aid from the MGC/V&A Purchase Grant Fund, London Goldsmiths' Company, Grosvenor Museum Society 1988.44

PUBLISHED: Ridgway 1985, p.124 Marrow Spoons no.2.

NOTES:

1. Snodin 1974, p.33; Wees, p.263; Clayton 1985 I, p.242; Pickford, p.186.
2. Moore 1984 I, no.59; Ridgway 1985, p.124; Ridgway 1996, p.183.
3. Ridgway 1985, pp.186-7; Ridgway 1996, pp.190, 192.

17 MARROW SPOON

Benjamin Pemberton I, Chester, 1728-9

Five marks on back of stem (maker's mark
Ridgway 1985, p.122 type 2)
Length 20.9 cm. (8.2 in.)
Weight 44 g. (1.55 oz.)

Sterling silver. The spoon is formed from a single piece of silver. The bowl is raised, with a single drop at its junction with the stem and a plain rat-tail extending more than half-way down its back. The lower third of the stem is rounded on the top but flat on its underside. The upper part of the stem is stamped to form a narrow scoop.

Although only two years apart, the bowls of Pemberton's two marrow spoons show one small step in the gradual transition to a slightly wider and shallower form.[1]

PROVENANCE: John ffoulkes Lowe, Chester; His sister, Miss Joyce Lowe, 1973; Purchased with grant aid from the MGC/V&A Purchase Grant Fund, London Goldsmiths' Company, Grosvenor Museum Society 1988.45

PUBLISHED: Ridgway 1968, p.148; Ridgway 1985, p.124 Marrow Spoons no.1.

NOTE:

1. Snodin 1974, pp.38-9.

18 SIX TEA SPOONS

Attributed to Benjamin Pemberton I of Chester, c.1740-54

Two marks on back of stem toward bowl: maker's mark BP, lion passant
Length: (1, 3, 5, 6) 11.3 cm. (4.45 in.), (2, 4) 11.2 cm. (4.4 in.)
Weight: (1) 9 g. (0.3 oz.), (2-6) 8 g. (0.25 oz.)

Sterling silver. Each spoon is formed from a single piece of silver. The raised egg-shaped bowl has a single drop at its junction with the stem. Below this the back of the bowl is stamped in low relief with a Rococo shell, having tiny beads between the five lobes and four graduated beads descending from the centre. There is a pronounced ridge along the upper half of the Hanoverian pattern stem, which turns sharply upward at the end. The back of the stem is engraved with the initials M·R in Roman lettering.

These spoons follow the standard practice between the early 18th century and the 1780s, when tea spoons were marked, near the base of the stem, with only the maker's mark and the lion passant. None of the marks are perfectly struck, since the stems are slender and

have been subjected to a certain amount of finishing. The BP maker's mark is similar to but smaller than Benjamin Pemberton I's type 1 mark, while the form of the lion passant is that used at Chester although contained within a simple rectangular frame.[1] According to Canon Ridgway, the spoons 'appear to be provincial in origin and belong to a 1735/50 period. If made in Chester they can only be the work of Benjamin Pemberton I as they are clearly too early for Benjamin Pemberton II.'[2] (A slightly later dating, on stylistic gounds, is discussed below.) Benjamin Pemberton I's dated silver falls within the period 1723-40, but these survivals may give a distorted picture of his output, since his business continued up to and beyond his death in 1754.[3]

From c.1600 English merchants and travellers were briefly in contact with the Japanese and almost continuously with the Chinese, and publicised their custom of drinking tea. Tea was sold in London coffee-houses from 1657, and from 1662 became fashionable at the court of Charles II's Portuguese queen, Catherine of Braganza. As the price of tea fell from 50s. per pound in 1660 to 12-14s. in the early 18th century (equivalent to one week's wages for a skilled craftsman), and to around 8s. for Bohea (black tea) in 1750, so the popularity of tea drinking grew and consumption increased dramatically.[4]

In the home, tea drinking became an established ritual and tea spoons became a standard element in its service. They are first referred to in 1685, and the earliest surviving examples date from around this time, but tea spoons made before the 1730s are very rare. The majority of tea spoons from all periods are smaller versions of the table spoons then in fashion. Small spoons are now usually called tea spoons, but they would also have been used for coffee and chocolate, the other new and fashionable beverages of the time.[5]

A tea spoon was used to stir a cup of tea, to which milk and sugar were being added by the early 18th century. The spoon was also used in teatime etiquette, being placed by the guest across or in the cup to indicate to the hostess that no further tea was required. The unrefined habit of sipping tea from one's saucer, which met with disapproval in polite society, meant that the tea spoon could not rest in the saucer. Instead, the inverted cover of the sugar bowl sometimes served as a spoon tray, and from the early 18th century small oval dishes were provided for used tea spoons.[6]

With the disappearance of the rat-tail from the back of the bowl of spoons in the 1730s, the resulting plain surface presented an area for decoration. This was achieved by hammering the bowl into a die in which a design had been cut in intaglio. Relief decoration on the back of the bowl was not a new idea, the same technique having been used for lace-back trifid spoons in the late 17th century. Die-stamped decoration is found on the bowls of spoons from the

18

1730s to the 1790s, known to collectors as fancy-back spoons, and the majority of examples are Hanoverian tea spoons. Many designs were used but the most popular motif was the shell, which began in the 1730s with a naturalistic representation and developed in the 1740s into a more decorative Rococo form, somewhat resembling a palmette, which remained in use until c.1780.[7] If these six spoons are indeed by Benjamin Pemberton I, a date between c.1740 and his death in 1754 seems most probable on stylistic grounds.

There are no other recorded tea spoons by Benjamin Pemberton I. All his silver is quite plain with one startling exception, a cream jug of 1725 which is an unusually sophisticated and elaborate piece of Chester silver.[8] Its flat-chased decoration is an extraordinarily precocious example of the English Rococo and, assuming that Pemberton remained conversant with the latest metropolitan fashions, significantly strengthens the probability that he made the spoons as well.

The Chirk Castle accounts for 1708 refer to six tea spoons in connection with Richard Richardson I, but there is no evidence that he had made them. The only other surviving 18th-century Chester tea spoons are a pair of c.1771-81 by Joseph Duke I (no.35) and a pair of 1797 by William Twemlow.[9] However, the Plate Duty Books record 292 tea spoons by Chester goldsmiths from the last 15 years of the 18th century: 143 by Richard Richardson IV in 1785-90, 38 by Thomas Hill in 1789, four by

Joseph Falconer in 1790, 67 by George Walker I in 1791-7 and 40 by William Twemlow in 1797-9.[10] There are no other recorded Chester fancy-back spoons from the 18th century.

PROVENANCE: S.J. Shrubsole, London; Purchased with grant aid from the Beecroft Bequest 1981.89.1-6

PUBLISHED: Moore 1984 I, p.9; Ridgway 1985, p.125 Note.

NOTES:

1. Pickford, p.42; Ridgway 1985, pp.28, 122.
2. Ridgway 1985, p.125. Benjamin Pemberton II became free in 1784 as a linendraper and has no recorded mark. There are no London goldsmiths with a BP mark before 1825 (Grimwade no.206).
3. Ridgway 1985, pp.122, 125; Ridgway 1996, p.183; Moore 1984 I, no.59.
4. Glanville 1987, pp.66, 68; Snodin 1974, p.32; Wees, p.268.
5. Wees, p.269; Glanville 1987, p.68; Oman 1967, pp.153-4; Snodin 1974, pl.18, p.32.
6. Wees, pp.269-70, 475; Glanville 1987, fig.34.
7. Pickford, p.212; Wees, p.478; Snodin 1974, pp.31, 41-2.
8. Ridgway 1968, p.147; illustrated Wark, no.120.
9. Ridgway 1996, p.185; Ridgway 1985, p.195.
10. Ridgway 1996, pp.81, 86, 96, 99, 101.

Daniel Kirkes

Daniel Kirkes became free in 1727-8. He was admitted to the Chester Goldsmiths' Company in 1728, serving as warden 1731-2, but disappeared from the company records thereafter.[1]

NOTE:

1. Ridgway 1985, pp.50, 94.

19 MARROW SCOOP

Attributed to Daniel Kirkes, Chester, 1742-3

Five marks on back of stem (maker's mark Ridgway 1985, p.94)
Length 20.8 cm. (8.2 in.)
Weight 53 g. (1.85 oz.)

Sterling silver. Formed from a single piece of silver, the two scoops are joined in the centre by a short stem. One scoop is wide, short and deep, while the other is narrow, long and shallow. 'No.1' is scratched on the stem beside the marks.

The marrow scoop, of which this is a typical example, developed from the marrow spoon (see no.16) in the early 18th century. Both varieties seem to have been called marrow spoons for some time, the term marrow scoop not being commonly used before the 19th century, but since the museum's collection includes both forms it seems useful to maintain the distinction. The two scoops of varying widths are designed to fit bones of different sizes. During the first half of the 18th century it would have been laid face down on the table in the French manner, as with Hanoverian pattern spoons, and, well into the 19th century, the marrow scoop appears to have been an object of communal use. Far more popular than marrow spoons during the 19th and 20th centuries, the end of the marrow scoop came with meat rationing in 1940-52, when it was not possible to buy joints of the size which would contain a bone from which marrow could be scooped.[1]

The maker's mark on this piece is well struck, but the quasi-Gothic letters are difficult to identify. They have been read as DK, and on this basis were tentatively attributed to Daniel Kirkes by Canon Ridgway in 1973 and 1985, although in 1989 he listed the mark as unidentified.[2] This marrow scoop bears the only known example of the mark and, since it was assayed at Chester, it was most probably made by Daniel Kirkes.

Twenty other 18th-century Chester marrow scoops have been recorded, made by Richard Richardson I from 1716-18, Benjamin Pemberton I from 1723-9, William Richardson I from 1724-33, Thomas Maddock in 1727, Richard Richardson II from 1731-69, Joseph Duke I in 1776 and Richard Richardson III in 1777.[3] The Chester Plate Duty Books record nine marrow scoops in 1788-9 and four marrow spoons in 1790 by

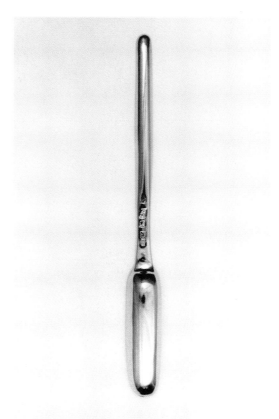

19

Richard Richardson IV, four marrow spoons in 1792 by George Walker I, and 12 marrow spoons in 1803 and five marrow scoops in 1809 by Robert Bowers I.[4]

PROVENANCE: John ffoulkes Lowe, Chester, by 1970; His sister, Miss Joyce Lowe, 1973; Phillips, London, 27 April 1984, lot 135; Purchased with grant aid from the V&A Purchase Grant Fund, Grosvenor Museum Society 1984.25

EXHIBITED: Chester 1984, no.68.

PUBLISHED: Ridgway 1973, pp.15-16; Ridgway 1976, illustrated p.18; Ridgway 1985, p.94; Moore 1985 III, illustrated p.71.

NOTES:

1. Pickford, pp.185-6; Davis, p.192; Wees, p.263; Clayton 1985 I, pp.241-2.
2. Ridgway 1973, pp.15-16; Ridgway 1985, p.94; Ridgway 1989, p.400.
3. Ridgway 1968, pp.174-5; Ridgway 1985, pp.79, 117, 124, 147, 160, 175, 186-7; Ridgway 1996, pp.183, 185-7.
4. Ridgway 1996, pp.77-8, 96, 101.

Robert Pyke

Robert Pyke was apprenticed to Thomas Maddock in 1723 and became free in 1730. He was admitted to the Chester Goldsmiths' Company in 1730 and died in 1740. He may also have worked in Wrexham, where he was married in 1730 and buried ten years later.[1]

NOTE:

1. Ridgway 1985, p.129.

20 THREE TABLE SPOONS

Robert Pyke of Chester and Wrexham, c.1730

Maker's mark only struck twice on back of each stem toward bowl (maker's mark Ridgway 1985, p.129)
Length: (1) 21.2 cm. (8.35 in.), (2) 21.5 cm. (8.45 in.), (3) 21.6 cm. (8.5 in.)
Weight: (1,2) 62 g. (2.2 oz.), (3) 61 g. (2.15 oz.)

Silver. Each spoon is formed from a single piece of silver. The raised bowl is deep and narrow, with a plain rat-tail extending nearly two-thirds of the way down its back. There is a pronounced ridge, forming hollows to either side, along the upper half of the Hanoverian stem, which turns sharply upward at the end.

The back of each stem is engraved in Roman lettering with the initials D over R - I. The engraving of the initials is identical to that on a marrow scoop of 1727 by Thomas Maddock, which also bears the Davenport crest of a felon's head couped. This was used by at least half of the 14 branches of the Davenport family in Cheshire, but the couple R. and I. Davenport remain unidentified.[1]

Robert Pyke appears to have lived in both Wrexham and Chester during his working life, being recorded as a Chester goldsmith when he was married and buried in Wrexham parish church, but also attending meetings of the Chester Goldsmiths' Company.[2] The fact that these spoons were not assayed at Chester, but were merely struck twice with the maker's mark, suggests that they may well have been made (and sold) in Wrexham. If this is so, they may be the only known examples of silver made in Wales in the 18th century.[3]

Only one other piece of silver has been convincingly attributed to Robert Pyke, a rat-tail spoon bearing this maker's mark and assayed at Chester in 1729.[4] Early Chester-made Hanoverian rat-tail table spoons are discussed at no.10 and, with the exception of the set specially commissioned from Richard Richardson II in 1763 (no.28), the spoon of 1729 is the latest firmly dated example. Nicholas Moore therefore dated these three spoons to c.1730.[5]

PROVENANCE: Probably R. and I. Davenport, Cheshire, c.1730; Sotheby's, Chester, 2 May 1984, lot 1239 (part); Purchased 1984.26.1-3

EXHIBITED: Chester 1984, no.69, illustrated.

PUBLISHED: Ridgway 1985, p.129; Moore 1985 III, p.71.

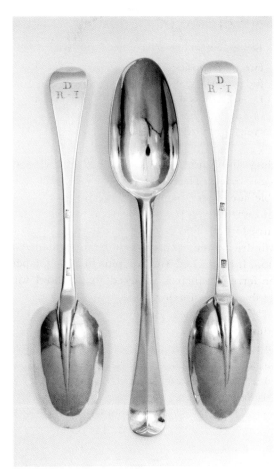

20

NOTES:

1. Moore 1984 I, nos.47, 69. None of the pedigrees in Ormerod suggest an identification for the couple.
2. Ridgway 1985, p.129.
3. Moore 1985 III, p.71; Oliver Fairclough, letter, 9 December 1999.
4. Jackson 1921, p.389.
5. Moore 1984 I, no.69.

Richard Richardson II

Richard Richardson II was born in 1712 and was apprenticed to his father Richard Richardson I (see no.10). His mark is first recorded in 1730 and he became free in 1732. He was admitted to the Chester Goldsmiths' Company in 1734, serving as warden 1736-61 and assay master 1761-9. He became sheriff of Chester in 1744-5, an alderman in 1754, and mayor in 1757-8. His son was Richard Richardson IV (see no.49), and George Walker I (see no.37) was apprenticed to him. He continued his father's workshop in Eastgate Street, but spent a great deal of time on his mining interests, and the 15 variants of his mark might signify individual craftsmen working for him. He died in 1769.[1]

NOTE:

1. Ridgway 1985, pp.132-3, 138-41; Ridgway 1989, p.399.

21 PUNCH LADLE

Richard Richardson II, Chester, 1732-3

Five marks inside base of bowl (maker's mark
Ridgway 1985, p.145 type 2)
Length across handle 37 cm. (14.55 in.), width
of bowl 7.9 cm. (3.1 in.)
Weight 109 g. (3.85 oz.)

Sterling silver with handle of stained English walnut
(*Juglans regia*).[1] The ovoid bowl is raised and has a
double line incised beneath the exterior of the rim. At
a right angle to its pouring side is an uplifted handle
of turned wood, having three sets of mouldings between
a cylindrical stem and a short baluster-shaped end
section. It is attached with two pins to a long, tapering
silver ferrule, which is soldered to the bowl with a
heart-shaped reinforcing plate.

The term 'punch' is believed to derive from the
Hindustani word for 'five', *paunch*, referring to the five
main ingredients of spirits, hot water or milk, lemons,
sugar, and spices. Punch was brewed in a large circular
bowl and was usually served hot. Introduced by
Englishmen returning from India, there are references
to punch from the 1650s. Its popularity spread rapidly,
and punch drinking became an important social habit
in the 18th century. The earliest surviving silver punch
bowl dates from 1680, but they were also made in glass
or pewter, and porcelain or tin-glazed earthenware
largely replaced silver after *c.*1735.[2]

A ladle was used for serving punch from the bowl
into individual punch cups or drinking glasses. An early
serving implement for punch was a small, shallow, oval
cup with a ring handle to one side: these are very rare,
but one of 1698 is known. Serving spoons were sometimes used, but the punch ladle with a circular bowl
and a tubular silver handle was in use by *c.*1685. The so-
called goose-egg bowl, of which Richardson's ladle is an
example, began in the 1720s and was one of the earliest departures from the circular type. From *c.*1730 silver handles were generally replaced by turned wood or,
more rarely, ivory. Large numbers of punch ladles were
made between *c.*1730 and the early 19th century, with
later developments bringing a variety of shaped bowls
and the use of whalebone for handles.[3]

This ladle is one of 194 recorded pieces of silver
bearing the mark of Richard Richardson II, whose workshop was by far the most productive in 18th-century
Chester.[4] Four of his punch ladles survive, made
between 1730 and 1735.[5] All are of the same type,
with an ovoid bowl and turned wood handle, making
them stylistically consistent with contemporary London examples.[6] They are the only known Chester punch
ladles of this type.

Although wooden-handled serving spoons were
made in Chester in the 1710s and '20s,[7] there are
only four other surviving Chester punch ladles. Two
were made in 1723, one with a silver handle by
Richard Richardson I and the other with a wooden
handle by William Richardson I, both having a strap
hook on the handle to catch on the rim of the punch
bowl.[8] Double-lipped punch ladles were made by
Richard Richardson IV in 1788 and by George Walker
I the following year: the former has a turned wood
handle but the latter has been converted into a pap
boat.[9] The Plate Duty Books record many more punch
ladles by Chester goldsmiths: 26 by Richard
Richardson IV in 1785-90, four by George Walker I
in 1791-7, 14 by George Lowe I in 1796-1823
(including one accompanying a punch bowl in 1798),
and four by William Twemlow in 1797-1801.[10]

PROVENANCE: J.H. Bourdon-Smith Ltd., London, 1984;
Purchased with grant aid from the MGC/V&A Purchase
Grant Fund, Beecroft Bequest 1985.102

PUBLISHED: Ridgway 1985, p.147 Ladles no.3.

NOTES:

1. Wood identified by Graham Usher, 13 November 1999.
2. Wees, p.43; Clayton 1985 I, pp.239, 287; Newman, p.251;
   Oman 1967, p.137; Glanville 1987, p.89; Snodin 1974, p.53.
3. Newman, p.252; Clayton 1985 I, p.239; Snodin 1974, p.53.
4. Ridgway 1985, pp.141-72; Ridgway 1996, pp.193-6.
5. Ridgway 1985, pp.147-8.
6. e.g. George Jones, 1730 (Sotheby's, Chester, 29 July 1980, lot
   175); William Darker, 1731 (Snodin 1974, pl.39).
7. There are five known examples: Richard Richardson I, 1713;
   William Richardson I, 1722; Benjamin Pemberton I, 1724

22

and undated (Ridgway 1968, pp.147, 171, 174; Ridgway 1985, p.123).

8. Ridgway 1968, p.xvi; Ridgway 1996, p.188.

9. Ridgway 1985, pp.200, 202; Ridgway 1996, p.197.

10. Ridgway 1996, pp.90-2, 96, 99, 101.

22 SAUCEPAN

Richard Richardson II, Chester, 1740-1

Five marks on base (maker's mark Ridgway 1985, p.150 type 5B)
Length across handle 12.6 cm. (4.95 in.), diameter of bowl 6.6 cm. (2.6 in.), height of bowl 4.6 cm. (1.8 in.)
Weight 72 g. (2.5 oz.)

Sterling silver with handle of stained holly (*Ilex aquifolium*).[1] The bulbous body is raised, with a flat, circular base, and has an incised line beneath the everted rim. The beak-shaped pouring lip, ending in a flattened bead, is cast and applied. At a right angle to the lip is an uplifted baluster handle of turned wood: a large split in its underside has been filled with wax

resin, and half of the finial is missing. The handle is attached with two pins to a long, tapering silver ferrule, which is soldered to the body with a heart-shaped reinforcing plate. There is a scratched inscription on the base: 'Lnt from Mr lLoyd 1823'.

The types of silver saucepans and their production at Chester are discussed at no.15. This example is one of four bulbous-bodied saucepans, dating between 1731 and 1765, by Richard Richardson II, who also made two cylindrical ones in 1732 and 1747.[2]

PROVENANCE: Lowe & Sons, Chester; Purchased with grant aid from the V&A Purchase Grant Fund, Beecroft Bequest 1980.48

EXHIBITED: Chester 1980; Chester 1982.

PUBLISHED: Ridgway 1985, p.153 Brandy Saucepans or Warmers no.1; Moore 1986, fig.6.

NOTES:

1. Wood identified by Graham Usher, 13 November 1999.

2. Ridgway 1985, pp.145, 148, 153, 164.

23 MILK JUG

Richard Richardson II, Chester, 1740-1

Five marks on base (maker's mark Ridgway 1985, p.150 type 5A)

Height 7.9 cm. (3.1 in.)

Weight 79 g. (2.8 oz.)

See Colour Plate III

Sterling silver. The pear-shaped body is raised, with a stepped circular foot-ring seamed once and soldered to the rounded base. The neck is boldly everted and has an incised line around the rim. The beak-shaped pouring lip is cast and applied, with a flattened double drop soldered beneath. On axis with the lip is a double-scroll handle with a thumbpiece, cast in two sections, and a triple drop is applied beneath its upper junction with the body. The jug is engraved beneath the lip with the initials TN over B in sprigged script, and on the base C-C in Roman lettering.

For the early history of tea drinking in England see no.18. Although European visitors in the 1650s recorded the Chinese as taking hot milk with tea, the English at first drank it plain rather than lose some of the flavour of this expensive beverage by mixing it with milk. From the beginning of the 18th century until the 1740s hot milk, served from small covered jugs, was sometimes taken with tea. Small jugs without covers also appear early in the 18th century, but they are scarce before 1720 and few were supplied with other tea wares until much later. They were used to serve cold milk with tea, and those with wide pouring lips seem to have been designed for cream, which was taken with dessert. Cream does not appear to have been taken with tea until later in the century, being still regarded as a novelty in 1780.[1]

The earliest example of a small jug without a cover dates from 1708: it has a pear-shaped body on a foot-ring, with a beak-shaped lip and an S-scroll handle. Similar in design to the contemporary beer jug, this shape was one of the most popular for milk jugs, and Richard Richardson II's example represents a later refinement of the form, with a more boldly everted neck and a more elaborate handle. An increasing variety of milk and cream jugs were made in the first half of the 18th century, including cast nautilus shells from the late 1710s, helmet-shaped or ovoid bodies on a foot from c.1720, pear-shaped or ovoid bodies on three legs around a decade later, and miniature sauce boats from the late 1730s (see no.41). Their capacity was modest, since tea was served in small cups and only a little milk or cream was required. Names for these and related vessels in the 18th century included cream ewers (see no.119), milk pots (probably with covers, for hot milk) and cream or milk boats (presumably those shaped like sauce boats). They could all have served milk, but the beak-shaped lip of Richardson's vessel would not have suited the slow pouring necessary with cream, hence its designation here as a milk jug.[2]

Richard Richardson II's jug of 1740 is close in both style and quality to contemporary and earlier London examples.[3] He also made an identical jug in 1731 and a similar one with an S-scroll handle the same year, a pear-shaped jug with three feet and a scalloped rim in 1737, and a squat jug with an S-scroll handle in 1750.[4]

Four other small jugs by Chester goldsmiths survive from the 1720s: one of c.1720 by Thomas Robinson with a bulbous body and S-scroll handle; an elaborate Rococo example of 1725 by Benjamin Pemberton I (discussed at no.18); and two of 1729 by Richard Richardson I, both pear-shaped, one with an S-scroll handle but the other altered. The only other surviving 18th-century example is of 1795 by George Lowe I.[5] The Chester Plate Duty Books record seven cream jugs by George Lowe I in 1794-7 and one by George Walker I in 1796.[6]

PROVENANCE: John ffoulkes Lowe, Chester; His sister, Miss Joyce Lowe, 1973; Purchased with grant aid from the MGC/V&A Purchase Grant Fund, London Goldsmiths' Company, Grosvenor Museum Society 1988.46

PUBLISHED: Ridgway 1976, illustrated p.21; Ridgway 1985, p.160 Jugs no.1; Schroder 1992, fig.1.

NOTES:

1. Clayton 1985 I, pp.115, 231; Wark, p.49; Oman 1967, pp.159-60; Wees, p.270; Davis, p.97.
2. Oman 1967, pp.160-1; Wees, pp.365, 368; Wills, p.80; Lomax, pp.120-1; Glanville 1987, p.92; Clayton 1985 I, p.115.
3. e.g. George Jones, 1725 (Davis, no.94); Francis Turner, 1726 (J.H. Bourdon-Smith Ltd., Catalogue No.39, Autumn 1997, p.12); unknown maker, 1738 (Wark, no.130); John Garner,

1739 (Clayton 1985 I, fig.154a); Dinah Gamon, 1741 (Wark, no.137).
4. Ridgway 1985, pp.146-7, 160, pls.9, 10, 12.
5. Ridgway 1968, pp.147, 177-8; Ridgway 1985, pp.106, 138.
6. Ridgway 1996, pp.90, 101.

24 CHAMBER CANDLESTICK

Richard Richardson II, Chester, 1752-3

Five marks on base (maker's mark Ridgway 1985, p.149 type 4). Extinguisher unmarked
Height to top of socket 6.8 cm. (2.7 in.), diameter of base 15.1 cm. (5.95 in.), height of extinguisher 7.4 cm. (2.9 in.)
Weight: candlestick 331 g. (11.7 oz.), extinguisher 30 g. (1.05 oz.)

Sterling silver candlestick with Sheffield Plate extinguisher. The circular drip-pan is raised, with a convex centre and an angled border having a moulded rim. A cast stem is attached with a pin to the centre of the drip-pan and supports a cylindrical socket, which has a plain band around its centre, a richly-moulded rim and a slot for the extinguisher. The cast ring handle has three projections, including a thumbpiece with two tiny volutes. The detachable extinguisher is conical, with a richly-moulded rim, a small spherical finial and an L-shaped hook.

The drip-pan is engraved opposite the handle with a lozenge-shaped shield of arms, denoting a spinster or widow, in a Rococo cartouche. The arms are those of Egerton of Tatton Park, Cheshire, for Elizabeth (1718-63), younger daughter of John Egerton (1679-1724) of Tatton by his wife Elizabeth Barbour (d.1743). In 1744 Elizabeth Egerton's personal fortune, comprising legacies from her mother and grandmother together with her own investments, was worth £3,360. This financial independence enabled her to move to Bath, where she bought a house in the late 1750s. She died unmarried and was buried at Rostherne Church in Cheshire, where she had been baptised 45 years before.[1]

Candles provided the essential form of artificial lighting until the development of oil lamps in the late 18th century. Candles of beeswax cost three times as much as those made of tallow (animal fat, the best being a mixture of mutton and beef), but they were preferred since tallow smoked, smelled, and needed constant trimming. During the 18th century candles of spermaceti (a wax derived from sperm-whales) were introduced, but proved hardly less expensive than beeswax.[2]

The chamber candlestick was the most portable type of candlestick, intended to be carried around the house after dark, especially when retiring to bed, and to light the bed chamber. It was therefore designed for easy carrying, with a handle, a low socket

24

for the candle, and a pan sufficiently broad to catch the melting wax. Originally called a low-footed or flat candlestick, it was later variously termed a bedroom, hand or night candlestick or a chamberstick. A 'hand candilstikke' is first recorded in 1438, but the earliest surviving example dates from 1652. Chamber candlesticks before 1700 are very rare and usually have flat or curved handles extending from the rim: an example from 1693 has a ring handle, but cast ring or scroll handles are uncommon before the 1720s. Numerous examples survive from the 18th century, when they become more decorative and are often equipped with a pair of snuffers and/or an extinguisher. At least one chamber candlestick was required by each person retiring to bed, and by the early 19th century London goldsmiths were making them in large sets.[3]

This chamber candlestick is one of eight surviving examples made by Richard Richardson II between 1739 and 1765: they include a pair dating from 1740, and a single one from the previous year which has the only recorded Chester-assayed snuffers.[4] The earliest surviving Chester chamber candlesticks are a pair of 1727 by Richard Richardson I, and the only other 18th-century example is one of 1771 by James Dixon (no.45).[5] The Plate Duty Books record no chamber candlesticks by Chester goldsmiths during the last 15 years of the 18th century.

The extinguisher is made of Sheffield Plate, a cheap substitute for solid silver made of copper rolled between and fused with films of silver, a process used commercially from c.1760-c.1840. Conical extinguishers, sometimes known as 'podkins', were used to put out the candle, and chamber candlesticks with detachable extinguishers were popular throughout the 18th century. On most London examples the extinguisher hooks onto the handle, although it is attached to the socket of one made in 1711.[6] The socket is the more usual location for the extinguisher on Chester examples, occuring on Richard Richardson II's pair of 1740 and James Dixon's of 1771, although it is found on the handle of Richard Richardson II's one of 1739.[7] The Sheffield Plate extinguisher with this chamber candlestick is undoubtedly a replacement of a lost or damaged original, which would have been of the same essential form but with the addition of an S-scroll handle, as on no.45.[8]

PROVENANCE: Miss Elizabeth Egerton of Tatton, Cheshire, c.1752; Her niece Elizabeth Tatton (1748-1803) of Wythenshaw, who married Sir Christopher Sykes (1749-1801), 2nd Baronet, of Sledmere, Yorkshire, in 1770; By descent to Sir Tatton Sykes, 8th Baronet; Sotheby's, London, 22 March 1979, lot 151; U. Schepers, Munster, Germany; Purchased with grant aid from the V&A Purchase Grant Fund, Beecroft Bequest, Mappin & Webb 1979.82

EXHIBITED: Chester 1980; Chester 1982; Chester 1984, no.84, illustrated.

53

PUBLISHED: Ridgway 1985, p.150 Chamber Stick, pl.30.

NOTES:

1. Gale Glynn, report, 22 March 1991; Ormerod, I, p.446; Burke's Peerage, p.2370; R.D. Johnson, 'The Egertons and Samuel Hill 1707-1780', unpublished essay, 1993.

2. Gilbert, p.5.

3. Wees, pp.498, 529-30; Gilbert, p.48; Newman, p.67; Oman 1967, pp.175-6; Clayton 1985 I, pp.63-4; Wills, p.69.

4. Ridgway 1985, pp.154-5; Moore 1984 I, no.75.

5. Ridgway 1985, pp.76, 137.

6. Fleming & Honour, p.729; Gilbert, p.52; Clayton 1985 I, p.63; Oman 1967, p.176.

7. Moore 1984 I, no.75; Ridgway 1985, pl.29.

8. All the other 18th-century Chester examples have these handles: Richard Richardson I, pair of 1727; Richard Richardson II, 1739 and pair of 1740 (Ridgway 1985, p.137, pl.29; Moore 1984 I, no.75).

25 PARCEL-GILT TUMBLER CUP

Richard Richardson II, Chester, 1752-3

Five marks on base (maker's mark Ridgway 1985, p.150 type 5D)

Height 4.2 cm. (1.65 in.)

Weight 54 g. (1.9 oz.)

Sterling silver with gilt interior. The cup is raised, with a setting-out point on its hemispherical base, and has slightly outcurved sides. The side is engraved with a single-masted ship, with the flag of St George flying from the stern and two labels flying from the mast, inscribed in Roman lettering 'SUCCESS TO / TRADE & NAVIGATION'. The cup retains its original fitted case with detachable lid, made of shaped and stitched leather and lined with scarlet velvet.

A tumbler cup is a short-sided drinking vessel, the thickness of whose rounded base provides sufficient weight to make the cup 'tumble' back to an upright position after it has been knocked. The earliest known example dates from 1625. Tumbler cups vary hugely in size and were used for a range of alcoholic drinks. Their use was probably confined largely to outdoor occasions, and they formed part of canteens, but they were also used at sea to withstand the rolling of a ship. Gold tumbler cups were presented as race trophies from the late 17th century, and one of the finest surviving examples is the Chester Gold Cup of 1766 (no.95).[1]

Tumbler cups may well have been originally introduced as part of travelling canteens, and little leather cases containing such canteens are known from the reign of Charles II. Surviving cases for individual cups, however, are rare, and this is the only known Chester example.[2]

This tumbler cup is one of 31 surviving examples made by Richard Richardson II between 1737

and 1768.[3] The earliest extant Chester tumbler cup was made by Peter Pemberton I c.1677-87,[4] and they continued to be made at Chester well into the 19th century. The other surviving examples are ten of c.1701-21 by Thomas Robinson, one of 1703 by Nathaniel Bullen, 11 of 1711-28 by Richard Richardson I, two of c.1721-6 by Thomas Maddock, one of c.1721-40 by Benjamin Pemberton I, six of 1768-73 by George Walker I, and one of 1780 by Richard Richardson IV.[5] The Plate Duty Books record a few later 'tumblers' made at Chester: two by Richard Richardson IV in 1785, two by George Walker I in 1787, two by William Twemlow in 1792, two by George Lowe I in 1796 and 1840, and one by Robert Bowers I in 1804.[6]

Chester tumbler cups are usually, but not always, parcel-gilt. As Canon Ridgway has explained, 'when contemporary this is found to be of an exceptionally pale lemon colour—almost a Chester characteristic—so thinly applied that it is often cleaned away.'[7]

The only comparable pictorial engraving on a Chester tumbler cup is found on one made by Richard Richardson II in 1750.[8] It bears a scroll with the inscription 'SUCCESS TO THE MINES', and depicts a miner operating the winding gear above a mine shaft.

Michael Stammers has observed that the vessel engraved on Richardson's cup of 1752 is 'a typical coasting sloop which could have plied between Chester and Dublin, or equally to London or North Wales. However, given the prestigious nature of the tumbler cup, it is likely that the artist had in mind a packet vessel which would be one that ran on a regular service, carrying passengers and high paying goods to specific destinations such as Dublin.'[9] According to Nicholas Moore, 'while this cup is not necessarily connected with Richardson's shipping interests, it is likely to have been used at a shareholders' meeting following successful voyages, or else it may have something to do with the River Dee Company, who had control of the river.'[10]

PROVENANCE: Phillip's, London, 30 January 1987, lot 93; Purchased through Spink & Son Ltd., London, with grant aid from the MGC/V&A Purchase Grant Fund, Grosvenor Museum Society 1987.41.1,2

PUBLISHED: Moore 1987, illustrated p.62; Schroder 1992, p.36.

NOTES:

1. Taylor 1956, pp.102-3; Clayton 1985 I, p.448; Wills, p.155; Newman, p.336; Ridgway 1985, p.165; Moore 1987, p.62.

2. Oman 1967, p.146. A tumbler cup by Thomas Jenkins (fl.1668-1706) retains its original shagreen case (mentioned but not illustrated in Warner, p.254). A silver-gilt beaker of 1738 by Paul de Lamerie retains its original leather case (mentioned but not illustrated in Hare, p.112).

3. Ridgway 1985, pp.144, 149, 165-8, 171-2.

4. Ridgway 1968, p.151.

5. Ridgway 1968, pp.xvi, 129, 145, 148, 151, 168-9, 179; Ridgway 1985, pp.117, 138, 185, 203; Ridgway 1996, pp.187-9, 190-1.

6. Ridgway 1996, pp.78, 90, 93, 96, 99, 101.

7. Ridgway 1985, p.56.

8. Ridgway 1985, p.166; Moore 1984 I, no.82.

9. Michael Stammers, letter, 26 October 1999.

10. Moore 1987, p.61.

26 CRUET FRAME

Richard Richardson II, Chester, 1753-4

Five marks beneath base (maker's mark Ridgway 1985, p.150 type 5F). Lion passant on handle and one foot

Height 25.3 cm. (9.95 in.)

Weight 995 g. (35.1 oz.), scratch weight 4162

See Colour Plate III

Sterling silver. The cinquefoil base of the frame is cut from sheet silver, strengthened by five rings cut from sheet and soldered beneath. Four cast shell feet with separately cast short legs support double-scroll stretchers, each cast in two parts. The stretchers extend from the rim of the base to seven circular moulded ring holders of four different sizes in a symmetrical arrangement. An asymmetrical Rococo cartouche, its high relief border reminiscent of splashing water, is cast and applied: the slightly pitted surface of the centre suggests that it once bore an engraved crest. The asymmetrical Rococo open handle, composed of scrolls and wave-like forms, joins a stem with an inverted-baluster head and four ring mouldings, the whole cast in several parts and soldered together. The stem's screw terminal threads through a central hole in the base, which is strengthened underneath with a circular applied moulding.

The back two rings held cruets for oil and vinegar, used to dress salad, which was an important part of the meal. They were small cut-glass bottles, whose slip-on silver covers were held in the adjacent small rings when the cruets were in use. The front three rings held casters, the larger one in the centre for sugar (roughly pounded loaf sugar), and the other two for pepper (black pepper or stronger cayenne) and mustard.[1] As Harold Newman has explained, 'the mustard was in the form of a ball of compressed powder, to be scraped or ground by an individual and mixed on his plate with vinegar', and its caster was therefore unpierced or blocked with an interior sleeve.[2]

The term 'Warwick cruet' has been used by collectors since the late 19th century, when it was believed that the earliest cruet frame was that of 1715 by Anthony Nelme, then at Warwick Castle. This is a three-tiered frame with five casters and two bottles, weighing 86 oz., but the term is applied indiscriminately to all cruets having three casters and two bottles.[3]

Among the earliest surviving casters are a single one dated 1658, a pair of 1672, and a set of three from 1683. The earliest form of cruet frame, holding

26

two silver-mounted bottles only, dates from c.1700. Cruet frames combined with casters appeared in England c.1707 as part of the French-inspired development of silver objects for dining. They were subsequently made in many different styles, with varying numbers of cruets and casters, but the Warwick cruet was the most popular type during the second quarter of the 18th century.[4]

As James Lomax has explained, 'cruets and casters were also incorporated into the fashionable centre-pieces and epergnes and (for supper at least) placed upon the dining table. Otherwise it would seem that these larger five-piece frames were intended for the sideboard and were passed around the diners by the servants during the meal.'[5]

This is the only surviving Chester-assayed cruet frame before 1832,[6] and none by Chester goldsmiths are recorded in the Plate Duty Books. With the exception of scroll handles, and the flower on the lid of a 1764 tea canister by Richard Richardson II,[7] it is also the only known item bearing the mark of an 18th-century Chester goldsmith to have cast, as distinct from engraved or chased, Rococo decoration.

Eighteenth-century provincial cruet frames are exceptionally rare,[8] and Richard Richardson II almost certainly acquired this frame (presumably with its cruets and casters) from London and had it assayed at Chester. The most likely maker is the London goldsmith Samuel Wood, who entered his first mark in 1733 and died in 1794. Almost 70 per cent of the Warwick cruets from the second quarter of the 18th century bear the mark of Samuel Wood, who must have been supplying them to the trade on a wholesale basis.[9] The Richardson cruet frame is very similar to examples by Wood:[10] for example, although different castings have been used, the cartouche is strongly reminiscent of that on a frame of 1751, and the asymmetrical handle is equally close to one of 1761.[11] The other notable examples of London-made silver retailed in Chester by Richard Richardson II are the St Martin Cup of 1755 (no.27) and a 1765 table basket, the latter almost certainly supplied by William Vincent and John Lawford.[12]

PROVENANCE: Michael Clayton, Edinburgh, by 1967; Purchased with grant aid from the MGC/V&A Purchase Grant Fund 1989.127

EXHIBITED: Chester 1984, no.85, illustrated.

PUBLISHED: Ridgway 1985, p.159, pl.46; Moore 1985 III, p.73; Schroder 1992, fig.1.

NOTES:

1. Glanville 1987, p.66; Taylor 1956, p.154; Newman, p.237; Clayton 1985 I, p.70.
2. Newman, p.219.
3. Glanville 1987, p.66; Clayton 1985 I, p.456; Lomax, p.95.
4. Glanville 1987, p.66; Clayton 1985 I, pp.70, 75, 118, 265; Lomax, p.95; Schroder 1988 II, p.326.
5. Lomax, p.95.
6. An oval cruet frame by Nicholas Cunliffe of Liverpool was assayed at Chester in 1832 (Ridgway 1985, p.74).
7. Ridgway 1996, p.195, pl.58.
8. They include Newcastle examples of 1743 and '44, and one of c.1740 from Aberdeen (Clayton 1985 I, p.118; Moore 1984 I, p.61).
9. Grimwade, p.709; Clayton 1985 I, p.118; Lomax, p.95.
10. e.g. one of 1752 in the Jackson Collection at the National Museum and Gallery Cardiff.
11. Davis, no.159; Lomax, no.86.
12. Illustrated Moore 1984 I, no.89; for attribution see Wees, no.108.

27 THE ST MARTIN CUP

Richard Richardson II, Chester, 1755-6

Five marks on base (maker's mark Ridgway 1985, p.150 type 5D). Lion passant inside foot ring. Maker's mark on handles.[1] Four marks (minus Chester mark) on bezel of cover. Figure group unmarked
Overall height 28.6 cm. (11.25 in.), height of cup 16.2 cm. (6.4 in.), width across handles 23.4 cm. (9.2 in.)
Weight 1,163 g. (41 oz.), scratch weight 37 14

See colour plate III
Sterling silver. The cup's spreading, stepped circular foot and low stem are raised. The foot is chased with diagonal flutes surrounded by matting within a wavy border, reminiscent of sea foam, and there is an incised line around the top of the stem. 'No.4' is scratched on the base. The raised, inverted bell-shaped cup has an incised line beneath its slightly everted rim and an applied horizontal moulding around its body. The lower part of the body is chased on one side with a turbanned figure (probably male) in a fur-lined jacket flanked by a rusticated obelisk and a curved wall with niches, and on the other side with a fishing lady in European dress beside a Rococo urn on a pedestal and a palm tree behind a curved wall. The upper part of the body is chased on each side with a different asymmetrical Rococo cartouche flanked by garlands of flowers and foliage. The S-scroll handles are of D-section, with a rounded underside soldered to a straight outer edge in two parts, the short top part curving upward to form a thumbpiece. Each handle tapers to a triangular heel with a circular air-hole beneath, and there is a large oval plate at its lower junction with the body.

The raised, high-domed cover has an applied bezel. The lower part of the cover is chased with a band of foliage and flowers. Its upper part is chased on one side with a single-storey Chinese pavilion and on the other with a rusticated obelisk, both flanked by trees and divided by scrolls. The cover, which has a 6 mm. diameter hole at its centre, is surmounted by a figure group. This is cast in several pieces, chased and soldered together, on a large, irregular circle of silver. The figure of St Martin is seated astride a horse with a fringed saddle cloth. The saint is wearing a plumed hat and a long cloak, and a tree trunk joins his rear boot. The top half of the sword in his right hand is missing, and with his left hand he presents the severed part of his cloak to a beggar. The latter wears a hat and a short tunic with a sash, rests his right hand on a crutch, and has his right leg in a stump.

The two cartouches on the body were intended to enclose crests, and there is evidence of previous engraving in both of them. One now bears the crest of a lion's head erased ducally crowned. The engraving appears to date from the early 19th century, and the crest was used by 36 different families.[2]

Two-Handled Cups
During the late 17th century the form of the functional two-handled cup (such as no.5) began to combine with that of the ceremonial (handleless) standing cup and cover, evolving to become one of the most typical vessels of the first half of the 18th century. As a drinking cup its use was now reserved for ceremonial occasions, but it became a favoured object for presentation and for display on the sideboard or table.[3]

Apart from four functional cups dating between c.1740 and 1755—each having strap handles and

27

an inverted bell-shaped body on a foot-ring—there are no other surviving two-handled cups by Richard Richardson II.[4] The only remotely comparable object from Georgian Chester is the two-handled cup of 1769 by George Walker I (no.37). The St Martin Cup is one of the few pieces of 18th-century Chester-assayed silver to have Rococo chasing,[5] and the only known example with Chinoiserie decoration.

The Figure Group

This cup takes its name from the figure group of St Martin of Tours (*c.*315-397) which surmounts the cover. As James Hall has explained, 'after enrolling in the Roman army Martin served in Gaul. Once he found a beggar shivering in the winter cold, and cut in half his *paludamentum*, or military cloak, and shared it with the poor man. That night he dreamed that Christ came to him wearing the piece he had given away.'[6] Martin later renounced his arms and became Bishop of Tours *c.*370. He was a preacher, the founder of the first monasteries in France, and a destroyer of pagan shrines.

One would expect to find a baluster finial on the cover,[7] and the figure group has previously been considered a later addition.[8] However, no part of the chasing on the cover is obscured by the irregular plate on which the figures stand, and testing by Inductively-Controlled Plasma Spectrometry has confirmed that the group is the original finial.[9]

The use of cast figures surmounting cups has always been rare, appearing occasionally on small numbers of particularly elaborate vessels. An especially early one dates from 1412,[10] and further specimens are found from the 16th and 17th centuries.[11] The cast figure on a mid-17th-century example—an equestrian warrior on a silver-gilt standing cup of 1663 by Francis Leake— bears a striking similarity to that of St Martin and especially his horse.[12] Covered cups surmounted by cast figures re-appear in the mid-18th century with, for example, comparatively small figures of the infant Bacchus on three cups of 1746-59.[13] Closer to the St Martin Cup, because larger and more elaborate, is the male figure on a cup of 1750 by Thomas Gilpin.[14] In all four cases these single, seated, secular figures of

pyramidal composition are fully integrated into their cup's sculptural form and decoration. The St Martin Cup is different, its group of standing religious figures having no thematic connection with the rest of the decoration on its simply-shaped cup. Although aesthetically less coherent, the sculptural group is in proportion to the overall size of the cup, and the rather stocky figure type accords well with the chased figures below. James Lomax has tentatively suggested that St Martin may have been chosen to reflect the original owner's name.[15]

The Chased Decoration

The handles of the St Martin Cup are its least fashionable feature and, while there are occasional examples of equally plain handles on London-made cups,[16] one would expect to find cast double-scroll handles on a cup of this date and elaboration.[17] However, the chasing is of metropolitan quality, employing a wide range of textures from very fine matting on an even ground to vigorous punching over an irregular embossed surface. The chasing must have been executed before the body was joined to the foot or the handles were applied, and the chaser clearly knew exactly where these parts were to go. It seems unlikely that the cup was made in Chester, sent in parts to London for chasing, and then returned to Chester for assembly and assay. Instead, as Timothy Schroder has concluded, it was presumably bought in from London by Richard Richardson II and only marked in Chester.[18]

Chinoiserie, a style inspired by European fantasies about China, developed as a branch of the international Rococo, but English Rococo Chinoiserie silver, decorated with chasing or casting, is an independent growth and its fully developed form has no parallel on the Continent. Chinoiserie appeared in the work of Paul de Lamerie from the early 1740s, reached its peak in England about 1755—the year of the St Martin Cup— and continued for a further two decades.[19] As Hugh Honour has observed, the designs are frequently 'reminiscent of prints by Jean-Baptiste Pillement; but none appears to have been copied precisely from these or any other known source. It seems probable that English silversmiths, inspired by some of the many decorative prints then available, let their fancies run free in these charming evocations of the land of Cathay.'[20] The St Martin Cup employs many elements from the repertoire of English Rococo Chinoiserie silver, including the rusticated obelisk,[21] the lady in European dress,[22] the turbanned figure,[23] the Rococo urn,[24] the palm tree,[25] and the single-storey Chinese pavilion.[26]

PROVENANCE: Lowe family, Chester, 19th century; By descent to Miss Joyce Lowe, 1973; Purchased through Sotheby's, London, with grant aid from the MGC/V&A Purchase Grant Fund, Beecroft Bequest 1986.170

PUBLISHED: Ridgway 1976, p.21; Ridgway 1985, pp.158-9, pl.40; Moore 1985 III, pp.70, 73; Schroder 1992, p.36, fig.1; Callaghan, illustrated p.32.

NOTES:

1. 'The maker's marks on both handles are unexpected as late as 1755' (Edmund Laird Clowes, letter, 14 May 1986).

2. The crest is that of Bampfylde; Barnfield, Shropshire & Devon; Bull; Cosard, Hampshire; Crown or Crowne; Darwell; Davies, Marrington Hall, Shropshire; Davis; Difford; Dikens; Dipford or Ditfod; Domvile, Ireland; Duperier, Totnes, Devon; Estwood; Geffry; Henley; Hutchings, Somerset; Jefferay, Malling, Sussex; Kift; Marsh, Middlesex; Mascal, Kent; Osborn or Osborne; Peache; Pechey, Kent; Peech; Penley or Penly; Perry; Pindall; Pindar; Baron Poltimore, Exeter, Devon; Pyndar,

Gloucestershire & Worcestershire; Simson; Sumner; Sympson, Kent; Wood; or Wynniatt, Guiting Grange, Gloucestershire (Gale Glynne, report, 22 March 1991).

3. Schroder 1988 I, pp.152, 154; Wees, p.43.

4. Ridgway 1985, pp.164, 190-1, the two earlier examples marked jointly with William Richardson II.

5. The principal examples are Benjamin Pemberton I's 1725 cream jug (Wark, no.120); five low two-handled cups of 1769-76 by George Walker I (Ridgway 1985, pp.200-1); and a pair of 1763 table candlesticks by Boulton & Fothergill of Birmingham (Moore 1984 I, no.172).

6. Hall 1985, p.202.

7. As on the simpler London-made covered cups of this period, e.g. one of 1747 by Ayme Videau (Brett, no.882) and another of 1752 by Fuller White (Wees, no.29).

8. Ridgway 1985, pp.158-9; Edmund Laird Clowes, letter, 14 May 1986.

9. While there are very slight differences in the impurity levels of the cover and finial, there are too many similarities for the finial to be a later addition (Paul Johnson, report of 28 January 2000 and telephone conversation on 2 February 2000). A conventional finial would not have contained enough silver to be re-cast into this figure group at a later date.

10. The Thomas Leigh Cup (Glanville 1987, fig.73).

11. Sixteenth-century examples, all except one with secular figures, include: the Howard Grace Cup of 1525, surmounted by St George and the dragon (Glanville 1990, no.7); the Parker Cup, c.1540 (Oman 1978, pl.25); cup of 1553, probably by Robert Danbe (Clayton 1985 I, fig.178); the Bowes Cup, 1554 (Taylor 1956, pl.8); cup of 1561 (Clayton 1985 II, p.30 fig.1); the Matthew Parker Cup of 1569, a covered coconut cup of 1577 and a covered standing bowl of 1584 (Glanville 1990, figs.115,133,193). Seventeenth-century examples, all with secular figures, include: the Sampson Leycroft Cup, 1608 (Glanville 1990, fig.52); cup of 1611 (Crighton, p.26); ostrich egg cup of 1623 (Glanville 1987, fig.112); the Richard Godfrey Cup of 1627 and the St John's Hampstead Cup of 1629 (Glanville 1990, no.24, fig.144); cup of 1666 by Arthur Manwaring and cup of 1683 (Oman 1970, pls.3B, 5B); cup of 1693 (Clayton 1985 II, p.90 fig.1).

12. Oman 1970, pl.2B.

13. Silver-gilt cup, Peter Taylor, 1746 (Schroder 1988 II, p.189); cup, Thomas Powell, 1758 (Mid-Georgian Domestic Silver, Victoria & Albert Museum, Small Picture Book No.28, 1976, pl.24); silver-gilt cup, Thomas Heming, 1759 (Oman 1965, pl.144).

14. Brett, no.866.

15. James Lomax, note, 6 March 2000.

16. e.g. Thomas Tearle, 1729 (Davis, no.49); William Skeen? 1766 (Wark, no.33).

17. As on the two London-made cups mentioned in note 7, and the Chester-made cup of 1769 (no.37).

18. Schroder 1992, p.36.

19. Fleming & Honour, pp.189-90; Lomax, p.134; Snodin 1984, p.272; Honour, p.306.

20. Honour, p.307. James Lomax (note of 6 March 2000) has recently discovered, but not yet published, an example of a figure taken from Pillement. Many suites and individual prints

after designs by Pillement (1728-1808) were published in London between 1755 and 1761 (Snodin 1984, p.274). For other sources of Chinoiserie design see Jervis 1984, p.110.

21. e.g. two tea canisters, Paul de Lamerie, 1751 (Brett, no.735); coffee pot, Francis Crump, 1769 (Lomax, no.135); three tea canisters, Louisa Courtauld & George Cowles, 1770 (Brett, no.948). 'In William de la Cour's *Book of Ornaments* published in 1741 there is a Chinese scene with a pyramid, but it is not very close to that on the St Martin cup' (Ridgway 1985, p.159). The rusticated obelisk is also found on Rococo work by Paul de Lamerie which otherwise lacks Chinoiserie elements, e.g. a dish of 1741 and a tea pot of 1743 (Hare, nos.91, 106).

22. e.g. a William Cripps coffee pot of 1755 (Schroder 1988 I, no.79), which also has a turbanned figure, a palm tree and a single-storey Chinese pavilion.

23. e.g. tea canisters of 1755 by Alexander Johnson and of 1763 by Augustin Le Sage (Grimwade 1974, pl.67B; Wees, no.294); and see note 22.

24. e.g. tea canisters of 1763 by Samuel Taylor and of 1765 by Thomas Freeman & James Marshall (Grimwade 1974, pl.67C).

25. e.g. two tea canisters and a sugar box, Paul de Lamerie, 1747 & 1750; sugar box, Paul Crespin, 1750; tea urn, Thomas Whipham & Charles Wright, 1766 (Grimwade 1974, pls.66B, 66A, 59); and see note 22.

26. e.g. tea canister, William Shaw & William Preist, 1759 (Oman 1965, pl.139); tea kettle, Thomas Whipham & Charles Wright, 1761 (Grimwade 1974, pl.57A); two tea canisters, Pierre Gillois, 1769 (Wees, no.295); and see note 22.

28 SIX TABLE SPOONS

(1,2) Two by John Millington, London, 1722-3
(3-6) Four by Richard Richardson II, Chester, 1763-4

Each marked on back of stem near bowl. (1,2) Four marks (maker's mark Grimwade no.1500). (3-5) Five marks (maker's mark Ridgway 1985, p.172 type 8). (6) Six marks, maker's mark struck twice
Length: (1,2) 19.9 cm. (7.8 in.), (3,4) 19.7 cm. (7.75 in.), (5,6) 19.8 cm. (7.8 in.)
Weight: (1,5) 70 g. (2.45 oz.), (2) 76 g. (2.7 oz.), (3) 73 g. (2.6 oz.), (4) 79 g. (2.8 oz.), (6) 78 g. (2.75 oz.)

Sterling silver. Each spoon is formed from a single piece of silver. The raised bowl is deep and narrow, with a plain rat-tail extending two-thirds of the way down its back: those by Richardson have a single drop above the rat-tail. There is a pronounced ridge along the upper half of the Hanoverian stem, which turns upward at the end.

The back of the stem is engraved with the crest of a garb environed by a serpent for the Dod family of Cheshire, whose three branches lived at Broxton, Edge and Shocklach.[1]

The distortion of the marks on John Millington's spoons may be due to the stems having been shaped after hallmarking, a common practice during the 18th century.[2]

28

Only five table spoons by Richard Richardson II are known, comprising these four of 1763 and one from the following year (no.30). The four spoons were specially commissioned by a Cheshire family from a Chester goldsmith to match the earlier London-made pair. The rat-tail, which fell from fashion in both London and Chester c.1730 (see no.20), was carefully reproduced by Richardson, albeit with the addition of a drop.

John Millington was probably the son of the London goldsmith Francis Millington, to whom he was apprenticed in 1710. He became free in 1718, entered his first mark as a largeworker in 1718 and his third mark in 1728.[3]

PROVENANCE: Dod family of Broxton, Edge or Shocklach, Cheshire, 1763; Christie's, London, 28 July 1982, lot 250; Purchased through Spink & Son Ltd., London, with grant aid from the V&A Purchase Grant Fund, Beecroft Bequest 1982.76.1-6

EXHIBITED: Chester 1984, no.87, one illustrated.

PUBLISHED: Ridgway 1985, pp.172-3 Spoons.

NOTES:

1. Gale Glynne, report, 22 March 1991; Ormerod, II, pp.673, 682, 688.

2. Wees, p.479.

3. Grimwade, p.597. A rat-tail dessert spoon of 1718 by John Millington is recorded (Jackson, p.168).

29 PAIR OF PARCEL-GILT TUMBLER CUPS

Richard Richardson II, Chester, 1764-5

Five marks on base (maker's mark Ridgway 1985,

p.150 type 5B)

Height: (1) 7.4 cm. (2.9 in.), (2) 7.3 cm. (2.85 in.)

Weight: (1) 157 g. (5.5 oz.), (2) 155 g. (5.45 oz.)

Sterling silver with gilt interiors. Each cup is raised, with a setting-out point on its hemispherical base, and has slightly outcurved sides. The bases have scratched inscriptions '1766 / Chester' and '17766'.

The side of each cup is engraved with the crest of a talbot's head erased. The engraving could be later than the cups, and the crest was used by 22 different families.[1]

Sixteen of Richard Richardson II's 31 known tumbler cups (see no.25) are in pairs, dating between 1737 and this pair of 1764.[2] Of the 33 other surviving Chester tumbler cups, eight are in pairs, comprising pairs of 1709 and 1715 by Thomas Robinson, of 1724 by Richard Richardson I and of 1772 by George Walker I.[3]

One of the largest tumbler cups, made at London in 1720, is 9.6 cm. high.[4] These, at 7.4 cm. high, are the largest known examples of Chester-made tumbler cups. The smallest, also made by Richard Richardson II and measuring just 3.8 cm. high, are a pair made in 1755.[4]

PROVENANCE: P. Watson; Sotheby's, London, 22 March 1973, lot 119; Private collection, U.S.A.; J.H. Bourdon-Smith, Ltd., London; Lowe & Sons, Chester; Purchased with grant aid from the V&A Purchase Grant Fund, National Art Collections Fund, Silver Society, and other donations 1980.95.1,2

EXHIBITED: Chester 1980; Chester 1982; Manchester 1983, no.73; London 1984, S.4; Chester 1984, no.94, illustrated.

29

PUBLISHED: NACF Report 1980, no.2842, illustrated; Ridgway 1985, p.167 Tumbler Cups nos. 15-16; Moore 1985 III, p.72; Moore 1986, fig.9; Moore 1987, p.63.

NOTES:

1. The crest is that of Allan; Blaydes, Yorkshire; Blaydes, Ranby Hall, Nottinghamshire; Blaydes-Marvel, Yorkshire; Chittinge; Clark; Clarke, Cambridgeshire; Clifford; Desbrowe; Griffin; Haigh; Hall, Worcestershire & Yorkshire; Jeafferson, Dallington House, Cambridgeshire; Jefferson; Kyrell; M'Killop, Scotland; Melveton; Morham; Tanner, Brannell, Cornwall; Tayloure; Watters, Edinburgh; or Wilson (Gale Glynn, report, 22 March 1991).
2. Ridgway 1985, pp.149, 166-8.
3. Ridgway 1968, pp.168, 174; Ridgway 1985, p.203; Ridgway 1996, p.191.
4. Clayton 1985 I, p.448.
5. Ridgway 1985, p.167 no.18.

30 TABLE SPOON

Richard Richardson II, Chester, 1764-5

Five marks on back of stem near bowl (maker's mark Ridgway 1985, p.150 type 5A)
Length 19.6 cm. (7.7 in.)
Weight 70 g. (2.45 oz.)

Sterling silver. The spoon is formed from a single piece of silver. The raised ovoid bowl has a double drop at its junction with the stem. There is a pronounced ridge along the upper half of the Hanoverian stem, which turns upward at the end.

The back of the stem is engraved with the crest of a boar passant fretty. The crest is that of Fitzgerald, Fitzgibbon or Hughes, and could possibly be a later addition.[1]

The motif of the single drop appeared in France *c.*1700 and was occasionally used on English spoons after 1715. It did not entirely supersede the rat-tail until *c.*1730, by which time the double drop had also been introduced. This was the commonest form of 'heel', as it was then called, and hardly changed throughout the 18th century.[2]

Chester-made table spoons having Hanoverian stems without rat-tails are very rare. The only other known examples are those of 1753 by the unknown maker EC and of 1774 by Richard Richardson III.[3]

PROVENANCE: Mr. B. Jefferis, by 1905; John ffoulkes Lowe, Chester; His sister, Miss Joyce Lowe, 1973; Purchased with grant aid from the MGC/V&A Purchase Grant Fund, London Goldsmiths' Company, Grosvenor Museum Society 1988.47

PUBLISHED: Jackson 1905, p.372; Ridgway 1985, p.164 Spoon.

30

NOTES:

1. Gale Glynne, report, 22 March 1991.
2. Snodin 1974, pp.40-1.
3. Ridgway 1985, pp.70, 179. A table spoon of 1770, maker's mark IW, is of unknown form (Ridgway 1985, p.213).

31 PARCEL-GILT DOUBLE BEAKER

Richard Richardson II, Chester, 1765-6

Five marks on each base (maker's mark Ridgway 1985, p.150 type 5B)
Height: 8.9 cm. (3.5 in.) each, 17.1 cm. (6.7 in.) together
Weight: (1) 148 g. (5.2 oz.), (2) 146 g. (5.15 oz.)

Sterling silver with gilt interiors. Each beaker has a tapering cylindrical body with an inset circular base. The side of the body is engraved with 20 vertical lines to simulate staves, and bound near either end with a group of five applied wire bands resembling hoops. The rim of beaker (1) is engraved with a cross-hatched roundel simulating a bung, and the rim of beaker (2) tapers inward above the hoops to fit within the other one, the two resembling a beer barrel when joined together.

The side of each beaker is engraved with a crest, opposite the bung and within the width of a stave. This is a 19th-century addition, and there is evidence of engraving having been removed from the opposite

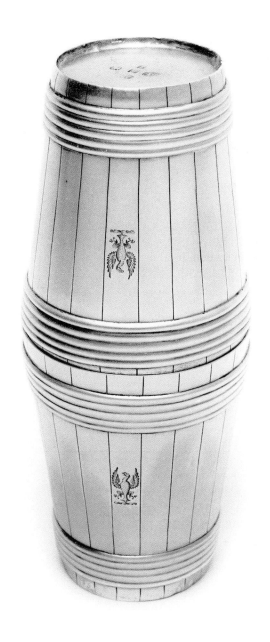

31

side and stave lines being re-engraved. The crest, a falcon displayed, was used by 57 different families.[1]

According to Charles Oman, 'it has been suggested that the beaker originated from the use of a straight section of an ox-horn with one end stopped up. The use of beakers can be traced in this country to the eleventh century by means of manuscript illuminations. By the fourteenth century they appear to have become very popular.'[2] Three medieval silver beakers survive, the earliest dating from 1496, and the tapering cylindrical beaker with a flared rim and sometimes a moulded base became the standard Elizabethan form.[3]

The only known English example before the 18th century of a barrel-shaped double beaker is by the London goldsmith RF and dates from 1572.[4] The idea of fitting together a pair of identical cups, rim to rim, enjoyed a brief vogue in the 1670s, when some tumbler cups were made which interlock to form a dumb-bell shape.[5] The double beaker in the form of a barrel was extremely popular with German goldsmiths, especially those of Nuremberg and Augsburg, who produced such vessels in great numbers between the late 16th and late 18th centuries,[6] and these inspired the revival of the form in 18th-century England.

Apart from the Grosvenor Museum's example, the only other surviving beaker in this style by Richard Richardson II is a single one from 1768, but another pair from 1765 (now lost) are recorded, and an unusual variant is a double beaker of 1741 whose sides are textured beneath a narrow band of vertical pales at the junction.[7] Nine beakers of other types, dating between 1750 and 1765, are also known to have been produced by Richard Richardson II.[8]

The only other barrel-shaped double beakers by a Chester goldsmith to survive are one pair and three single examples from 1796-1800 by George Walker I.[9] The Plate Duty Books record just two entries for a 'barrel' by a Chester maker: by George Walker I in 1801 and by William Twemlow in 1803.[10] Three pairs and three single beakers were made in 1779-83 by Joseph Walley of Liverpool,[11] and another pair, marked only by an unknown maker SW,[12] is likewise extremely close to the Chester examples. Double beakers were also made in London between the 1770s and the 1800s and in Sheffield in the 1770s, some with hoops and staves but others having only hoops.[13]

The idea of the simulated barrel, seen in the London double beaker of 1572 referred to above, also appears in a few tankards at this date, some having two horizontal ribs and others engraved with hoops and staves.[14] After a brief re-appearance in the 1640s,[15] the concept was revived again, with a few tankards having hoops and staves from the 1740s and hoops alone in the early 19th century.[16] The motif of hoops and staves was also applied to a range of silverwares from the mid-18th century: it is found, for example, on a barrel-shaped tobacco stand, a mustard pot and a nutmeg grater,[17] and on bucket-shaped wine coolers, an ice pail and a butter dish.[18] The use of hoops alone began a little earlier in the 18th century, being found, for example, on bucket-shaped cream pails and a butter dish,[19] and on barrel-shaped mugs.[20] Different in origin, yet related in effect, are the tea canisters of the 1760s and '70s engraved with slats, which simulate the wooden packing crates in which tea was shipped.[21]

PROVENANCE: J.H. Bourdon-Smith Ltd., London; Purchased with grant aid from the MGC/V&A Purchase Grant Fund, London Goldsmiths' Company, Grosvenor Museum Society 1985.101.1,2

PUBLISHED: J.H. Bourdon-Smith Ltd., Catalogue, Spring 1984, illustrated p.32; Ridgway 1985, pp.151-2 Beakers no.4; Moore 1985 III, p.72, illustrated p.71; Moore 1986, p.1294, fig.10.

NOTES:

1. The crest could be that of Aldhouse; Aldhowse; Aldehowse; Aldous or Aldis; Ainsworth; Atkinson; Aynesworth; Bolton; Brown; Burrow; Carpenter; Chalmers; Chambers; Chappan; Chesham, Lancashire; Chirnside; Clagstone; Clark; Cleland, Scotland; Colepeter; Congrave, Berkshire & Kent; Congreve, Staffordshire; Cooke; Culpepper; Cunliffe; Doig; Drummond; Eastfield; Eld; Elliott; Falconer; Fallon; Finucave; Gargrave; George; Glenham, Suffolk; Halhead; Hanmer, Shropshire; Harding, Devon; Harris, Rosewarne, Cornwall; Hay; Henly; Jennings, Reigate, Surrey; Lanyon, Cornwall; Le Mesurier; Lowe; Pape; Partington; Paton, Grandhome, Aberdeenshire;

Pepe; Pole, Derbyshire; Pool or Poole, Essex, Staffordshire & Derbyshire; Read, Buckinghamshire; Slaughter, Worcestershire; Straton; Throckmorton; or Willis, Hungerford Park, Bedfordshire (Gale Glynn, report, 22 March 1991).

2. Oman 1967, p.18.

3. Oman 1967, pp.18-19, 58. Nineteen such beakers are illustrated in the advertisement of the prizes to be awarded in the State lottery of 1567 (Glanville 1987, fig.11).

4. Oman 1978, pl.27.

5. e.g. maker OS, 1671 or '73 (Oman 1970, pl.22A); maker RW, 1672 (Wark, no.12); maker DG, 1676 (Clayton 1985 II, p.76 fig.5).

6. Muller, pp.288-9; e.g. Nicolaus Emmerling, Nuremberg, c.1600 and Esaias Busch I, Augsburg, 1650 (Brett, nos.16, 48). The German examples also inspired parcel-gilt beakers made at Neusohl from copper mined at Herrengrund in Slovakia (Muller, nos.93-5).

7. Ridgway 1985, pp.34, 152, 168.

8. Ridgway 1985, p.151; Ridgway 1996, p.195.

9. Ridgway 1985, p.198, pl.22.

10. Ridgway 1996, pp.99, 102.

11. Moore 1984 I, p.114, nos.191, 196; Ridgway 1985, pp.208-10, pl.21.

12. Phillips, London, 29 April 1994, lot 133.

13. London beakers with hoops and staves include: John Lambe, 1783, and Hester Bateman, 1786 (J.H. Bourdon-Smith Ltd., Catalogue, Autumn 1994, p.32); Peter & William Bateman, 1806 (Shure, pl.LXXXVI). London beakers with only hoops include: Charles Aldridge & Henry Green, 1771 (Wark, no.16); William Champion, 1780 (J.H. Bourdon-Smith Ltd., Catalogue, Autumn 1994, p.32); Duncan Urquhart & Naphtali Hart, 1803 (Asprey 1994, no.61); maker SH, 1809 (J.H. Bourdon-Smith Ltd., Catalogue, Spring 1984, p.32). A Sheffield example with only hoops is by John Rowbotham & Co., 1775 (Clayton 1985 I, fig.29).

14. e.g. three tankards of 1572 with two horizontal ribs (Glanville 1987, p.41); and tankards of 1572 and 1597 engraved with hoops and staves (Schroder 1988 II, p.72; Clayton 1985 I, p.396).

15. e.g. tankard with hoops and staves, maker CR, 1649 (Oman 1970, p.41, pl.25B).

16. Tankards having hoops and staves include: Edward Feline, 1746 (Clayton 1985 II, p.172 fig.1); Louisa Courtauld & George Cowles, 1772 (Taylor 1956, pl.19d). Tankards with hoops alone include one by Rebecca Emes & Edward Barnard I, 1811 (Wees, no.13).

17. Tobacco stand, Phillips Garden, 1757 (Crighton, p.87); mustard pot, John Bridge, 1825 (Clayton 1985 I, fig.384); nutmeg grater, Nathaniel Mills, Birmingham, 1830 (Ransome-Wallis, no.160).

18. Pairs of wine coolers by Thomas Heming, 1766, and by John Wakelin & Robert Garrard I, 1801 (Clayton 1985 II, p.232 fig.1; Brett, no.1005); ice pail, Benjamin Laver, 1785 (Newman, p.175); butter dish, maker JH, Greenock, c.1800 (Wills, fig.26).

19. Cream pails of 1733 by Ayme Videau, of 1750 by John Alderhead, and of 1752 by Samuel Herbert (Brett, no.87b; Wark, no.226; Newman, p.30); butter dish, Rebecca Emes & Edward

32

Mugs of the blackjack form appear to be unique to Chester. Eight are known to have been made by Richard Richardson II between 1751 and this example of 1767, including a pair of 1765 which have a band of engraved decoration.[3] The other surviving examples are one of 1769 by George Walker I and thirteen, including three pairs, of 1772-6 by Richard Richardson III.[4] Other types of mug were also made in 18th-century Chester: two in 1721 by Richard Richardson I, one in 1725 by Benjamin Pemberton I, 11 between 1730 and 1765 by Richard Richardson II, two in 1769 by James Dixon and one in 1771 by George Walker I (no.38).[5] However, no mugs by Chester goldsmiths are recorded in the Plate Duty Books from 1784.

PROVENANCE: Farthings Antiques, Nantwich, Cheshire, 1982; Purchased with grant aid from the V&A Purchase Grant Fund, Beecroft Bequest, Grosvenor Museum Society 1984.24

PUBLISHED: Ridgway 1985, p.170 Mug.

NOTES:

1. Chester 1951 exhibition catalogue, p.33; Moore 1984 I, p.72; Newman, p.41. 'The word jack or blackjack appears to derive from archaic French possibly referring to the possessions of a peasant man' (Lomax, p.71). Made since at least the 16th century, some 17th- and 18th-century ones have silver mounts (e.g., Newman, p.42 and Lomax, no.58, all straight-sided). For a pair of Victorian novelty milk jugs modelled as blackjacks with simulated leather surfaces (by Edward Hutton, London, 1887) see Phillips, London, 19 January 1999, lot 168.
2. Ridgway 1985, pp.160, 175-6.
3. Banister 1973, pl.2; Ridgway 1985, pp.161-2, pl.14.
4. Ridgway 1985, pp.176-7, 200.
5. Ridgway 1968, pp.147, 171; Ridgway 1985, pp.75-6, 144, 148, 161-3.

Richard Richardson II & William Richardson II

For Richard Richardson II see no.21

William Richardson II was apprenticed in 1734 to his father William Richardson I (see no.14). Since part of the Chester freedom list for 1740-1 is indecipherable, there is no record of his name, nor does he appear in the Goldsmiths' Company book. Canon Ridgway suggests that William Richardson II marked some silver jointly with his cousin Richard Richardson II between 1740 and 1748. His date of death is unknown.[1]

NOTE:

1. Ridgway 1985, pp.132-3, 188.

Barnard I, 1822 (J.H. Bourdon-Smith Ltd., Catalogue, Autumn 1999, p.50).

20. Mugs of 1785 by maker WB, of 1810 by Crispin Fuller, and of 1815 by William Bateman I (Wark, nos.72, 74-5).

21. See Wees, p.409 n.5 for list of examples.

32 MUG

Richard Richardson II, Chester, 1767-8

Five marks on base (maker's mark Ridgway 1985, p.168 type 6)

Height 8.1 cm. (3.2 in.)

Weight 136 g. (4.8 oz.)

Sterling silver. The bulbous cylindrical mug flares outward to the applied foot-ring with an inset circular base, and has an incised line around the everted rim. The applied S-scroll handle is of oval section, widening slightly toward either end. Scratched on the base are the date 1767 and the numbers 297.4 and 411.

Charles Brocklehurst and Nicholas Moore called mugs of this type the blackjack form. Their shape resembles the blackjack, a type of jug or tankard for beer, made of treated leather and having a distinctive bulge midway on the body.[1]

Canon Ridgway categorised Richard Richardson II's mugs into four types. The blackjack form is type B, having an 'ogee outline, often so slight that the curves are almost imperceptible. These are sometimes referred to as the "Chester type" … In most cases their capacity is so little that one must accept the suggestion that they were either christening gifts, or used for some drink popular at the time, perhaps brandy to accompany the brandy warmer saucepans of the period. The "Chester type", though attractive, required less skill and time to make than either of the other groups.'[2]

33

33 TEA CANISTER

Richard Richardson II & William Richardson II, Chester, 1741-2

Five marks on base (maker's mark Ridgway 1985, p.149 type 3B). Four marks inside cover (minus maker's mark)
Height 9.3 cm. (3.65 in.), length of base 9.5 cm. (3.75 in.)
Weight 265 g. (9.35 oz.)

Sterling silver. The oval body is constructed from sheet silver, seamed vertically opposite the hinge and incurved beneath an applied vertical rim. The edge of the base is moulded to form a spreading foot, and a convex moulding is applied around its junction with the body. The flat stepped cover is raised, with an applied bezel seamed opposite the hinge. The cover joins the body with a five-part hinge on the short axis, opposite which is a small crescent-shaped extension of the rim.

For the early history of tea drinking in England see no.18. The closed container for dry tea leaves was called a tea 'canister' from at least 1711, the term having been applied since 1704 by the tea trade to a box of tea weighing between 75 lbs. and 1 cwt. The word 'caddy', by which it is now generally known, was introduced in the 1780s. This derives from the Malay *kati*, the weight equivalent to 1⅓lb. by which tea was sold in the East. The term 'caddy' is also used today for the wooden container which held the canisters, known in the 18th century as a 'tea chest'.[1]

What may be the earliest surviving tea canisters are a pair of 1682: such vessels are extremely rare

before 1700 but their use spread rapidly thereafter. They were usually made in pairs for different types of tea, most commonly Viridis (green) and Bohea (black), to be chosen or blended according to taste. A matching third canister, frequently larger, was often supplied to hold lumps of sugar. Due to the high price of both tea and sugar, the canisters were kept in locked chests of wood, often covered with shagreen and having silver mounts. Canisters with their own locks appeared *c.*1750, but the absence of a lock on the Richardson canister shows that it was originally housed in a chest.[2]

The fact that tea canisters were intended to fit into chests strongly influenced their design. In the early 18th century they were usually rectangular, octagonal or oval, later blossoming with the Rococo into a great diversity of ornament and form. The early canisters have a flat top with a hole covered by a domed, pull-off cap suitable for measuring the tea. Most examples also have a sliding base or top to enable the insertion of a lead liner, which helped to retain freshness and which could be slipped out and refilled.[3] An alternative design, in use by 1719,[4] has a hinged cover which bends right back to facilitate access to the lead liner.

The Richardson canister employs the oval body of the popular early 18th-century type,[5] but replaces the domed cap with the more convenient hinged cover. The resulting form, pared of all extraneous projections, seems to anticipate the streamlined elegance of some 1920s and '30s design.[6]

Only one other 18th-century Chester tea canister survives. Made by Richard Richardson II in 1764, it is a lockable cylinder with beaded edges, having a flat hinged cover with a cast flower handle.[7] The Chester Plate Duty Books also record two tea canisters made by George Walker I in 1787.[8]

PROVENANCE: Sotheby's, London, 5 October 1972, lot 116; H.R. Jessop Ltd., London; Purchased with grant aid from the V&A Purchase Grant Fund, Beecroft Bequest 1973.25

EXHIBITED: Chester 1973 II, p.44 no.20; Chester 1979 I, no.4; Chester 1980; Chester 1984, no.76, illustrated.

PUBLISHED: Thomas, p.16; Ridgway 1985, p.191 Tea Caddy, pl.28.

NOTES:
1. Newman, p.317; Hare, p.40; Oman 1967, pp.154-5; Wills, p.140; Davis, p.104; Banister 1967, p.44. The Chester Plate Duty Books first refer to a 'caddy spoon' in 1784 (Ridgway 1996, p.96).
2. Clayton 1985 I, pp.405, 407; Newman, p.317; Davis, p.103; Taylor 1956, p.134.
3. Oman 1967, p.155; Wees, p.397.

4. e.g. Paul de Lamerie's earliest known canisters, a rectangular pair of 1719 (Hare, no.12).

5. It is particularly close to a pair of 1728 by John Newton (Clayton 1985 I, fig.616) and, despite their tighter base mouldings, to a pair of 1746 by Samuel Taylor (Davidson, fig.3).

6. The features of tall, incurving forms and stepped mouldings are found in silver, e.g.: tea & coffee set designed by Harold Stabler for Adie Bros., Birmingham, 1925; covered bowl, H.G. Murphy, London, 1935 (Brett, nos.1543, 1546); Ascot Gold Vase designed by R.G. Baxendale for Wakeley & Wheeler, Birmingham, 1939 (Jones 1981, fig.223). They are also found in other media, e.g.: a gilded mahogany desk designed by Sir Edward Maufe, 1924 (Hogben, p.95); the polished granite Leverhulme Memorial, Port Sunlight, Wirral, designed by James Lomax-Simpson, 1930 (Hubbard & Shippobottom, fig.19); and earthenware vessels designed by Keith Murray for Wedgewood, c.1933-4 (Garner, p.163).

7. Ridgway 1996, pp.195-6, pl.58.

8. Ridgway 1996, p.101.

Richard Richardson II
or Richard Richardson III

For Richard Richardson II see no.21
For Richard Richardson III see no.47

34 BOTTLE TICKET

Richard Richardson II of Chester, c.1764-9
or Richard Richardson III of Chester, c.1769-79

Maker's mark only on back (Ridgway 1985, p.168 type 6)
Length 4.2 cm. (1.65 in.)
Weight 6 g. (0.2 oz.)

Silver. The ticket is a narrow rectangle, cut from sheet silver and slightly curved. The inscription, 'MADEIRA', is stamped and pierced in Roman lettering. The circular link chain is attached to rings, which pass through holes pierced in the two eyelets extending from the ticket's upper edge.

Now commonly called a wine label, this was known as a bottle ticket in the 18th century. Silver bottle tickets for wine were an English innovation, first recorded in 1735-6. At first, they were intended to replace the scrap of paper or parchment attached to the side of a bottle, which had served to identify the contents as it lay on the cellar shelf below stairs, and to add grace to its appearance when it came up to the dining room.[1] Later, as Philippa Glanville has explained, 'once the value of storing wine in one's cellar to mature was recognised, some more elegant method of bringing it to the table than the common green wine bottle was inevitably required, and by 1750 clear lead glass decanters were common ... A predecessor of the decanter label may be seen in certain tin-glazed earthenware serving bottles of the mid-seventeenth century which are painted with 'sack' and other terms for wine.'[2] The use of decanters, together with the variety of wines and liquors becoming available and the increasing tendency to offer as much choice as possible, led to a great increase in bottle tickets from c.1760, and they remained popular up to the mid-19th century. Large numbers were also made in Staffordshire and Battersea enamel in the 18th century, and in the 19th century bottle tickets in porcelain and mother-of-pearl were produced.[3]

Most bottle tickets, like the Richardson one, were suspended around the neck of the bottle or decanter by a chain, and are slightly curved so as to fit closely on the vessel. The narrow rectangular form is one of the 20 types of bottle ticket identified by Norman Penzer. The holes for the chains are either contained within the rectangle or, as here, pierce two eyelets extending above it, a feature found from the early 1760s.[4]

More than 500 different names appear on bottle tickets, but one of the most common is madeira, a fortified white wine from the Portuguese island of Madeira in the Atlantic. Wines were imported into Chester from Portugal throughout the 18th century.[5]

Bottle tickets were exempt from assay and their marking was voluntary until 1790, so most examples before this date are unmarked or only partially marked. According to Captain Sir Thomas Barlow, there are escutcheons which can be reasonably dated to c.1750-5 with the type 5D maker's mark of Richard Richardson II, making him the earliest recorded maker of bottle tickets in Chester.[6] The type 6 maker's mark was used by Richard Richardson II from 1764 until his death in 1769, and continued to be used by the family firm under Richard Richardson III until Richardson IV took over in 1779.[7] The same mark appears on a rectangular bottle ticket with a gadrooned border and, according to Sir Thomas, on an escutcheon and some ovals and crescents. The museum's ticket and one of these crescents are the only known examples from 18th-century Chester with pierced inscriptions.[8]

Several bottle tickets by Richard Richardson IV, including a reeded escutcheon of c.1782-8 and a pair of trefoil-capped rectangles from c.1786-96,[9] are the only other Chester-made examples to survive before those by William Twemlow (no.51) and George Lowe I (nos.53 and 58). Many more were made in the city before 1800 as recorded, with varying nomenclature, in the Plate Duty Books: 61 labels and a bottle label by Richard Richardson IV in 1785-90, 16 bottle labels by Thomas Hill in 1789, 13 bottle tickets and 12 labels by George Walker I in 1792-6, 18 bottle tickets by George Lowe I in 1793 and 24 labels by Robert Bowers I in 1797.[10]

34

PROVENANCE: John Phillips, Toronto; Sotheby's, Chester, 19 October 1983, lot 793; Purchased 1983.77

EXHIBITED: Chester 1984, no.97, illustrated.

NOTES:

1. Wills, p.64; Glanville 1987, p.88; Clayton 1985 I, p.469; Davis, p.75; Captain Sir Thomas Barlow, letter, 7 March 2000. The Chester Plate Duty Books first record the term 'wine label' in 1828 (Ridgway 1996, p.92).
2. Glanville 1987, p.88.
3. Davis, pp.75-6; Clayton 1985 I, p.469; Barlow, *op.cit.*
4. Wills, p.164; Clayton 1985 I, p.469; Penzer 1974, pp.70-1; Barlow, *op.cit.*
5. Davis, p.76 n.1; Kennett, p.17; Barlow, *op.cit.*
6. Davis, p.76; Barlow, *op.cit.*
7. Ridgway 1985, pp.168, 170, 174.
8. Ridgway 1985, p.171; Barlow, *op.cit.*
9. Ridgway 1985, pp.182, 184; Barlow, *op.cit.*
10. Ridgway 1996, pp.77, 86, 90, 96, 101.

Joseph Duke I

Joseph Duke I was in business by 1762, entered the Chester Goldsmiths' Company in 1764, and became free in 1779. He served the company as warden 1765-6, 1767-8, 1769-70, 1771-2, 1773-*c.*1800 and 1808-10. His shop was in Pepper Street and he died in 1810.

The later Chester goldsmith Joseph Duke II was probably related but was not his son.[1]

NOTE:

1. Ridgway 1985, pp.77-8, 80; Ridgway 1996, p.147.

35 PAIR OF TEA SPOONS

Joseph Duke I of Chester, c.1771-81

Two marks on back of stem near bowl: lion passant and maker's mark (Ridgway 1985, p.77 type 2)
Length: both 12.3 cm. (4.85 in.)
Weight: (1) 12 g. (0.45 oz.), (2) 11 g. (0.4 oz.)

Sterling silver. Each spoon is formed from a single piece of silver. The deep oblong bowl is raised, with an extended single drop at its junction with the stem. The Hanoverian pattern stem turns sharply upward at the end, and the back of the stem is engraved with the initials M·P in Roman lettering. The bowl of (2) is damaged.

Up to the 1780s most tea spoons were marked with only the lion passant and the maker's mark. The lion passant on these spoons is that used at Chester between 1762 and 1781. All of Joseph Duke I's recorded silver falls within the period 1771-81, which is therefore the most likely date range for these spoons.[1]

They are among the 11 known pieces by Duke, which include a sugar caster, a wine funnel, sauce boats

35

and a sauce ladle, a badge and a marrow scoop.[2] For a discussion of tea spoons and the other 18th-century Chester examples see no.18.

PROVENANCE: Miss Amy Smith (died 1955); Chester City Treasurer (appointed Receiver); Transferred to Museum 1980.33.7,8

EXHIBITED: Chester 1980 (as Joseph Duke); Chester 1984, no.105 (as James Dixon).

PUBLISHED: Ridgway 1985, p.79 Tea Spoons (as Joseph Duke I).

NOTES:
1. Ridgway 1985, pp.28, 78-9.
2. Ridgway 1985, pp.78-9; Ridgway 1996, pp.192-3.

36 SAUCE LADLE

Joseph Duke I, Chester, 1780-1

Five marks on back of stem near bowl (maker's mark Ridgway 1985, p.77 type 2)
Length 16.6 cm. (6.5 in.)
Weight 52 g. (1.8 oz.)

Sterling silver. The ladle is formed from a single piece of silver. The raised circular bowl has a double-ring drop, struck with a ridge across the end of the long central strap, at its junction with the stem. The Old English pattern stem rises at a sharp angle to the bowl and curves backward, with a vestigial ridge behind the turned down end.

Smaller than soup ladles, sauce ladles were used with sauce boats, gravy boats and sauce tureens. The earliest true ladles, with curved stems rising at a sharp angle to the bowl, date from the 1730s, and sauce ladles are recorded from 1743. The Old English pattern, where the end of the stem turns down instead of up, is probably of English origin. It may have been initially intended for ladles, occurring on a soup ladle

of 1752, and became the standard form after *c.*1760. Sauce ladles increased in popularity from the 1760s with the introduction of the Neo-Classical sauce tureen, which had no pouring lip and therefore required a ladle to serve the contents.[1]

This is the only surviving ladle by Joseph Duke I. Seven other sauce ladles by 18th-century Chester goldsmiths are known: pairs from 1783 and 1785 by Richard Richardson IV, and single ones from 1791 by George Walker I and from 1791 and 1797 (no.56) by George Lowe I.[2] The Chester Plate Duty Books also record 51 sauce ladles by Richard Richardson IV in 1785-90, eight by James Dixon in 1788, nine by Thomas Hill in 1789, 29 by George Walker I in 1793-8 and six by George Lowe I in the same period.[3]

PROVENANCE: John ffoulkes Lowe, Chester: His sister, Miss Joyce Lowe, 1973; Phillips, London, 21 June 1985, lot 114; Purchased through J.H. Bourdon-Smith Ltd., London 1985.126

PUBLISHED: Ridgway 1985, p.79 Ladle.

NOTES:
1. Newman, p.274; Snodin 1974, pp.46-7; Wees, p.256; Wills, p.118.
2. Ridgway 1985, pp.106, 183, 200.
3. Ridgway 1996, pp.80, 86, 90, 96, 101-2.

George Walker I

George Walker I was apprenticed to Richard Richardson II (see no.21). He became free in 1767 and his mark is first recorded in 1768. He was admitted to the Chester Goldsmiths' Company in 1770, serving as warden 1771-2, 1773-91 and assay master 1791-1809. His sons George Walker II and John Walker I were apprenticed to him. He lived in Eastgate Street and died in 1809.[1]

NOTE:
1. Ridgway 1985, pp.196-7, 203; Ridgway 1996, p.100.

36

37 TWO-HANDLED CUP

George Walker I, Chester, 1769-70

Five marks below rim (maker's mark Ridgway 1985, p.197 type 1). Three marks beneath foot rim: maker's mark, lion passant twice

Height 14.5 cm. (5.7 in.), width across handles 18.1 cm. (7.1 in.)

Weight 572 g. (20.2 oz.)

See Colour Plate IV

Sterling silver. The domed, stepped circular foot and low stem are raised. They support the raised, inverted bell-shaped cup, which has a setting-out point on its base and an incised line around its everted rim. The two cast double-scroll handles have plain thumbpieces. Each joins the body with two oval plates, that near the rim being larger. Beneath the foot is scratched 'No 3', '5/5 352' and '18 19 at p 11'.

The side of the body is engraved with an elaborate, asymmetrical Rococo cartouche composed of scrolls, wave-like forms, foliage and flowers. The motto

'PATRIAE FIDELIS ET CONSTANS AMICUS' (Loyal to his country and a constant friend) is apparently unrecorded for any family. The engraving of the cartouche and motto looks contemporary with the cup, but the arms and crest of Courtney appear to be 20th-century additions.[1]

This cup may have been made for drinking on ceremonial occasions but, like the St Martin Cup (no.27), it was probably intended primarily for display on the sideboard or table. Inverted bell-shaped cups with cast double-scroll handles were made in London between the 1720s and '50s, and in Dublin from the 1720s until the end of the century, but they usually have leaf-capped handles and a central moulding around the body.[2] The design of George Walker's cup is untouched by the emerging taste for Neo-Classicism, but looks backward to such pieces as the Walpole Gold Cup of 1739 by David Willaume II,[3] where the absence of the central moulding gives free rein to the engraving which decorates the body.

Thirty-five pieces of silver by George Walker I survive, including flatware, double beakers, saucepans, tumbler cups, a coconut cup and a nutmeg grater.[4] Six other two-handled cups are known to have been made by Walker between 1769 and 1776: they have inverted bell-shaped bodies, but strap handles and no feet and, while one is plain, the others are chased with fluting and gadrooning. A further eight cups by Walker, of unspecified form, are recorded in the Chester Plate Duty Books for 1785-1801.[5] The only remotely comparable two-handled cup from Georgian Chester is the St Martin Cup.

PROVENANCE: Courtney family, 20th century; John ffoulkes Lowe, Chester; His sister, Miss Joyce Lowe, 1973; Purchased with grant aid from the MGC/V&A Purchase Grant Fund, London Goldsmiths' Company, Grosvenor Museum Society 1988.50

PUBLISHED: Ridgway 1976, illustrated p.20; Ridgway 1985, pp.201-2 Porringers no.7, pl.42.

NOTES:

1. Gale Glynn, report, 22 March 1991.
2. London examples include: Paul de Lamerie, 1720 (Clayton 1985 II, p.110); Fuller White, 1752 (Wees, no.29). Dublin cups are discussed at no.114.
3. Clayton 1985 II, p.133.
4. Ridgway 1985, pp.197-203; this catalogue, no.39.
5. Ridgway 1985, pp.200-1; Ridgway 1996, pp.101-2.

38 PARCEL-GILT MUG

George Walker I, Chester, 1771-2

Five marks beneath base (maker's mark Ridgway 1985, p.197 type 1)
Height 8.7 cm. (3.4 in.)
Weight 144 g. (5.1 oz.)

See Colour Plate IV

Sterling silver with gilt interior. The domed, spreading circular foot is raised, with a narrow concave moulding applied around its junction with the body. The baluster-shaped mug is raised, with a setting-out point on its base and an incised line around its slightly everted rim. The double-scroll handle, with a plain thumb-piece, is cast in identical halves and seamed down the centre. The side of the body opposite the handle is engraved with the monogram CHEL in ornamental script above a pattern of spigs.

The interior has presumably been regilded, since its very rich colour is quite different from the exceptionally pale lemon characteristic of 18th-century Chester gilding.

For the early history of mugs see no.9. The plain mug with a tulip-shaped body, having an everted rim

and a tuck-in base on a moulded foot, had appeared in London by 1715. The cast handle was at first a single scroll, but the double-scroll began to replace this from *c.*1725. At about the same time, the body began to assume the baluster form and, sometimes tending towards a pear shape, this type of mug remained very popular until the 1770s.[1] George Walker's mug is particularly close to many London examples from the 1730s.[2]

This mug is the only known example of the type by George Walker I, although he also made one of the blackjack form (see no.32) in 1769.[3] As Nicholas Moore has observed, a pair of baluster mugs made by James Dixon in 1769 employ the same handle castings as those used by Walker two years later.[4] The other surviving Chester-assayed baluster mugs comprise seven of 1736-65 by Richard Richardson II (the earliest of which has an S-scroll handle), and two of 1782 and '85 by Joseph Walley of Liverpool (which have leaf-capped handles).[5] No mugs by Chester goldsmiths are recorded from 1784 in the Plate Duty Books.

PROVENANCE: The Rev. Canon Maurice H. Ridgway, Bowdon, Cheshire; Purchased with grant aid from the V&A Purchase Grant Fund, National Art Collections Fund, Grosvenor Museum Society 1982.88

EXHIBITED: Chester 1984, no.107.

PUBLISHED: NACF Review 1983, no.2990, illustrated; Ridgway 1985, p.200 Mugs no.2; Moore 1985 III, illustrated p.71; Moore 1986, fig.11.

NOTES:

1. Clayton 1985 I, p.258; Taylor 1956, p.150; Wark, p.27.
2. e.g. pair by William Darker, 1732 (Christie's, New York, 28 October 1986, lot 36); Ayme Videau, 1734 (J.H. Bourdon-Smith Ltd., Catalogue, Autumn 1999, p.26); Thomas Mason, 1735, with a leaf-capped handle (Lomax, no.46); Richard Zouch, 1737, with an engraved body (Clayton 1985 II, p.173 fig.12); Humphry Payne, 1739 (Wark, no.69).
3. Ridgway 1985, p.200.
4. Moore 1984 I, nos.99, 107.
5. Ridgway 1985, pp.144, 162-3, 211-12.

39 PAP BOAT

George Walker I, Chester, 1771-2

Five marks beneath base (maker's mark Ridgway 1985, p.197 type 1)
Length 12.3 cm. (4.85 in.)
Weight 58 g. (2.05 oz.)

Sterling silver. The shallow boat-shaped vessel is raised, with a flat oval base, a curved holding end, and the feeding end shaped as an extended, tapering and slightly rising lip.

38

Pap was a mixture of stale white bread-crumbs or flour, cooked to a sloppy mush in water, with the possible addition of a little wine, beer, beef-stock or milk. It was fed to infants as young as three months old in order to provide them with some solid nourishment and to aid the process of weaning. However, there was little real nourishment in pap, which one 17th-century childcare expert compared unfavourably with bookbinders' paste, and which an 18th-century French writer condemned as 'the most dangerous of all the foods for infants'.[1]

Pap boats were used for feeding pap and administering medicine to infants and invalids. The vessel could be gently tipped, and its contents introduced into a mouth via the lip of the feeding end. Silver pap boats were made between c.1710 and the mid-19th century. London-made examples are almost invariably marked on the rim opposite the lip, but this provincial one is marked beneath the base. Pap boats were also made in several other materials, including horn, wood, salt-glazed stoneware, creamware, earthenware, Sheffield Plate and pewter.[2]

Silver feeding utensils for invalids included feeding cups, feeding tubes and medicine spoons as well as pap boats. A wide range of other medical implements was also made in silver, including surgical and diagnostic instruments, bleeding bowls, and aids to personal health and hygiene.[3]

No other pap boats by George Walker I survive,[4] but the Chester Plate Duty Books record one in 1794.[5]

39

Fifteen other Chester pap boats are known, including one of *c*.1727 by Richard Richardson I, eight of 1730-69 by Richard Richardson II, ones of 1733 by William Richardson I, of 1742 by Thomas Maddock and of 1775 by Richard Richardson III, and three of 1828-37 by George Lowe I.[6] The Plate Duty Books record 41 pap boats by Chester goldsmiths, comprising 12 by Richard Richardson IV in 1786-90, 28 by George Lowe I in 1793-1837 and one by H.M. & S. Huntingdon in 1826.[7]

PROVENANCE: Lowe & Sons, Chester; Purchased with grant aid from the MGC/V&A Purchase Grant Fund, Beecroft Bequest, Grosvenor Museum Society 1985.100

NOTES:

1. Kevill-Davies.
2. Newman, p.233; Davis, p.199; Wills, p.109; Kevill-Davies; Clayton 1985 I, p.269.
3. Newman, p.209.
4. A vessel of 1789, which now resembles a double-lipped pap boat, was originally the bowl of a punch ladle (Moore 1984 I, no.110).
5. Ridgway 1996, p.101.
6. Ridgway 1985, pp.106-7, 117, 144, 148, 163-4, 170, 178, 187, 190; Ridgway 1996, p.188.
7. Ridgway 1996, pp.86, 90-3, 96.

40 TAPER BOX

George Walker I, Chester, 1790-1

Six marks on base (maker's mark Ridgway 1985, p.197 type 1). Three marks inside cover and on extinguisher: maker's mark, sovereign's head, lion passant

Total height (extinguisher on cover on box) 8.4 cm. (3.3 in.), height with cover but without extinguisher 6.1 cm. (2.4 in.), height of extinguisher 3.3 cm. (1.3 in.)
Total weight 91 g. (3.2 oz.)

See Colour Plate IV

Sterling silver. The straight-sided cylindrical body is made of sheet silver, seamed behind the handle. It has a flat base, and narrow mouldings are applied around the foot and beneath the cover. The S-scroll moulded strap handle has a small lozenge-shaped panel at its lower junction with the body. The raised slip-on cover has an applied bezel with a narrow moulding applied around the shoulder, rising to a short cylindrical funnel extending upward from an opening in its centre. Attached to the cover by a long silver chain of circular links is a conical extinguisher with a moulded base and finial. The side of the body is engraved in Roman lettering: 'Trifles shew regard'.

Sealing wax, a mixture of shellac and rosin, was used for sealing letters before the introduction of the gummed envelope in the mid-19th century,[1] and for attaching impressions of seals to documents. The stick of sealing wax was melted by a lighted length of wax taper, which was held on the writing desk in a number of ways. The taper stick, made between *c*.1685 and *c*.1775, resembled a small candlestick and held a straight length of taper. The wax jack, made from *c*.1680, held a tight coil of taper, either horizontally or vertically, in such a way that it extended upward while burning. Because the coiled taper tended to adhere, the wax jack was superseded in the 1770s by the wax-ball taper holder, a frame which held a loosely wound ball of taper.[2]

40

An alternative device was the taper box. One of the earliest examples dates from *c*.1690 and, although comparatively few survive from the first half of the 18th century, it later increased in popularity. The cylindrical box held a loose coil of taper, which emerged from a funnel in the centre of the cover. Because it protected the taper when not in use, the taper box was especially favoured for travelling writing cases. The taper, of wax treated with turpentine, was non-odorous, burned clearly, and did not crack or scale when bent. Taper boxes usually have a single loop handle and some have an extinguisher attached by a chain. Earlier examples have a flat cover, but later ones are conical or domed: the cover of George Walker's taper box is a transitional form. The device was also known as a bougie box, after *bougie*, the French word for 'candle', which derived in turn from B(o)ugia, the Algerian town which exported the wax.[3]

The inscription makes clear that this box was a gift, albeit quite a cheap one.[4] Only one other Chester-assayed taper box survives, likewise made by George Walker I *c*.1790, but having a hinged cover and a pivoted crescent-shaped drip pan.[5] The Chester Plate Duty Books use the terms 'wax candle box' or 'candle box', and record three in 1792-3 by George Walker I and three in 1797-1800 by George Lowe I.[6]

PROVENANCE: John ffoulkes Lowe, Chester; His sister, Miss Joyce Lowe, 1973; Purchased with grant aid from the MGC/V&A Purchase Grant Fund, London Goldsmiths' Company, Grosvenor Museum Society 1988.51

EXHIBITED: London V&A 1989.

PUBLISHED: Banister 1973, p.1877; Ridgway 1976, illustrated p.19; Ridgway 1985, p.198 Bougie Boxes no.1, pl.33.

NOTES:

1. Envelopes were known in Britain in the 1830s, but were rarely used before 1840. Gumming of the flap was first mentioned as a possibility in 1840, being introduced shortly thereafter, and gummed envelopes were probably in general use by 1850 (Douglas Muir, letter, 4 January 2000; David Beech, letter, 24 December 1999).

2. Clayton 1985 I, pp.65-6; Oman 1967, pp.178-9; Wills, p.139; Newman, pp.315, 352.

3. Clayton 1985 I, p.403; Oman 1967, p.179; Wills, p.139; Newman, pp.45, 315. A broadly comparable London-made taper

41

box of 1790 by Joseph Heriot (Rowe 1965, pl.87A) has a slightly more elaborate handle and funnel, but its extinguisher hooks onto the side of the body.

4. Rowe 1965, p.80.
5. Ridgway 1985, p.199.
6. Ridgway 1996, pp.90, 101-2.

41 CREAM BOAT

George Walker I, Chester, 1791-2

Six marks beneath pouring lip (maker's mark Ridgway 1985, p.197 type 1)
Length 14.7 cm. (5.8 in.)
Weight 119 g. (4.2 oz.)

Sterling silver. The deep, oval body is raised, extending at one end into a long everted pouring lip, and having a rounded moulding applied to the rim, which dips midway on the sides. The body rests on three shell-headed hoof feet, cast and applied, one beneath the lip and two at either side of the handle. The leaf-capped flying double-scroll handle is cast in two parts and applied on axis with the lip.

Although the Chester Plate Duty Books contain numerous references to sauce ladles (discussed at no.36), they mention only one sauce boat. However, they record 18 cream boats and a further four unspecified 'boats'.[1] There can be little doubt that this vessel is the one cream boat by George Walker I which was assayed in 1792.[2]

Cream boats were used to serve cream with dessert. Modelled on sauce boats, but smaller, the most common form had three legs and a scroll or flying-scroll handle. Sauce boats of this type were made from the mid-1720s and had become the dominant form by 1740, but they are also found with a single spreading foot and in extravagant Rococo designs, which likewise influenced some smaller vessels. In London, cream boats were made from the late 1730s and, although declining in popularity from the 1760s, continued into the late 1790s.[3] George Walker's cream boat is very close to certain London examples of the 1770s and '80s.[4]

The Chester Plate Duty Books record 17 cream boats by George Walker I in 1786-93, but only one other example survives. Dating from 1784, this is very close to the museum's cream boat, its only difference being a scalloped rim.[5]

The other surviving 18th-century Chester-assayed examples comprise: a cream boat of 1741 by John Brancker of Liverpool;[6] a sauce boat of 1743 by Richard Richardson II and William Richardson II; five cream boats of 1771-5 by Joseph Duke I; and a sauce boat of 1794 by George Lowe I.[7] All follow the same basic form, with the flying double-scroll handle featuring on those of 1741-3 and 1794; the shell-headed hoof feet on those of 1772-5 and 1794; and the rounded rim-moulding also being employed in 1794.

PROVENANCE: The Rev. Canon Maurice H. Ridgway, Bowdon, Cheshire; Purchased with grant aid from the

V&A Purchase Grant Fund, Beecroft Bequest, Grosvenor Museum Society 1983.48

EXHIBITED: Chester 1984, no.111, illustrated.

PUBLISHED: Ridgway 1985, p.202 Sauce Boats no.2.

NOTES:

1. The two goldsmiths concerned are George Walker I, whose work is discussed below, and George Lowe I, by whom six vessels are recorded in 1795-6 (Ridgway 1996, p.90).
2. Ridgway 1996, p.101.
3. Newman, p.92; Clayton 1985 I, pp.113, 324; Oman 1967, pp.161-2.
4. e.g. cream boat, probably Thomas Smith or Thomas Satchwell, 1777 (Davis, no.100); pair of sauce boats, Hester Bateman, 1781 (Shure, pl.LIV): the only notable difference is that all three have punched rims.
5. Ridgway 1996, p.101; Moore 1984 I, no.109.
6. Wark, no.138; maker confirmed by Elizabeth Pergam (letter, 15 December 1999).
7. Ridgway 1985, pp.79, 107, 191; Moore 1984 I, no.103. Both sauce boats are over 6 in. long.

42 CHEESE SCOOP

George Walker I, Chester, 1792-3

Six marks on back of blade (maker's mark Ridgway 1985, p.197 type 1)
Length 22.7 cm. (8.9 in.)
Weight 88 g. (3.1 oz.)

Sterling silver with green-stained ivory handle. The blade and stem are formed from a single piece of silver. The wide blade is raised in a curved section, with a rounded end and two notches to either side near the stem. The straight stem, tapering toward the blade, is cast and soldered to a tapering silver ferrule, to which the handle is attached with two pins.

Cheese scoops were used to scoop an individual portion from a large cheese. Made from the late 18th century, early examples like George Walker's most commonly have ivory handles, although bone and wood were also used.[1]

This is the only surviving cheese scoop by George Walker I. The Chester Plate Duty Books, which use the terms cheese scoop and cheese digger interchangeably, record six examples by Walker between 1792 (when he submitted two) and 1797.[2] The Duty Books also record three by Richard Richardson IV in 1785 and one by George Lowe I in 1839.[3] No other cheese scoops by Chester goldsmiths are known to survive from the 18th or early 19th centuries, although a later example is that of 1852 by John Lowe I (no.69).

42

PROVENANCE: John ffoulkes Lowe, Chester; His sister, Miss Joyce Lowe, 1973; Purchased with grant aid from the MGC/V&A Purchase Grant Fund, London Goldsmiths' Company, Grosvenor Museum Society 1988.52

EXHIBITED: London V&A 1989.

PUBLISHED: Ridgway 1985, p.199 Cheese Scoop.

NOTES:

1. Newman, p.71; Wills, p.71.
2. Ridgway 1996, p.101.
3. Ridgway 1996, pp.93, 96.

43 SUGAR SIFTER SPOON

George Walker I, Chester, 1794-5

Six marks on back of stem near top (maker's mark variant of Ridgway 1985, p.197 type 2)[1]
Length 16.4 cm. (6.45 in.)
Weight 38 g. (1.35 oz.)

Sterling silver. The spoon is formed from a single piece of silver. The raised circular bowl is pierced with a double row of comma shapes near the rim and a square of crosses and small circles in the centre. The bowl has a single drop at its junction with the Old English pattern stem, which rises at a sharp angle and curves backward, with a vestigial ridge behind the turned down end.

Sugar had been used in England since the Middle Ages, and increasing quantities were imported after 1660. The loaf of sugar, a moulded conical mass about 60 cm. high, was the normal form in which sugar was purchased until the early 20th century. Lumps of sugar were cut from a loaf in the kitchen with a sugar chopper, and these lumps could then be powdered with a sugar crusher.[2]

The sugar sifter spoon was also known as a sifter spoon, sugar spoon, sugar sifter or sugar ladle. It was used to sprinkle powdered sugar, from a container, over fruit or other desserts. Ladle-shaped spoons, smaller than sauce ladles and having pierced bowls, were introduced *c.*1750 to accompany the deep vessels, often vase- or urn-shaped, which were used for sugar. By the end of the 18th century sugar sifter spoons had reached the same size as sauce ladles and formed part of the dessert service, following the flatware styles of the period. The bowls were pierced with holes in various sizes and patterns, and the delightful piercing of George Walker's spoon follows contemporary London examples.[3]

This is the only known Chester-assayed sugar sifter spoon, and the only surviving example of the 13 by George Walker I which appear in the Duty Books between 1791 and 1804.[4] The Duty Books, which use the terms sugar ladle and sugar spoon interchangeably, also record four by Richard Richardson IV in 1785-8, 55 by George Lowe I in 1812-38 and five by John Walker I in 1814-27.[5]

PROVENANCE: John ffoulkes Lowe, Chester; His sister, Miss Joyce Lowe, 1973; Purchased with grant aid from the MGC/V&A Purchase Grant Fund, London Goldsmiths' Company, Grosvenor Museum Society 1988.53

EXHIBITED: London V&A 1989.

PUBLISHED: Ridgway 1985, p.202 Sifter.

NOTES:
1. With two cut corners to the left as well as the lower right.
2. Oman 1967, p.107; Wees, p.120; Newman, p.307; Clayton 1985 I, p.392.
3. Newman, p.307; Snodin 1974, p.51; Clayton 1985 I, p.393; Pickford, p.198, fig.353.
4. Ridgway 1996, pp.101-2.
5. Ridgway 1996, pp.91-3, 96, 102.

James Dixon

James Dixon was born *c.*1738 and became free in 1770. He entered his mark in 1769, although he did not join the Chester Goldsmiths' Company, He lived in Eastgate Street, later moved to Northgate Street, and died in 1807.[1]

NOTE:
1. Bennett 1908, p.370; Ridgway 1985, p.75; Ridgway 1989, p.400.

43

44 PAIR OF SALT SHOVELS

James Dixon of Chester, c.1769-79

Maker's mark only on back of stem near bowl
(Ridgway 1985, p.75 type 1)
Length: both 9.9 cm. (3.9 in.)
Weight: both 6 g. (0.2 oz.)

Silver. Each shovel is formed from a single piece of silver. The plain shovel-shaped bowl is raised, and joins the stem without a drop. There is a ridge along the upper half of the Hanoverian pattern stem, which turns sharply upward at the end. The back of the stem is engraved with the initials E·I in Roman lettering.

Since the Middle Ages, magnificent vessels had been made to hold salt for the dinner table, but during the course of the 17th century these were gradually superseded by small individual salt-containers set by each diner. From the late medieval period salt was taken with the tip of the knife, but a salt spoon is first recorded in 1643. The earliest existing type appears to be the salt shovel, although some miniature spoons may also have been intended for salt. Among the first surviving examples are four shovels of *c.*1730 with baluster finials, but datable shovels before *c.*1750 are very rare. Those with a wavy-edged bowl are perhaps the earliest, but the lighter plain-bowled type—as exemplified by James Dixon's pair—was made from *c.*1750 and remained popular into the 20th century.[1]

Before *c.*1784 salt shovels usually bear only two marks, the correct form being the maker's mark and a standard mark. These by James Dixon have just the maker's mark and were presumably never assayed. His surviving silver dates from 1769-75, but the Chester Plate Duty Books record that he also sent silver for assay in 1785-8. According to Ian Pickford, the majority of Hanoverian pattern salt shovels were produced up to the 1770s, which suggests a dating for this pair of *c.*1769-79.[2]

Seventeen pieces of silver by James Dixon survive, including flatware, mugs and a snuff mull. No other salt shovels are known to have been made by him, and his other flatware—two serving spoons of 1771 and six dessert spoons of 1772—has Old English pattern stems.[3] The Chester Plate Duty Books record 26 salt shovels by Richard Richardson IV in 1786, four by George Walker I in 1792, four by John Walker I in 1806 and two by George Lowe I in 1816.[4] Their production was evidently sporadic, and the two by James Dixon are the only surviving 18th-century Chester salt shovels, although exactly the same form was used again by John Lowe I in 1849 (no.68).

PROVENANCE: John ffoulkes Lowe, Chester; His sister, Miss Joyce Lowe, 1973; Purchased with grant aid from

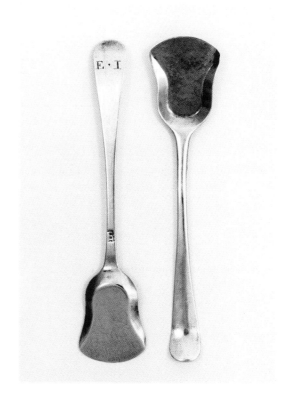

44

the MGC/V&A Purchase Grant Fund, London Goldsmiths' Company, Grosvenor Museum Society 1988.49.1,2

PUBLISHED: Ridgway 1985, p.77 Spoons no.3.

NOTES:

1. Pickford, p.189; Wills, p.113; Snodin 1974, p.52; Newman, p.273; Clayton 1985 I, p.381. Examples of salt shovels with Hanoverian stems, identical to those by James Dixon, include one of *c.*1760-70 by maker TW (Snodin 1974, p.52) and a pair of *c.*1770 by Thomas Foster (J.H. Bourdon-Smith Ltd., Catalogue, Autumn 1999, p.17). Other variants include 12 cast Chinoiserie shovels of *c.*1760 by Emick Roemer (Clayton 1985 I, fig.451) and one of 1792 with an Old English stem by Peter & Ann Bateman (Wills, pl.13).

2. Pickford, pp.42, 189; Ridgway 1996, p.80.

3. Ridgway 1985, pp.75-7; Ridgway 1996, p.192.

4. Ridgway 1996, pp.91, 96, 101-2.

45 CHAMBER CANDLESTICK

James Dixon, Chester, 1771-2

Five marks on base of drip-pan (maker's mark Ridgway 1985, p.75 type 1). Lion passant on nozzle and extinguisher
Height of candlestick alone 7.2 cm. (2.8 in.), diameter of drip-pan 11.6 cm. (4.55 in.), diameter of nozzle 4.3 cm. (1.7 in.), height of extinguisher 7.3 cm. (2.9 in.)
Weight: candlestick alone 191 g. (6.7 oz.), nozzle and extinguisher 18 g. (0.6 oz.) each

45

Sterling silver. The circular drip-pan is raised, with a convex centre and a cast and applied rope moulding around the rim. The cylindrical stem is pierced with a slot and supports the socket, whose raised bulbous base carries a slot for the extinguisher, and whose cylindrical upper part has applied mouldings at either end. The flying C-scroll handle, with a thumbpiece, is cast and applied. The detachable nozzle, with a seamed cylindrical bezel, has a raised circular drip-pan with a chased rope moulding around its rim. The detachable extinguisher is conical and applied with a moulded rim, a cast finial, an S-scroll handle and an L-shaped hook. 'TO' is scratched on the base.

The drip-pan is engraved opposite the handle with a lozenge-shaped shield of impaled arms, denoting a widow, in a Rococo cartouche. The arms are: on a chevron between three leopard's heads a roundel, impaling barry of six azure and ermine, on a canton a fleur-de-lys. These may be the arms of Hale, Helly, Hely, Nix or Nykke impaling Comberbach (a Cheshire family) or Cumberledge.[1]

The slot through the stem was intended to house a pair of snuffers, which were essential before the development of the self-consuming candle wick in the 19th century. The wick, particularly of tallow candles, needed to have its burnt end snipped off or 'snuffed' every few minutes, otherwise the wick would burn too slowly and topple over, extinguishing the flame in a pool of melting wax. The snuffers were of scissor form with a box-like compartment, to catch the bits of wick, attached to one blade.[2] The only known Chester-assayed snuffers are found with a chamber candlestick of 1739 by Richard Richardson II.[3]

This is the sole surviving chamber candlestick by James Dixon. The other 18th-century Chester examples are described at no.24.

PROVENANCE: John ffoulkes Lowe, Chester; His sister, Miss Joyce Lowe, 1973; Purchased with grant aid from the MGC/V&A Purchase Grant Fund, London Goldsmiths' Company, Grosvenor Museum Society 1988.48

EXHIBITED: London V&A 1989.

PUBLISHED: Ridgway 1985, p.76 Chamber Stick, pl.32.

NOTES:
1. Gale Glynn, report, 22 March 1991. The Comberbach pedigree in Ormerod III, p.561, does not provide an identification.
2. Gilbert, pp.11, 152; Wees, p.498.
3. Ridgway 1985, p.155, pl.29.

46 PAIR OF TABLE CANDLESTICKS

James Dixon, Chester, 1771-2

Five marks on one side of each base (maker's
mark Ridgway 1985, p.75 type 1). Lion passant
only on nozzles
Height: (1) without nozzle 31.3 cm. (12.3 in.),
with nozzle 31.5 cm. (12.4 in.); (2) without
nozzle 31.1 cm. (12.2 in.), with nozzle 31.4 cm.
(12.4 in.)
Weight: (1) without nozzle 752 g. (26.5 oz.),
nozzle 27 g. (0.95 oz.); (2) without nozzle 676 g.
(23.8 oz.), nozzle 29 g. (1 oz.)

Sterling silver. The square upwardly-curving bases have
die-stamped ornament in the form of beaded borders,
with beribboned oval medallions between leafy festoons.
One medallion on each base is engraved and the others
are stamped with oval paterae. The nine-sided cluster-
column stems taper upward, with two pairs of horizontal
rings, and single rings before the columns flare outward
at either end. The capitals act as sconces, each formed
from two tiers of nine stylised palm leaves and
terminating in a nine-sided scalloped and gadrooned
rim. The detachable nozzles, with tapering cylindrical
bezels, have wide nine-sided scalloped drip pans with
gadrooned edges.[1] The bases are loaded with wood,
each having a turned circular moulding and a central
silver button.

One medallion on each base is engraved with a
lion sejant erect, a crest used by 15 different families.[2]

The table candlestick has a flat-bottomed base for
resting on a table and, although recorded from the
early 16th century, very few survive before 1660. The
cluster-column candlestick first appeared in the 1660s
and '70s, the only aspect of a tentative Gothic Revival
to affect both ecclesiastical and secular silver, its
columns usually square in section and encircled by
bands.[3] The first 18th-century revival of the square
cluster-column candlestick was by Paul de Lamerie in
1738,[4] and a large number of circular cluster-column
candlesticks were made in the 1760s and '70s.[5] The
great majority of mid-18th century cluster-column
candlesticks have either square stepped bases,[6] or
square upwardly-curving bases, often with Neo-Classical
ornament, like this pair bearing James Dixon's mark.[7]
The capitals are usually formed from stylised acanthus
or palm leaves, not closely copied from any Classical
model.[8]

Despite being one of the most popular patterns of
the mid-18th century, Robert Rowe derided the cluster-
column candlestick as 'an art historical nightmare'![9]
The cluster-columns of the James Dixon pair are
entirely in the spirit of Rococo Gothic, being based on
the Fourth Order in Batty Langley's *Gothic Architecture,
Improved by Rules and Proportions* of 1742.[10] The bases,
however, are a pure example of Adamesque Neo-
Classicism.[11] Whilst undoubtedly a stylistic hybrid, they

might also be said to show 'how the eighteenth century
could mix its aesthetic metaphors with charming
results', to quote Robert Rowe again.[12]

In addition to James Dixon's surviving work (outlined at no.44), the Chester Plate Duty Books record
his production of buttons, spoons and sauce ladles.[13]
These are all small pieces, which could well have been
made by Dixon himself. The table candlesticks,
however, were almost certainly made in Sheffield.
Finished but unmarked, they would have been bought
by Dixon, acting as a retailer, to be struck with his
'maker's mark' and assayed at Chester.

Many of the candlesticks at this time were made
in Sheffield, where the development of die stamping
made possible their mass production. Candlestick
parts were stamped from thin sheet silver with the
same steel dies as those used for Sheffield Plate,[14]
and the sections soldered together and loaded with
an iron rod and resin to provide strength and
stability. Although the majority of early
Sheffield-assayed candlesticks bear the marks of John
Winter, Thomas Law, Tudor & Leader or Matthew
Fenton, it is not possible to associate a particular
design exclusively with one maker, since plate-work-
ers exchanged dies and traded parts.[15] An identical
base is seen on a plain column candlestick of 1778
by Thomas Law,[16] and Sheffield-assayed examples
similar to the James Dixon pair, with cluster-columns
and varied festoon bases, were made by Samuel
Roberts in 1773 and by Tudor & Leader in 1774.[17]

Before the opening of the Sheffield Assay Office
in 1773, Sheffield silver was nearly always assayed in
London. Most of the larger London firms acted as
retailers and sold the work of other goldsmiths as well
as their own products. John Carter, in particular, sold
large numbers of Sheffield candlesticks under his own
mark. Even after 1773, large amounts of Sheffield silver
were sold to London firms, and John Winter was a
notable supplier of candlesticks.[18]

In contrast, it is generally assumed that Chester goldsmiths before the 1790s produced the wares bearing
their marks in their own workshops. The James Dixon
candlesticks are among the clearest exceptions to this
presumption. Richard Richardson II occasionally retailed
pieces made elsewhere, the most notable examples being the 1753 cruet frame (no.26), the St Martin Cup of
1755 (no.27) and a 1765 table basket. In addition, five
Chester-assayed dish crosses of 1780-90, bearing the
marks of the Liverpool goldsmiths Joseph Walley and
Robert Jones I,[19] were possibly made elsewhere.

The James Dixon candlesticks are the only known
example of 18th-century Chester-assayed silver in the
Gothic style. Although ten table candlesticks by Boulton
& Fothergill of Birmingham were assayed at Chester in
1768-9,[20] the James Dixon pair are the only surviving
or recorded examples marked by an 18th-century
Chester goldsmith.

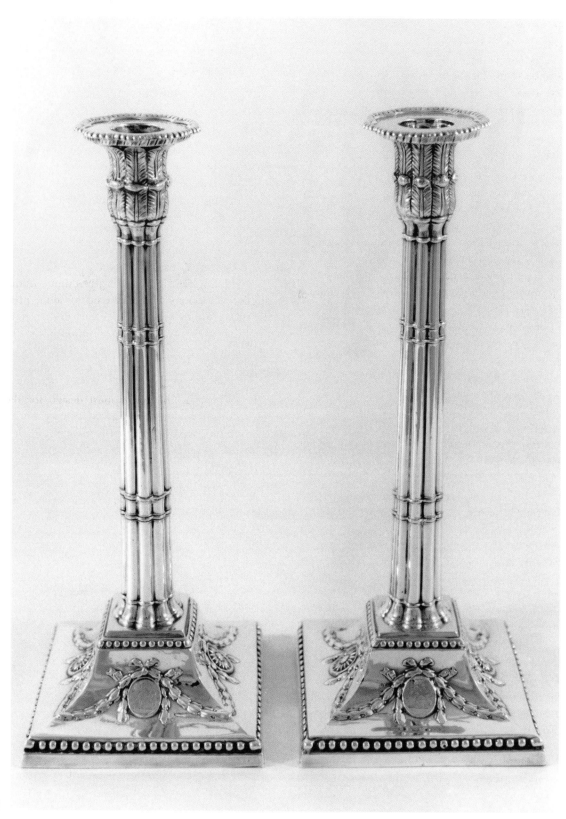

46

PROVENANCE: Kayes of Chester, 1992; Purchased with the assistance of the MGC/V&A Purchase Grant Fund, Kayes of Chester, Beecroft Bequest, Grosvenor Museum Society 1995.89.1,2

PUBLISHED: *The Silver Society Journal*, Autumn 1996, pp.524-5, illustrated; Ridgway 1996, p.192, pls.56-7.

NOTES:

1. 'The general use of detachable nozzles seems to be an innovation of the 1740s, perhaps because of the difficulty of cleaning wax from the more decorative examples' (Clayton 1985 I, p.56).

2. The crest is that of Blithe, London; Bond; Bonde, Dorchester; Chamond, Cornwall; Elvet; Eyston, East Hendred, Berkshire;

Fell; Kempethorne; Lee, Cornwall & Wiltshire; Legatt; Le Hunte, co. Wexford; Ley; Salmon; Shershall; or Silly, Cornwall (Fairbairn, pl.126, cr.15).

3. e.g. a pair of 1670, maker BP (Clayton 1985 I, fig.69).

4. Hare, no.32.

5. Wholly Gothic examples include a pair with domed hexafoil bases by Francis Crump, 1766 (Sotheby's, 30 November 1978, lot 43), and a pair with cinquefoil lobed bases by John Barbe (?), 1765 (Lomax, no.174). A variant of the square cluster column was used by Frederick Kandler for a set of four Gothic candlesticks, 1765 (Brett, no.834).

6. e.g. a set of four made in Sheffield but overstruck by John Carter in 1775 (Rowe 1965, pl.61A).

7. A variant design with a circular stepped base appears in Boulton & Fothergill of Birmingham's pattern books (Book 1, p.49, no.336; Victoria & Albert Museum). A further variant, by John Winter, Sheffield, 1774, has a spiral cluster-column (Rowe 1965, pl.60).

8. An example of 1770 by Thomas Law of Sheffield has a conventional Corinthian capital (Bradbury, p.220).

9. Rowe 1965, p.68.

10. Langley, pl.X for the column and pl.XII for the capital.

11. e.g. a Sheffield Plate sauce tureen designed by Robert Adam and possibly produced by John Hoyland of Sheffield c.1774, on which beribboned oval paterae are linked by leafy festoons between beaded borders (Manchester City Art Gallery).

12. Rowe 1965, p.42, speaking of Chinoiserie.

13. Ridgway 1996, p.80.

14. Illustrated in Bradbury, pp.102-3.

15. Bradbury, p.189; Rowe 1965, p.67.

16. Bradbury, p.223.

17. Oman 1967, pl.XXIX, no.119; Christie's, 14 October 1992, lot 191.

18. Rowe 1965, pp.84-5.

19. Ridgway 1985, pp.92, 210-11.

20. Ridgway 1985, pp.63-4; Ridgway 1996, p.192.

Richard Richardson III

Richard Richardson III was the son of William Richardson I (see no.14) and the brother of William Richardson II (see no.33). He became free in 1747 as a chandler, and later moved to London as a broker. When his cousin Richard Richardson II (see no.21) died in 1769, the latter's son Richard Richardson IV (see no.49) was only fourteen. Richard Richardson III returned to Chester to run the family workshop in Eastgate Street until 1779 when Richard Richardson IV became free. He was admitted to the Chester Goldsmiths' Company in 1773. He may have returned to London as a chandler and died there at an unknown date.[1]

A bottle ticket (no.34) may also be by him.

NOTE:

1. Ridgway 1985, pp.132-3, 173.

47 PAIR OF TABLE SPOONS

Richard Richardson III, Chester, 1775-6

Five marks on back of stem near bowl (maker's mark Ridgway 1985, p.173 type 1)
Length: both 22.6 cm. (8.9 in.)
Weight: (1) 76 g. (2.7 oz.), (2) 78 g. (2.75 oz.)

Sterling silver. Each spoon is formed from a single piece of silver. The raised ovoid bowl has a single drop at its junction with the stem. The Old English pattern stem is long and narrow, rectangular in cross-section, and has a vestigial ridge behind the turned down end. The front of the stem is decorated with feather-edging, and the end is engraved with the initial C in sprigged script beneath a baron's coronet.[1]

'Old English' is a late 19th-century trade term applied to spoons with this type of stem, previously described simply as 'plain'. The earliest form of Old English spoon was made in London from the late 1750s, but this pair by Richard Richardson III is typical of the type made from c.1770 until the end of the century. Shortly after 1800 the Fiddle pattern superseded it as the commonest design for flatware, but Old English spoons continued to be made in a modified form for another 20 years. Unlike the Hanoverian pattern, the rounded end of the stem turns up. From the introduction of this pattern, spoons were placed on the table open bowl up, and it was now the smooth front of the stem which was engraved.[2]

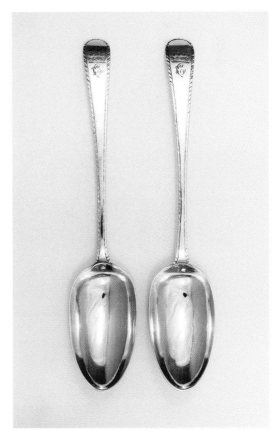

47

The stems of Old English spoons were often enhanced with various decorative borders, of which the earliest was feather-edging. This facetted ornament, produced by bright-cut engraving, was popular between 1760 and 1790.[3]

Thirty-nine pieces of silver, produced by the family workshop under Richard Richardson III, are known to survive. They include flatware, communion cups and patens, mugs, buttons and a pap boat.[4] His only other known spoons are a Hanoverian pattern table spoon of 1774 and an Old English pattern serving spoon with an illegible date letter. The museum's pair of spoons was made to match three assayed at London in 1769, which bear the unidentified makers' mark TE above GS.[5]

The only other Old English table spoons known to survive from 18th-century Chester are a plain pair of 1779 by Richard Richardson IV.[6] The Chester Plate Duty Books for 1784-99 record the following table spoons, which were probably Old English: 82 by Richard Richardson IV in 1785-90, seven by Thomas Hill in 1789, 13 by George Walker I in 1791-4 and 11 by George Lowe I in 1793-6.[7]

PROVENANCE: Brian Battersby, 1969; Boodle & Dunthorne, Chester; Purchased 1979.83.1,2

EXHIBITED: Chester 1980; Chester 1982; Chester 1984, no.114, illustrated.

Published: Ridgway 1985, pp.178-9 Spoons nos.2,3; Moore 1985 III, p.72.

NOTES:

1. 'There is no way of identifying which of at least 12 English Barons, not to mention any Scottish or Irish Barons this might be' (Gale Glynn, report, 22 March 1991).
2. Snodin 1974, pp.14, 48-9, 55, 57; Newman, p.228; Pickford, p.95.
3. Davis, p.179; Snodin 1974, p.48; Clayton 1985 I, pp.46, 186.
4. Ridgway 1985, pp.174-9; Ridgway 1996, p.196; this catalogue, no.48.
5. Ridgway 1985, pp.178-9.
6. Ridgway 1985, p.181.
7. Ridgway 1996, pp.86, 90, 96, 101.

48 BEAKER

Richard Richardson III, Chester, 1776-7

Five marks on base (maker's mark Ridgway 1985, p.173 type 1)
Height 5.6 cm. (2.2 in.)
Weight 48 g. (1.7 oz.)

Sterling silver. The tapering cylindrical body has an incised line beneath its slightly everted rim, and an applied moulding surrounds the inset circular base.

48

For the early development of the beaker in England see no.31. The vessel retained its popularity throughout the 17th century, but relatively few silver beakers were made during the 18th century, when glass could be obtained with less difficulty and expense. Except for an armorial engraving and a moulded foot, 18th-century beakers are usually plain, and by 1755 even the moulded foot was generally omitted.[1]

One other beaker by Richard Richardson III survives, likewise dating from 1776 but parcel-gilt, identical to both the museum's example and some London-made beakers known to have been used as christening gifts.[2] Apart from double beakers (see no.31), the other surviving beakers by Chester goldsmiths comprise one of 1715 by Richard Richardson I, nine of 1750-65 (including a straight-sided pair) by Richard Richardson II, two of 1781-7 by Richard Richardson IV, one of 1795 by George Lowe I (no.55) and seven of 1802-3 by Robert Bowers I.[3] In addition, the Chester Plate Duty Books record three beakers by George Lowe I in 1793-6 and three by William Twemlow in 1805-7.[4]

PROVENANCE: Phillips, London, 25 January 1991, lot 100; Purchased 1991.98

NOTES:

1. Glanville 1987, p.60; Oman 1967, p.146; Wills, p.55; Clayton 1985 I, p.33.
2. Ridgway 1985, p.174.
3. Ridgway 1985, pp.67, 151, 181, 183; Ridgway 1996, pp.185, 195.
4. Ridgway 1996, pp.90, 99.

Richard Richardson IV

Richard Richardson IV was born in 1755, the son of Richard Richardson II (see no.21). Although he never served a proper apprenticeship to the trade, he became free in 1779. He was admitted to the Chester Goldsmiths' Company in 1779, serving as assay master 1785-91 and warden 1791-4, after which he attended no further meetings. He was elected a common councilman in 1780 and an alderman in 1798, having served as sheriff in 1784-5. He was the last member of the family to run the workshop in Eastgate Street. He retired from business in 1790, when he purchased the manor of Capenhurst in Wirral, and he died in 1822.[1]

NOTE:

1. Ridgway 1985, pp.133, 179-80; Ridgway 1996, p.96.

49 SERVING SPOON

Richard Richardson IV, Chester, 1785

Six marks on back of stem near top (maker's mark Ridgway 1985, p.182 type 2A)
Length 29.2 cm. (11.5 in.)
Weight 86 g. (3 oz.)

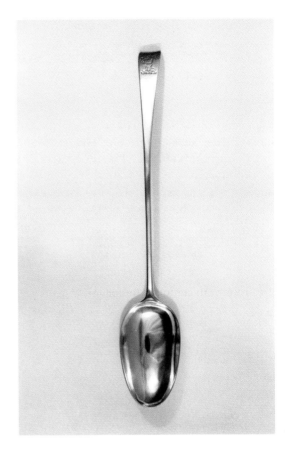

49

Sterling silver. The spoon is formed from a single piece of silver. The raised ovoid bowl has a single drop at its junction with the stem. The Old English pattern stem is long and narrow, rising at a slight angle to the bowl and curving backward, with a vestigial ridge behind the turned down end.

The front of the stem is engraved with the crest of a lion's jamb erect erased holding a key from which a chain is reflexed. The crest is that of Pownall of Lancashire, or Pownall of Pownall, Cheshire: the latter branch of the family seems slightly more likely to have been the original owner.[1]

The date letter 'i' on this spoon was only used between 28 January and 20 July 1785. The piece also bears the first duty mark used at Chester, an incuse head, which was introduced on 1 December 1784 and was succeeded by a cameo head in 1785-6 during the date letter 'k'.[2]

Twenty-nine pieces of silver, produced by the family workshop under Richard Richardson IV, are known to survive. They include flatware, bottle tickets, badges, beakers, communion cups, a paten and a tumbler cup.[3]

Early 18th-century Chester serving spoons are discussed at no.6. They were known as gravy spoons in late 18th-century Chester, and the Plate Duty Books record 100 submitted by seven Chester goldsmiths between 1785 and 1828. Their most prolific maker was Richard Richardson IV, who sent 66 for assay during 1785-90. The museum's spoon is one of four surviving examples, along with an identical pair from the same year, 1785, and another of 1782.[4]

The surviving Old English serving spoons by other Chester goldsmiths comprise an undated example (*c.*1769-79) by Richard Richardson III, a pair of 1771 by James Dixon, a pair of 1787 by Thomas Hill and one of 1803 by Robert Bowers I. The Chester Plate Duty Books record the following gravy spoons: 13 by Thomas Hill in 1789, five by George Walker I in 1792-1804, nine by Robert Bowers I in 1804-6, three by William Twemlow in 1808-17, three by John Walker I in 1811-17 and one by George Lowe I in 1828.[5]

PROVENANCE: Pownall family, *c.*1785; Christie's, London, 23 July 1980, lot 183; Purchased through Spink & Son Ltd., London, with grant aid from the Beecroft Bequest 1980.82

EXHIBITED: Chester 1980; Chester 1982; Chester 1984, no.119.

PUBLISHED: Ridgway 1985, p.184 Spoons no.2, marks pl.81.

NOTES:

1. Gale Glynn, report, 22 March 1991.
2. Ridgway 1985, pp.29-30, 35.
3. Ridgway 1985, pp.181-5; Ridgway 1996, p.197.
4. Ridgway 1996, p.96; Ridgway 1985, pp.181-2, 184.
5. Ridgway 1985, pp.68, 76, 87, 178; Ridgway 1996, pp.78, 86, 92, 99-102. The 1785 pair, previously recorded as maker TH, are now confirmed as Thomas Hill (Canon Ridgway, letter, 4 December 1999).

50 DESSERT SPOON

Richard Richardson IV, Chester, 1788-9

Six marks on back of stem near top (maker's
mark Ridgway 1985, p.182 type 2A)
Length 17.6 cm. (6.9 in.)
Weight 48 g. (1.7 oz.)

50

Sterling silver. The spoon is formed from a single piece
of silver. The raised ovoid bowl has a single drop at its
junction with the stem. The Old English pattern stem
is long and narrow, rectangular in cross-section, and
has a vestigial ridge behind the turned down end.

The front of the stem is engraved with the crest of a
stork, and the back with the monogram PGE in sprigged
script. Since the crest and initials appear to have been
engraved by the same hand, the crest could be that of
Eaton of Rainham in Essex, or the Irish family of
Elrington.[1]

The development of dessert spoons, and their
production in 18th-century Chester, is discussed at
no.14. The Plate Duty Books record 72 dessert spoons
by Richard Richardson IV in 1785-90, but this is the
sole surviving example.[2]

PROVENANCE: John ffoulkes Lowe, Chester; His sister, Miss
Joyce Lowe, 1973; Purchased with grant aid from the
MGC/V&A Purchase Grant Fund, London Goldsmiths'
Company, Grosvenor Museum Society 1988.58

PUBLISHED: Ridgway 1985, p.183 Spoons no.1.

NOTES:
 1. Gale Glynn, report, 22 March 1991. This crest was also used
     by 33 other families whose names do not begin with E.
 2. Ridgway 1996, p.96.

William Twemlow

William Twemlow was living at Nantwich in southern
Cheshire in 1786. He had moved to Chester by 1795,
when he became free as a victualler, and is recorded
under the same occupation in 1812. He also practised
as a goldsmith between 1787 and 1823, although he
never joined the Goldsmiths' Company. He lived in
the suburb of Boughton, where his son John Twemlow
(see no.66) continued the goldsmithing business.[1]

NOTE:
 1. Bennett 1908, p.412; Ridgway 1985, p.194; Ridgway 1993 II,
     p.331; Ridgway 1996, pp.99-100.

51 BOTTLE TICKET

William Twemlow of Chester, c.1787-90

Maker's mark only struck twice on back (Ridgway
1985, p.194 type 1)

Width 3.9 cm. (1.5 in.)
Weight 8 g. (0.3 oz.)

Sterling silver. The ticket is a convex crescent with
incurving horns, cut from sheet silver and raised. The
border is decorated with feather-edging; the inscription
'PORT' is engraved in Roman lettering; and each horn
is flat-chased with a bunch of grapes and foliage. The
circular link chain is attached to rings, which pass
through holes pierced in the horns.

Port is a sweet red fortified wine, named after the
town of Oporto in the Douro region of northern
Portugal. The crescent form is one of the 20 types of
bottle ticket identified by Norman Penzer, and the
feather-edge border and decorated horns are among
the most popular of the many variant designs.[1]

Many English goldsmiths were using the crescent
shape with the same borders and decoration from
c.1765 onwards. An almost identical design for a bottle
ticket in Sheffield Plate, lacking only the grapes, appears in a catalogue of c.1770-90, and William Twemlow
may have copied either this illustration or an actual
example.[2] The fact that it bears only the maker's mark
suggests that it was made before the assaying of bottle
tickets became compulsory in 1790, and since Twemlow
is first recorded as a goldsmith in 1787 a dating of
c.1787-90 seems most likely.

Ten pieces of silver by William Twemlow survive,
including flatware, medals, a mug and a tobacco box.[3] At
least one other bottle ticket by him is known, another

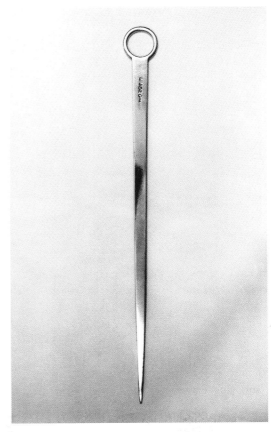

51   52

crescent of *c.*1787-90, but none are recorded in the Chester Plate Duty Books.[4] The only other known crescent-shaped bottle tickets from 18th-century Chester were made by Richard Richardson II or Richard Richardson III (see no.34).

PROVENANCE: Phillips, London, 30 May 1984, lot 76; Purchased with grant aid from the Grosvenor Museum Society 1984.52

PUBLISHED: Ridgway 1985, p.195 Wine Label.

NOTES:

1. Penzer 1974, p.71.
2. Captain Sir Thomas Barlow, letter, 7 March 2000. Illustration reproduced in Bradbury, p.399. The same catalogue may have inspired his son to make a pair of salts in 1827 which, as Nicholas Moore has observed, copy a form popular in Sheffield in the 1770s (Moore 1984 I, no.143; Ridgway 1985, p.194).
3. Ridgway 1985, pp.194-5.
4. Barlow, *op.cit.*

Maker's Mark ST

52   SKEWER

Maker's mark ST, Chester, 1788-9

Six marks at top of blade (maker's mark Ridgway 1985, p.193)

Length 29.8 cm. (11.7 in.)
Weight 69 g. (2.4 oz.)

Sterling silver. The tapering blade, of rectangular section, is stamped in one piece with the circular ring handle.

Crude wooden skewers were used to retain the shape of meat while it was roasted, but these were replaced with silver skewers when the food was served at the table. The most common and functional finial was the ring handle, which provided a good grip when withdrawing the skewer from the meat, and which enabled the skewer to be hung on a hook. A silver skewer of 1702 is known, but there are few hallmarked examples before 1745, and the majority date between the mid-18th and mid-19th centuries. The earlier skewers have blades of rectangular section. Large skewers like this one were used with large joints of meat.[1]

This skewer is the only piece of Chester-assayed silver bearing the maker's mark ST. Although it carries the duty mark, no one with these initials appears in the Chester Plate Duty Books, and the maker remains unidentified.[2]

All the known skewers by the Richardson family—four of 1768-9 by Richard Richardson II, four of 1772-8 by Richard Richardson III and one of 1787 by Richard Richardson IV—have a rounded head pierced to hold a separate draw ring.[3] With one exception, the other surviving skewers by

Chester goldsmiths have circular ring handles, and comprise two of 1787 by Thomas Hill (one with an oval ring), one of 1792 by George Walker I, more than five between 1797 and 1836 by George Lowe I (including no.61), two undated ones by William Twemlow and one of 1823 by Mary Huntingdon (no.65).[4]

Skewers were clearly in great demand in Chester, since more than 300 are recorded in the Plate Duty Books: 41 by George Walker I in 1786-1803, 39 by Richard Richardson IV in 1787-90, 20 by Thomas Hill in 1789, 152 by George Lowe I in 1792-1832, 23 by Robert Bowers I in 1800-6, 11 by William Twemlow in 1805-20, five by John Walker I in 1809-29, four by Mary Huntingdon in 1821, four by H.M. & S. Huntingdon in 1824 and two by Thomas Walker in 1831.[5]

PROVENANCE: John ffoulkes Lowe, Chester; His sister, Miss Joyce Lowe, 1973; Purchased with grant aid from the MGC/V&A Purchase Grant Fund, London Goldsmiths' Company, Grosvenor Museum Society 1988.56

PUBLISHED: Ridgway 1985, p.193 Skewer.

NOTES:

1. Wees, p.259; Newman, p.286; Wills, p.122; Clayton 1985 I, p.355.
2. Nicholas Moore has suggested that the maker might be a member of the Twemlow family of Chester goldsmiths.
3. Ridgway 1985, pp.170-1, 178, 181.
4. Ridgway 1985, pp.70, 87, 107, 195, 202. Those listed on pp.70 and 87 are now both confirmed as being by Thomas Hill (Canon Ridgway, letter, 13 March 2000).
5. Ridgway 1996, pp.77-8, 86, 90-2, 96, 99-103.

George Lowe I

George Lowe I was born in 1768. He served his apprenticeship in London, possibly under the Bateman family (see nos.94 and 96), for whom he later acted as agent in Chester. In 1791 he registered his mark in London, became a freeman of Chester, and was admitted to the Chester Goldsmiths' Company. He first established his business at the Cross in 1791, and in 1804 moved to Bridge Street Row East. He served the Goldsmiths' Company as warden 1794-7 and 1808-40, and as assay master 1840-1. Four of his sons became goldsmiths: he took John Lowe I (see no.67) and Thomas Lowe into partnership in 1826, but George Lowe II (see no.63) worked in Gloucester and Robert Lowe in Preston. George Lowe I died in 1841.[1]

NOTE:

1. Ridgway 1985, pp.97-103; Ridgway 1996, pp.18, 90.

53 PAIR OF BOTTLE TICKETS

George Lowe I of Chester, c.1791-1810

Maker's mark only on back (Ridgway 1985, p.104 type 1)
Width: both 3.7 cm. (1.45 in.)
Weight: both 7 g. (0.25 oz.)

Silver. Each ticket is a narrow rectangle, cut from sheet silver and slightly curved. The inscriptions, 'MADEIRA' and 'PORT', are engraved in Roman lettering. Each has a circular link chain attached to rings, which pass through holes pierced in the two eyelets extending from the ticket's upper edge.

The back of each ticket is engraved, beneath the left eyelet, with the ancient arms of the City of Chester within a circle. The same engraving is also found on another George Lowe I bottle ticket, which dates from 1804 and is of a different type.[1] The city arms strongly suggest that all three tickets once belonged to Chester's civic plate, and this pair may have formed part of a much larger purchase from George Lowe by the corporation in 1799.[2]

Eighty-four pieces of silver by George Lowe I survive, including flatware, pap boats, toast racks, goblets, a communion cup and paten cover, and a tea pot, saucepan, chamber candlestick, cream jug, sauce boat, souvenir box, trowel, butter tester and wine funnel stand.[3] The only mark on these tickets is the type 1 maker's mark of George Lowe I, which is found on silver between 1791-2 and 1824-5.[4] The 1972 Sotheby's auction catalogue (see Provenance) suggested a dating of *c*.1810, while Nicholas Moore dated them to *c*.1805, but Captain Sir Thomas Barlow does not think that one can be more specific than 'turn of the century', and a dating of *c*.1791-1810 therefore seems prudent.[5]

Thirty-one bottle tickets by George Lowe survive, of which the 11 dated examples span the period

53

1800-34. They comprise this pair, 17 other rectangular tickets of different forms (including no.60), a crescent-shaped one, and 11 bottle rings (including no.58).[6] This pair is of the same type as the Richard Richardson bottle ticket of *c.*1764-79 (no.34). An indication of the price is provided by the day books from the first years of George Lowe's business, which record '2 Bottle tokets 11/-'.[7] The Chester Plate Duty Books record 234 bottle tickets, labels, decanter labels and wine labels by George Lowe between 1793 and 1839.[8]

Eighteenth-century Chester-made bottle tickets are discussed at no.34. Only four other early 19th-century examples survive, two octagonal and two rectangular, comprising one of *c.*1815-23 by Mary Huntingdon and three of *c.*1825 by Robert Bowers I.[9] The Duty Books record a great many more by early 19th-century Chester goldsmiths: 36 by Robert Bowers I in 1801, six by George Walker I in 1802-5, eight by William Twemlow in 1818-20, four by John Walker I in 1821, 16 by Mary Huntingdon in 1821-2 and two by H.M. & S. Huntingdon in 1825, four by John Twemlow in 1826 and six by Joseph Duke II in 1839.[10]

PROVENANCE: 'Madeira' ticket only, Sotheby's, London, 3 February 1972, lot 72; both tickets, Sotheby's, London, 14 December 1989, lot 76 (part); Purchased through Spink & Son Ltd., London 1990.5.1,2

PUBLISHED: 'Madeira' ticket only, Ridgway 1985, p.112 Wine Labels Type 4.

NOTES:

1. Gale Glynn, report, 22 March 1991; Ridgway 1985, p.112 Type 3.
2. The Chester Corporation Treasurers' Account Books do not survive for the period 1790-8. For 1798-1827, with the exception of expenditure on the City Plate race trophy, they record only two purchases from George Lowe: unspecified bills of £35 12s. 7d. in 1799, and £28 8s. in 1807 for knives and forks (Chester Record Office, TAB/9/8r,88r). The Corporation's favoured goldsmith at this time was Robert Bowers I, from whom they made purchases totalling £295 8s. 7d. in 1801-15 (TAB/9/27r, 56r, 76r, 76v, 78v, 89v, 145r, 159r, 180r, 181r). They later spent £2 12s. 6d. with Mary Huntingdon in 1821 (TAB/9/250v) and £1 17s. 6d. with John Walker I in 1827 (TAB/10/56r).
3. Ridgway 1985, pp.105-12; Ridgway 1996, p.193; Moore 1984 I, nos.130, 133, 135, 150-1; Wees, no.369(145); this catalogue, nos.53-4, 56, 59-61.
4. Ridgway 1985, p.106; this catalogue, no.62. Ridgway 1985, p.108, also records a jam spoon of 1837 with the type 1 mark, but this date has probably been mistaken, since the letter T for 1815 looks very similar.
5. Nicholas Moore, letter, 18 December 1989; Captain Sir Thomas Barlow, letter, 7 March 2000.
6. Ridgway 1985, pp.111-12; Moore 1984 I, no.133.

7. Ridgway 1985, p.102.
8. Ridgway 1996, pp.90-3. For the record of bottle rings see no.58.
9. Ridgway 1985, pp.68, 90.
10. Ridgway 1996, pp.77, 80, 86, 99-100, 102.

54 SALT SPOON

George Lowe I of Chester, c.1793-4

Three marks on back of stem at top: maker's mark (Ridgway 1985, p.104 type 1), sovereign's head, lion passant.
Length 10.2 cm. (4 in.)
Weight 6 g. (0.2 oz.)

Sterling silver. The spoon is formed from a single piece of silver. The raised circular bowl has a single drop at its junction with the stem. The Old English pattern stem rises at an angle to the bowl and curves backward to its turned down end. The front of the stem is engraved with the script monogram EN surrounded by sprigs: the same monogram appears on the two salt spoons by Robert Bowers I (no.64), which formed part of the same lot when purchased at auction by the museum.

A salt spoon is first recorded in 1643, although the earliest existing type appears to be the salt shovel (see no.44). Some miniature spoons may also have been intended for salt, and one surviving example— unmarked but probably dating from the first decade of the 18th century—has a shallow circular bowl and a stem of ribbon-scroll form. The salt spoon with a small circular bowl emerged in the 1730s, co-existing with the salt shovel and later surpassing it in popularity.[1] The earliest examples have whip handles,[2] while slightly later variants include shell bowls with whip or coral handles.[3] Following the introduction of the Old English pattern stem in the late 1750s the salt spoon took on the form seen in George Lowe I's example, which remains the most popular to this day. All the subsequent major flatware patterns have also been used, and a transverse oval bowl became an alternative to the circular one from the early 19th century (e.g. no.129).[4]

Most modern writers make a distinction between salt shovels and spoons, but some also employ the term salt ladle. Its current usage is inconsistent: Harold Newman reserves 'ladle' for those with oval bowls; Ian Pickford uses the terms spoon and ladle interchangeably; while Michael Snodin generally refers to straight-stemmed implements as spoons and ones with curved stems as ladles.[5] The Chester Plate Duty Books refer to both salt spoons and ladles, and it seems unlikely that there was a meaningful and consistent distinction between the terms.

The three marks on this spoon suggest a dating of *c.*1791-7: the George Lowe I type 1 maker's mark

54

55

is found an silver from 1791-1824;[6] the duty mark of the sovereign's head is the form used at Chester in 1785-97; and the lion passant is that used from 1781-1800.[7] However, the only salt spoons by George Lowe recorded in the Duty Books during this period are 28 in 1793 and four the following year, so this one almost certainly dates from c.1793-4. The Duty Books record a further 111 salt spoons by George Lowe in 1828-38, but this is his only surviving example.[8]

The only other known pre-1840 Chester salt spoons are two of c.1803-5 and c.1813 by Robert Bowers I (no.64). However, this meagre survival is out of all proportion to the vast number produced in Chester, where the Duty Books record 788 between 1785 and 1838: 331 by Richard Richardson IV in 1785-90, 47 by George Walker I in 1786-1804, 39 by William Twemlow in 1800-22, 76 by Robert Bowers I in 1803-13, 102 by John Walker I in 1807-30, four by Mary Huntingdon in 1821 and four by H.M. & S. Huntingdon in 1823, 14 by John Twemlow in 1824-5, 24 by Thomas Walker in 1831, two by Joseph Duke II in 1838 and two by Joseph Dutton the same year.[9] Their production reflected the demands of etiquette, which required a spoon for the small individual salt-container set by each diner.

PROVENANCE: Sotheby's, Chester, 10 November 1982, lot 367 (part); Purchased 1982.75.3

NOTES:

1. Snodin 1974, p.52; Clayton 1985 I, pp.312, 381.
2. e.g. four of 1733 by Paul de Lamerie (Clayton 1985 II, p.176 fig.2).
3. e.g. one of c.1740-50 with a whip handle (Snodin 1974, pl.38); four of 1739 by Paul de Lamerie with coral handles (Wees, no.143).
4. Pickford, p.190.
5. Newman, p.273; Pickford, pp.42, 189-90; Snodin 1974, p.52 (although he calls one of c.1775 by Hester Bateman with an Old English stem a 'spoon').
6. See no.53, note 4.
7. Ridgway 1985, pp.28-9.
8. Ridgway 1996, pp.90, 92-3.
9. Ridgway 1996, pp.77-8, 80-1, 86, 96, 99-103.

55 PARCEL-GILT BEAKER

George Lowe I, Chester, 1795-6

Six marks beneath base (maker's mark Ridgway 1985, p.104 type 1)
Height 7.8 cm. (3.1 in.), diameter of rim 6.7 cm. (2.6 in.)
Weight 141 g. (4.8 oz.)

Sterling silver with gilt interior. The tapering cylindrical body is seamed once and has a very slightly everted rim. The applied circular base is slightly concave.

The interior has presumably been re-gilded, since its very rich colour is quite different from the exceptionally pale lemon characteristic of 18th-century Chester gilding. The perfectly plain form of this beaker is typical of those made in the second half of the 18th century.

Three beakers by George Lowe I are recorded in the Chester Plate Duty Books in 1793-6, of which this is the latest and only surviving example.[1] The other Chester beakers are discussed at no.48.

PROVENANCE: John ffoulkes Lowe, Chester: His sister, Miss Joyce Lowe, 1973; Purchased with grant aid from the MGC/V&A Purchase Grant Fund, London Goldsmiths' Company, Grosvenor Museum Society 1988.59

PUBLISHED: Ridgway 1985, p.105 Beaker.

NOTE:
1. Ridgway 1996, p.90.

56 SAUCE LADLE

George Lowe I, Chester, 1797-8

Six marks on back of stem at top (maker's mark Ridgway 1985, p.104 type 1)
Length 14.4 cm. (5.65 in.)
Weight 32 g. (1.1 oz.)

Sterling silver. The ladle is formed from a single piece of silver. The raised circular bowl has a long single drop, struck with an indentation across its centre, at the junction with the stem. The Old English pattern stem rises at a sharp angle to the bowl and curves backward, with a vestigial ridge behind its turned down end.

The front of the stem is engraved with a lion rampant holding between his paws a fleur-de-lys, which is probably the crest of the Pugh family.[1]

The development of sauce ladles is outlined at no.36. Only one other example by George Lowe I survives, dating from 1791 and having a longer feather-edged stem.[2] The Chester Plate Duty Books record 14 sauce ladles by George Lowe from 1793-1823

and 12 small ladles in 1801.[3] Sauce ladles by 18th-century Chester goldsmiths are discussed at no.36. No examples by early 19th-century Chester goldsmiths survive, although the Duty Books record six by Robert Bowers I in 1803 and six by John Walker I in 1811-22.[4]

PROVENANCE: Probably Pugh family, c.1797; John ffoulkes Lowe, Chester; His sister, Miss Joyce Lowe, 1973; Purchased with grant aid from the MGC/V&A Purchase Grant Fund, London Goldsmiths' Company, Grosvenor Museum Society 1988.60.

EXHIBITED: London V&A 1989.

NOTES:
1. Gale Glynn, report, 22 March 1991.
2. Ridgway 1985, p.106.
3. Ridgway 1996, pp.90-2.
4. Ridgway 1996, pp.77, 102.

57 CADDY SPOON

George Lowe I of Chester, c.1801-5

Three marks on back of stem near top: maker's mark (Ridgway 1985, p.104 type 1), sovereign's head, lion passant
Length 7.9 cm. (3.1 in.)
Weight 15 g. (0.5 oz.)

Sterling silver. The spoon is formed from a single piece of silver. The transverse oval bowl is raised and has a single drop at its junction with the stem. The Old English pattern stem rises at an angle to the bowl and curves backward to its turned down end. The front of the stem is engraved with the monogram WE in sprigged script.

A caddy spoon was used to measure dry tea leaves into the tea pot from the canister, the container now generally known as a caddy (see no.33). The early canisters had a domed, pull-off cap, which could be used for measuring the tea. An alternative was the so-called mote or strainer spoon, made from the end of the 17th century: with its pierced bowl and long stem, it was the only type of spoon which could pass a

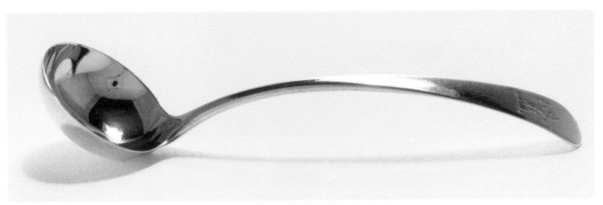

57

from 1829-37: one has a wide Fiddle pattern stem and an oval bowl; another has a wide, flat handle and an oval bowl; and the third is of unknown form.[6] An indication of their price at the beginning of George Lowe's career is provided by his early day books, which record 'caddy spoon 3/-'.[7] George Lowe appears to have enjoyed a near-monopoly on the production of caddy spoons in Chester, but the Duty Books record a handful by other goldsmiths in the late 18th and early 19th centuries: one by Richard Richardson IV in 1784, two by William Twemlow in 1790-7, seven by George Walker I in 1794-6 and one by Joseph Duke II in 1840.[8] None are known to survive.

PROVENANCE: Sotheby's, Chester, 21 July 1981, lot 468; Purchased 1981.38

EXHIBITED: Chester 1984, no.132

PUBLISHED: Ridgway 1985, p.108 Caddy Spoons b.

NOTES:
1. Wees, p.487; Oman 1967, pp.154, 157; Glanville 1987, p.97; Clayton 1985 I, p.375.
2. Glanville 1987, p.97; Wees, p.487; Pickford, pp.202-3, 210; Oman 1967, p.157. For illustrations of the variety of designs see: Pickford, figs. 363-4; Wark, no.324; Wees, no.369.
3. See no.53, note 4.
4. Ridgway 1985, pp.28-9.
5. Ridgway 1996, pp.90-3.
6. Ridgway 1985, p.108; Wees, no.369 (145); Alexis Goodin, letter, 29 March 2000.
7. Ridgway 1985, p.102.
8. Ridgway 1996, pp.80, 96, 99, 101.

canister's narrow neck. Some of the vase-shaped canisters of the mid-18th century were accompanied by small ladles with shell-shaped bowls, and the so-called medicine spoons of the 1750s could have had a secondary use for tea.[1]

The earliest caddy spoons were made in the 1760s, when canister openings had become wider and could accommodate a broad, short-stemmed spoon. They were first produced in large numbers in the 1770s, and the earliest known fully-marked example dates from 1781. Their immense popularity lasted well into the 19th century, and a vast variety of forms was adopted, including shells, leaves, wings, hands, acorns, jockey caps and shovels. With the exception of Birmingham caddy spoons, most provincial examples—like this one—follow the standard patterns such as Old English and Fiddle.[2]

The three marks on this spoon suggest a dating of c.1799-1806: the George Lowe I type 1 maker's mark is found on silver from 1791-1824;[3] the duty mark of the sovereign's head is the form used at Chester in 1797-1837; and the lion passant is that used from 1799-1806.[4] However, the only relevant spoons by George Lowe recorded in the Chester Plate Duty Books during this period are five caddy spoons in 1801, six caddy ladles in 1802 and 15 in 1805, so this one almost certainly dates from c.1801-5. The Duty Books record a further 91 caddy spoons and ladles (the terms are probably interchangeable) between 1793 and 1837, together with 21 caddy shells in 1796-1817.[5] Three other caddy spoons by George Lowe survive, dating

58 FIVE BOTTLE RINGS

George Lowe I of Chester, c.1802-5

Three marks inside each ring, those on 'Hock' smaller than the rest: maker's mark (Ridgway 1985, p.104 type 1), sovereign's head, lion passant

(1) Hock
Diameter 7.4 cm. (2.9 in.)
Weight 28 g. (1 oz.)

(2) Port
Diameter 7.4 cm. (2.9 in.)
Weight 21 g. (0.75 oz.)

(3) White Wine
Diameter 7.5 cm. (2.95 in.)
Weight 20 g. (0.7 oz.)

(4) Sherry
Diameter 7.5 cm. (2.95 in.)
Weight 20 g. (0.7 oz.)

(5) Madeira
Diameter 7.4 cm. (2.9 in.)
Weight 20 g. (0.7 oz.)

Sterling silver. Each ring is a splayed hoop with a V-shaped seam. The lower edge is squared, but the outside of the upper edge is bevelled. Each ring is inscribed twice with the name of the wine: 'HOCK', 'PORT', 'W. WINE', 'SHERRY' and 'MADEIRA'. The engraving is in Roman lettering, filled with a niello-substitute.

Hock is a German white wine, named after Hochheim in the Rhine valley, and sherry is a white fortified wine, named after the province of Jerez de la Frontera in southern Spain. For madeira and port see nos.34 and 51.

'Neck rings' are among the 20 types of bottle ticket identified by Norman Penzer, and the form seen here—splayed hoops like those used on a cooper's barrel—represents one of the three varieties of this type.[1] The Chester Plate Duty Books use the term 'bottle rings' for these objects. The predecessor of the bottle ring is shown in William Hogarth's painting of 'An Election Entertainment' (1754-5), which depicts two bottles with inscribed parchment neck labels.[2]

Silver bottle rings in the form of splayed hoops are uncommon, but include a set of five from 1802 by the London goldsmith Elizabeth Morley, which are very close to George Lowe's but with the addition of reeded borders.[3] As Captain Sir Thomas Barlow has noted, 'the Phipps and Robinson partnership in London [active 1783-1816] made quite a number of usually plain rings, and some London makers made some elaborate examples later in the 19th century. A few Irish ones are known, and a couple from Edinburgh, but none seem to have been recorded from any other provincial office.'[4] They were also made in Sheffield Plate, electro-plate, ivory and bone.[5]

The three marks on these rings by George Lowe I suggest a dating of c.1799-1806: the type 1 maker's mark is found on silver from 1791-1824;[6] the sovereign's head is the form used at Chester in 1797-1837; and the lion passant is that used from 1799-1806.[7] However, the Duty Books during this period only record bottle rings by George Lowe for the years 1802 (11), 1803 (10), 1804 (unspecified number) and 1805 (4), so the museum's five almost certainly date from c.1802-5.[8]

Only six other bottle rings by George Lowe I survive, one with very worn marks, a pair of 1810 and three of 1815: all eleven examples were in the collection of John ffoulkes Lowe in 1970.[9] In addition to those noted above, the Duty Books record a further four in 1817 and two in 1826.[10]

According to Canon Ridgway, 'the type was repeated by the firm of Lowe and Sons, Chester, in the present [20th] century, and more recently modern examples have been produced elsewhere and assayed at Birmingham.'[11] For some years from 1988 Lowe & Sons commissioned the Chester jewellery company Orocraft to make replicas of these bottle rings, which were assayed at Sheffield and bear the Chester city of origin mark. Replicas of those in the museum have also been produced by Simon Beer of Cooksbridge, East Sussex, who made about 400 London-assayed rings in 1986-92.[12]

PROVENANCE: John ffoulkes Lowe, Chester; His sister, Miss Joyce Lowe, 1973; Phillips, London, 2 May 1984, lot 170; Purchased with grant aid from the V&A Purchase Grant Fund, Grosvenor Museum Society 1984.51.1-5

EXHIBITED: Chester 1984, no.134, illustrated.

PUBLISHED: Ridgway 1985, p.111 Wine Labels Type 1, Hock bottle ring illustrated pl.36; Moore 1985 III, p.72, illustrated p.73.

NOTES:

1. Penzer 1974, p.79.
2. Penzer 1974, p.29. Hogarth's painting is reproduced in colour in Einberg (no.196), and the parchment labels are shown even more clearly in the engraving in Trusler (The Election, Plate I).
3. J.H. Bourdon-Smith Ltd., Catalogue no.35, Autumn 1992, p.46.
4. Captain Sir Thomas Barlow, letter, 7 March 2000.
5. Penzer 1974, p.79. Ivory rings were cut concentrically from the tusk. A Sheffield Plate example of 1810 by Nathaniel Smith & Co. of Sheffield has an incised line around each rim (Bradbury, p.303).
6. See no.53, note 4.
7. Ridgway 1985, pp.28-9.
8. Ridgway 1996, p.91.
9. Ridgway 1985, p.111.
10. Ridgway 1996, pp.91-2.
11. Ridgway 1985, p.111. 'No silver was made at Lowe's after the [Second World] war. They used William Comyns & Sons and E. Barnard & Sons of London to supply orders which were sent to Chester for assay until 1962.' (Ridgway 1996, p.133).
12. Walton 1989, p.115; Peter Lowe, telephone conversation, 21 January 2000; Simon Beer, telephone conversation, 23 June 1995.

59 SILVER-MOUNTED COCONUT CUP

George Lowe 1 of Chester, c.1807-17

Three marks beneath foot: maker's mark (Ridgway 1985, p.104 type 1), sovereign's head, lion passant. Rim band unmarked
Height 11 cm. (4.3 in.)
Weight 113 g. (4 oz.)

See Colour Plate V

Sterling silver and coconut shell. The raised trumpet-shaped foot has an applied vertical foot-ring, and its upper edge is soldered to a small hemispherical cup. This supports the polished, semi-ovoid-shaped coconut shell, which is secured with a brass screw and washer. The silver rim band is drawn over the edge of the nut and secured with four pins. The rim is crudely engraved with the initial B in Roman lettering, and '8090' is scratched beneath the foot.

Coconut shell is non-porous and, with its fibrous husk removed, is capable of taking a high polish. On the Continent coconuts were frequently carved with scenes, and they could also be engraved, but in England they were generally left plain. Mounted in silver, the shell was an ideal material for drinking and pouring vessels. These usually took the form of standing cups, with or without a cover, although some two-handled cups and ox eye cups were also made. Early explorers brought back coconuts from the tropics to Europe, where they were highly prized as rare and exotic objects. During the Middle Ages they were also believed to possess miraculous powers, such as the ability to reveal the presence of poison or neutralise its effects.[1]

A coconut cup is first recorded in England in 1259, but the earliest surviving examples date from the mid-15th century.[2] One of the finest is an exquisite silver-gilt cup of c.1490, in which the coconut is clasped by oak branches growing from a paled enclosure.[3] In 1523 coconuts were worth as much as their weight in silver-gilt, but during the course of the 16th century, with the opening of the New World to trade, they became the cheapest and most widely available exotic material for mounting. The status of coconut cups had slumped by the late 16th century and very plain examples, foreshadowing some 18th-century ones, are found from 1580 onwards. Belief in the coconut's supposed magical properties declined, although as late as 1640 it was credited with protective powers against colic, epilepsy and rheumatism.[4]

Despite the loss of its rarity and reputed supernatural qualities, the coconut cup continued to enjoy periods of popularity for both its practicality and its historical associations.[5] An early instance of the latter is one by John Plummer of York, probably from 1665, which was almost certainly conceived as a deliberate piece of romantic antiquarianism.[6] Early 18th-century examples vary from a very plain pair, with deep rims and small feet, to a richly decorated cup of c.1730, with cast handles and a type of cut-card ornament.[7] The later 18th century is equally varied, ranging from an elaborate Adamesque cup with silver-gilt and Wedgwood mounts to one of 1787 by Hester Bateman, quite close to George Lowe's example with its plain trumpet-shaped foot and rim, but with engraved decoration on the shell.[8]

The foot of this coconut cup bears three marks: the George Lowe I type 1 maker's mark is found on silver from 1791-1824;[9] the duty mark of the sovereign's head is the form used at Chester in 1797-1837; the lion passant is poorly struck, but its frame has a straight base with docked corners, and is therefore one of the marks used from 1781-1800 or 1806-19.[10] Thus the marks suggest a dating of c.1797-1800 or c.1806-19.

However, the only coconut mounts by George Lowe recorded in the Chester Plate Duty Books during either of these periods are 18 between 1807 and 1817, so this one almost certainly dates from c.1807-17. The Duty Books record two further coconut mounts by George Lowe, one each in 1802 and 1821, but this is his only surviving example. Seven of the entries in the Duty Books refer to feet alone, while only one records

59

'a foot and rim to cocoa shell' and the other entries simply mention mounts.[11] As in the case of the museum's cup, sometimes the foot alone was sent for assay, but every coconut cup had a silver rim to protect the shell's brittle edge.[12] An indication of their price at the beginning of George Lowe's career is provided by his early day books, which record 'mounting a cocoanut shell with square foot £1.5s.0d.'.[13]

Only two other coconut cups by Chester gold-smiths are known to survive, both with trumpet-shaped stems and deckled rims: one of *c.*1720-5 by William Richardson I, whose circular foot is linked to the rim by four bands; and one of 1794 by George Walker I, which has a square base.[14] Coconut cups were not particularly rare in late 18th- and early 19th-century Chester, since the Duty Books record several by other goldsmiths in the city: seven by Richard Richardson IV in 1785-8, four by George Walker I in 1801-5 (including two with covers), one by Robert Bowers I in 1805, two by William Twemlow in 1808-10, nine by John Walker I in 1808-18 and one by Mary Huntingdon in 1815.[15]

PROVENANCE: Hennell, London; Purchased 1987.44

NOTES:

1. Schroder 1988 II, p.44; Newman, p.79; Clayton 1985 I, p.252; Schroder 1988 I, p.500.

2. Clayton 1985 I, p.95; Oman 1967, p.27.

3. Glanville 1987, fig.4.

4.   Glanville 1987, pp.20, 33; Schroder 1988 I, p.500; Glanville 1990, p.325; Clayton 1985 I, p.252; Oman 1967, p.27.

5.   Schroder 1988 II, p.44; Clayton 1985 I, p.96.

6.   Lomax, no.38.

7.   Lomax, no.41; Clayton 1985 I, fig.371b.

8.   Oman 1965, pl.166; Shure, pl.XXXVIII.

9.   See no.53, note 4.

10.   Ridgway 1985, pp.28-9.

11.   Ridgway 1996, pp.91-2.

12.   Newman, p.79.

13.   Ridgway 1985, p.102.

14.   Ridgway 1985, pp.199, 221; Ridgway 1996, p.189.

15.   Ridgway 1996, pp.78, 86, 96, 99, 102

60 BOTTLE TICKET

George Lowe I, Chester, 1816-17

Four marks on back: maker's mark (Ridgway 1985, p.104 type 1), sovereign's head, lion passant, date letter
Width 4.1 cm. (1.6 in.)
Weight 7 g. (0.25 oz.)

60

Sterling silver. The ticket is a broad rectangle with slightly rounded corners, stamped with a single line border which is bevelled toward the centre. It is slightly curved and the inscription, 'CLARET', is engraved in Roman lettering and filled with a niello-substitute. The circular link chain is attached to rings, which pass through holes pierced beneath the border.

Claret is an English term for the red wines from the region around the city of Bordeaux in south-western France.

The broad rectangular form is one of the 20 types of bottle ticket identified by Norman Penzer, and the straight sides with slightly rounded corners represent one of its four variant shapes. The broad rectangle developed later than the narrow rectangular form (see nos.34 and 53).[1]

Thirty-one bottle tickets by George Lowe I survive, of which 19 are rectangular (see no.53). The example closest to the museum's ticket is one of 1834 for 'gooseberry', although this has right-angled corners.[2] This type of broad rectangle with a single line border is rather late for its actual date, and the proportions are also slightly unusual, being deep in relation to its width. Roughly the same proportions are found with Mary Huntingdon's sole surviving bottle ticket of *c.*1815-23.[3]

PROVENANCE: Lowe & Sons, Chester; Purchased with grant aid from the Grosvenor Museum Society 1983.63

EXHIBITED: Chester 1984, no.128 (misplaced under Robert Bowers I), illustrated.

NOTES:

1.   Penzer 1974, p.74.

2.   Ridgway 1985, p.112 Type 2; Phillips, London, 2 May 1984, lot 171 (illustrated).

3.   Captain Sir Thomas Barlow, letter, 7 March 2000.

61 SKEWER

George Lowe I, Chester, 1820-1

Six marks at top of blade (maker's mark Ridgway 1985, p.104 type 1)
Length 28.1 cm. (11.05 in.)
Weight 109 g. (3.85 oz.)

Sterling silver. The tapering blade, of lozenge section, is cast in one piece with the circular ring handle.

The earlier skewers, such as no.52, have blades of rectangular section, but blades of lozenge section emerged in the late 18th century: they had become the most common form by 1790 and remained so throughout the 19th century.[1]

More than seven skewers between 1797 and 1837 by George Lowe I survive, all with circular ring handles, and the Chester Plate Duty Books record 152 in the period 1792-1832.[2] An indication of their price at the beginning of George Lowe's career is provided by his early day books, which record 'one scewer £1 6s. 6d.'.[3] Skewers by other Chester goldsmiths are discussed at no.52.

PROVENANCE: John ffoulkes Lowe, Chester; His sister, Miss Joyce Lowe, 1973; Purchased with grant aid from the

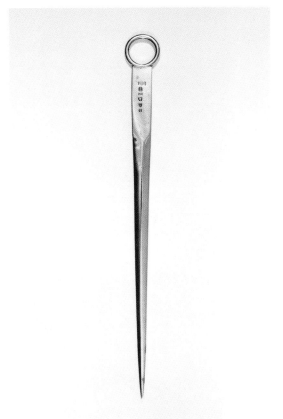

61   62

MGC/V&A Purchase Grant Fund, London Goldsmiths' Company, Grosvenor Museum Society 1988.61

PUBLISHED: Ridgway 1985, not in text, but marks illustrated pl.89 (mis-dated on caption).

NOTES:

1. Pickford, p.192; Clayton 1985 I, p.355; Wees, p.260.
2. Moore 1984 I, nos.150-1; Ridgway 1985, p.107; Ridgway 1996, pp.90-2.
3. Ridgway 1985, p.102.

62 PARCEL-GILT EGG SPOON

George Lowe I, Chester, 1824-5

Five marks on back of stem at top: maker's mark (Ridgway 1985, p.104 type 1), lion passant, sovereign's head, Chester mark, date letter
Length 12.2 cm. (4.8 in.)
Weight 12 g. (0.4 oz.)

Sterling silver with gilt interior to the bowl. The spoon is formed from a single piece of silver. The elongated bowl is raised, and has a single long drop at its junction with the stem. The Fiddle pattern stem, with a bevelled edge and a turned down end, has two projecting shoulders at its junction with the bowl.

The front of the stem is engraved with the crest of Hughes. With the possible exception of ermine, it is very unusual to find crests with tinctures on silver, and this engraving may well date from the latter part of the 19th century.[1]

Egg spoons are small spoons used for eating boiled eggs. Their bowls were often gilded to prevent the egg-yolk from staining the silver. A tiny egg spoon is recorded in 1479, but the surviving examples date from the last quarter of the 18th century up to the present day. The stems usually follow contemporary flatware patterns, and two bowl shapes are found. Egg spoons with elongated bowls—as in George Lowe's example—are similar to mustard spoons only larger, while the shield-shaped bowl became a popular alternative in the 19th century. Egg spoons were frequently made to accompany egg cup frames or flatware services.[2]

The Fiddle pattern is so called because the top of the stem resembles, in outline, part of a violin, known colloquially as a fiddle. As Ian Pickford has noted, 'perhaps the earliest example is to be found among the Esquiline Treasure of late Roman silver in the British Museum. Its production in England did not however stem directly from this source but from France where, in the mid-eighteenth century, it was the most popular pattern.'[3] A London spoon of 1739, probably made to replace a lost piece from a French service, is the earliest known English example, but its popularity in England dates from the 1780s. A variant of the Fiddle pattern was introduced in Scotland as early as the 1730s, and it was also made in Dublin from the 1750s. Shortly after 1800 the Fiddle pattern superseded the Old English as the most popular 19th-century style, but today it is the only major flatware pattern not in production. Plain examples often have the bevelled edge seen on George Lowe's spoon.[4]

George Lowe made the vast majority of egg spoons in early 19th-century Chester, the Duty Books recording 187 examples between 1812 and 1838.[5] Only one other spoon survives, almost identical and dating from 1821.[6] No other examples by Chester goldsmiths survive before the mid-19th century (see no.70), although the Duty Books record 11 by Robert Bowers I in 1803, four by George Walker I in 1804, three by John Walker I in 1825, six by H.M. & S. Huntingdon in 1826 and four by John Twemlow in 1827.[7]

PROVENANCE: Hughes family, probably late 19th century; Mrs. Applegate, Welwyn, Hertfordshire; Purchased 1981.33

EXHIBITED: Chester 1984, no.135.

PUBLISHED: Moore 1985 III, illustrated p.73.

NOTES:

1. Gale Glynn, report, 22 March 1991.
2. Snodin 1974, p.62; Newman, p.119; Glanville 1987, p.14; Pickford, p.204; Clayton 1985 I, p.167. Mustard spoons became popular from the third quarter of the 18th century, but William Richardson I of Chester made a documented and surviving example c.1732 (Clayton 1985 I, p.380; Ridgway 1985, p.187).
3. Pickford, p.108.
4. Clayton 1985 I, p.378; Pickford, pp.108-9; Snodin 1974, pp.54-5.
5. Ridgway 1996, pp.91-3.
6. Ridgway 1985, p.108.
7. Ridgway 1996, pp.77, 86, 99, 102.

63 HOT WATER JUG

George Lowe I, Chester, 1830-1

Six marks below rim (maker's mark Ridgway 1985, p.104 type 2). Sovereign's head and lion passant on lower handle socket
Height 17 cm. (6.7 in.)
Weight 447 g. (15.75 oz.)

See Colour Plate V
Sterling silver with two ivory insulation fillets. The ovoid body is raised and has a vertical foot-ring, with incised lines top and bottom, applied around the inset circular base. The waisted neck rises to a boldly everted rim, which is applied with a wire moulding and shaped to form a wide pouring lip. The cast loop handle, of flattened oval section, is on axis with the lip. It rises above the rim, beneath which is a cast and applied acanthus leaf. The handle is connected to two sockets by ivory

insulation fillets, each having four pins with projecting heads. '14 10' is scratched on the base.

The George Lowe I type 2 maker's mark is found on silver between 1826-7 and 1837-8.[1] According to Canon Ridgway, this is the mark of George Lowe II.[2] The eldest son of George Lowe I, he was born in 1793 and admitted to the Chester Goldsmiths' Company on 24 September 1827, but worked as a goldsmith at Gloucester from at least 1817-44. George Lowe II ran his own shop at Chester in Eastgate Row South from at least 1844-57, was re-admitted to the Goldsmiths' Company in 1847, and was weigher at the assay office from 1861-76.[3] However, his younger brothers John and Thomas Lowe were admitted to the goldsmiths' company on 11 December 1826.[4] Noting that the GL maker's mark changed between 1824-5 and 1826-7, Nicholas Moore has convincingly suggested that George Lowe I took his sons John and Thomas into partnership in December 1826, and changed his mark to type 2 to denote this.[5] The business was known as George Lowe and Sons by 1834.[6]

The ivory insulation fillets show that the jug was intended for a hot liquid, but the absence of a cover would not have kept it hot for long. Nevertheless, the only possible reference to this piece in the Chester Plate Duty Books is the entry for '1 water jug' in 1832. Nicholas Moore has plausibly suggested that it may have been specially commissioned to match a tea service, probably London-made, which lacked a hot water jug. It would have held hot water to dilute the strong tea made in the tea pot.[7]

The shape of George Lowe's jug is derived from the *oenochoe*. This simple one-handled jug, with the lip pulled out to make a pouring spout, was a very common type in the ancient world. It was in use from the 4th century BC in Greek states through to the Roman period, and was usually made of pottery, but is also found in silver and bronze.[8] From the mid-18th century the collection and publication of Classical antiquities was highly fashionable in Britain, and they became widely known and copied by artisans of the day. Greek vases were particularly popularised by Sir William Hamilton (see no.72): his first collection, sold to the British Museum in 1772, was published in four volumes of engravings by the Baron d'Hancarville from 1767 and inspired pottery reproductions by Josiah Wedgwood from 1769, and his second collection was published in four volumes by Wilhelm Tischbein from 1793. The connoisseur Richard Payne Knight bequeathed his large collection of Classical metalwork to the British Museum in 1824.[9]

The taste for exact replicas or adaptations of antique vessels for modern uses is one of the most characteristic features of English silver in the period 1800-37.[10] The *oenochoe* was adapted for coffee pots,

ewers and hot water jugs;[11] the *rhyton* was copied for cups,[12] the *ascos* for jugs,[13] the bell *krater* for vases;[14] and the Roman oil lamp inspired lamps, ink wells and tea pots.[15] The Warwick Vase, one of the most popular Regency forms, was copied in various sizes for salt cellars, sugar basins, presentation cups, wine coolers, soup tureens and punch bowls.[16] Vases, wine coolers and race trophies were also modelled on the Medici Vase,[17] the Portland Vase,[18] the Buckingham Vase,[19] and others engraved in Giovanni Battista Piranesi's *Vasi, candelabri, cippi* of 1778.[20]

The gauge of silver, heavier than was usual for London at this date, confirms that the jug was provincially made.[21] Similarly, the pin heads which secure the ivory fillets are slightly larger and more prominent than those on contemporary London pieces (e.g. nos.109 and 123). In their undisguised functionalism, they seem to anticipate the almost brutalist penchant for exposed rivets in Christopher Dresser's designs for silver and electroplate of the 1870s and '80s.[22] The cast acanthus leaf, however, belongs unequivocally to the repertoire of Regency silver.

The jug is the largest surviving example of Chester-made silver from the first half of the 19th century, and a suprisingly sophisticated piece.[23] The only other surviving jugs by George Lowe are two cream jugs of 1795 and 1816,[24] although the Duty Books record six jugs by him from 1796-1832, plus the water jug referred to above and a 'water pot' in 1836.[25] The motif of the cast acanthus leaf was also used by George Lowe on a trowel in 1826, and Neo-Classical ornament appears on the feet of two toast racks, elegantly incised in 1828 and cast in 1832.[26] No jugs by other Chester goldsmiths survive from the early 19th century, and none are recorded in the Duty Books.

PROVENANCE: Sotheby's, Chester, 27 July 1982, lot 282; Purchased with grant aid from the V&A Purchase Grant Fund, London Goldsmiths' Company, Grosvenor Museum Society, Boodle & Dunthorne, Mappin & Webb, Lowe & Sons 1982.55

EXHIBITED: Chester 1984, no.139, illustrated (as George, John & Thomas Lowe).

PUBLISHED: Wainwright, p.984, illustrated (as George Lowe II); Ridgway 1985, p.106 Hot Liquid Jug, pl.18 (as George Lowe II); Moore 1985 III, p.73, illustrated p.72 (as George Lowe I); Moore 1986, fig.15 (as George Lowe I); Ridgway 1996, pl.7 (as George Lowe II).

NOTES:

1. Ridgway 1985, pp.109, 111. Ridgway 1985, p.109, also records a pair of sugar tongs of 1820 with the type 2 mark, but the date letter or maker's mark has probably been mistaken.

2. Ridgway 1985, p.104.

3. Ridgway 1985, pp.97, 100, 103-4; Ridgway 1996, pp.19-20. George Lowe is recorded as a goldsmith in Gloucester trade directories between 1820-39 (Mr. P.R. Evans, letter, 21 February 2000); and in Gloucester street directories between 1828-44, although he does not appear in the 1841 Census (Graham Baker, letter, 3 March 2000). According to Dowler (p.126) he was active in Gloucester from 1817-42.

4. Ridgway 1985, p.112.

5. Moore 1984 I, pp.77, 79; Moore 1985 III, p.73. It seems highly unlikely that no silver survives from the last 16 years of George Lowe I's business in Chester, and that all the known pieces with the type 2 mark were made in Gloucester. The identification of this mark as belonging to George Lowe I is further reinforced by a surviving trowel, used on 1 October 1827 and bearing the type 2 mark, which was described by a Chester historian in 1831 as 'executed by Mr Lowe, goldsmith' (Ridgway 1985, p.110): this must refer to the head of the Chester business rather than to his son in Gloucester.

6. Pigot's Chester Directory 1834.

7. Ridgway 1996, p.92; Nicholas Moore, letter of 17 June 1982 and undated note; Newman, p.171. 'The usual early nineteenth-century service was limited to three pieces - teapot, cream jug, and sugar basin (although a five-piece version with coffeepot and tray en suite was occasionally made). The four-piece service, with the addition of a coffeepot, did not become common until after about 1825' (Schroder 1988 I, p.374).

8. Moore 1984 I, no.139; Edmund Southworth, letter, 1 February 2000; Dr. Paul Roberts, letter, 21 February 2000. For a Greek silver *oenochoe* of 350-325 BC see Blair, p.14.

9. Edmund Southworth and Dr. Paul Roberts (see n.8); Jenkins & Sloan, pp.46-9, 55-60. One of d'Hancarville's engravings of an *oenochoe* from Hamilton's collection (Rowe 1965, pl.44) inspired a jug of 1840 by Charles Reily & George Storer (Brett, no.1348). Other Victorian variants of the *oenochoe* include an 1838 coffee jug by William Bateman II, an 1861 ewer by Edward Barnard & Sons, and an 1867 ewer by Charles Thomas & George Fox (Brett, nos.1187, 1391, 1337).

10. Lomax, p.27.

11. e.g. coffee pot of 1828 by John Bridge and ewer of 1829 by William Elliott (Brett, nos.1165, 1257); hot water jug of 1833 by John Bridge (Lomax, no.162).

12. e.g. stirrup cup of 1821 by Philip Rundell (Brett, no.1159).

13. e.g. jug of 1836 by Paul Storr (Clayton 1985 II, p.256 fig.3).

14. e.g. vases of 1827 by John Bridge (Brett, no.1166).

15. e.g. spirit lamp of 1823 by John Edward Terrey (Wees, no.391); ink well of 1804 by Digby Scott & Benjamin Smith II (Brett, no.1117); tea pot of 1809 by Paul Storr (Schroder 1988 I, no.98).

16. Schroder 1988 II, p.243; Glanville 1987, p.250; Clayton 1985 II, p.239. For a presentation cup of 1814 by Paul Storr see Schroder 1988 I, no.107.

17. e.g. wine coolers of 1810 by Benjamin & James Smith (Clayton 1985 II, p.266 fig.2).

18. e.g. replica of 1820 by Philip Rundell (Brett, no.1158).

19. e.g. race trophy of 1828 by Rebeccah Emes & Edward Barnard I (Lomax, no.16).

20. e.g. wine coolers of 1811 by Benjamin Smith II & James Smith III and vase of 1824 by Rebeccah Emes & Edward Barnard I (Schroder 1988 I, nos.103, 121).

21. Moore 1984 I, no.139; Nicholas Moore, undated note.

22. Fleming & Honour, p.258; e.g. a plated toast rack made by Hukin & Heath (Glanville 1987, fig.53).

23. Moore 1985 III, p.73; Nicholas Moore, letter, 17 June 1982.

24. Ridgway 1985, p.106; private collection, on loan to Grosvenor Museum.

25. Ridgway 1996, pp.90-2.

26. Moore 1984 I, nos.136, 138, 140.

Robert Bowers I

Robert Bowers I became free as a watchmaker in 1781, and his work as a goldsmith is recorded in the Chester Plate Duty Books from 1787-1814. He worked closely with George Lowe I (see no.53) from 1792. He was admitted to the Chester Goldsmiths' Company in 1795 and served as warden 1797-c.1803. He first worked in Bridge Street and later moved to Eastgate Street. His son Robert Bowers II was apprenticed to him. He was elected a common councilman in 1794 and alderman in 1810, serving as sheriff in 1798-9 and mayor in 1811-12. He died in 1829.[1]

NOTE:

1. Ridgway 1985, pp.64-6; Ridgway 1989, p.401; Ridgway 1996, pp.77-8.

64 TWO SALT SPOONS

Robert Bowers I of Chester, c.1803-5 and c.1813

Three marks on back of stem at top: maker's mark (Ridgway 1985, p.64), sovereign's head, lion passant
Length: (1) 9.9 cm. (3.9 in.), (2) 10 cm. (3.95 in.)
Weight: (1) 10 g. (0.35 oz.), (2) 8 g. (0.3 oz.)

Sterling silver. Each spoon is formed from a single piece of silver. The deep, circular bowl is raised, and joins the stem without a drop. Both have an Old English pattern stem, that of (2) having a vestigial ridge behind its turned down end. The front of each stem is engraved with the script monogram EN surrounded by sprigs: the same monogram appears on the salt spoon by George Lowe I (no.54), which formed part of the same lot when purchased at auction by the museum.

Eighteen pieces of silver by Robert Bowers I survive, including badges, beakers, bottle tickets, a box, a buckle and flatware.[1] In addition to the maker's mark and the duty mark of the sovereign's head, each spoon bears a lion passant: that on (1) is the form used at Chester in 1799-1806, while the mark on (2) is the type used from 1806-19.[2] However, the only salt spoons by Robert Bowers recorded in the Chester Plate Duty Books during the first period are 74 from 1803-5, and for the second period two in 1813:[3] so (1) almost certainly dates from c.1803-5 and (2) from c.1813. These two salt spoons are his sole surviving examples, and the only other known pre-1840 Chester salt spoon is the almost identical one of c.1793-4 by George Lowe I (no.54). For a discussion of salt spoons and the other recorded Chester examples see no.54.

PROVENANCE: Sotheby's, Chester, 10 November 1982, lot 367 (part); Purchased 1982.75.1,2

EXHIBITED: Chester 1984, no.129.

NOTES:
1. Ridgway 1985, pp.66-8.
2. Ridgway 1985, p.28.
3. Ridgway 1996, pp.77-8.

Mary Huntingdon

Mary Huntingdon or Huntington may have been the widow of William Huntington of Bridge Street Row, who appears in the Chester directories as a cutler in 1789-92 and as a hardwareman in 1795-7. The trade directories and the Chester Plate Duty Books record Mary Huntingdon as a silversmith in Bridge Street Row from 1806-22, the business becoming H.M. & S. Huntingdon from 1822-30 and finally appearing as Hannah Maria Huntingdon in 1834.[1]

64

NOTE:
1. Ridgway 1985, p.89; Walton 1989, p.103; Ridgway 1993 II, p.331; Ridgway 1996, p.86.

65 SKEWER

Mary Huntingdon, Chester, 1823-4

Six marks at top of blade (maker's mark Ridgway 1985, p.89)
Length 35.4 cm. (13.9 in.)
Weight 110 g. (3.9 oz.)

Sterling silver. The tapering blade, of lozenge section, is cast in one piece with the circular ring handle.

The only other surviving piece of silver by Mary Huntingdon is a bottle ticket.[1] The Chester Plate Duty Books record four skewers by Mary Huntingdon in 1821 and another four by H.M. & S. Huntingdon in 1824:[2] the museum's skewer is presumably one of the latter. Although it was made two years after the name of the business changed, it still bears the MH mark of Mary Huntingdon. It is very similar in form to a skewer of 1820 by George Lowe I (no.61). Skewers by other Chester goldsmiths are discussed at no.52.

PROVENANCE: Sotheby's, London, 8 March 1973, lot 97; Silver Lyon Ltd., London; Purchased 1974.131

EXHIBITED: Chester 1979 I, no.20; Chester 1980; Chester 1984, no.145.

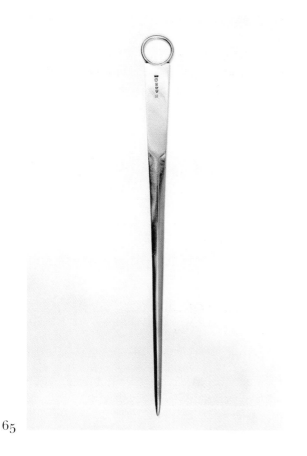

65

PUBLISHED: Thomas, p.17; Ridgway 1985, p.89 Skewer, pl.91 (marks).

NOTES:

1. Ridgway 1985, p.90.
2. Ridgway 1996, p.86.

John Twemlow

John Twemlow was the son of the victualler and goldsmith William Twemlow (see no.51). Like his father, he did not join the Chester Goldsmiths' Company, but he worked as a goldsmith in Boughton, a suburb of Chester, between 1814 and 1844. He then followed his father's other trade, being recorded as the landlord of the *Black Lion* public house in Boughton from 1846-57, also appearing as a watchsmith in the latter year.[1]

NOTE:

1. Ridgway 1985, p.194; Ridgway 1996, p.99; Chester Trade Directories.

66 RATTLE

John Twemlow, Chester, 1828-9

Three marks on ferrule: date letter, lion passant, maker's mark (JT with pellet between, variant of Ridgway 1985, p.194)
Length 8.4 cm. (3.3 in.)
Weight 35 g. (1.2 oz.)

Sterling silver, with traces of gilding on the smooth parts of the whistle and bells, and a fragment of red coral. The thin silver is elaborately chased and engraved in a debased Rococo Revival style. The upper part of the pear-shaped whistle has a pierced aperture and a ring pendant, while its lower section is chased with four almond-shaped panels between scrolls. The compressed spherical knop is chased with 16 ribs, alternately floral and plain. It has five rings from which hang bells of different sizes, their tops chased with swirling foliage, and their smooth hemispherical undersides pierced with two small holes. The lower part of the rattle comprises a smaller compressed sphere and another pear-shaped section, both chased with six panels of foliage, and terminating in the four-part ferrule holding the coral, of which only a fragment remains.

Rattles for infants comprise a satin-smooth coral stick to hold or suck as a teether; a central knop hung with spherical bells to shake as a rattle; a whistle to blow; and a ring for a retaining chain or ribbon. They are found in silver, silver-gilt or even gold. As Berenice Ball has explained, 'coral had been regarded from ancient times as a potent amulet against every ill suffered by man. Folklore linked the miraculous hardening of coral, once it leaves the water, to the mysterious process of the eruption and hardening of human teeth,' and it was therefore used in nearly all teethers. Such rattles were often elaborately chased, reflecting their status as a favourite christening gift. (The Rococo Revival style, seen in this example, is discussed at no.88.) They were known as a 'whistle with coral and bells', a 'coral and bells' or merely a 'coral'. A coral teether is referred to c.1600, but most extant examples date from after c.1760, and they continued to be made until the end of the 19th century.[1]

John Twemlow's only other surviving pieces are a pair of salts, which are also decorative, but with cast feet and pierced sides rather than chasing.[2] The rattle is so close to Birmingham examples that it seems highly likely to have been bought in by Twemlow and only marked in Chester.[3] It does not bear the duty mark, and the Chester Plate Duty Books record no rattles by him. Indeed, the only ones by a Chester goldsmith to appear in the Duty Books are two 'corrals' by George Lowe I in 1805-6,[4] but neither survives, and Twemlow's rattle remains the sole example.

66

into partnership by their father. John and Thomas Lowe registered joint marks in 1839 and 1841, but in 1842 Thomas Lowe became assay master and John Lowe I registered a separate mark. He ran the family business in Bridge Street Row East after the death of his father in 1841, living above the shop until 1861. Three of his sons were apprenticed to him: John Foulkes Lowe (see no.71), James Foulkes Lowe, and George Bennett Lowe (see no.72). John Lowe I served the city as sheriff in 1841-2 and the company as prime warden from 1841 until his death in 1864.[1]

NOTE:

1. Moore 1984 I, pp.77, 79, 86; Moore 1985 III, p.73; Ridgway 1985, pp.112-13; Ridgway 1996, pp.36-7, 90, 126-8.

67 SUGAR TONGS

John Lowe I, Chester, 1843-4

Marked inside handle: maker's mark (Ridgway 1989, p.402) one side, four marks other side
Length 14.1 cm. (5.55 in.), width 4 cm. (1.6 in.)
Weight 31 g. (1.1 oz.)

Sterling silver. The tongs are made from a single piece of silver, bent in a U-shape forming two spring arms. The ovoid bowls of the grips are raised and each Fiddle pattern stem, with a bevelled edge, has two projecting shoulders at its junction with the bowl.

Sugar tongs were used to transfer a lump of sugar from a container to the tea cup. Tea drinking in England had grown rapidly from the mid-17th century (see no.18), and by the early 18th century the addition of sugar to tea had become widespread, perhaps due to its increased availability or to the gentility associated with both imported commodities. Loaves of sugar (see no.43) were cut in the kitchen with heavy iron shears into small lumps. These were served in a range of containers, more than one type being produced concurrently: boxes from the 1650s, bowls from the 1670s, vases from the 1740s, baskets from the 1760s and basins from the 1790s.[1]

The earliest form of sugar tongs, introduced *c.*1685 and made until the 1720s, resembles miniature fire tongs. Another type, called sugar nippers or nips, had evolved by *c.*1715 and resembles a pair of scissors. These, in turn, were gradually superseded between *c.*1755 and *c.*1775 by U-shaped tongs, whose two spring arms resume their parallel position when hand pressure is released. Known as bow tongs or spring tongs by collectors, they were generally called tea tongs in the 18th century although, with the exception of one reference in 1804, the Chester Plate Duty Books use the term sugar tongs from 1789. Early examples were usually made in three pieces, with cast openwork arms and a sprung end section. By the 1780s they were

PROVENANCE: Sotheby's, Chester, 25 August 1981, lot 407; Purchased 1981.102

EXHIBITED: Chester 1984, no.144.

PUBLISHED: Ridgway 1985, p.194 Rattle.

NOTES:

1. Ball 1961, pp.552-4; Holland, pp.238-9; Clayton 1985 I, p.296; Newman, pp.258, 358-9.

2. Moore 1984 I, no.143.

3. e.g. one by George Unite, Birmingham, 1837 (Ransome-Wallis, no.158). 'Rattles of this type are the virtual preserve of Birmingham' (Moore 1984 I, no.144).

4. Ridgway 1996, p.91.

John Lowe I

John Lowe I was born in 1804. He and his brother Thomas (1806-66) were apprenticed to their father George Lowe I (see no.53) in 1819. They became free in 1826, were admitted to the Chester Goldsmiths' Company later that year, and were then taken

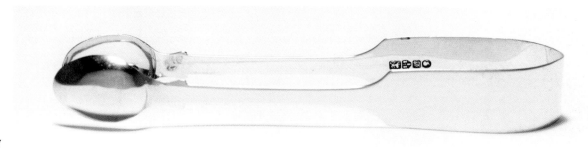

mostly formed from one piece of metal, with the grips generally shaped like small spoons, and during the 19th century they were produced in almost all the flatware patterns.[2]

John and Thomas Lowe jointly marked three silver-mounted horn snuff boxes, and silver marked by John Lowe I alone includes flatware, a mustard pot, five flask labels, a magnifying glass, and an identical pair of sugar tongs dating from 1847.[3] For John Lowe I's use of the Fiddle pattern see no.69. The Duty Books show that his father, George Lowe I, had been the principal maker of sugar tongs in Chester, producing 230 pairs between 1794 and 1840, but a large number were made by other Chester goldsmiths: 52 by Thomas Hill in 1789, 32 by George Walker I in 1791-9, eight by William Twemlow in 1802-17, 18 by Robert Bowers I in 1804-5, five by John Walker I in 1806, three by H.M. & S. Huntingdon in 1824-8 and three by Joseph Duke II in 1838-9.[4] Of these 351 pairs of sugar tongs only six survive, comprising five of 1820-37 by George Lowe I and one of 1824 by John Walker I.[5]

PROVENANCE: John ffoulkes Lowe, Chester; His sister, Miss Joyce Lowe, 1973; Pickwick Antiques, Mold, Flintshire; Purchased 1980.58

EXHIBITED: Chester 1980; Chester 1984, no.154.

NOTES:

1. Newman, p.306; Wees, pp.269-70; Clayton 1985 I, pp.391-3.
2. Wees, p.486; Newman, p.306; Clayton 1985 I, p.393; Pickford, pp.194, 198-9; Wills, p.133; Ridgway 1996, p.78.
3. Moore 1984 I, p.86; Ridgway 1996, pp.127-8, pls.15-16.
4. Ridgway 1996, pp.77-8, 80, 86, 90-3, 99-102.
5. Ridgway 1985, pp.109, 214.

68   THREE SALT SHOVELS

John Lowe I, Chester, 1849-50

Five marks on back of stem toward bowl (maker's mark Ridgway 1989, p.402)
Length: (1,2) 8.7 cm. (3.4 in.), (3) 8.8 cm. (3.45 in.)
Weight: each 5 g. (0.2 oz.)

Sterling silver. Each shovel is formed from a single piece of silver. The plain shovel-shaped bowl is raised, and joins the stem without a drop. There is a vestigial ridge below the upturned end of the Hanoverian pattern stem.

The back of the stem is engraved with the crest of Aldersey of Cheshire, London and Kent. The same crest appears on a cheese scoop of 1852 by the same maker (no.69). These pieces almost certainly belonged to the Cheshire branch of the family, whose head at this time was Samuel Aldersey (1776-1855) of Aldersey and Spurstow, who lived at Aldersey Hall and had been sheriff of Cheshire in 1816.[1]

Plain-bowled salt shovels were made from c.1750 and remained popular into the 20th century, but the majority of Hanoverian pattern salt shovels were produced up to the 1770s. These three of 1849 by John Lowe I follow exactly the same form as James Dixon's pair of c.1769-79 (no.44), if on a slightly reduced scale, and are clearly a deliberate reproduction of this 18th-century pattern. Indeed, they may have been commissioned to match an incomplete 18th-century set belonging to the Aldersey family.

A pair of salt spoons and a pair of mustard spoons, both in the Old English pattern, were made by John and Thomas Lowe in 1840.[2] No other salt shovels are known, and the rest of John Lowe I's recorded flatware employs the Fiddle pattern (see no.69).

PROVENANCE: Probably Samuel Aldersey of Aldersey and Spurstow, Cheshire, c.1849; John ffoulkes Lowe, Chester; His sister, Miss Joyce Lowe, 1973; Purchased with grant aid from the MGC/V&A Purchase Grant Fund, London Goldsmiths' Company, Grosvenor Museum Society 1988.63.1-3

PUBLISHED: Ridgway 1996, p.127.

NOTES:

1. Gale Glynn, report, 22 March 1991; Fairbairn, p.8; Ormerod, II, pp.739-40.
2. Moore 1984 I, no.153; Ridgway 1996, p.128.

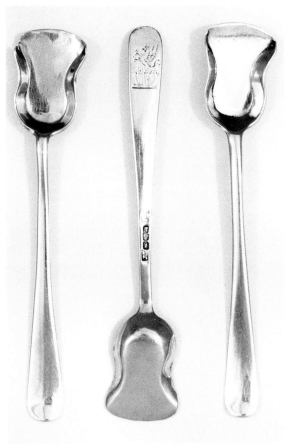

68   69

69 CHEESE SCOOP

John Lowe I, Chester, 1852-3

Five marks on back of stem at top (maker's mark
Ridgway 1989, p.402)

Length 20.7 cm. (8.15 in.)

Weight 57 g. (2 oz.)

Sterling silver. The scoop is formed from a single
piece of silver. The blade is raised in a wide semicircular section and has rounded lower corners.
The Fiddle pattern stem, with a bevelled edge, has
two projecting shoulders at its junction with the
blade and a short ridge behind its turned down
end.

The front of the stem is engraved with the crest of
Aldersey, as discussed at no.68.

Like George Walker I's cheese scoop of 1792
(no.42), most 18th- and some 19th-century
examples have ivory handles. From the early 19th
century they were usually made completely of silver,
matching the flatware patterns of the day, and John
Lowe I's cheese scoop employs the most popular
design of the mid-19th century, the Fiddle pattern.[1]

This is the only known cheese scoop by John Lowe
I. Most of his recorded flatware employs the Fiddle
pattern, including a mustard spoon, sugar tongs, a
serving fork, a fish slice and egg spoons made between
1839 and 1860.[2]

PROVENANCE: Probably Samuel Aldersey of Aldersey
and Spurstow, Cheshire, *c.*1852; John ffoulkes Lowe,
Chester; His sister, Miss Joyce Lowe, 1973; Purchased
with grant aid from the MGC/V&A Purchase Grant
Fund, London Goldsmiths' Company, Grosvenor
Museum Society 1988.62

NOTES:

1.   Pickford, p.181.
2.   Moore 1984 I, nos.152, 155-6; Ridgway 1996, p.127; this
catalogue, nos. 67, 70.

70 EGG SPOON

John Lowe I, Chester, 1859-60

Five marks on back of stem at top (maker's mark
Ridgway 1909, p.402)

Length 16.3 cm. (6.4 in.)

Weight 19 g. (0.7 oz.)

Sterling silver. The spoon is formed from a single
piece of silver. The elongated bowl is raised, and
joins the stem without a drop. The Fiddle pattern
stem, with a bevelled edge, has two projecting
shoulders at its junction with the bowl and a
vestigial ridge behind its turned down end. The
front of the stem is engraved with the script
monogram RHP.

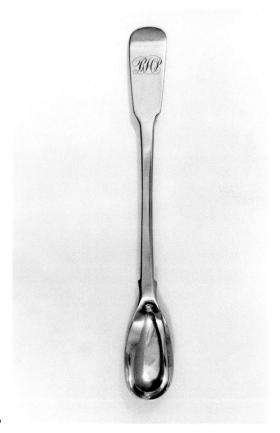

70

in 1864. Working in partnership with his brother George Bennett Lowe (see no.72), they first registered a joint mark in 1896. He was sheriff of Chester in 1896-7. His son George Frederick Lowe was apprenticed to him and continued the business after his death in 1911.[1]

NOTE:

1. Ridgway 1973, pp.19-20; Moore 1984 I, p.87; Ridgway 1996, pp.27, 124, 129-30.

71 CREAM JUG

John Foulkes Lowe, Chester, 1878-9

Five marks on base (maker's mark Ridgway 1996, pl.27)
Height 5.2 cm. (2.05 in.), length across handle 9.5 cm. (3.75 in.)
Weight 58 g. (2.05 oz.)

Sterling silver. The compressed globular body is raised and has a slightly convex circular base. The upturned pouring lip is shaped and applied. The loop handle, cast in identical halves and seamed down the centre, is on axis with the lip and rises above the rim.

The jug's pouring lip is rounded rather than beak-shaped, and is therefore suited to the slow pouring necessary with cream. The serving of cream with tea and dessert is discussed at nos.23 and 41.

The surviving silver marked by John Foulkes Lowe alone includes flatware, an alms dish, a mustard pot, a box and a regatta shield.[1] For work marked in partnership with his brother see no.72. The shape of the jug is surprisingly advanced for its date, bearing comparison with some of Christopher Dresser's contemporary designs for metalwork, and anticipating by a quarter of the century the form of certain cream jugs produced by Liberty & Co.[2] Pared of all extraneous ornament, the unpretentious simplicity of this little jug is in marked contrast to some of J.F. Lowe's other pieces, such as the late 18th-century-style beading and engraving an a set of four parcel-gilt boat-shaped salts from the same year, 1878.[3] A slightly later tea service of 1881, although decorated, is equally far from the polite conventions of slavish historicism, being chased with domed bosses and zigzags of almost barbaric vigour.[4]

PROVENANCE: John ffoulkes Lowe, Chester; His sister, Miss Joyce Lowe, 1973; Purchased with grant aid from the MGC/V&A Purchase Grant Fund, London Goldsmiths' Company, Grosvenor Museum Society 1988.64

PUBLISHED: Ridgway 1996, p.131.

NOTES:

1. Ridgway 1996, pp.130-1; Moore 1984 I, nos.159-60.
2. e.g.: an electroplated kettle with stand and burner, designed by Christopher Dresser in 1878 and made by Hukin & Heath;

According to Nicholas Moore, this is a preserve spoon or possibly a long-handled egg spoon, but Ian Pickford has confirmed that it is most probably an egg spoon.[1] By comparison with George Lowe I's example of 1824 (no.62), the stem is thicker and the bowl narrower. John and Thomas Lowe jointly marked an egg spoon in 1839,[2] and another Fiddle pattern egg spoon of 1860 bears the mark of John Lowe I.[3]

PROVENANCE: Sotheby's, Chester, 21 July 1981, lot 453; Purchased 1981.37

EXHIBITED: Chester 1984, no.158 (misplaced under John Foulkes Lowe).

NOTES:

1. Moore 1984 I, no.158; Ian Pickford, telephone conversation, 3 February 2000.
2. Ridgway 1996, p.127: this may be the same piece as a Fiddle pattern mustard spoon of 1839 (Moore 1984 I, no.152).
3. Moore 1984 I, no.155.

John Foulkes Lowe

John Foulkes Lowe was born in 1836 and was apprenticed to his father John Lowe I (see no.67). He became free in 1857 and was admitted to the Chester Goldsmiths' Company in 1858. He succeeded his father as prime warden from 1864-1911, also serving the company as auditor up to 1864 and drawer from 1874. He took over the family business of Lowe & Sons on his father's death

71

a pewter cream jug designed by Archibald Knox in 1903 for Liberty & Co. (Rudoe, nos.85, 134).

3. Ridgway 1996, p.131, pl.13.

4. Ridgway 1996, pls.24-6.

John Foulkes Lowe
& George Bennett Lowe

For John Foulkes Lowe see no.71.

George Bennett Lowe was born in 1843 and was apprenticed to his father John Lowe I (see no.67). He was admitted to the Chester Goldsmiths' Company in 1864, serving as auditor from that date. Working in partnership with his brother John Foulkes Lowe, they first registered a joint mark in 1896, and ran the family business of Lowe & Sons. He died in 1911.[1]

NOTE:

1. Ridgway 1973, pp.19-20; Ridgway 1996, pp.35, 129.

72 SILVER PLAQUE ON OAK BLOCK

John Foulkes Lowe & George Bennett Lowe, Chester, 1898-9

Four marks (maker's mark of 1896 described but not illustrated, Ridgway 1996, p.129)

Silver plaque: height 4.5 cm. (1.8 in.), width 8.5 cm. (3.35 in.)

Weight 293 g. (10.3 oz.)

Sterling silver plaque on block of English oak (*Quercus petrae*).[1] The rectangular plaque has canted corners and is secured to the wood with three dome-headed silver pins: a fourth pin is missing from the lower left corner. The plaque is engraved with the inscription: 'This Block was made from a beam from a house / where Lady Hamilton lived at Hawarden', (in Roman lettering) and 'Bought from / Messrs. Lowe & Sons, / Oct: 27. 1894.' (in script).

Lady Hamilton was born in Denhall, in the parish of Neston on the Wirral peninsula in Cheshire. The daughter of Henry Lyon, an illiterate blacksmith, and his wife Mary, she was most probably born in 1765. She was christened Amy but, after trying variations of Emily, eventually adopted the name Emma Hart. Henry Lyon died later in 1765, and Mary returned with her infant daughter to her mother, Mrs. Sarah Kidd, in her native village of Hawarden in Flintshire. Here they lived in a small thatched and whitewashed cruck cottage, known as The Steps.[2] While still young Emma became under-nursemaid to the family of a surgeon in Hawarden, and in 1777 moved to London as nursemaid to another doctor's family. After successive occupations of varying virtue, she gave birth to a daughter c.1780, and then lived with Sir Harry Fetherstonhaugh at Uppark in Sussex. Pregnant again, possibly by the Hon. Charles Greville, Emma returned to her grandmother in Hawarden in 1781 and the following year gave birth, but the child was probably stillborn. She then lived with Greville in London, and

72

her last recorded visit to Hawarden was with her mother and daughter in 1784.[3] Emma's extraordinary beauty captivated George Romney, who painted her more than 20 times from 1782, and she also sat to Sir Joshua Reynolds, Gavin Hamilton, Elisabeth Vigee-Le Brun, Sir Thomas Lawrence and Angelica Kauffman.[4]

Greville's uncle was Sir William Hamilton (1730-1803), British Minister Plenipotentiary to the Kingdom of the Two Sicilies and a renowned antiquary, connoisseur and natural historian. He met Emma in 1783 and described her as 'better than anything in nature. In her particular way she is finer than anything that is to be found in antique art.'[5] In 1786 Greville sent her to Naples to be his uncle's mistress in return for Hamilton's payments of Greville's debts, and in 1791 Hamilton married her. In Naples she gained a European reputation for her 'Attitudes', a kind of Romantic aesthetic posturing achieved with the aid of shawls and classical draperies and, following her marriage, Lady Emma Hamilton became the diplomatic intermediary between her husband and her close friend Queen Maria Carolina. In 1793 she met Horatio Nelson (1758-1805), who was knighted in 1797, created a baron the following year and viscount in 1801. Emma became Nelson's mistress in 1798 after his victory over the French in the Battle of the Nile. In 1800, when the British government recalled Hamilton, Nelson

returned with him and Emma to England, where she flaunted her control over the admiral. They had two daughters, one of whom survived infancy. After Hamilton's death in 1803 she lived with Nelson until he perished at the Battle of Trafalgar two years later. Although she inherited money from both men she squandered most of it, was imprisoned for debt, and died in impecunious exile in Calais in 1815.[6]

The surviving silver marked jointly by John Foulkes Lowe and George Bennett Lowe includes a communion cup and paten, a bowl and a gold snuff box.[7] It is surprising that this silver plaque was made some four years after the block of wood was bought, and that the inscription gives greater prominence to the name of the vendor and the date of the purchase than to the explanation of the relic's significance. A comparable piece had been made by John and George Lowe's grandfather, George Lowe I, who in 1837 added silver mounts to a box made of wood from the Nannau oak.[8]

PROVENANCE: John ffoulkes Lowe, Chester; His sister, Miss Joyce Lowe, 1973; Purchased with grant aid from the MGC/V&A Purchase Grant Fund, London Goldsmiths' Company, Grosvenor Museum Society 1988.65

PUBLISHED: Boughton 1992 III, p.15, illustrated; Ridgway 1996, p.130.

NOTES:

1. Wood identified by Graham Usher, 13 November 1999.

2. The cottage has long since disappeared. For a photograph see Fraser opposite p.210.

3. *Dictionary of National Biography*, vol.24, p.148; *The Cheshire Sheaf*, 5th series, no.29, December 1976; Fraser, pp.1-4, 44-5; Jenkins & Sloan, pp.18, 175.

4. *DNB*, vol.24, p.149; Jenkins & Sloan, pp.254, 266, 269, 271-2, 275; Ryskamp, p.110. Although later cruelly caricatured by James Gillray (Jenkins & Sloan, no.189), her most ravishing portrait is Romney's 'A Bacchante', commissioned by Sir William Hamilton in 1783 (Jenkins & Sloan, no.167).

5. *DNB*, vol.24, p.149.

6. *The New Encyclopaedia Britannica* (Chicago), 1998, vol.5, p.662; Ryskamp, p.110.

7. Ridgway 1996, pp.130-1; Moore 1984 I, no.161.

8. Ridgway 1985, pp.107-8. In the early 15th century, according to legend, Owain Glyndwr, the last independent prince of Wales, murdered his cousin Hywell Sele of Nannau, Merioneth, and hid his body inside this hollow oak, which blew down in 1813.

Francis Maurice Lowe

Francis (known as Frank) Maurice Lowe was born in 1916 and was apprenticed to his father James Foulkes Lowe (a grandson of John Lowe I). He became free in 1937 and was admitted to the Chester Goldsmiths' Company later that year. He worked in the assay office, and served the company as deputy warden from c.1954 and later as alderman. His nephew Grahame Jones (now alderman of the company) and his son Peter James Lowe (now steward) were apprenticed to him. Between the closure of the assay office in 1962 and his retirement in 1981 he worked for the jewellers Boodle & Dunthorne in Chester, and died in 1991.[1]

NOTE:

1. Ridgway 1996, pp.30-1, 36, 47, 124-5; Janet Lowe, letter, 26 October 1993.

73 DISH

Francis Maurice Lowe, Chester, 1962

Four marks on central surface (maker's mark of Arthur Vincent Ward, Ridgway 1996, pl.42)
Diameter 29.5 cm. (11.6 in.)
Weight 798g. (28.15oz.)

See Colour Plate V

Sterling silver. The circular dish is raised from a single sheet of silver, with a smooth, slightly convex centre and a broad upturned rim with an unplanished surface. The centre is engraved in block letters: 'ASSAY OFFICES ACT, 1962 / 10 and 11 ELIZABETH 2 /

This was the last piece of / silver Hallmarked at the / CHESTER ASSAY OFFICE / before closure 24th August / 1962. / Witness A. Vincent Ward, / Assay Master.'[1]

Great quantities of silver were assayed at Chester after the Second World War, but in 1955 the Board of Trade appointed a Departmental Committee on Hallmarking chaired by Sir Leonard Stone. The committee's report, presented to Parliament in 1959, recommended the dissolution of both the Chester Assay Office and the Chester Goldsmiths' Company. John ffoulkes Lowe conducted an unsuccessful campaign to retain the assay office but, thanks to a speech in the House of Lords by the Bishop of Chester, Dr. Gerald Ellison, the legislation was amended to preserve the company. The Act became law, the last Chester date letter began on 1 July 1962, and much London-made silver and gold was sent for marking before the Chester Assay Office closed an 24 August 1962.[2]

Francis Maurice Lowe, who made and engraved this dish, had not registered his own mark, and instead borrowed that of Arthur Vincent Ward.[3] A.V. Ward was born in 1885 and was apprenticed to his grandfather Thomas Woolley (a descendant of the Duke family of Chester goldsmiths). He was admitted to the Chester Goldsmiths' Company in 1906, serving as senior warden 1946-53, prime warden 1953-4 and Chester's last assay master 1954-62. He died in 1972.[4]

Francis Maurice Lowe was responsible for a limited amount of silver, all bearing the maker's mark of Arthur Vincent Ward. His work includes a pair of Britannia standard salt and mustard spoons made in 1953, a jam spoon from the same year, a scallop-edged dish of 1958 and a five-light candelabrum of 1959. In 1962 he purchased blanks from the Sheffield Smelting Company and made a small canteen of Old English pattern cutlery, comprising six table forks, dessert forks, tea spoons, dessert spoons and table spoons, plus two serving spoons.[5] His nephew Grahame Jones also made a silver dish, hallmarked on the day the Chester Assay Ofice closed and inscribed accordingly.[6]

PROVENANCE: Francis Maurice Lowe, Great Boughton, Chester; Purchased with grant aid from the V&A Purchase Grant Fund, Grosvenor Museum Society 1984.54

EXHIBITED: Chester 1984, no.165, illustrated.

PUBLISHED: Moore 1986, pp.1296-7; Ridgway 1996, pp.34, 125, 143.

NOTES:

1. A letter in the museum's archive reads: 'Assay Offices Act. 1962. 10 and 11. Elizabeth 2. This is to certify that I witnessed the last hallmark struck on the silver dish, so engraved, made and owned by Mr. F.M. Lowe, Deputy Warden of the Chester Goldsmiths' Company, and bearing my maker's mark, before

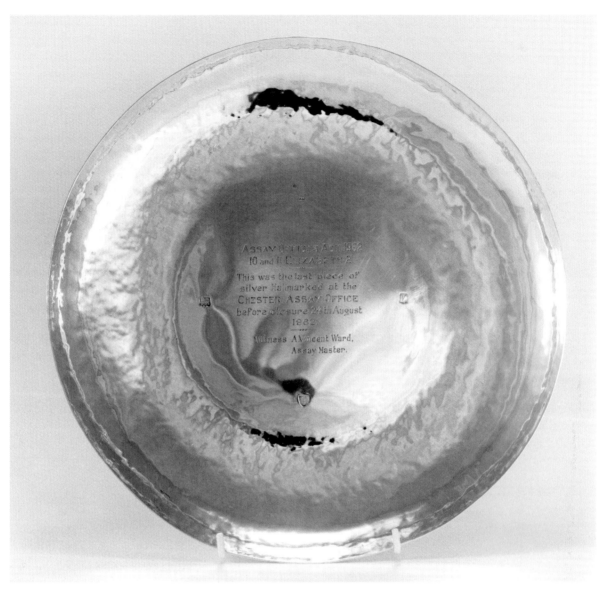

73

the closure of the Chester Assay Office, by the above Act of Parliament, on 24th August, 1962. Signed. A. Vincent Ward Assay Master.'

2. Ridgway 1996, pp.32-3.

3. Ridgway 1996, p.34, and pl.46 for a photograph of the two men marking the dish.

4. Ridgway 1996, pp.31-2, 36-7, 60, 143; Mr. A.G. Ward, letter, 24 July 1993.

5. Ridgway 1996, pp.34, 125.

6. Ridgway 1996, p.123.

Lowe & Sons

The business was established in 1791 by George Lowe I (see no.53). It was run successively by John Lowe I (see no.67) and Thomas Lowe (1806-66); by John Foulkes Lowe (see no.71) and George Bennett Lowe (see no.72); by George Frederic Lowe (1871-1934) and then by his widow Martha Elizabeth Lowe (1882-1966); and by John ffoulkes Lowe (1921-73) and his

sister Margaret Joyce Lowe (born 1916). In 1977 Joyce Lowe sold the shop as a going concern to James Walker Ltd. In 1985 they were taken over by H. Samuel Ltd., who were in turn taken over by the Ratner's Group in 1986. Since 1988 Lowe & Sons has been owned by Walton's the Jewellers of Chester, who retain the shop's own identity.[1]

NOTE:

1. Culme I, p.402; Walton 1989, p.102; Ridgway 1996, p.124; Miss Joyce Lowe, letter, 6 December 1993.

74 THE SPIRIT OF CHESTER BOWL

Lowe & Sons of Chester, hallmarked Sheffield, 1992
Designed by Rachel Walton and made by Hugh Crawshaw

Five marks on rim of bowl: sponsor's mark (L & S within shield, illustrated Walton 1998), Sheffield assay office mark, lion passant, date

letter, Chester city of origin mark. Lion passant and date letter on separate stand

Diameter of bowl 20.4 cm. (8 in.), diameter of stand 6.2 cm. (2.45 in.), total height 5cm. (1.95 in.)

Weight: bowl 326 g. (11.5 oz.), stand 64 g. (2.25 oz.)

Sterling silver. The circular bowl is raised from a single sheet of silver with a deep, concave well and a wide, flat rim. The centre of the well is engraved with a six-pointed star and the rim with six half-timbered gables, having alternately vertical and diagonal timbering. The inner edge of the rim is engraved in Old English lettering: 'Presented by Lowe & Sons Ltd / To Commemorate the Opening of the Ridgway Gallery 1992'. The underside of the rim is engraved in script: 'Designed by Rachel Walton'. The separate stand is a slightly tapering seamed ring, with a vertically-reeded moulding applied around its foot.

This bowl was presented to mark the opening of the Ridgway Gallery at the Grosvenor Museum by H.R.H. The Prince of Wales an 20 June 1992. The gallery displays the museum's permanent collection of silver, together with a number of loans, and is named after Canon Maurice Ridgway in recognition of his outstanding contribution to the study of Chester silver.

The Spirit of Chester Bowl was designed by Rachel Walton, daughter of Edward Walton,

managing director of Waltons the Jewellers (Chester) Ltd., the present owners of Lowe & Sons. Born in 1967, Rachel Walton took a foundation course in art and design at the North East Wales Institute, Wrexham, in 1985-6, and in 1986-90 took a degree in jewellery design at Middlesex Polytechnic. She was manager of Reema Pachachi's fashion jewellery workshop in Fulham from 1990-1, worked as a jewellery designer and precious stone sorter with Fred E. Ullmann in Hatton Garden from 1991-4, then worked with antique jewellery at Bentleys in Bond Street for three years. Now married with two small children, she is a part-time jewellery designer and consultant for Waltons the Jewellers.

Rachel Walton has written:[1] 'As part of my degree course in Jewellery Design, I had written my thesis about the history of Chester silversmithing from the Middle Ages through to 1962, when the Assay Office closed. I enjoyed designing the bowl because, to me, it was the perfect culmination of all my thesis research and a lasting tribute to all the long-dead Chester silversmiths whose work I had so much admired'.

'Inspired by the simplicity and boldness of the silver articles designed by previous local craftsmen, I wanted to create a striking yet uncomplicated piece ... The rim of the bowl is engraved with a geometric pattern representing the stunning black and white gables for which Chester is so well known,[2] and in the middle of the bowl there is a six pointed star shape that is seen on the face of the Eastgate clock.[3] These architectural features evoke the 'spirit' of Chester, hence the name.

'The original bowl is now an permanent display in the museum. Lowe and Sons have made smaller replicas to special order. [Each has three small feet, and approximately 60 were made from 1992-8.] Each year a 'Spirit of Chester' bowl has been presented as an award to The Chester Business Woman of the Year, and the Lord Mayor of Chester has taken them as gifts when visiting foreign dignitaries abroad, even as far away as Japan. I am especially proud to know that the bowl has been used in this way, as a token of civic friendship.'

The original Spirit of Chester Bowl was made by the Sheffield goldsmith Hugh Crawshaw. Born in 1945, he began work in 1960 as an apprentice with James Dixon & Sons Ltd., the well-known Sheffield firm of manufacturing silversmiths. He set up in partnership with Pater Perry in 1977 and formed his own company ten years later.[4]

The bowl bears the Chester city of origin mark. At Canon Ridgway's suggestion, the Chester Goldsmiths' Company obtained permission from the Committee of Assay Offices of Great Britain to stamp on Chester-made gold, silver and platinum a special mark to denote the place of origin, and since 1988 the mark of a single wheatsheaf has been stamped by the company's alderman, Grahame Jones.[5]

A special Millennium mark was authorised for use an all articles of silver and gold made between 1 January 1999 and 31 December 2000. To celebrate the new millennium, Lowe & Sons produced a limited edition of the Spirit of Chester Bowl, bearing the millennium mark and comprising 250 four-inch diameter bowls, 50 six-inch and 10 eight-inch bowls to be made in each year.[6]

PROVENANCE: Presented by Lowe & Sons of Chester to mark the opening of the Ridgway Gallery 1992.33

PUBLISHED: Schroder 1992, p.36; Ridgway 1996, p.48; Walton 1998, illustrated.

NOTES:

1. Walton 1998.
2. 'In the popular view Chester is the English medieval city *par excellence*. It has preserved its walls all around, and within them are half-timbered houses galore ... [but] Chester is not medieval, it is a Victorian city. What deceives is the black and white. 95 per cent is Victorian and after.' (Pevsner & Hubbard, pp.130-1).
3. Designed by John Douglas, Chester's greatest Victorian architect, and erected in 1899, the Eastgate Clock, with its four faces, has become Chester's most famous landmark (Boughton 1997, no.78).
4. Walton 1998; Edward Walton, fax, 27 March 2000.
5. Ridgway 1996, pp.46-7, the mark illustrated in pl.48 and the four punches in pl.49.
6. Walton 1998.

LIVERPOOL GOLDSMITHS

The first goldsmith in Liverpool, 17 miles north of Chester, was recorded in 1415, and a second died in 1628. Following the restoration of peace after the Civil War a Chester goldsmith, Edward Lewis, settled in Liverpool in 1672. He died in 1691 and his assistant, Robert Shields, married his widow and continued his business. Benjamin Brancker, active by 1704, took over the shop of Robert Shields (who died in 1716): although elected a freeman of Chester in 1715, he did not join the Chester Goldsmiths' Company. He was succeeded in 1734 by his son John Brancker, who was the first Liverpool goldsmith to have his work assayed at Chester. John Brancker died in 1752 and the business was continued by Robert Jones, who died in 1756 and whose widow married Joseph Walley in 1760. By 1766 Walley was one of eight goldsmiths in Liverpool, and he was among the 49 recorded in the Chester Plate Duty Books between 1784 and 1840. Seventy-eight Liverpool goldsmiths registered their marks at Chester from 1863-85 and 63 did so in 1894-1921. The earliest Liverpool watchcase maker was active from 1696, and by the 1780s an increasing number of watchcases were being sent to Chester. A large-scale watchmaking industry developed in and around Liverpool, and hallmarking watchcases became a very important source of revenue for the Chester Assay Office until the demise of the pocket watch after the First World War.[1]

NOTE:

1. Moore 1984 I, pp.104-8, 124; Moore 1986, p.1292; Ridgway 1989, pp.410-16; Ridgway 1996, pp.56, 62-3.

Joseph Walley

Joseph Walley came from Tatton, near Knutsford in Cheshire. In 1760 he married Maria, the widow of Robert Jones, who ran the business originally established in Liverpool in 1672 by Edward Lewis. Walley's mark is first recorded in 1777, and he worked in partnership with his stepson Robert Jones I in 1785-8. Joseph Walley died in 1801.[1]

I Parcel-Gilt Communion Cup, William Mutton, *c.*1570 (no.1); Communion Cup and Standing Paten, Richard Richardson I, 1723-4 (no.12).

II Tankard, Ralph Walley, 1687-90 (no.7); Two-Handled Cup, Thomas Robinson, 1690-2 (no.5); Jug, Ralph Walley, 1690-2 (no.8).

III Richard Richardson II: Cruet Frame, 1753-4 (no.26); The St Martin Cup, 1755-6 (no.27); Milk Jug, 1740-1 (no.23).

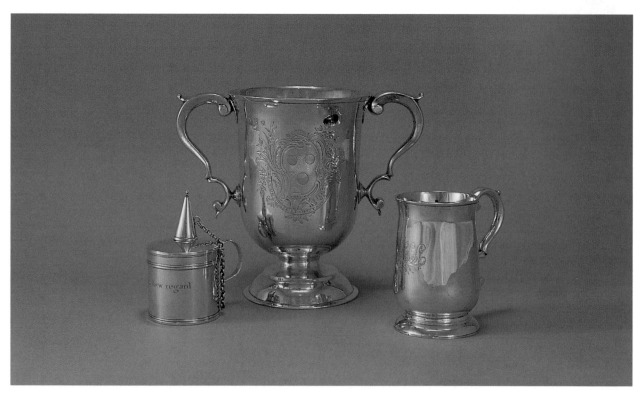

IV George Walker I: Taper Box, 1790-1 (no.40); Two-Handled Cup, 1769-70 (no.37); Parcel-Gilt Mug, 1771-2 (no.38).

V Silver-Mounted Coconut Cup, George Lowe I, *c.*1807-17 (no.59); Dish, Francis Maurice Lowe, 1962 (no.73); Hot Water Jug, George Lowe I, 1830-1 (no.63).

VI Flagon, Seth Lofthouse, 1701-2 (no.99); Silver-Gilt Flagon, Hugh Roberts, 1697 (no.101); Ewer/ Flagon, Humphrey Payne, 1728-9 (no.100).

VII Silver-Gilt Covered Cup, Peter & William Bateman, 1813-4 (no.96); Gold Tumbler Cup, probably Joseph Steward II, 1765-6 (no.95); Silver-Gilt Covered Cup, William Bateman I, 1815-6 (no.97).

VIII Paul Storr: Covered Vegetable Dish, 1807-8 (no.118); Parcel-Gilt Cream Ewer, 1808-9 (no.119); Tea Pot, 1813-14 (no.123).

NOTE:

1. Ridgway 1985, pp.91, 205-6; Ridgway 1989, pp.400, 416; Ridgway 1996, p.88.

75 SERVING FORK

Joseph Walley of Liverpool, hallmarked Chester, 1778-9

Five marks on back of stem near bowl (date letter double struck; maker's mark Ridgway 1985, p.208 type 1)
Length 30.8 cm. (12.1 in.)
Weight 137g. (4.8 oz.)

Sterling silver. The fork is formed from a single piece of silver. The raised bowl is pierced to form six wide, flat tines, with a slightly deeper division between the two central ones, and joins the stem without a drop. The Old English pattern stem has a short ridge behind its turned down end. The front of the stem is engraved with the monogram WL in ornamental script.

The earliest surviving English fork, dating from 1632, has two tines or prongs, and two-pronged examples were still being made in the 1710s. Three tines appeared in the 1680s and became the standard form for the Hanoverian fork. Four tines were known as early as the 1670s, but became general with the introduction of the Old English pattern *c.*1760.[1]

This large fork, with six tines, is called a potato fork by Nicholas Moore and Harold Newman, who maintain that potato forks are otherwise only known from London and Dublin.[2] Ian Pickford illustrates a near-identical fork by George Smith & William Fearn (active 1786-*c.*1796), which he calls a salad fork, quoting a 1772 entry from the Parker & Wakelin ledgers for '6 pronged Salad Forks'.[3] It seems prudent to follow Canon Ridgway in calling this a serving fork, since it could clearly be used for more than one type of food.

Fifty-four pieces of silver by Joseph Walley survive, including flatware, barrel beakers, dish crosses, mugs and a jug, lemon strainer, saucepan and toastrack.[4] Twenty-three of his table forks survive, six made in 1777 with Hanoverian stems and 17 in 1781 in the Old English pattern.[5] Those of 1777 are described by Nicholas Moore as the earliest extant table forks by an English provincial goldsmith, and according to Canon Ridgway their shape 'suggests that they were destined for Ireland or influenced by an Irish fashion'. Nicholas Moore has also seen this serving fork as evidence of Irish influence.[6] No other Chester-assayed serving forks survive from the late 18th or early 19th centuries, nor are any recorded in the Chester Plate Duty Books.

PROVENANCE: Lowe & Sons, Chester; Purchased with grant aid from the Beecroft Bequest 1981.36

EXHIBITED: Chester 1984, no.193, illustrated.

75

PUBLISHED: Ridgway 1905, p.209 Serving Fork; Moore 1985 I, illustrated p.55.

NOTES:

1. Clayton 1985 I, p.192; Pickford, pp.84, 95, fig.92.
2. Moore 1984 I, no.193; Moore 1985 I, p.55; Newman, p.248.
3. Pickford, p.189.
4. Ridgway 1985, pp.208-13.
5. Ridgway 1985, pp.209, 211.
6. Moore 1985 I, p.55; Ridgway 1985, p.209; Moore 1984 I, no.193.

76 SKEWER

Joseph Walley of Liverpool, hallmarked Chester, 1780-1

Five marks at top of blade (maker's mark Ridgway 1985, p.208 type 2)
Length 26.5 cm. (10.4 in.)
Weight 51g. (1.8 oz.)

Sterling silver. The tapering blade, of rectangular section, is stamped in one piece with a vertical oval disk beneath the horizontal oval ring handle. Both sides of the disk and the shoulders of the blade are decorated with sub-Rococo engraving, and the disk has feather-edging.

Like the anonymous Chester example of 1788 (no.52), Joseph Walley's skewer takes the earlier form of a stamped flat blade. The disk's feather-edging was a popular decorative border at this time (see no.47).

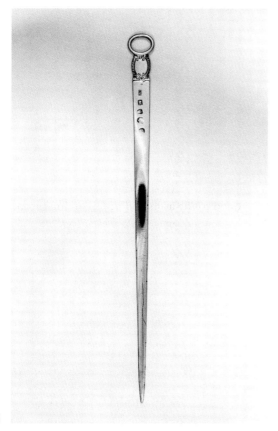

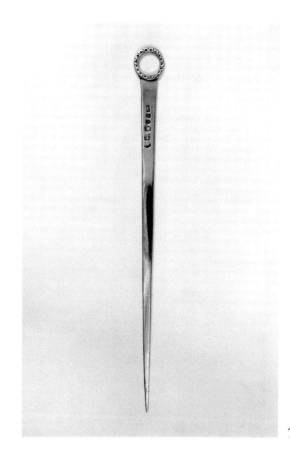

76
77

Five skewers by Joseph Walley survive, dating between 1777 and 1783.[1] Three have a conventional ring handle, but one of 1783 takes the same form as the museum's example, with an engraved crest on its oval disk, demonstrating the intended purpose of this otherwise non-functional feature.[2] The Chester Plate Duty Books record 24 skewers made by the partnership of Joseph Walley and Robert Jones I in 1785-7:[3] these presumably included a surviving skewer of 1786 which bear's Jones's mark and has an oval disk beneath its ring handle.[4]

With one exception, the other surviving skewers by late 18th- and early 19th-century Liverpool goldsmiths have circular ring handles, and comprise two of 1782 by John Fisher, one of 1789 by Joseph Hewitt (no.77), and eight of 1794-1810 by Robert Jones I (including one of 1807 with an octagonal ring).[5] Jones clearly dominated their production in Liverpool at this time, since the Duty Books record 275 skewers by him between 1788 and 1811. They also record one by John Fisher in 1784, 10 by Joseph Hewitt in 1791, six by Robert Green in 1793-1803, nine by Nicholas Cunliffe in 1800, six by R. Jones & Son in 1828, two by John Coakley in 1829 and four by John Sutter in 1839.[6]

PROVENANCE: John ffoulkes Lowe, Chester; His sister, Miss Joyce Lowe, 1973; Purchased with grant aid from the MGC/V&A Purchase Grant Fund, London Goldsmiths' Company, Grosvenor Museum Society 1988.55

PUBLISHED: Ridgway 1985, p.212 Skewers no.3.

NOTES:
1. Moore 1984 I, no.194; Ridgway 1985, pp.209, 212.
2. Ridgway 1985, p.212 Skewers no.1. Hester Bateman made a very similar skewer, with a circular ring handle above an oval disk, in 1788 (Phillips, London, 17 July 1998, lot 100).
3. Ridgway 1996, p.88.
4. Ridgway 1985, p.93 Skewers no.3.
5. Ridgway 1985, pp.82, 93.
6. Ridgway1996, pp.79, 80-1, 83, 86-8, 98.

Joseph Hewitt

Joseph Hewitt (also spelled Hewit or Hewett) is recorded as a working jeweller and silversmith in Liverpool between 1787 and 1796.[1]

NOTE:
1. Ridgway 1996, p.86; Liverpool Trade Directories.

77 SKEWER

Joseph Hewitt of Liverpool, hallmarked Chester, 1789-90

Six marks at top of blade (maker's mark Ridgway 1985, p.86)
Length 22 cm. (8.65 in.)
Weight 28g. (1 oz.)

Sterling silver. The tapering blade, of rectangular section, is cast in one piece with the circular ring handle, which is decorated with bright-cut engraving.

Smaller skewers like this one are generally known as poultry or game skewers. Bright-cut engraving was sometimes used to decorate the utilitarian ring handle.[1]

Canon Ridgway previously attributed the IH mark, used on work of 1789-91, to John Helsby of Liverpool (active 1823-64), while noting that the mark had also been attributed to Isaac Hadwen or Joseph Hewitt.[2] The Chester Plate Duty Books show that there were two gold-smiths at this date with these initials. Isaac Hadwen of Liverpool, although active from 1777-94, only appears in the Duty Books in 1792 with gold rings.[3] However, Joseph Hewitt is recorded in 1790-2 with a range of wares, including ten skewers and pieces like the other two surviving ones with this mark, a spout cup of 1789 and a communion cup of 1790.[4] Skewers by other Liverpool goldsmiths are discussed at no.76.

Provenance: Lloyd Tyrell-Kenyon, 5th Baron Kenyon of Gredington; Sotheby's, London, 19 June 1969, lot 179; John ffoulkes Lowe, Chester; His sister, Miss Joyce Lowe, 1973; Purchased with grant aid from the MGC/V&A Purchase Grant Fund, London Goldsmiths' Company, Grosvenor Museum Society 1988.57

Published: Ridgway 1985, p.86 Skewer (as ? John Helsby).

Notes:
1. Newman, p.286; Wees, p.260.
2. Ridgway 1985, p.86.
3. Liverpool Trade Directories; Ridgway 1996, p.84.
4. Ridgway 1996, p.86; Ridgway 1985, pp.86-7. John & Thomas Lowe's type 2 mark shows that the initial J could appear as the letter I on a maker's mark as late as 1840 (Ridgway 1985, pp.112-3).

Nicholas Cunliffe

Nicholas Cunliffe of Liverpool is recorded as a working jeweller and silversmith from 1790-1829, with surviving silver up to 1832. He had retired by 1835 and had died by 1837.[1]

Note:
1. Liverpool Trade Directories; Ridgway 1985, p.74; Ridgway 1996, p.80.

78 SILVER-MOUNTED COWRIE SHELL SNUFF BOX

Nicholas Cunliffe of Liverpool, hallmarked Chester 1800-1

Six marks inside cover (maker's mark Ridgway 1985, p.74)

Length 9 cm. (3.5 in.)
Weight 119 g. (4.2 oz.)

Sterling silver and cowrie shell. The cowrie shell has been cut off flat on the side of its natural opening. It is edged with a broad silver band, seamed once and shaped to the curvature of the shell but not pinned. The flat cover has a seven-part flush hinge, and its rim fits into the encircling band.

The lid is engraved with a variant of the arms, crest and motto of Gartshore of Dumbarton, with a border added to the arms and the 'I' omitted from the motto 'I renew my age'. Gale Glynn has commented that 'Dumbarton being a west coast port on the Clyde, the owner of this box may very well have been a cadet member of the family and a ship owner or merchant plying between Liverpool and Dumbarton. Borders can be used to designate cadency on occasions in Scotland.'[1]

The shell is a tiger cowrie (*Cypraea tigris* Linnaeus, 1758). This is found in the Indo-Pacific region, a vast area between the Cape of Good Hope in the west and the mid-Pacific in the east, extending north to Japan and south to New Zealand.[2] The shell was presumably imported directly into the great port of Liverpool. As well as snuff boxes, cowrie shells were also transformed, by the addition of silver mounts, into sauce boats, nutmeg graters, pap boats and spoons.[3]

Snuff is a preparation of powdered tobacco for inhaling through the nostrils. Snuff boxes have been made, from a wide variety of materials, since the 17th century. Pocket boxes, which have a hinged lid, generally held between a quarter and half an ounce of snuff. Cowries were found to be admirable retainers of snuff's freshness and savour. Their lids needed to be almost airtight, to permit neither the escape of snuff nor the entrance of unnecessary air.[4]

Nicholas Cunliffe's other surviving silver comprises a covered milk jug, a cruet frame and a bottle ticket.[5] The Chester Plate Duty Books record two boxes by him in 1807 and 1812.[6] The top of his silver-mounted cowrie shell snuff box follows the standard form of the late 18th century, although the shell's edging and the cover's rim are deeper and simpler than some other examples.[7]

Snuff box making was a recognised and highly profitable branch of the jeweller's trade in the 18th and early 19th centuries.[8] The closest Liverpool example is a mounted cowrie shell snuff box by James Barton (active 1785-1816), its hinged cover set with an agate.[9] There also survive two parcel-gilt table snuff boxes of 1815 and 1819 by Thomas and John Helsby.[10] The Duty Books record a number of shell mounts by Liverpool goldsmiths during the first third of the 19th century: one by Robert Jones in

78

1803, one by John Clarke in 1819, 17 by Thomas Helsby & Son in 1820, five by Thomas Woolfield in 1835, and specifically a 'mounting for shell box' by W. Ellison in 1815 and a 'shell snuff box top' by John Helsby in 1830.[11] The Duty Books record 395 unspecified boxes by 22 Liverpool goldsmiths, together with the following snuff boxes: 13 by John Adamson in 1785-7, one by Robert Jones in 1799, one by Edward Maddock in 1815, two by J. Abbott in 1817, six by Thomas Helsby & Sons in 1817-27, one by Hugh Adamson in 1820, one by Jones & Reeves in 1821, one by J. Helsby & Son in 1826 and one by C. Jones in 1830.[12]

PROVENANCE: Probably Gartshore family, Dumbarton, c.1800; Nicholas Shaw Antiques, London; Purchased with grant aid from the Grosvenor Museum Society 1994.23

PUBLISHED: Ridgway 1996, p.192.

NOTES:

1. Gale Glynn, letter, 5 March 1995.
2. Dr. Ian Wallace, examination on 8 November 1999.
3. Newman, p.92.
4. McCausland, pp.100, 103, 110, 113.
5. Ridgway 1985, p.74.
6. Ridgway 1996, p.80.
7. e.g.: undated one (pre-1794) by Hester Bateman (Shure, pl.XLVI); unmarked one, probably Scottish c.1800 (Davis, no.234).

8. McCausland, p.101.
9. Ridgway 1985, p.59; Ridgway 1996, pp.76-7.
10. Ridgway 1985, pp.88-9; Ridgway 1996, pp.84-5.
11. Ridgway 1996, pp.78, 81, 84-5, 87, 103.
12. Ridgway 1996, pp.75, 84-5, 87-9, 93.

John Coakley

John Coakley of Liverpool sent silver to Chester between 1828 and 1833. He also registered his mark at Exeter in 1828 and at London in 1832.[1]

NOTE:

1. Grimwade, p.721; Moore 1984 I, p.120; Jackson, p.306; Ridgway 1996, p.79.

79 SUGAR TONGS

John Coakley of Liverpool, hallmarked Chester, 1828-9

Six marks inside handle, three each side (maker's mark Ridgway 1985, p.71)
Length 14.7 cm. (5.8 in.), width 5 cm. (1.95 in.)
Weight 38 g. (1.35 oz.)

Sterling silver. The tongs are made from a single piece of silver, bent in a U-shape forming two spring arms. The ovoid bowls of the grips are raised and each Fiddle pattern stem, with a bevelled edge, has two projecting shoulders at its junction with the bowl. One side of the handle is

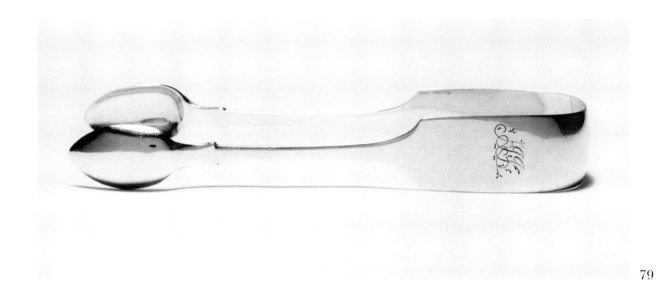

engraved with the script monogram AJJ surrounded by sprigs.

Sugar tongs are discussed in the entry for John Lowe I's pair of 1843 (no.67), and John Coakley's pair of 1828 are almost identical. The 17 recorded pieces of Coakley's surviving silver are all Fiddle pattern flatware, including a gravy spoon, ladles, a fish slice, oyster forks, a jam spoon and a table spoon.[1] The Chester Plate Duty Books record 534 pairs of sugar tongs by Coakley in 1828-32, including 93 in 1828 and a peak of 194 the following year.[2] Two of these have survived, the other example being almost identical and likewise dating from 1828.[3]

Coakley was succeeded by John Sutter as the principal producer of Liverpool flatware, and his sugar tongs are discussed at no.81. No other sugar tongs by early 19th-century Liverpool goldsmiths appear to have survived, although the Duty Books record one pair by Nicholas Cunliffe in 1800 and 15 by John Helsby in 1832.[4]

PROVENANCE: Sotheby's, Chester, 29 July 1980, lot 32; Lowe & Sons, Chester; Purchased 1980.75

EXHIBITED: Chester 1980; Chester 1984, no.208.

PUBLISHED: Ridgway 1985, p.72, Tongs no.2 (as maker JC); Moore 1985 I, illustrated p.55.

NOTES:

1. Ridgway 1985, pp.71-3.
2. Ridgway 1996, p.79.
3. Ridgway 1985, p.72.
4. Ridgway 1996, pp.80, 85.

80 TEA SPOON

John Coakley of Liverpool, hallmarked Chester, 1829-30

Four marks on back of stem at top: maker's mark (Ridgway 1985, p.71), sovereign's head, lion passant, date letter
Length 14.4 cm. (5.65 in.)
Weight 17 g. (0.6 oz.)

Sterling silver. The spoon is formed from a single piece of silver. The raised ovoid bowl has a single drop at its junction with the stem. The Fiddle pattern stem, with a bevelled edge, has two projecting shoulders at its junction with the bowl and a vestigial

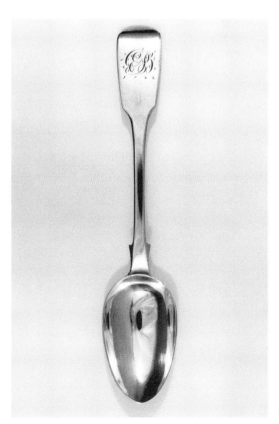

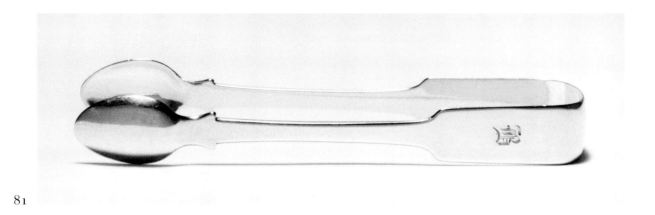

81

ridge behind its turned down end. The front of the stem is engraved with the script monogram EB surrounded by sprigs.

The use of tea spoons is discussed at no.18. The Chester Plate Duty Books record 6,791 tea spoons by John Coakley in 1828-33, his production peaking at 2,025 in 1829.[1] Several of these have survived, mostly—like the museum's example—lacking the Chester mark, and including an almost identical set of six from 1830.[2]

Coakley was succeeded by John Sutter (see no.81) as the principal producer of Liverpool flatware, the Duty Books recording 5,135 tea spoons by him from 1834-40. They also record one tea spoon by Thomas Helsby & Son in 1821, 359 by John Helsby in 1832, 11 by Hugh Adamson in 1833, 24 by R. Adamson the same year, and 12 by Henry Close in 1837.[3] Tea spoons of 1836 by John Sutter are known, but no others by Liverpool goldsmiths appear to have survived.[4]

PROVENANCE: Sotheby's, Chester, 19 October 1983, lot 794; Purchased 1983.78

EXHIBITED: Chester 1984, no.209.

NOTES:
1. Ridgway 1996, p.79.
2. Ridgway 1985, p.73.
3. Ridgway 1996, pp.75, 79, 84-5, 97-8.
4. Ridgway 1985, p.193.

John Sutter

John Sutter first registered his mark at Newcastle in 1832 and had his silver assayed there for a year. In 1834 he registered his mark at Chester, and is recorded as a goldsmith in Liverpool up to 1874.[1]

NOTE:
1. Moore 1984 I, pp.107, 120; Ridgway 1985, p.193; Ridgway 1996, pp.97-8.

81 SUGAR TONGS

John Sutter of Liverpool, hallmarked Chester, 1835-6

Six marks inside centre of handle (maker's mark Ridgway 1985, p.193)
Length 15.1 cm. (5.95 in.), width 5.1 cm. (2 in.)
Weight 52 g. (1.8 oz.)

Sterling silver. The tongs are made from a single piece of silver, bent in a squared U-shape forming two spring arms. The ovoid bowls of the grips are raised and each Fiddle pattern stem, with a bevelled edge, has two projecting shoulders at its junction with the bowl. One side of the handle is engraved with the initial B in Old English lettering.

Sugar tongs are discussed at no.67, and John Sutter's pair is of the same type as those by John Coakley (no.79). Many pieces of flatware by John Sutter have survived, mostly in the Fiddle pattern, including caddy, tea, egg, jam, dessert, table, gravy and serving spoons; miniature, oyster and table forks; sauce and toddy ladles; and a butter tester.[1] John Sutter had one pair of sugar tongs assayed at Newcastle in 1832-3, and the Chester Plate Duty Books record 196 pairs by him from 1835-40, but this appears to be the only extant example.[2] Sutter succeeded John Coakley as the principal producer of Liverpool flatware, and two pairs by Coakley appear to be the only other surviving early 19th-century Liverpool sugar tongs (see no.79).

PROVENANCE: Phillips, Chester, 21 September 1984, lot 318 (part); Purchased 1984.53

PUBLISHED: Ridgway 1985, p.193.

NOTES:
1. Moore 1984 I, pp.120-1; Ridgway 1985, p.193; Ridgway 1996, p.98.
2. Gill, p.258; Ridgway 1996, p.98.

82 BADGE

John Sutter of Liverpool, hallmarked Chester, 1842-3

Five marks on back (maker's mark Ridgway 1985, p.193)

Diameter 10.5 cm. (4.1 in.)

Weight 31 g. (1.1 oz.)

Sterling silver. The flat, circular 16-pointed star is cut from sheet silver. The points of the star are engraved with two alternating patterns of rays, and enclose two concentric rings of engraved ornament. Between these rings is engraved in script: 'Presented to Br William Waddington, P.C.R of Court 1030. / A Token of Esteem'. The centre of the badge is engraved with a stag's head issuing from a ducal coronet, the crest of the Ancient Order of Foresters.[1] Three slightly raised strips of silver, one large and two small, are soldered to the back, which is lightly inscribed with a circle.

The Ancient Order of Foresters, one of Britain's oldest and largest friendly societies, evolved from an earlier organisation, the Royal Foresters. The first dated reference to the Royal Foresters is a gathering at Knaresborough in Yorkshire in 1745, but the undisputed history of Forestry began in 1790 with the opening of Court No.1 in Leeds. Over the next decade they developed the principles and rituals of Forestry, whose rule book defined a brotherhood which 'while wandering through the Forest of this World' might 'render mutual aid and assistance to each other'. 408 courts were opened between 1813 and 1834, when the Royal Foresters re-organised as the Ancient Order of Foresters. The contributions of members provided benefits for sickness, old age, funerals, widows and orphans, and often medical assistance.[2]

Each of the Order's branches, which eventually exceeded 10,000, was called a court. This was identified by the serial number of its establishment, and the founders chose a name which gave additional identification. The early courts nearly always met in public houses, and their members were called brothers. The president of the court was the Chief Ranger, elected for one year, who was known as a Past Chief Ranger (PCR) after his term of office. In early years the PCR would receive a silver medal (valued at 8s. in 1835), which was worn on a neck ribbon (a feature introduced in 1834). The medals of the Ancient Order of Foresters vary greatly in style, but include circular eight-pointed stars.[3]

Court 1030 was called 'Working Men's Dependence'. It opened in 1840 and met at the Strugglers Inn, High Street, Eagle, Lincolnshire. The court left the Order in 1881, probably due to the Order's insistence on the adoption of more viable contributions and benefits. According to the 1881 census William Waddington was then 71 years old and a retired farmer, living in Kirton but born in Eagle.[4]

The Chester Plate Duty Books, which survive up to 1840, record '1 medal' by John Sutter in 1838, but the museum's badge is his only known example.[5] The Duty Books usually refer to these items as medals, specifying those which were masonic, and record their production by other Liverpool goldsmiths: 13 by Richard Morrow in 1787-92 (including 7 masonic jewels), seven by William Hull in 1798, 43 by Nicholas Cunliffe in 1800-11, five by Hugh Adamson in 1805-8, one gold medal by Thomas Helsby in 1811, 11 by J. Abbott in 1819-26, five by Jones & Reeves in 1820, four by John Coakley in 1830, nine by Henry Close in 1830-7, six by Richard Lucas in 1832-9, three by John Helsby in 1834-5, two by Joseph Lewis Samuel in 1834-8 (including a gold medal), two by Samuel Close in 1838 and one by William James Hemming in 1839.[6] None of these 112 badges appear to survive, and the only other extant Liverpool badge from this period is one of 1838 by John Helsby (no.83).

PROVENANCE: Presented by the Ancient Order of Foresters, Court 1030, Eagle, Lincolnshire to William Waddington, Past Chief Ranger, c.1842-3; Sotheby's, Chester, 23 July 1986, lot 1285; Purchased 1986.167

NOTES:
1. Gale Glynn, report, 22 March 1991; Audrey Fisk, letter, 14 January 2000.
2. Cooper 1984, pp.2, 5-7, 9, 11.

3. Cooper 1984, pp.4, 9, 16, 25, pl.13; Audrey Fisk, letter, 14 January 2000.
4. Audrey Fisk, letter, 14 January 2000.
5. Ridgway 1996, p.98.
6. Ridgway 1996, pp.75, 79-80, 84-6, 89, 93-4, 97.

John Helsby

John Helsby was the son of Thomas Helsby, a Liverpool watchcase maker and goldsmith. Thomas Helsby was active from 1793, and was in partnership with his son by 1815. Although the partnership appears to have continued until at least 1832, John Helsby was working at a separate address by 1823, and is recorded as a watchcase maker until 1862 and as an assayer of gold and silver in 1864.[1]

NOTE:
1. Ridgway 1985, pp.88-9; Ridgway 1996, pp.84-5; Liverpool Trade Directories.

83 BADGE

John Helsby of Liverpool, hallmarked Chester, 1838-9

Five marks on front (maker's mark JH)
Length 7.2 cm. (2.8 in.)
Weight 12 g. (0.4 oz.)

Sterling silver. The slightly convex, oval eight-pointed star is die-stamped from sheet silver. The points of the star have a radiating pattern of diamond facets. A burnished oval band encloses the matted ground of the centre, which is stamped with a stag's head pierced by two arrows in saltaire, all on a branch of bay above crossed keys.[1] Two slightly raised strips of silver are soldered to the back.

This badge is almost certainly connected with the Ancient Order of Foresters (AOF). The Order's official crest, a stag's head issuing from a ducal coronet, is engraved on no.82. The symbol of a stag's head with crossed arrows on a branch is found on early membership certificates of the Order, although with a hunting horn hanging from a bow in the branch rather than the crossed keys.[2]

Audrey Fisk has suggested that the museum's badge could have been made for 'either the AOF or their antecedents the Royal Foresters. Those Royal Foresters' Courts which did not secede to the AOF in 1834 did continue in existence for some time in parallel with the AOF.' The badge may also refer to the second degree of Forestry, the Ancient Order of Shepherds, introduced in 1815 and continuing after 1834, which provided additional benefits in return for additional contributions. Audrey Fisk has concluded, 'that in the early days of the establishment of the AOF standardisation took time to establish and that local variations abounded.'[3]

One of the badges illustrated in the Order's official history is identical to the museum's example, and presumably used the same die, the only difference being areas of plain silver joining the points of the star.[4] In keeping with the chivalric character of the Ancient Order's title, the facetted decoration on this eight-pointed star emulates the eight rays of silver or diamonds seen on the stars of the great orders of British chivalry—oval for the Most Ancient and Most Noble Order of the Thistle, and circular for the Most Noble Order of the Garter and the Most Illustrious Order of St Patrick.[5]

John Helsby is the only goldsmith with the initials JH recorded in the Chester Plate Duty Books as a maker of 'medals' near the date of this one.[6] The known work from his partnership with Thomas Helsby comprises two parcel-gilt table snuff boxes and a watch-case. The other surviving pieces marked by John Helsby alone are a silver-mounted meershaum pipe and a cylindrical box. The Duty Books record three medals by him in 1834-5, but this is his only surviving example and, along with that by John Sutter (no.82), one of only two known Liverpool badges from this period.[7]

PROVENANCE: Christopher Warner, Harrogate, North Yorkshire; Purchased 1982.89

EXHIBITED: Chester 1984, no.206.

NOTES:

1. Gale Glynn, report, 22 March 1991.

2. Membership certificates of 1834 and 1843 illustrated Cooper 1984, p.11, pl.1.

3. Audrey Fisk, letter, 14 January 2000; Cooper 1984, pp.4, 7.

4. Cooper 1984, p.25.

5. Boutell, pp.286-9.

6. The Duty Books record a badge by James Hemming, who appears in 1837-9, plus a goldsmith called William Hemming in 1827-36 (Ridgway 1996, p.85): however, the Liverpool Trade Directories show that this was one person, William James Hemming, active from 1827-41.

7. Moore 1984 I, no.207; Ridgway 1985, pp.88-9; Ridgway 1996, p.85.

MANCHESTER GOLDSMITHS

The first goldsmith in Manchester, 40 miles east of Chester, was recorded in 1568, with six others later in the 16th century and an eighth in 1698. Both John Ollivant (who worked from 1749-95) and William Harwick (active 1771-80) had silver assayed at Chester, and 14 Manchester goldsmiths are recorded in the Chester Plate Duty Books between 1784 and 1840. Although the majority of Manchester goldsmiths had their work assayed at Chester, a few also registered their marks at London from 1789, at York from 1802, and at Birmingham and Sheffield from 1839. Four Manchester goldsmiths registered at Chester between 1841 and 1862, 29 did so from 1863-85 and 133 in 1894-1921.[1]

NOTE:

1.   Moore 1984 I, pp.132-4; Ridgway 1989, pp.406, 410, 417-18; Ridgway 1996, pp.62-3, 72-4.

William Hardwick

William Hardwick of Manchester had entered his mark at Chester by 1771, but had died by 1781.[1]

NOTE:

1.   Moore 1984 I, p.132; Ridgway 1985, p.85; Ridgway 1989, p.400.

84 SKEWER

William Harwick of Manchester, hallmarked Chester, 1779-80

Five marks on back of blade at top (maker's mark Ridgway 1985, p.85)
Length 24.1 cm. (9.5 in.)
Weight 55 g. (1.95 oz.)

Sterling silver. The tapering blade, of rectangular section, is stamped in one piece with the two horizontal scrolls which form the handle. The top of the blade is crudely engraved with an oval containing the crest of a lion's head couped.

The most common finial was the ring handle (discussed at no.52), but the unusual form seen here—described by Canon Ridgway as a 'horned terminal'—enabled the skewer to be withdrawn from the meat with the strength of two fingers.[1]

William Hardwick's surviving work comprises a bottle ticket and two other skewers, dating from 1771 and '74, which also have unusual finials in the form of cast fan-like shells.[2]

The only other surviving skewers by an 18th-century Manchester goldsmith are two of 1783-4 with plain rings by John Ollivant. The sole record of Manchester skewers in the Chester Plate Duty Books is the 45 made by James France in 1785-96.[3]

PROVENANCE: John ffoulkes Lowe, Chester; His sister, Miss Joyce Lowe, 1973; Purchased with grant aid from the MGC/V&A Purchase Grant Fund, London Goldsmiths' Company, Grosvenor Museum Society 1988.54

PUBLISHED: Ridgway 1985, p.86 Skewers no.3.

NOTES:

1.   Ridgway 1985, p.86.

2.   Ridgway 1985, p.85; Captain Sir Thomas Barlow, letter, 7 March 2000.

3.   Ridgway 1985, p.119; Ridgway 1996, p.82.

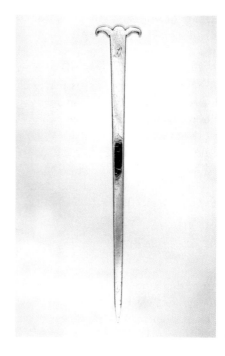

84

Thomas Armitt

Thomas Armitt is known to have produced silver between 1824 and 1835. He is recorded as an earthenware dealer in Salford in 1824-32, and as a glass and china dealer in Manchester in 1836-43.[1]

NOTE:

1. Manchester Trade Directories; Ridgway 1996, p.76.

85 BADGE

Thomas Armitt of Manchester, hallmarked Chester, 1834-5

Six marks on back (maker's mark Ridgway 1985, p.57)
Length 12 cm. (4.7 in.), width 9.2 cm. (3.6 in.)
Weight 71 g. (2.5 oz.)

Sterling silver. The slightly convex escutcheon-shaped badge is cut from sheet silver, with an engraved border of scrolls around its elaborately shaped rim. A circular wire moulding is applied with three pins to the centre of the badge, and contains an engraved portrait bust of William Shakespeare, above which is engraved in block letters 'SHAKESPEARE LODGE.' The badge is engraved in Roman lettering: 'PRESENTED by the OFFICERS & BROTHERS of the Loyal Shakespeare / Lodge to P.G. GEORGE LOVITT on the 16th. Decr. 1834 for his valuable. / services to the said Lodge.' A short horizontal tube is applied with two pins to the back of the badge, beneath which is scratched '1079'.

William Shakespeare (1564-1616) is often called the English national poet and considered by many to be the greatest dramatist of all time. His portrait on this badge derives from the monument in Westminster Abbey, although there are some differences. The monument, designed by William Kent and executed by Peter Scheemakers, dates from 1740. The head of the monument is, in turn, modelled an the 'Chandos' portrait of Shakespeare, which was painted *c*.1610 by John Taylor and is now in the National Portrait Gallery. Several different engravings of the monument were made in the following hundred years, but perhaps the closest to the portrait on the badge is the engraving by B. Hall published in Abraham Wivell's *An Inquiry into the history of the Shakespeare Portraits* (1827).[1] However, the image on the badge includes tassels (not shown in Hall's engraving) and drapery across the right shoulder, and these features relate more closely to a number of 19th-century busts of Shakespeare, which are likewise derived from the Scheemakers monument.[2]

As Roger Pringle has explained: 'Shakespeare's cultural supremacy was established in the eighteenth century, with his popularity in the theatre, the widespread availability of his works for the first time, and growing pride in Britain's past. By the time this badge was made in the 1830s, the Romantic writers had confirmed Shakespeare's position as the national poet and, with Britain emerging as the most advanced industrial state in the world, the Bard was increasingly being adopted as an icon symbolising his country's greatness. The existence in the first part of the 19th century of Shakespeare festivals, societies, reading clubs and masonic lodges was all part of the popular manifestation of the dramatist's status as a national treasure.'[3]

This badge is almost certainly connected with the Order of Odd Fellows, a secret benevolent and social society. The term 'Odd Fellows' was used in the 18th and 19th centuries to describe workers who did not belong to a recognised trade body, but instead joined together to form a mutual self-help society in order to provide for themselves and their families in the event of sickness, unemployment or death. The society of Odd Fellows is mentioned in the early 18th century, and the oldest recorded lodge met in London in 1745. The lodges gradually adopted a common ritual and formed a confederation called the Patriotic Order. Towards the end of the 18th century many of the lodges were suspected of sedition and were broken up, but the society continued to exist as the Union Order of Odd Fellows until 1809. In 1810, at a convention in Manchester, was formed the Manchester Unity of the Independent Order of Odd Fellows, to which the majority of lodges have since belonged.[4]

Each of the Order's branches, of which there are now over 800, was called a lodge. The early lodges nearly always met in public houses, and the Shakespeare Lodge was probably named after such a meeting place.[5] The members of a lodge were called brothers, and their president was the Noble Grand (NG), elected for one year. The following year he became the Immediate Past Noble Grand (IPNG), and thereafter was accorded the rank of Past Noble Grand (PNG), which was quite often quoted as simply Past Grand (PG). He would sometimes receive a silver medal.[6]

This badge was formerly attributed to Thomas Appleby of Manchester, but the TA mark has now been identified as that of Thomas Armitt. The Chester Plate Duty Books record his entire output as 158 medals in 1832-5.[7] His surviving work comprises seven badges made between 1824 and 1834, including at least one each for the Foresters and the Odd Fellows.[8] The majority of these resemble the museum's example in being of escutcheon shape with an engraved border and, while most have cast heraldic centres, one of 1832 has an engraved roundel of the Good Samaritan, comparable with the portrait of Shakespeare in its unsophisticated execution.[9]

Thomas Armitt appears to have been the principal producer of 'medals' in Manchester at this

85

time, but the Duty Books also record 88 by Thomas Newton in 1827-32, 54 by John Armstrong in 1833-4 and 34 by Joseph Armstrong in 1833-9.[10] The only other surviving pieces of friendly society silver by Manchester goldsmiths, both made for the Odd Fellows, are a gorget of 1828 by Thomas Newton[11] and a badge of 1844 by Patrick Leonard,[12] the latter having an even richer border than the museum's example.

PROVENANCE: Presented by the Shakespeare Lodge (probably of the Manchester Unity of the Independent Order of Odd Fellows) to George Lovitt, Past Noble Grand, 1834; Ivan Mazure, London; Purchased 1975.92

EXHIBITED: Chester 1979 1, no.16 (as Thomas Appleby).

PUBLISHED: Thomas, p.17 (as Thomas Appleby); Ridgway 1985, p.58 Badges no.6 (as Thomas Appleby); Ridgway 1996, p.76 (as Thomas Armitt).

NOTES:

1. Wivell, opposite p.250. For the monument by Scheemakers see Whinney, pl.130. For the 'Chandos' portrait see Simon, fig.16: it was much prized in the 18th century, since it was held to have been painted from the life by Shakespeare's fellow-actor, Richard Burbage (Whinney, p.190). The works by Scheemakers and Hall were identified as sources by Roger Pringle (letter, 14 January 2000).

2. e.g. marble bust, circle of Benjamin Cheverton (with Historical Portraits, London, 1991), and plaster busts (Christie's, T. Crowther & Son Collection, 12-14 October 1992, lot 824; Christie's, South Kensington, 6-7 July 1999, lot 895): identified by Jill Springall (letter, 3 February 2000).

3. Roger Pringle, letter, 14 January 2000.

4. Dr. Dan Weinbren, telephone conversation, 16 February 2000; Peter Sedgley, letter, 16 February 2000; Information Leaflet No.18 from the Library and Museum of Freemasonry.

5. Dr. Dan Weinbren, telephone conversation, 16 February 2000. There were at least seven Shakespeare Lodges in the period 1860-75: at South West Brompton, New Brompton and St John's Wood in London; and at Durham, Stratford-upon-Avon, Middlesbrough and Newcastle upon Tyne. None of their lodge numbers correspond with the number an the back of this badge: if this was the lodge number or the individual's lodge membership number or roll number, it would more probably be engraved rather than scratched (Peter Sedgley, letter, 16 February 2000).

6. Peter Sedgley, letters of 16 February and 17 March 2000

7. Ridgway 1996, p.76.

8. Ridgway 1985, pp.57-8; Moore 1984 I, p.136.

9. Moore 1984 I, no.234.

10. Ridgway 1996, pp.76, 95.

11. Ridgway 1985, pl.52; for maker's identification see Moore 1984 I, p.137 and Ridgway 1996, p.95.

12. Moore 1984 I, no.232.

BIRMINGHAM GOLDSMITHS

The Neo-Classical silver manufacturers Boulton & Fothergill and the watchcase makers Gimlet & Vale had their work hallmarked at Chester before the Birmingham Assay Office was opened in 1773. Mass-production thrived as new methods of manufacture were patented and, although a wide range of objects was made, smallware dominated Birmingham's output. Until 1854 no goldsmith living within 30 miles of the Birmingham Assay Office was allowed to send his work to Chester, although two did so in 1810-19. After the lifting of this ban Birmingham provided the Chester Assay Office with the majority of its business, although many of those who registered their marks were pipe mounters, jewellers, umbrella manufacturers, tobacconists, stick mounters and importers of fancy goods. The number of Birmingham firms registering at Chester grew from five in 1863-76 to 286 in 1877-85, 260 in 1894-1904 and 123 in 1905-21.[1]

NOTE:

1. Newman, p.41; Ridgway 1985, pp.10-1, 63-4; Ridgway 1989, p.404; Ridgway 1996, pp.21, 62-3, 74.

Nathan & Hayes

The firm of Nathan & Hayes, manufacturing silversmiths, was established in Birmingham in 1885 by George Nathan (c.1855-1935) and Ridley Hayes. The firm registered 16 marks at Birmingham between 1888 and 1913, and registered at London, where they had showrooms, in 1893. The firm also registered at Chester in 1894 and 1912. In 1917 Nathan & Hayes were taken over by the large silver and jewellery firm of S. Blanckensee & Son Ltd. (which had been founded in 1826 and, after further mergers, became the Albioncraft Co. Ltd. in 1967 and still existed in 1987).[1]

NOTE:

1. Jones 1981, pp.202, 212, 308, 339, 359; Culme, I, pp.7, 340; Culme, II, p.120; Phyllis Benedikz, letters of 12 September 1991, 22 July 1993 and 13 March 2000; Ridgway 1996, p.136.

86 SILVER-GILT CUP

Nathan & Hayes of Birmingham, hallmarked Chester, 1903-4

Four marks beneath bowl (maker's mark Jones 1981, p.339 2nd mark)

Height 10 cm. (3.9 in.), diameter 11.8 cm. (4.65 in.)

Weight 329 g. (11.6 oz.)

Sterling silver, gilt (the gilding recently renewed). The 'font-shaped' standing cup is made in two raised parts. The vertical foot-ring is stamped with alternate diagonal oak leaves on a matted ground between applied horizontal mouldings. The upper part of the spreading foot is chased with bulbous-ended lobes, and the slightly tapering cylindrical stem is chased with narrow vertical gadroons. The stem is soldered to the bowl, and a narrow rope moulding is applied at the junction. The bowl's slightly rounded base is stamped externally with an outer band of circles and an inner band of pentagons, creating a honeycomb effect. The sides of the shallow bowl flare outward, and the lower two-thirds are flat-chased with three rows of imbricated scale pattern, the bottom two tiers having matted centres. The upper third is flat-chased on a diagonally-hatched ground with an inscription, 'BENEDICTVS DEVS IM DONA SVIS AME', in Lombardic lettering with a lozenge between each word.

The underside of the foot-ring is inscribed 'DOBSON, PICCADILLY, W'. Dobson & Sons were a London firm of retail jewellers and silversmiths, which had been established in or before 1814 and which closed after 1916. They were located at 32 Piccadilly from 1821 and at 200 Piccadilly from 1905-11. Despite having their own London showrooms, Nathan & Hayes were among the manufacturing silversmiths supplying goods to Dobson & Sons, the other known example being a silver-gilt cup after a Mycenean gold original, hallmarked at Chester in 1905.[1]

According to a writer in 1911, George Nathan co-founded the firm, 'perceiving the great commercial

86

possibilities in the manufacture of artistic-looking silver articles at a moderate price ... In the endeavour to produce goods of a special character, Mr. George Nathan used to the utmost of his knowledge of styles and design, gathered from the various art collections so far abroad as Italy and Greece so that, today, one of the special features of Nathan and Hayes' output is their clever reproductions of ancient classic cups, vases, &c.'[2] In 1915 another writer noted that the firm exhibited a wide range of domestic silverware, but 'the pieces which made this exhibit one of the best ... were the replicas of ancient drinking cups which Messrs. Nathan & Hayes make a speciality of reproducing in silver-gilt.'[3] In addition to this archaeological work, the firm made reproductions of old English silver,

including the Bodkin Cup of 1521, a Tudor bowl, and late 17th-century pieces.[4]

The market for antique silver between the mid-18th and mid-19th centuries is discussed at no.3. The demand for old English silver continued to grow, and by 1900 the collectors' market was flourishing, stimulated by important exhibitions and supporting specialist periodicals. The prevailing taste was for silver made before 1700, particularly ornate Elizabethan pieces, and the museum's cup reflects this fashion.[5]

It is a reproduction of the Holms Cup, a silver-gilt vessel assayed at London in 1521, which is now in the Royal Museum, Edinburgh. 'The inscription, in which IM DONA is a mistake for IN DONIS, is the first phrase of a Benedictine monastic grace for use after meals, and it might suggest that the [original] cup was used at table by a Benedictine abbot or prior. The blunder in the Latin however may point rather to a layman's imperfect memory of a grace heard when staying in a monastery.'[6]

The Holms Cup had been on loan from John Dunn-Gardner to the Victoria and Albert Museum from 1870, until sold at Christie's (29-30 April 1902, lot 131) to Chrichton Brothers, dealers in antique and reproduction silver. Its record price of £4,100 received considerable publicity and Nathan & Hayes, seeing the opportunity to capitalise upon this, presumably approached Chrichton Brothers for permission to reproduce it.[7]

Nathan & Hayes produced numerous replicas of the Holms Cup, all apparently hallmarked in Chester, with early examples recorded from 1902-4, 1906-7 and 1910.[8] It remained in stock for many years, appearing in an S. Blanckensee & Son catalogue of c.1938 available in silver at £7 10s. and in silver-gilt at £8 15s., thus bringing the glories of Tudor silver to a mass market. The copies were not entirely accurate,[9] and there were variations between them.[10]

PROVENANCE: Lowe & Sons, Chester; Purchased 1991·99

NOTES:

1. Culme, I, p.124.
2. *The Watchmaker, Jeweller and Silversmiths' Trade Journal*, 1 December 1911, p.1493.
3. *The Jeweller and Metalworker*, 1 June 1915, p.676. Examples of these archaeological replicas include cups of 1906 (Ridgway 1996, pl.34) and 1908 (Jones 1981, fig.195). A precursor of their work is a silver-gilt cup of 1884, based on a Greco-Roman original, by Edward Barnard & Sons of London (Brett, no.1397). Earlier 19th-century replicas and adaptations of Classical vessels are discussed at no.63.
4. Jones 1981, p.202. Nathan & Hayes were not alone in copying Tudor silver: Thomas Bradbury & Sons of Sheffield advertised a reproduction Elizabethan salt cellar in 1907 (Culme, I, fig.27).
5. Glanville 1987, pp.295, 297-8.
6. *NACF Annual Report 1958*, p.28, pl.IXA.
7. Glanville 1987, p.298; Godfrey Evans, letter, 23 August 1993; Culme, I, p.102.
8. Godfrey Evans, letter, 23 August 1993; Jones 1981, fig.196; Ridgway 1996, p.137.
9. The original is 10.6 cm. high, 12.1 cm. in diameter, and weighs 440.7 g. (Godfrey Evans, letter, 23 August 1993). The original is larger and heavier, the sides of its bowl are less flared, some of the letters are more elaborate, and the lozenges are undecorated. The original inscription is engraved rather than flat-chased, and the scale pattern is composed of thicker crescents, with alternate diagonal hatching instead of matting. The underside of the original bowl has incised rather than stamped circles, and a much thicker rope moulding. The original stem is more cylindrical and has thinner gadroons, while the lobes on the foot are shorter. The original foot-ring is half the depth and has a thicker rim.
10. One of 1910 (Jones 1981, fig.196) has a pronounced break between the lobes of the foot and the stem, and omits the inscription.

Stokes & Ireland Ltd.

The firm of Stokes & Ireland was established in Birmingham *c.*1872 by William Henry Stokes and Arthur George Ireland. The partnership was dissolved in 1881, but the business was continued under the same name by A.G. Ireland. It became a limited company in 1892, and by 1894 Ireland was joint managing director with Theodore Schwarck (who changed his name to Stokes in 1918). The firm registered 11 marks at Birmingham between 1878 and 1902, and eight marks at London between 1889 and 1904. They also registered at Chester in 1896 and 1898, and opened a London showroom in 1898. In 1926 the firm was taken over by S. Blanckensee & Son Ltd. of Birmingham (see no.86) who, trading as Stokes & Ireland, registered the S&I mark at Birmingham and Chester that year.[1]

NOTE:

1. Jones 1981, pp.363, 365; Culme, I, p.435; Culme, II, pp.12, 274; Phyllis Benedikz, letters of 22 July 1993 and 13 March 2000.

87 TELESCOPIC BEAKER

Stokes & Ireland Ltd. of Birmingham, hallmarked Chester, 1907-8

Four marks beneath base (maker's mark variant of Jones 1981, p.363). Lion passant and date letter on each of four rings
Height when fully extended 6.5 cm. (2.55 in.)
diameter of base and rim 5.8 cm. (2.3 in.)
Weight 80 g. (2.8 oz.)

Sterling silver. The flat, circular foot has a turned-over rim moulding. The body is an outward-tapering cylinder, comprising five rings of equal depth but graduated diameter, each seamed once. The lowest ring is soldered to the base and the others can be collapsed in concentric circles around it or opened to form a beaker. The top ring has an applied rim moulding.

The origin of the beaker's shape is discussed at no.31. This type can be collapsed to fit into a pocket or opened, by pulling the rings upward, to form a beaker which may then be filled from a flask. However, the museum's example is more novel than useful, since it leaks! The usual application of the telescopic principle to silverware is the adjustable-height candlestick, first patented in 1795, whose cylindrical stem has between two and five interior telescopic slides rising from a base.[1]

87

Apart from the detailing of the beaker's moulded rim, every aspect of the design is intended to be purely functional, in contrast to the decoration—in whatever style—found on most Edwardian silver. In its stark angularity this beaker strikingly anticipates some designs of the 1930s, which employ the motif of tapering rings for purely aesthetic effect in the quest for a truly modern style.[2]

This telescopic beaker would have complemented the flasks mentioned by Stokes & Ireland when they advertised in 1894 as 'silversmiths, Flask Makers, & Spinners ... Large Assortment of Typical Tea & Fruit Spoons, Sugar Sifters & Tongs ... Specialities: Tea Sets, Muffineers, Mustard Pots, Salts, Match Boxes, Card Cases, Cigar and Cigarette Cases, Fancy Candlesticks, Snuff and Tobacco Boxes, Trinket Boxes, Dessert and Fish Knives and Forks, Cream Ewers, and Sugar Bowls. Waiters, Cups, &c. Tortoiseshell and Glass Articles Mounted.'[3]

PROVENANCE: Lowe & Sons, Chester; Purchased 1991.233

NOTES:
1. Newman, p.321.

2. A most notable case is a tea and coffee set of 1934/9 by Viners Ltd., but other examples of the same tendency include a tazza of 1930 by Adie Brothers and a covered bowl of 1935 by H.G. Murphy (Brett, nos.1545-6).
3. Culme, I, p.435.

Jones & Crompton

This business was established in Birmingham by Edward Samuel Jones in 1895. In 1899 he was joined by Hubert Crompton (born 1874), trading as Jones & Crompton. Howard Ashwell Wallis subsequently joined as an additional partner, and Hubert Crompton's brother, Francis Hilary Crompton, joined the firm when E.S. Jones retired in 1904. Jones & Crompton registered numerous marks at Birmingham from 1899-1932, and single marks at Chester in 1899 and at London in 1907. As well as their factory in Birmingham, they had shops in London, Manchester and Glasgow by 1912, but the firm probably closed before or during the Second World War.[1]

NOTE:
1. Culme, I, p.263; Culme, II, p.171; Jones 1981, pp.334, 354; Philip Priestley, fax, 12 February 2000; Phyllis Benedikz, letter, 13 March 2000.

88 SHOE HORN

Jones & Crompton of Birmingham, hallmarked Chester, 1913-14

Four marks on front of handle (maker's mark, J&_)
Front of horn stamped 'SHEFFIELD / STEEL'
Total length 18 cm. (7.1 in.)
Weight 42 g. (1.5 oz.)

Sterling silver handle with horn of close plated steel. The handle has a curvaceously shaped outline and is stamped in two identical halves, seamed down the sides and filled (presumably with resin). It is decorated in the Rococo Revival style, with trelliswork between cartouches, and flowers and foliage within scrolls, but has only modest elements of asymmetry at either end. There is a small, separately cast, spherical steel knop between the handle and the slightly concave horn, which tapers outward to a wide, rounded end.

The technique of close plating, used on the horn, involved a small article of iron or steel being first dipped into a sal ammoniac flux and then into molten solder. Silver foil was pressed onto the surface, the object heated again to remelt the solder, and the work finished by burnishing. As sometimes happens with close plated pieces, the silver foil on this horn has blistered.[1]

The maker's mark is poorly struck on the thin, hollow silver of the handle, and only 'J&' is legible. Philip Priestley has suggested that the maker was almost certainly Jones & Crompton of Birmingham, since theirs was the only 'J&_' mark to be registered at Chester between 1863 and 1913.[2] The shoe horn is highly characteristic of their work, as described in 1915: 'a very comprehensive show of the smaller goods in Sterling silver ... The firm are great on manicure sets, and an almost endless variety of ideas in these articles was on view. The pierced cake stands and sweet dishes were very attractive, and also the bowls and vases are well made and finished. Mounted glass goods, too, were a feature, as also were the brush sets.'[3]

The first flowering of the Rococo is found in English silver between the late 1720s and the early 1770s, and William Abdy's candlesticks of 1770 (no.111) are a late but typical example of the style. The Rococo Revival began in England in the early 19th century, probably as a reaction against the Neo-Classicism associated with Revolutionary and Napoleonic France. Like the original style, this affected interior decoration and the decorative arts, but was seen first in silver from the early 1800s. The Rococo Revival rapidly descended the social scale in the 1830s, and remained popular for the rest of the century. The museum's collection includes representative examples from the upper end of the market, dating from various decades between the

88

1800s and the 1870s (nos.113-4, 117, 121). The style was particularly favoured in Edwardian England, as exemplified by the luxurious interior of the *Ritz Hotel* in London, and this shoe horn is a tiny relic of that era.[4] Silver has been made at Birmingham in every phase of the Rococo Revival throughout its history.[5] The Rococo has continued to inspire designers, reaching a pinnacle of brilliance in the art of Rex Whistler during the second quarter of the 20th century, and enduring today at levels both creative and banal.[6]

PROVENANCE: Mr. B.S. James, Connah's Quay, Flintshire; Presented 1985.125

NOTES:
1. Savage, p.78.
2. Philip Priestley, fax, 12 February 2000.
3. *The Jeweller and Metalworker*, 1 June 1915, p.674.
4. Fleming & Honour, pp.693-4; Jervis 1984, p.416; Savage, p.277.
5. e.g. a silver-gilt snuff box of 1816 by Matthew Linwood with cast decoration, and a silver-plated supper dish of 1966 by Barker Ellis with flat-chased ornament (Jones 1981, figs.51, 232).
6. For some of the more imaginative aspects of the 20th century Rococo Revival see Calloway.

SHEFFIELD GOLDSMITHS

The Sheffield Assay Office was opened in 1773, and the town produced a great variety of wares for both domestic and decorative purposes. Until 1854 no goldsmith living within 30 miles of the Sheffield Assay Office could send his work to Chester, and no Sheffield goldsmiths registered at Chester during 1863-85, but 39 did so from 1894-1921.[1]

NOTE:

1. Newman, p.238; Ridgway 1996, pp.21, 53, 63.

James Deakin & Sons Ltd.

This firm of manufacturing silversmiths, platers and cutlers was established in Sheffield *c.*1865 by James Deakin.

By 1878 he was joined in partnership by his three sons, William Pitchford, John and Albert, and the firm was styled James Deakin & Sons, becoming a limited company in 1897. They registered their mark at Sheffield in 1878, and registered ten marks at London between 1888 and 1909. The firm also registered three marks at Chester between 1898 and 1913. They had showrooms in Belfast, Glasgow and Paris by 1886, opened one in London in 1888, and by 1898 had works in both Sheffield and London. The firm closed *c.*1940.[1]

NOTE:

1. Culme, I, pp.114-15; Culme, II, pp.174-5; Jackson, p.450; Phyllis Benedikz, letter, 22 July 1993; Ridgway 1996, p.119.

89

89 PHOTOGRAPH FRAME

James Deakin & Sons Ltd. of Sheffield, hallmarked Chester, 1905-6

Four marks in lower left corner (maker's mark JD over WD)[1]
Height 21.5 cm. (8.45 in.), width 17.7 cm. (6.95 in.)
Total weight 192 g. (6.8 oz.)

Sterling silver on wooden frame. The frame's inner opening is rectangular, with rounded lower corners and concave upper ones. The frame's outer rim has concave sides, swelling outward to highly asymmetrical lower and upper edges. The thin sheet of silver is stamped and chased in low relief in the Art Nouveau style. To either side, poppy heads on delicate stems emerge from sinuous foliage against a textured ground, with flowing wave-like lobes between them. The silver is secured with eight brass pins onto a wooden frame covered in emerald green velvet, and the hinged backing for the photograph is lined with olive green silk. The original hinged stand is missing.

Free-standing silver frames for photographs were popular from the second half of the 19th century, and remain in production today. This example is typical of those from the 1890s and 1900s in having a thin sheet of stamped and chased silver on a velvet covered wooden mount. Its asymmetry, although not rare, is less common and, while a range of styles is found, Art Nouveau was not as popular as Rococo Revival.[2]

This frame exhibits many of the most distinctive features of Art Nouveau, in its asymmetry, its intertwining flowers and leaves, and its swaying and curving lines, all in very shallow relief. Art Nouveau, which affected all the decorative arts, flourished most strongly in the decade 1895-1905 but, as George Savage has noted, 'after 1900 commercial manufacturers increasingly began to adopt the style's motifs in quantity production … and the original impetus was soon lost.'[3]

A visitor to James Deakin & Sons' Sheffield factory in 1886 described the three showrooms as 'replete with every description of goods, from a tea service to a salt spoon, and from a handsome three-tier centrepiece to an inkstand', executed in silver, nickel and Britannia silver, plus mounted glass and pottery. The factory included 'the mixing shop, where the metal is alloyed, and afterwards either made into ingots or rolled between heavy steel rollers into sheets suitable for stamping'. This was done in stamping-presses, after which the silver was chased—the sequence of production used 19 years later for this frame. The visitor in 1886 noted that 'the tendency is to copy the old silver patterns', but the use of Art Nouveau in 1905 indicates a move toward greater stylistic variety.[4]

PROVENANCE: Dr. S. Lang, London; Presented in 1983 1984.1

NOTES:

1. For John Deakin & William Deakin: identified by Phyllis Benedikz, letter, 3 October 1991.
2. For a range of typical photograph frames of 1898-1909 see Holland, pp.222-3.
3. Fleming & Honour, p.43; Jervis 1984, p.33; Newman, p.24; Savage, pp.15-16. For examples of Art Nouveau silver from 1897-1908 see Brett, pp.315-20.
4. Culme, I, pp.114-15. For a Rococo Revival string box of 1900 by James Deakin & Sons Ltd. see Ridgway 1996, pl.37.

KESWICK SCHOOL OF INDUSTRIAL ARTS

The Keswick School of Industrial Arts was founded in 1884 by Canon Hardwicke Drummond Rawnsley (1851-1920), Vicar of Crosthwaite near Keswick, and his wife Edith (d.1916). Inspired by John Ruskin, they began with evening classes in woodcarving, metalwork, drawing and design. The classes were held in the parish room at Crosthwaite until purpose-built premises were opened in 1894. Mrs. Rawnsley superintended the metalwork classes for the first ten years. Harold Stabler was the first-full time teacher from 1898-1900, and continued to contribute designs until at least 1902. Herbert J. Maryon was the first director from 1900-4, followed by Robert Hilton until 1921. In addition to woodcarving and linen production, the school made copper, brass and silverware, and stainless steel was introduced in the 1930s. The school sent its work to the shows of the Arts and Crafts Exhibition Society, and sold its products through the Home Arts and Industries Association and the Rural Industries Co-Operative Society. Early silver does not appear to have been assayed, but the school registered marks at Birmingham in 1888 and 1891, and at Chester in 1898 and 1905. The school registered a mark at London in 1964, but the registration was not renewed in 1976 and the school closed in 1984.[1]

NOTE:

1. Phyllis Benedikz, letter, 22 July 1993; Rudoe, p.61; Shrigley, p.49; Ian Bruce, letters of 18 July 1998 and 11 January 2000.

90 SPOON

Keswick School of Industrial Arts, hallmarked Chester, 1914-15

Four marks on back of bowl (maker's mark Rudoe, pl.132)
Length 17.1 cm. (6.7 in.)
Weight 61 g. (2.15 oz.)

90

91

Sterling silver. The bowl and stem are formed from a single piece of silver. The raised bowl is fig-shaped and slightly up-curved, with an unplanished surface on the back. The flattened hexagonal stem is straight and tapers from the bowl to the applied finial. The plain, circular seal-top finial is cast and turned. 'P719A7' is engraved in tiny letters at the top of the stem.[1]

The Keswick School of Industrial Arts belonged to the Arts and Crafts Movement, which sought to revive handicrafts and improve standards of decorative design in Victorian England. Born in the wake of the 1851 Great Exhibition and in opposition to industrial design and the automatic processes of mass production, the movement is named after the Arts and Crafts Exhibition Society of 1888-99. Although highly influential in the last quarter of the 19th century, the movement came to be regarded as a cul-de-sac after 1900.[2]

The unplanished surface is one of the most characteristic features of Arts and Crafts metalwork. *The Studio* commented on the work of the Guild of Handicrafts, which had been founded by the movement's main organiser, C.R. Ashbee: 'The hammer marks on the plain metal surfaces are retained throughout, for Mr. Ashbee has justly a strong objection to the abrasive process of treating silver with the polishing wheel, or buffers.'[3] Liberty & Co. was one of the firms which sold metalwork in the Arts and Crafts manner, but at a far lower price, their 'Cymric' silver (launched 1899) and 'Tudric' pewter (introduced 1901) being largely machine-made and only then hammered to give a hand-crafted appearance.[4] Their publicity explained the appeal of the hammered finish, 'which secures that individuality which is so attractive, and which is an essential condition to secure the production of a real work of art'.[5]

Produced under Robert Hilton's directorship, this spoon is based on the traditional English form of the 'seal-top', originally made between the mid-15th and late 17th centuries. The fig-shaped bowl and hexagonal stem are copied directly from historical examples, such as William Mutton's spoon of c.1580-4 (no.3). Circular seal-top finials were originally produced for about a century from c.1575, but the cast and turned example on this spoon is further from its source of inspiration. An early 20th-century Keswick School catalogue lists seal-top spoons at 21s. each.[6]

PROVENANCE: Boodle & Dunthorne, Chester; Purchased 1985.82

NOTES:

1. This is not the school's job number and is not necessarily connected with the school (Ian Bruce, letter, 11 January 2000).
2. Fleming & Honour, p.45; Savage, pp.16-17; Culme 1977, p.220.
3. *The Studio*, April 1900, p.165.
4. Culme 1977, pp.220-1; Shrigley, p.50.
5. Quoted in Culme 1977, p.221.
6. The undated catalogue, in the Cumbria Record Office, predates the introduction of stainless steel in the 1930s (Ian Bruce, letter, 11 January 2000).

91 SPOON

Keswick School of Industrial Arts, hallmarked Chester, 1918-19

Four marks on back of bowl (maker's mark Rudoe, pl.132)

Length 15.3 cm. (6 in.)

Weight 36 g. (1.25 oz.)

92

Sterling silver. The raised bowl is fig-shaped, with an unplanished surface on the back. The flat, straight stem is rectangular in section, and clasps both sides of the bowl with two openwork lobes beneath projecting shoulders. The top of the stem is pierced with asymmetrical interlacing, and has additional engraving on the front.

Produced under Robert Hilton's directorship, the fig-shaped bowl is based on English spoons of the mid-15th to late 17th centuries, but the interlacing of the finial is derived from Celtic designs. Celtic art had flourished in England between the 7th and 9th centuries. In Ireland it had continued into the 12th century, and was revived there from the mid-19th century as an expression of national identity. The Celtic Revival in late 19th-century England was seen principally in metalwork, above all in the silver and pewter designed by the Manxman Archibald Knox and mass-produced by Liberty & Co. from the turn of the century (see no.90). The entangled curvilinear surface ornamentation of Celtic art had much in common with elements of Art Nouveau (see no.89), but that style was regarded as suspiciously foreign by the English design establishment, whereas Celtic ornament could be seen as reassuringly British.[1]

The most overt manifestation of the Celtic Revival in Chester-hallmarked silver is found in the work of Iverna Cubbin, the daughter of a Manxman and resident of the Wirral, whose masterpiece is a bowl of 1922, richly decorated with interlacing.[2] An early 20th-century Keswick School catalogue lists cased pairs of Celtic spoons at 37s.[3] A different form of Celtic-inspired interlacing to that on the museum's example is found on a Keswick spoon of 1942.[4]

PROVENANCE: Lowe & Sons, Chester; Purchased with grant aid from the Grosvenor Museum Society 1983.71
EXHIBITED: Chester 1984, no.236, illustrated.

NOTES:

1. Fleming & Honour, pp.165, 483; Harbison, pl.18; Sheehy, fig.73; Jervis 1987, p.19; Savage, p.178.
2. Ridgway 1996, pp.118-19, pl.40.
3. See no.90 note 6.
4. Ian Bruce, letter, 18 July 1998.

92 TEA SPOON

Keswick School of Industrial Arts, hallmarked Chester, 1959-60

Five marks on back of stem near bowl (maker's mark Rudoe, pl.132, and stamped KESWICK)
Length 11.8 cm. (4.65 in.)
Weight 14 g. (0.5 oz.)

Sterling silver. The raised bowl has an elongated fig-shape, extending to the point where it is soldered to the stem. The tapering stem of lozenge-section is shaped at the end to form the finial, with two bands beneath a bud knop. 'P723A71' is engraved in tiny letters at the base of the stem.[1]

This spoon was produced under the directorship of Thomas Hartley, a metalworker at the school from 1905, who was appointed acting manager in 1952 and manager secretary from 1953-62.[2] Its shape is derived from early Roman spoons in silver and bronze,[3] but the finial is based on English acorn-knop spoons of the early 14th to early 16th centuries.[4] These features have been given a streamlined angularity, which imparts an Art Deco flavour to the design.

This design was in production by 1915,[5] and a cased set of six survives from 1917:[6] these early examples differ from the museum's only in having an unplanished bowl and a slightly more rounded end to the knop. An early 20th-century Keswick School catalogue lists three styles of tea spoon available in cased sets of six, and the style of the museum's spoon is almost certainly the 'Etruscan', which cost 37s.6d.[7]

PROVENANCE: Boodle & Dunthorne, Chester; Purchased 1985.83

NOTES:

1. See no.90 note 1.
2. Ian Bruce, letter, 11 January 2000.
3. Dr. Paul Roberts, letter, 21 February 2000.
4. Snodin 1974, p.18.
5. A spoon of 1915, 15.5 cm. long, sold at Phillips, London, 17 November 1998, lot 199 (part).
6. They are 11.7 cm. long (Rudoe, no.132, pl.86).
7. See no.90 note 6.

CHESTER RACE TROPHIES

The City Plate

Adjacent to Chester's western city wall, and bounded by the broad curve of the river Dee, is an expanse of low-lying land called the Roodee. The name means rood island, and it seems probable that there was a cross (or 'rood') on an island in the Dee, which once flowed beside the city wall. By the 16th century the Roodee had become common grazing land and a place of recreation.

In January 1540 the city assembly replaced the annual Shrove Tuesday football match on the Roodee by an archery contest and races on foot and on horseback. This order is usually taken to mark the beginning of the Roodee's use for officially organised horse racing, and thus Chester has a longer continuous history than any other racecourse in the British Isles. Most British horse racing trophies before the Civil War took the form of silver bells, copied from the bell customarily worn by the lead pack horse, which could be hung from the winning horse's tack. The trophy for Chester's Shrove Tuesday race was originally 'a bell of sylver' worth 3s.4d. provided by the Sadlers' Company, but no Chester bells are known to survive.[1]

The Shrove Tuesday race continued until 1609, when the date was changed to St George's Day, 23 April,[2] with three cups as the prizes.[3] This is a very early example of the 17th-century move from bell trophies to cups, a change probably due to the custom of toasting the winner. In 1624 the three silver cups were replaced by one 'faire silver cup' worth £8.[4] The Chester races fell into abeyance during the Civil War and Commonwealth, but the St George's Day race was revived soon after the Restoration of 1660, although its date subsequently varied.

The race course originally stretched from the Water Tower to the Castle, but the present oval course has remained little changed since the early 18th century.[5] In the 18th century each race took up a whole day,[6] and consisted of eliminating heats,[7] which were normally four miles long.[8] This form of racing continued at Chester well into the 19th century,[9] and placed emphasis on the stamina rather than the speed of the horse.

The races became a major social event for the local aristocracy and gentry, as well as for the citizens of Chester. In addition to horse races there were cock fighting contests, assemblies, balls, dinners and theatrical performances.[10]

The trophy for the St George's Day race, still referred to as the St George's Plate in 1785, was also known as the City Plate from at least 1743.[11] Held during Easter Week in 1728, the races took place around St George's Day from 1729, and during the first week of May from 1756. The number of race days grew from three in 1728 to five in 1758, and additional meetings were held in the summer of 1744 and 1754 and in the autumn of 1739, 1755 and 1774-81.[12] The City Plate was jointly funded by the mayor, the city assembly and the 26 trade companies.[13] Worth £30 from at least 1728, it was worth £50 from at least 1768 until 1807, and from at least 1777 comprised a trophy worth £30 with a 'purse' (cash prize) of £20.[14]

Punch bowls were a favourite race prize in England.[15] From at least 1723 up to 1803, and in 1805, the trophy for the City Plate at Chester was a large silver punch bowl, but silver cups were awarded in 1804 and 1806-7.[16] Nine examples survive, all engraved with the city arms, the name of the mayor and the date of presentation.

1723
Punch Bowl, Timothy Lee, London, 1722-3
inscribed: Lawrence Gother Esqr: Mayor, 1723
Private Collection, Cheshire[17]

1762
Punch Bowl, Fuller White, London, 1761-2
inscribed: Thos. Cholmondley, Esq., Mayor 1762
Christie's, London, 4 October 1950, lot 126

1763
Punch Bowl, Fuller White, London, 1762-3
inscribed: Henry Hesketh Esq. Mayor 1763
Grosvenor Museum, no.93

1768
Punch Bowl, John Kentesber, London, 1767-8
inscribed: John Kelsall Esqr. Mayor 1768
Christie's, New York, 15 October 1985, lot 1196[18]

1780
Punch Bowl, Hester Bateman, London, 1779-80
inscribed: Gabriel Smith Esqr. Mayor 1780
With Bracher & Sydenham, Reading, 1951[19]

1785
Punch Bowl, Hester Bateman, London, 1784-5
inscribed: Henry Hegg Esq. Mayor 1785
Grosvenor Museum, no.94

1786
Punch Bowl, Hester Bateman, London, 1785-6

inscribed: John Bennett Esqr. Mayor 1786
Chester Civic Plate[20]

1787
Punch Bowl, Hester Bateman, London, 1786-7
inscribed: Thomas Edwards, Esqre Mayor 1787
Chester Civic Plate

1790
Punch Bowl, Hester Bateman, London, 1789-90
inscribed: Robt. Howell Vaughan Esqr. Mayor 1790
Christie's, New York, 27 October 1992, lot 295[21]

A silver-gilt punch bowl by Thomas Heming, London, 1771-2 (National Museum and Gallery Cardiff), commissioned by Sir Watkin Williams Wynn of Wynnstay in Denbighshire and designed by Robert Adam, is inscribed 'Chester Plates won by Fop in the years 1769 & 1770'.[22]

All the recorded punch bowls were made in London. However, at least some and probably all were supplied through either the Chester Goldsmiths' Company or individual Chester goldsmiths.[23]

The last trophy for the City Plate was presented in 1807, and from 1808 it was replaced by a cash prize of £63.[24] The Municipal Corporations Act of 1835 made it illegal for public funds to be used for such purposes as racing, and the City Plate was last run for in 1836.[25]

A number of new races were gradually introduced, some short-lived but others becoming well-established: the Maiden Plate of £50 from 1780;[26] the Members' Plate of £50 from 1784;[27] the Earl of Chester's Plate of 100 guineas from 1802-19; the Ladies' Plate of £50 from 1803;[28] and His Majesty's Plate of 100 guineas from 1821. Despite being called Plates these new races were for cash prizes, the only trophies being the City Plate and the Gold Cup.[29] The Palatine Stakes and the Dee Stakes were introduced in 1813. The first grandstand was built in 1816, and the Stand Cup was presented between 1817 and 1877.[30] The Tradesmen's Cup was introduced in 1824 and became the Chester Cup in 1893.[31]

Trophies at Chester continued to follow national trends, a splendid example of High Victorian design being the Cheshire Welter Cup of 1846 by Edward Barnard & Sons, comprising a silver sculptural group of two Arabs with a horse beneath a palm tree supporting a bowl.[32] In the 20th century trophies have often been supplied by Chester firms, particularly Lowe & Sons, but they have tended to re-use old cups and add new inscriptions: for example, the Chester Cup of 1939 is a covered cup of 1850 by J.-V. Morel & Co., gilded and mounted by Lowe's.[33] The Chester races now take place on 11 days between May and September.

NOTES:

1. Clifford, pp.44, 153; Bevan, p.15; Moore 1982. According to Clifford, p.32, 'The first [British] racing trophy was offered by the promoters of the Chester Fair in 1512. It took the form of a wooden ball, adorned with flowers. This inexpensive symbol of success was replaced, in the following year, by a silver ball and later by a gold one.' Two small silver bells of 1590 and 1599, which 'doubtless correspond in form to those awarded at Chester at the same time' (Ridgway 1968, p.11, pl.8), survive in Tullie House Museum & Art Gallery, Carlisle.

2. Bevan, p.17. According to Moore 1982, races were held twice a year on Shrove Tuesday and St George's Day from the 16th until the early 18th centuries, when they were amalgamated to form the May meeting. This somewhat unlikely scenario is supported by the Chester Corporation Assembly Book (Chester Record Office, A/B/3/140v,158v), which records in 1706 that 'the race hitherto run on the Roodee on St. George's Day yearly should in future take place on Easter Tuesday, and that the plate which was usually run for on Shrove Tuesday should henceforth be added to the Easter Tuesday's plate.' However, the Assembly Book records in 1708 'that in future the annual race should be run on the Roodee on St. George's day according to ancient custom', implying that there was only one race.

3. The cups were held by the winners for one year (Bevan, p.17). This is said to be the earliest example of the practice of awarding first, second and third prizes (Clifford, p.32) although, according to Moore 1982, the prizes were recorded in 1598 as being a large and a small silver bell and a silver cup.

4. Clifford, p.46; Bevan, p.18. In 1635 this was made by the Chester goldsmith Griffith Edwardes II, who was paid £8 6s.8d. by the city assembly for a 'Cupp waying 23oz.1qr. and a dramme of Gilt plate' (Ridgway 1968, p.37).

5. Moore 1982. It is shown in an engraving of 1728 and an aerial view of 1855, reproduced in Boughton 1997, nos.5, 10.

6. For example, there were five races in five days in 1758, although by 1800 this had increased to eight races over five days (Tushingham, pp.3-4, 70-2).

7. Between two and 12 horses entered the first heat. A distance post was used and, after the initial heats, those horses which had not passed the distance post when the winner had crossed the finishing line were disqualified (Moore 1982). Heats were run until the same horse had won twice: there were usually three heats, but occasionally four or five.

8. Tushingham sometimes specifically records 'Four mile heats', although 'two mile' also appears.

9. A single race without heats was first run in 1791 (Tushingham, p.56) and became increasingly common, and by 1816 eight of the 13 races were run without heats. In 1845 twelve of the sixteen races were run without heats, and by 1856 there were no heats (The Racing Calendar).

10. See Tushingham, pp.32, 37 for descriptions of social activities.

11. The trophy is recorded by Cheny as the St George's Plate in 1728 and 1741; a free Plate of £30 value from 1729-40; and the City Plate from 1743-50. It is recorded by Pond as the Legacy Plate of £30 from 1751-7. It is recorded by Tushingham (covering the period 1758-1815) as the City Plate; as the City

and Corporation Plate in 1793, 1803 and 1805; as the Corporation Plate from 1808-14; but called the City Plate again in 1815.

12. Cheny; Pond; Tushingham. Autumn meetings did not resume until 1845 (*The Racing Calendar*).

13. Kennett, p.38; Moore 1979, p.11; Moore 1982. The Chester Corporation Assembly Book (Chester Record Office, A/B/3/159,212) records in 1708 that owners had to pay to enter their horses: 40s. if only two horses ran, 30s. if three horses were entered, and 20s. each if there were more than three horses. The Assembly Book records in 1714 that the companies should contribute toward the St George's Plate, 'The sums were not to be less than they had usually contributed for the greatest part of the last twenty years' and 'the Mayor and Citizens would ... pay £10 a year out of the Treasury towards the plate'. The Goldsmiths' Company subscribed 'Five shillings towards St. George's Plate' in 1670 (Ridgway 1968, p.87), and paid 15s. 'for the Race plate' annually from 1749 until well into the 19th century (Ridgway 1985, p.54). See also note 23.

14. Tushingham records (with slightly varying phraseology): 'A Subscription Purse of 20l. added to the Annual City Plate of 30l.' from 1777-9; 'The Annual City Plate of 30l. with a Purse of 20l. given by the Corporation' in 1781-91, 1798, 1800, 1802 and 1806-7; and 'The City Plate, value 30l. with a purse of 20l.' in 1796. The Chester Corporation Treasurers' Account Book (Chester Record Office, TAB/9) consistently records a £30 trophy with a £20 purse from 1798-1807.

15. An early example of a punch bowl as race prize is the Basingstoke monteith of 1688 (Clifford, pp.48-50).

16. For the 1796 punch bowl see Ridgway 1985, p.102. The Corporation Account Book (see note 14) records punch bowls in 1798-1803 and 1805, but cups in 1804 and 1806-7 (TAB/9/4v, 8r, 13v, 24v, 34v, 44r, 53v, 63v, 73v, 84v). By the second quarter of the 18th century silver punch bowls were competing with less costly ceramic versions, and they are uncommon from *c.*1775 (Wees, p.43; Clayton 1985 I, p.287).

17. Exhibited Chester 1951, no.81, pl.XVII.

18. Grimwade 1974, pl.11.

19. Advertisement in *Apollo*, January 1951, p.vii. Illustrated Clayton 1985 I, pl.420, and Holland, p.78, both wrongly describing the hallmark as 1784.

20. Moore 1979, pl.13.

21. Previously unsold Sotheby's, London, 2 June 1992, lot 148.

22. Evans & Fairclough, pl.55.

23. The Goldsmiths' Company Minute Book (Chester Record Office, G12/2) records in 1703: 'we have Annually contributed to the Plates given by this Citty to be run for upon the Rood Dee, wch said Plates have hitherto been sold by one or two psons of said Company ... [in future] the said Plates shall be annually sold by each Brother in his Turn according to Seniority'. The Goldsmiths' Company Account Book (Chester Record Office, G12/5) refers to the supply of 'the Race Plate' in 1759 and 'the Bowl' for 13 years from 1777-89. The punch bowl for 1796 was made by the Batemans and sold to the Corporation by George Lowe I (Lowe Day Book, quoted in Ridgway 1985, p.102). The Corporation Account Book (see note 16 for page references) records the suppliers of the last 10 trophies: George Walker I in 1798, 1800-1, 1803 and 1806; Robert Bowers I in 1799, 1804 and 1807; George Lowe I in 1802 and 1805.

24. The Corporation Account Books (Chester Record Office, TAB/9-11) consistently record £63 'Paid to the Winner of the City Plate' from 1808-36.

25. 'A Purse, value 80gs, in specie (in lieu of the Annual City Plate) the gift of a portion of the Town Council and its Officers' was run for in 1837, and a similar prize of 60 sovereigns was offered the following year but lapsed thereafter (*The Racing Calendar*).

26. Run in 1780, 1783-1806, 1808-9, 1811-24, 1826-8 and 1835-6 (Tushingham; *The Racing Calendar*).

27. Run in 1784 and 1785; as the City Members' Plate of £50 run in 1806 and 1808, then raised to 60 guineas and run in 1811, 1815 and most years from 1821 until at least 1856 (Tushingham; *The Racing Calendar*).

28. Run in 1803-4 and annually from 1818 until at least 1856 (Tushingham; *The Racing Calendar*).

29. This is graphically illustrated in a printed card for the 1791 races, reproduced in Bevan, p.23.

30. Hanshall, p.202. The original grandstand is depicted in a painting of 1843 and a lithograph of 1858, reproduced in Boughton 1997, nos.199, 200. The grandstand was enlarged several times later in the 19th century, rebuilt in 1899-1900, and again in 1985-8. The Stand Cup was called the Gold Cup in 1817; the Stand Gold Cup in 1818 and 1820; the Stand Cup in 1819, 1821-37 and 1840-41; the Stand Cup Sweepstakes in 1838; and the Dee Stand Stakes from 1842 (*The Racing Calendar*). The Stand Cup of 1817 was a silver-gilt two-handled cup and cover by William Bateman I, London, 1816 (illustrated in *The Cheshire Sheaf*, 5th series, no.136, March 1978). The Stand Cup of 1819 was a silver-gilt two-handled cup and cover by William Bateman I, London, 1818 (Sotheby's, London, 18 March 1982, lot 85). The Stand Cup of 1835 survives in a private collection in Cheshire.

31. In 1830 the Tradesmen's Cup was 'a beautiful salver, richly gilt on both sides, exquisitely chased in the middle, and having a rich classical border' (Bevan, p.36). It was called the Tradesmen's Plate from 1834.

32. Assayed at London in 1846, 50 cm. high, engraved with the arms of Chester and inscribed 'Cheshire Welter Cup 1846 / Stewards / The Marquis of Normanby / The Earl of Chesterfield / J. Stanley, Esq.' (Private Collection, Dumfriesshire). It is stylistically very close to the much larger Russian Imperial Ascot Trophy of the same year by Hunt & Roskill (Clifford, p.63).

33. Private Collection, on loan to Grosvenor Museum.

93 PUNCH BOWL

Fuller White, London, 1762-3

Four marks beneath base (maker's mark
Grimwade no.733)
Height 22.9 cm. (9 in.), maximum diameter 33.5
cm. (13.2 in.)
Weight 2,501 g. (88.2 oz.)

Sterling silver. The stepped, spreading circular foot is
raised and has an applied foot-ring. The raised hemispherical bowl is incurved slightly below the applied
rim moulding. The side of the bowl is engraved with
the ancient arms of the City of Chester within an elaborate, asymmetrical Rococo cartouche. It is engraved in
script either side of the armorial: 'Henry Hesketh Esqr,
/ Mayor 1763'.

The 1763 City Plate comprised this silver punch
bowl worth £30 with a cash prize of £20. The
corporation accounts record in August 1763, 'paid
the City's contribution to St. George's plate' £10 and
'paid the Leavelookers Fees to Do. [ditto]' 6s.8d.[1]
The remaining cost was met by the trade companies
and the mayor.[2] The punch bowl was probably
supplied to the mayor by the Chester Goldsmiths'
Company.

The City Plate was presented to the winner by the
mayor, Henry Hesketh, a wine merchant. Born c.1715,
he became a freeman of Chester and was elected a
councilman in 1746, serving as sheriff 1749-50. He
was elected an alderman in 1762 and served as mayor
1762-3. He had already been involved with the races
just before his mayoralty, when in May 1762 he was
appointed to 'a committee to view the condition of
the starting chair and distance chair on the Roodee'.
On his death in 1788 he bequeathed £120 to endow
one of Chester's gownsmen or pensioners.[3]

Tushingham (p.10) records the race on Wednesday
4 May 1763:
'For the CITY PLATE
J. Smith Barry, Esqr's b h Schemer, 2 1 1
Mr. Egerton's ch h Rattlesnake, 1 2 2'

This punch bowl was won by the Hon. John Smith-
Barry (1725-84), the youngest son of James Barry, 4th
Earl of Barrymore. In 1746 he married the heiress Dorothy
Smith of Weald Hall, Essex, adding her surname to his
own, and building Belmont Hall, Cheshire in 1749-55. In
addition to the 1763 City Plate his horses also won the
Gold Cup in 1763, 1765, 1769 and 1771, and six other
races at Chester between 1754 and 1781. He was a leading
member of the Tarporley Hunt Club, won the Doncaster
Cup in 1773, and owned the famous hound Bluecap.[4]

The vast majority of early 18th-century punch bowls have handles, including that which formed the 1723 City Plate, but handles largely disappear after 1730.[5] The punch bowl which forms the 1763 City Plate closely follows the pattern established by the late 1720s, and is thus somewhat archaic for its date.[6] The 1768 City Plate has a bowl of very similar shape but on a much simpler foot, its even more exuberant Rococo cartouche compensating for this plainness.

Fuller White was apprenticed to Edward Feline in 1734. In 1744 he became free and entered his first mark as a largeworker. He was in partnership with John Fray from 1745, but this was apparently dissolved by 1748. He was elected to the Livery in 1750 and died in 1775.[7] Fuller White also made a very similar punch bowl for the previous year's City Plate in 1762.

PROVENANCE: Presented by Henry Hesketh, mayor of Chester, and won by the Hon. John Smith-Barry of Belmont Hall, Cheshire, in 1763; With Bracher & Sydenham, Reading, in 1953;[8] Boodle & Dunthorne, Chester, 1973; Purchased with the assistance of the V&A Purchase Grant Fund, National Art Collections Fund, Cheshire County Council, Boodle & Dunthorne 1974-77

EXHIBITED: Chester 1980; Manchester 1983, no.72.

PUBLISHED: NACF Report 1974, no.2537; Thomas, p.16; Moore 1979, p.11; Schroder 1992, p.36.

NOTES:

1. Chester Corporation, Treasurers' Account Book (Chester Record Office, TAB/7). The two leavelookers, elected annually, were regarded as the leaders of the 40 common councilmen: their name derives from one of the tolls they collected, a maritime tax called leave-lookerage (Lewis & Harrison, p.14).

2. For example, the Goldsmiths' Company Account Book (Chester Record Office, G12/5) records on 29 May 1763, 'pd. towards the Race plate' 15s. Henry Hesketh, the mayor in 1762-3, was well able to afford a substantial contribution, having lent £1,500 to the city in 1758 (Chester Record Office, CHD/6/33).

3. Hanshall, p.179; Gerrard Barnes, report, 12 January 2000; Chester Corporation, Fourth Assembly Book (Chester Record Office, A/B/4/116, 199, 201); Bennett 1908, p.326; Brown, p.L. The silver badge which commemorates this benefaction, made by Robert Bowers I at Chester in 1800-1, is on loan to the Grosvenor Museum from the Trustees of the Chester Municipal Charities.

4. Treuherz, p.56; Moore 1982; de Figueiredo & Treuherz, pp.31, 34; Sotheby's auction catalogue, London, 9 July 1959, lot 144. See also the following discussion of the Gold Cup.

5. Clayton 1985 I, p.287.

6. It is very close to London-made punch bowls of 1726 by George Wickes and of 1728 by Edward Vincent (Davis, no.34; Wees, no.48).

7. Grimwade, p.698. A tankard of 1760 and a saucepan of 1766 are at Williamsburg (Davis, nos.53, 165).

8. Illustrated advertisement, *Country Life*, 20 August 1953, p.578.

94 PUNCH BOWL

Hester Bateman, London, 1784-5

Five marks beneath base (maker's mark Grimwade no.960)
Height 31.4 cm. (12.4 in.), maximum diameter 34.2 cm. (13.5 in.)
Weight 2,234 g. (78.8 oz.)

Sterling silver. The stepped, spreading circular foot is raised in two sections and has an applied horizontal foot-ring. The inverted pear-shaped bowl is raised, incurving slightly below the applied rim moulding. The side of the bowl is engraved with the heraldic achievement of the City of Chester (as granted in 1580). It is engraved in script either side of the armorial: 'Henry Hegg / Esqr. Mayor 1785'.

The 1785 City Plate comprised this silver punch bowl worth £30 with a cash prize of £20. The corporation accounts record on 6 May 1785, 'Paid the Leavelookers Contribution to Saint George's Plate' 6s.9d., 'The City's do. [ditto]' £10, and 'Paid with the Punch Bowl' £20 (i.e. the cash prize).[1] The remaining cost was met by the trade companies and the mayor.[2] The punch bowl was supplied to the mayor by the Chester Goldsmiths' Company. It is one of 13 bowls acquired for the company by Richard Richardson IV (see no.49 for a biographical note): the profit was shared between the company and 'Mr Richardson for his trouble sending & paying for it'.[3]

The City Plate was presented to the winner by the mayor, Henry Hegg, a druggist. Admitted to the freedom of the city in 1758 and elected a councilman in 1762, he served as sheriff 1770-1, treasurer 1781-3 and mayor 1784-5. He died in 1792.[4]

Tushingham (p.46) records the race on Wednesday 4 May 1785:
'The Annual City Plate, value 30l. with 20l. given by the Corporation. - Four-mile heats.

Mr. Roylance's ch h Trimmer, 5 yrs		4 4 1 1
Mr. Wilbraham's b h Cheshire-Round,		1 5 2 2
Mr. Lloyd's ch h Tommy, aged		3 1 4 3
Col. Radcliffe's b g Johnny-lad, aged		2 3 3
Mr. Gatfield's b h Joe Andrews, aged		5 2 dr'

The Mr. Roylance, whose horse won the trophy, was probably James Roylance of Newton Manor House, Middlewich, Cheshire, who died in 1812 aged 67.[5] The 1785 City Plate was his only win at Chester.

This is one of five surviving Hester Bateman punch bowls which formed the annual City Plate between 1780 and 1790. The 1796 City Plate was by Peter & Ann Bateman,[6] and it is reasonable to assume that the Bateman family firm supplied a punch bowl each year

94

between at least 1780 and 1796. The 1780 City Plate has a compressed inverted pear-shaped bowl with an elaborate Rococo cartouche to the armorial, a feature seen in the surviving City Plates of the 1760s and so outmoded by 1780 as to suggest that it may have been deliberately archaic. The four other bowls are very similar to each other: their only variations are beading to the rim and foot-ring of the 1786 and 1787 ones, and a depression to the spreading foot of the 1787 and 1790 examples. All four have near-identical armorials by the same hand, which may suggest that they were engraved in Chester.[7]

Hester Bateman, née Neden, was born in 1708. In 1732 she married John Bateman, a chainmaker, who died in 1760 leaving her all his property. She entered her first mark as a smallworker in 1761, and subsequent marks as a spoonmaker and plateworker. She retired in 1790 and died in 1794.

Her sons Peter (see no.96) and Jonathan became goldsmiths.[8]

PROVENANCE: Presented by Henry Hegg, mayor of Chester, and won by Mr. Roylance (probably James Roylance of Newton Manor House, Cheshire) in 1785; Major A.P.R. Rolt, M.C.; Sotheby's, London, 2 June 1962, lot 27; Purchased in 1962 with grant aid from the National Art Collections Fund, Mr. G.D. Lockett; Accessioned as 1998.15

EXHIBITED: Chester 1973 I.

PUBLISHED: *Sotheby's Annual Review 1961-2*, illustrated p.115; NACF Report 1962, no.2109; Banister 1973, p.1877, fig.4; Thomas, p.11; Moore 1979, p.14, pl.13; Chapel & Gere, illustrated p.145; Schroder 1992, p.36.

Notes:

1. Chester Corporation, Treasurers' Account Book (Chester Record Office, TAB/8).

2. For example, the Goldsmiths' Company Account Book (Chester Record Office, G12/5) records a 15s. 'Subscription for the plate' in 1785. The mayor in 1785 probably made a comparatively modest contribution.

3. Goldsmiths' Company Account Book (Chester Record Office, G12/5): the company's profit in 1785 was £2 2s.

4. Hanshall, p.179; *Sotheby's Annual Review 1961-2*, p.115; Chester Corporation, Treasurers' Account Book (Chester Record Office, TAB/8); Bennett 1908, p.420; Gerrard Barnes, report, 12 January 2000.

5. Ormerod, III, p.244.

6. Ridgway 1985, p.102.

7. The inverted pear-shaped form, much enriched, was later used by Paul Storr for a pair of punch bowls in 1814 (Penzer 1971, p.185).

8. Grimwade, p.433. For a fuller study of her work see Shure.

The Gold Cup

In 1677 Sir Thomas Grosvenor, 3rd Baronet, of Eaton Hall near Chester, married a London heiress, Mary Davies. This marriage united the already substantial Grosvenor fortunes, founded on land and lead-mines, with vast London estates, which were subsequently developed as Mayfair, Belgravia and Pimlico. As the principal landowner in and around Chester, the Grosvenors were highly influential in the city and were great benefactors, a situation which, as dukes of Westminster since 1874, continues in large measure to this day.[1] Between 1741 and 1820, the head of the Grosvenor family annually presented a gold cup as a prize at the Chester races.[2] The practice was begun by Sir Robert Grosvenor (1695-1755), 6th Baronet, and was continued by his son and grandson.

In 1734, the year after his accession to the baronetcy, Sir Robert Grosvenor presented a £10 Plate and a £30 Plate at the Chester Races, and these prizes continued until 1740.[3] Between 1741 and 1800 the prize was a gold tumbler cup worth £50.[4] Gold tumbler cups had appeared as race trophies by the late 17th century, and were *de luxe* versions of the drinking vessels that would have been used at *al fresco* meals beside the race track.[5] Eighteenth-century gold trophies were usually made with the maximum weight and the minimum amount of workmanship because the recipient almost invariably sent them straight to be melted and turned into cash.[6] The three extant Chester Gold Cups,[7] detailed below, are of great rarity, since only three other English gold tumbler cups before 1830 are known to survive.[8]

1744

Gold Tumbler Cup, Richard Bayley, London, 1743-4
inscribed: The Gift of Sir Robert Grosvenor Bart. 1744 / Won at Chester by Darling

National Trust, Harpur-Crewe Collection, Calke Abbey, Derbyshire[9]

1766

Gold Tumbler Cup, probably Joseph Steward II, London, 1765-6
inscribed: The Gift of the Right Honourable Lord Grosvenor to the City of Chester 1766
Grosvenor Museum, no.95

1792

Gold Tumbler Cup, Peter & Ann Bateman, London, 1791-2
inscribed: The Gift of the Right Honble Earl Grosvenor to the City of Chester 1792
Private Collection, on loan to Victoria and Albert Museum, London[10]

A gold cup and cover by John Parker & Edward Wakelin, London, 1772-3 (Manchester City Art Galleries), commissioned by the Hon. John Smith-Barry of Belmont Hall in Cheshire, was made from the four gold tumbler cups which his horses had won at Chester in 1763, 1765, 1769 and 1771.[11]

The three surviving Grosvenor gold cups were all made in London. However, the Eaton Hall Accounts and the Chester Plate Duty Books suggest that some, at least, of these cups were supplied through Chester goldsmiths.[12] This was certainly the case with George Lowe I, who established his business in 1791 and acted as agent for the Bateman family in Chester.[13]

The cups became lighter as the price of gold rose,[14] and the tumbler cup was superseded by a two-handled cup, which had been the most popular form of race trophy since the 1690s. From 1801 Earl Grosvenor's trophy was a silver or silver-gilt two-handled cup, but it was still sometimes called the Gold Cup.[15] The value of this prize, originally £50, rose to £60 in 1808, 60 guineas in 1809, and £70 in 1811. Twelve of these later Gold Cups survive.

1802

Silver Two-Handled Cup and Cover, Peter, Ann & William Bateman, overstruck by George Lowe I, London, 1801-2
inscribed: The Gift of the Right Honble Earl Grosvenor to the City of Chester. 1802
Later converted into a tea urn
Chester Civic Plate[16]

1806

Silver-Gilt Two-Handled Cup and Cover, Peter & William Bateman, London, 1805-6
inscribed: Gift of the Rt. Honble Earl Grosvenor to the City of Chester, 1806
With J.C. Vander (Antiques) Ltd., London, 1984

1808
Silver-Gilt Two-Handled Cup and Cover, Peter & William Bateman, London, 1807-8
Sotheby's, London, 10 October 1946, lot 78; purchased by Kaye[17]

1809
Silver-Gilt Two-Handled Cup and Cover, Peter & William Bateman, London, 1809-10
Sotheby's, London, 10 October 1946, lot 79; purchased by Kaye

1812
Silver-Gilt Two-Handled Cup and Cover, Peter & William Bateman, London, 1811-12
inscribed: Chester Races / Robt Bowers Esq Mayor 1812
Private Collection, London

1814
Silver-Gilt Two-Handled Cup and Cover, Peter & William Bateman, London, 1813-14
inscribed: Chester Races, 1814
Grosvenor Museum, no.96

1815
Silver-Gilt Two-Handled Cup and Cover, William Bateman I, London, 1815-16
inscribed: Chester Races, 1815
Grosvenor Museum, no.97

1816
Silver-Gilt Two-Handled Cup and Cover, William Bateman I, London
At Oulton Park, Cheshire in 1953[18]

1817
Silver-Gilt Two-Handled Cup and Cover, William Bateman I, London, 1816-17
Sotheby's, London, 10 October 1946, lot 80; purchased by Kaye[19]

1818
Silver-Gilt Two-Handled Cup and Cover, William Bateman I, London, 1817-18
Sotheby's, London, 10 October 1946, lot 81; purchased by W. Walter

1819
Silver-Gilt Two-Handled Cup and Cover, William Bateman I, London, 1818-19
inscribed: Chester Races 1819
Castle Museum, Nottingham

1820
Silver-Gilt Two-Handled Cup and Cover, William Bateman I, London
At Oulton Park, Cheshire in 1953[20]

The last Gold Cup was presented by Earl Grosvenor in 1820, after which it became a cash prize.[21]

NOTES:

1. Egerton, p.66; Ridgway 1985, p.53.
2. It was run for at the May races, except for the years 1774-80, when it formed the highlight of the short-lived Autumn meetings.
3. Cheny 1734, p.35. The same prizes are recorded in Cheny 1735-40, but without reference to their presentation by Sir Robert Grosvenor. The £10 Plate in 1738 was a London-assayed silver waiter of 1737, recorded in a 1950s inventory of the Williams-Wynn silver but now unlocated (Cheny 1738; Oliver Fairclough, letter, 17 June 1999).
4. Cheny 1741, p.13. The race for the Gold Cup in 1779 was not run because only one horse was entered (Tushingham, p.35).
5. Wills, p.155. A gold tumbler was won at Newmarket in 1691 (Clayton 1985 I, p.448), and 'A gold cup, which may have been a tumbler cup, was mentioned as a Chester race prize in 1700' (Moore 1987, p.61).
6. Michael Clayton, letter, 17 March 1978.
7. The Gold Cup for 1774 is said to survive in Clayton 1985 I, p.295, but it is not recorded in Jones 1907 or Grimwade 1951 III, and no illustration or sale record has yet been found. It is described as 'of beaker form. The sides, tapering inwards from the base, give a solid if inelegant effect' (Clayton 1985 I, p.33).
8. Grimwade 1951 III, p.89, lists a 17th-century English gold tumbler cup owned by the Worshipful Company of Cooks. A gold tumbler cup by Pierre Harache, London, 1702, is in the Museum of Fine Arts, Boston (Glynne, pl.1). A London-made gold tumbler cup of 1766, commissioned by the Rev. William Sandys, a Fellow of All Souls College, Oxford, was with Spink & Son Ltd., London in 1970 (Moore 1987, p.61; Thomas Seaman, letter, 8 October 1999).
9. National Trust: East Midlands Region, telephone conversation, 17 November 1999.
10. Sold Christie's, London, 16 October 1963, Lot 172. Illustrated Wills, fig.93; Clayton 1985 I, fig.705 (wrongly describing hallmark as 1792); Clayton 1985 II, p.228 fig.1 (wrongly described as the Chester Gold Cup for 1791).
11. Illustrated Treuherz, no.43.
12. The Eaton Hall Accounts contain references to three gold cups, costing £50 and run for at Chester, purchased from Richard Richardson II in 1762 and from Joseph Duke I in 1762 and 1776 (Ridgway 1996, p.147). The Grosvenor archives in the Eaton Estate Office and the City of Westminster Archives Centre unfortunately do not record the expenditure on race trophies in 1766, 1814 or 1815. The Chester Plate Duty Books record five gold cups, presented for assaying at Chester by Richard Richardson IV in 1785, 1787, 1789 and 1790, and by George Walker I in 1791, just before the May races and similar in weight to the surviving cups (Ridgway 1996, pp.96, 101). Silver tumbler cups were made by Richard Richardson II, Richard Richardson IV, George Walker I and George Lowe I but, although they were technically capable of making gold tumbler cups, all the Grosvenor gold cups were probably made in London.

13. Ridgway 1985, pp.54, 101. The 1793 Gold Cup was made by Peter & Ann Bateman but sold to Earl Grosvenor for £50 by George Lowe I (Ridgway 1985, p.54). The 1802 Gold Cup was made by Peter, Ann & William Bateman but overstruck by George Lowe I.

14. The 1744 cup is 4 in. high. The 1766 cup is 3.35 in. high and weighs 11.8 oz., but the 1792 cup is 3.5 in. high and weighs 9 oz. 11 dwt.

15. Recorded by Tushingham as: 'A Silver Cup' in 1801, 1807 and 1813; 'The Gold Cup' in 1802 (although the surviving cup is silver), 1808 and 1812; 'A Piece of Silver Plate' in 1803-6; 'A Cup' in 1809 and 1810; and 'The Cup' in 1811, 1814 and 1815. It is recorded in *The Racing Calendar* as 'A Cup' from 1816-20. By the 19th century many so-called 'Gold Cups' were in fact silver-gilt (Clayton 1985 I, p.296).

16. Moore 1979, pl.9. The hot iron rod holder has no date letter, but bears the mark which Paul Storr registered in 1807 (Ridgway 1985, p.110).

17. Jones 1935, pl.VI. According to Jones 1935, p.16, the Chester Gold Cup for 1807 was owned by Sir Watkin Williams-Wynn in 1935. However, whilst the five cups for 1808, 1809, 1817, 1818 and 1819 appear in the Williams-Wynn silver inventory of 1885, and were sold at Sotheby's in 1946, the 1807 cup is not mentioned, nor does it feature in a 1950s inventory of the silver remaining in the family (Oliver Fairclough, letter, 17 June 1999).

18. Recorded in Oulton Inventory in 1953 (Sir John Grey Egerton, letter, 5 August 1999).

19. For the 1817 and 1818 cups, Sotheby's followed Jones 1935, p.16, in wrongly giving the maker as William Bell.

20. Recorded in Oulton Inventory in 1953 (Sir John Grey Egerton, letter, 5 August 1999).

21. *The Racing Calendar* is fairly consistent in its terminology, using the word 'value' when referring to trophies and 'of' for cash prizes. It records 'A Cup, value 70l. the gift of Earl Grosvenor' up to and including 1820, but thereafter: 'Earl Grosvenor's Plate of 70l.' in 1821; 'Seventy Pounds, the gift of the Right Hon. Earl Grosvenor' in 1822-7 and 1830; 'A Cup, value 70l. in specie, the gift of the Right Hon. Earl Grosvenor' in 1828; 'A Cup, value 70l. the gift of the Right Hon. Earl Grosvenor' in 1829 (it is highly unlikely that a trophy was presented after a gap of eight years, and it is more probable that the words 'in specie', meaning 'in coin', were accidentally omitted from the record); 'A gold Cup, value 70 sov. in specie, the gift of the Right Hon. Earl Grosvenor' in 1831; 'A Plate of 70l. the gift of the Marquis of Westminster' in 1832-4; 'A Plate, value 70l. in specie, the gift of the Marquis of Westminster' in 1835; and 'The Marquis of Westminster's Plate, value 100 sov. in specie' in 1836, 1838 and from 1840 until at least 1856.

95 GOLD TUMBLER CUP

Probably Joseph Steward II, London, 1765-6

Four marks beneath base (maker's mark Grimwade no.3682)

Height 8.5 cm. (3.35 in.), diameter 9.3 cm. (3.65 in.)

Weight 335 g. (11.8 oz.)

See Colour Plate VII

22 carat gold. The cup is raised, with an hemispherical base and slightly incurved sides. The side is engraved with the heraldic achievement of Richard, 1st Baron Grosvenor, with an almost symmetrical Rococo frame to the shield. It is engraved in script either side of the armorial: 'The Gift of the Right Honourable Lord / Grosvenor to the City of Chester 1766'.

Lord Grosvenor paid £50 for this cup, which may have been supplied through a Chester goldsmith although it was made in London. Richard (1731-1802) was the son of Sir Robert Grosvenor, whom he succeeded as 7th Baronet in 1755. He became a freeman of Chester in 1752, M.P. for the city 1754-61 and mayor 1759-60. In 1761 he was created Baron Grosvenor of Eaton and was Cupbearer at the Coronation of George III. In 1764 he married Henrietta (died 1828), daughter of Henry Vernon of Hilton Park, Staffordshire, from whom he separated in 1770 following her adultery with the King's brother, H.R.H. The Duke of Cumberland. In 1784 he was created Viscount Belgrave and Earl Grosvenor. He was one of the richest men in England and a great art collector, but his greatest enthusiasm was racing and the breeding of racehorses. His horses won his own Gold Cup in 1776 and 16 other races at Chester between 1769 and 1789. He also won the Oaks five times between 1781 and 1799 and the Derby three times between 1790 and 1794.[1]

Tushingham records the race on Thursday 8 May 1766:

'A GOLD CUP, given by the Right Hon. Ld. Grosvenor, six years old, was run for.

Mr. Hutton's b h Lofty,	1	1
Mr. Brandlin's b h Helvidius,	2	4
Mr. Southeron's bl h Cherokee	4	2
Mr. Price's b h Gamester	5	3
P. Egerton, Esqr's r h Aurihanus,	3	dr'[2]

This Gold Cup was won by John Hutton (1691-1768), son of John Hutton of Marske Hall near Richmond, Yorkshire. He married firstly in 1720 Barbara (died 1723), daughter and co-heiress of Thomas Barker of York, and secondly in 1726 Elizabeth (died 1739), daughter of James Conyers, Lord Darcy of Navan. He built the stables at Marske, which he had inherited on his father's death in 1730. His horses won gold cups at Newcastle in 1730 and at Edinburgh *c.*1755, the Chester City Plate in 1762,

and a silver-gilt trophy at Richmond in 1764. Lofty, the horse which won the 1766 Chester Gold Cup, also won the Chester City Plate in 1768 for his son John Hutton (1730-83).[3]

This is one of the three surviving gold tumbler cups from the 60 presented by the Grosvenors at the Chester races. It is larger than most tumbler cups,[4] and the quality of the engraving surpasses that on the 1792 Gold Cup, making this one of the finest of all tumbler cups.

To celebrate 1900 years of Chester's recorded history in 1979, Mappin & Webb of 32 Eastgate Row, Chester, offered limited edition replicas of this cup, 250 in sterling silver with gilt linings 2.25 inches high and 19 in silver-gilt 3.5 inches high.

Grimwade lists mark no.3682 as 'Joseph Steward II(?)'. The son of Joseph Steward I, he was apprenticed to Richard Pargeter in 1746 and turned

over to Richard Bayley (the maker of the 1744 Gold Cup) in 1751. His freedom is unrecorded, but he entered his first mark as a largeworker in 1755 and subsequent marks as a smallworker. He entered his last mark in 1783. The same mark as that on the gold tumbler cup is also found on a tankard of 1765 and a hot water jug of the following year.[5]

PROVENANCE: Presented by Richard, 1st Baron Grosvenor (later 1st Earl Grosvenor), and won by John Hutton of Marske Hall, Yorkshire, in 1766; By descent to the executors of John T. D'Arcy Hutton of Marske Hall; Christie's, London, 4 October 1950, lot 148; Mrs. Ian G. Menzies; Christie's, London, 10 March 1965, lot 105; Spink & Son Ltd., London, 1975; Purchased with grant aid from the V&A Purchase Grant Fund, National Art Collections Fund, London Goldsmiths' Company, Duke of Westminster through the

Westminster Foundation, Viscount Leverhulme, James Walker Ltd., Boodle & Dunthorne and a public appeal 1978.96

EXHIBITED: Chester 1951, no.99, pl.XXI; Chester 1979 II, no.21; Manchester 1983, no.74.

PUBLISHED: Grimwade 1951 III, p.86 no.XXIX, illustrated p.84; *Christie's Review of the Year 1964-65*, pp.134-5, illustrated; Grimwade, no.3682; Spink, *Octagon*, vol.13, no.1, Spring 1976, illustrated p.6; NACF Report 1978, no.2721, illustrated; *The Cheshire Sheaf*, 5th series, no.168, August 1978, illustrated; Moore 1979, p.14; Moore 1982, illustrated; Ridgway 1985, p.53; Moore 1987, p.62, illustrated p.60; Schroder 1992, p.36, fig.2; Callaghan, illustrated p.33; Ridgway 1996, p.148.

NOTES:

1. Hanshall, p.179; Complete Peerage, vol.6, pp.209-10; Bennett 1908, p.347. For his art collecting see Boughton 1992 II, pp.39-40.
2. According to a racing broadsheet (quoted in *Christie's Review 1964-65*, p.135), Lofty was ridden by 'John Hutchurs in stripe'.
3. Mr. M.Y. Ashcroft, letter, 27 July 1999; Christie's auction catalogue, London, 4 October 1950, lots 122-50. The Newcastle gold cup illustrated Grimwade 1951 II, p.13 no.XX; the Edinburgh gold cup illustrated Grimwade 1951 III, p.83 no.XXVII.
4. It is bigger than the largest known examples of Chester-made tumbler cups (no.29, 7.4 cm high), but smaller than a 9.6 cm high London-made cup of 1720 by John White (Clayton 1985 I, p.448).
5. Grimwade, no.3682, pp.670-1.

96 SILVER-GILT CUP AND COVER

Peter & William Bateman, London, 1813-14

Five marks on side of body (makers' mark Grimwade no.2143). Three marks on bezel of cover: date letter, lion passant, makers' mark
Total height 32.5 cm. (12.8 in.), width across handles 32.2 cm. (12.7 in.), diameter 20.8 cm. (8.2 in.)
Total weight 1,987 g. (70.1 oz.)

See Colour Plate VII

Sterling silver, gilt.[1] The stepped, spreading circular foot is raised, and has a cast and applied inner border of tiny diamond facets between bands of braiding. The foot rises to a short stem with a chased calyx of matted acanthus leaves beneath an applied moulding. The hemispherical bowl is raised, and its lower part chased with a calyx of matted alternating stiff and acanthus leaves. In the centre of one side is a cast and applied oval medallion encircled by husks, containing the heraldic achievement of Robert, 2nd Earl Grosvenor on a slightly convex matted ground.[2] The other side is engraved in Old English lettering, 'Chester Races. / 1814', within a matching cast and applied oval of husks. The upper edge has a cast and applied frieze of Greek key pattern on a matted ground between bands of braiding. Each handle has cast decoration on a matted ground, with vine branches on the two curved sections and an oval patera of acanthus leaves on the straight section between. The lower part of the handle has a cast and applied stiff leaf with a palmette terminal. The raised, domed lid has an applied bezel and rim, and rises to a chased calyx of matted alternating stiff and acanthus leaves. The cast finial is in the form of a naturalistic wheat sheaf, a feature common to the arms of both the City of Chester and the Grosvenor family.

Lord Grosvenor paid £70 for this cup, which was almost certainly supplied through George Lowe I of Chester (see no.53 for a biographical note). Robert (1767-1845) was the son of the 1st Earl Grosvenor. He became a freeman of Chester in 1783, was M.P. for East Looe 1788-90 and for Chester 1790-1802, and was mayor of Chester 1807-8. He served as a Lord of the Admiralty 1789-91 and became a Privy Councillor in 1793. In 1794 he married Eleanor (1770-1846), only daughter and heiress of Thomas Egerton, 1st Earl of Wilton. In 1798 he became Major Commandant of a regiment of Volunteers which he raised in Westminster and was made Colonel of the Flintshire Militia. He was Lord Lieutenant of Flintshire 1798-1845. He succeeded his father as 2nd Earl Grosvenor in 1802 and was created Marquess of Westminster in 1831. He was bearer of the Third Sword at Queen Victoria's Coronation in 1838, and was made a Knight of the Garter in 1841. Like his father, he was a great art collector and a major patron of the turf. At Chester his horses won the Tradesmen's Cup in 1825 and 1839; the Stand Cup in 1835; the Dee Stakes in 1834, 1838 and 1840; the Palatine Stakes in 1837, 1838 and 1842; and 20 other races between 1803 and 1843. He also won the Oaks in 1805 and 1841, the Doncaster Gold Cup in 1835 and 1836, the Ascot Gold Cup in 1836 and 1837, and the St Leger three times between 1834 and 1841.[3]

Tushingham (pp.110-111) records the race on Thursday 5 May 1814:
'A Cup, value 70l. the gift of the Right Hon. Earl Grosvenor - Heats thrice round.

Mr. Egerton's br h Hit-or-Miss, 6 yrs	1	3	1
Lord Derby's Rinaldo, 4 yrs (bolted)	4	1	dis
Mr. Shaw's br h Don Julian, 5 yrs	3	2	dr
Sir W.W. Wynn's ch c by Tityrus 4yrs	2	dr	

3 to 1 agst Hit-or-Miss.'

This trophy was won by John Egerton (1766-1825), eldest son of Philip Egerton of Egerton and Oulton, who inherited Oulton Park, Cheshire, on his father's death in 1786. In 1794 he became a freeman of Chester,

and in 1795 he married Maria (1777-1830), daughter and sole heiress of Thomas Scott Jackson, a director of the Bank of England. In 1814 he became 8th Baronet on the death of his distant cousin Thomas Egerton, 1st Earl of Wilton,[4] and assumed the additional surname of Grey. He was a founding governor of the British Institution and Provincial Grand Master of the Freemasons. Despite being related to the 2nd Earl Grosvenor's wife, he fought four bitterly contested Parliamentary elections in Chester as an 'Independent' opposed to the Grosvenors' monopoly of power, winning in 1807 and 1812 but losing in 1818 and 1820. His horse Hit-or-Miss won a Handicap Stakes on the same day as the 1814 Gold Cup, and other horses of his won

the Gold Cup again in 1815, 1816 and 1820; the City Plate in 1810, 1819 and 1822; and nine other races at Chester between 1806 and 1825.[5]

The Bateman family firm had a long history of supplying Chester race trophies: they probably produced the City Plate between at least 1780 and 1796 and the Stand Cup between at least 1817 and 1819. The Batemans also enjoyed the patronage of the Grosvenors,[6] probably producing the Gold Cup between at least 1792 and 1819. The later Bateman Gold Cups, like most early 19th-century sporting trophies, are derived from Classical vases and urns. The almost identical vase-shaped Gold Cups of 1802 and 1806 are attenuated and minimally decorated, stylistically close to work of the previous two decades.[7] The surviving cups of 1808-19, all of the same form with slight differences in ornamentation, have more ample proportions and far richer decoration, yet remain fully within the Neo-Classical vocabulary of design. These, in turn, appear restrained and elegant by comparison with William Bateman I's heavy and florid Chester Stand Cups of 1817 and 1819.[8]

Peter Bateman was born in 1740, the son of Hester Bateman (see no.94). He was apprenticed to his sister's husband Richard Clarke. His first mark was entered in partnership with his brother Jonathan in 1790. On Jonathan's death in 1791 Peter entered in partnership with Jonathan's widow Ann, and her son William I was added to the partnership in 1800. Ann retired in 1805, and Peter probably retired in 1815, dying in 1825.[9]

William Bateman I was born in 1774, the son of Jonathan and Ann Bateman (see no.103). He was apprenticed in 1789 to his father, and turned over on the latter's death in 1791 to his mother. He became free in 1799. His first mark was entered in partnership with Peter and Ann in 1800, his second in partnership with Peter in 1805, and his third mark alone in 1815. He was elected to the Livery in 1816 and to the Court of Assistants in 1828. He served as warden 1833-5, 1847-9 and prime warden 1836. He sold the family business c.1840 and died in 1850.[10]

PROVENANCE: Presented by Robert, 2nd Earl Grosvenor (later 1st Marquess of Westminster), and won by John Egerton (later Sir John Grey-Egerton, 8th Baronet) of Oulton Park, Cheshire; By descent to Sir Philip Grey Egerton, 14th Baronet;[11] Lowe & Sons, Chester, 1980; Purchased with grant aid from the V&A Purchase Grant Fund, National Art Collections Fund, Grosvenor Museum Society, Mrs. E.M. Bell, Duke of Westminster, Richard Green, Spink & Son, David Beaton, Marks & Spencer and a public appeal 1981.25.1

EXHIBITED: Manchester 1983, no.78; London 1984, S.5.

PUBLISHED: 'Trophies for Grosvenor Museum', *Country Life*, 23 April 1981, p.1101, illustrated; NACF Report 1981, no.2914, illustrated; Moore 1982, illustrated; Schroder 1992, fig.2; Callaghan, illustrated p.33.

NOTES:

1. Re-gilded by Lowe's before purchased by museum (Nicholas Moore, fax, 19 August 1999).

2. There is a mistake in the tinctures, the field of the shield being shown as gules when it should be azure, and the word Nobilitatis in the motto has been shortened to

Nobilitas (Gale Glynn, report, 22 March 1991). The tinctures are correct on the following year's cup (no.97) but the error in the motto is repeated.

3. Bevan, p.67; Hanshall, p.179; Complete Peerage, vol.12, part 2, pp.538-9; Bennett 1908, p.385; Tushingham; *The Racing Calendar*. For his art collecting see Boughton 1992 II, pp.40-1.

4. Sir Thomas Egerton of Heaton, 7th Baronet, created Baron Grey de Wilton in 1784 and Viscount Grey de Wilton and Earl of Wilton in 1801 (Ormerod, II, p.629).

5. Ormerod, II, pp.218, 221-2; Kennett, pp.20, 22, 24-5; Burke's Peerage, p.827; Bennett 1908, p.410; Tushingham; *The Racing Calendar*.

6. And not only at Chester: a silver-gilt two-handled cup by Peter & Anne Bateman of 1792, in the Cleveland Museum of Art, is engraved with the arms of Earl Grosvenor but not inscribed for a particular race (James Lomax, letter, 17 June 1993).

7. The form is essentially that used by Hester Bateman for a tea urn in 1785 (Shure, pl.XXII).

8. The Stand Cup of 1817 is illustrated in *The Cheshire Sheaf*, 5th series, no.136, March 1978. The Stand Cup of 1819 was sold Sotheby's, London, 18 March 1982, lot 85. An even more massive racing trophy of 1820 by William Bateman I is illustrated in Cornforth, pl.95.

9. Grimwade, pp.433-4.

10. Grimwade, p.434.

11. Recorded in Oulton Inventory in 1953 but sold before his death in 1962 (Sir John Grey Egerton, letter of 5 August 1999 and telephone message of 8 October 1999).

97 SILVER-GILT CUP AND COVER

William Bateman I, London, 1815-16

Five marks of side of body (maker's mark Grimwade no.3037). Three marks on bezel of cover: date letter, lion passant, maker's mark
Total height 31.8 cm. (12.5 in.), width across handles 31.1 cm. (12.25 in.), diameter 20.6 cm. (8.1 in.)
Total weight 1,971 g. (69.5 oz.)

See Colour Plate VII

Sterling silver, gilt.[1] The high foot-ring is separately formed and has an applied moulding to its lower edge. The stepped, spreading circular foot is raised, and has a cast and applied inner border of tiny diamond facets between bands of braiding. The foot rises to a short stem with a chased calyx of matted acanthus leaves beneath an applied moulding. The hemispherical bowl is raised, and its lower part chased with a calyx of matted alternating stiff and acanthus leaves. In the centre of one side is a cast and applied oval medallion encircled by husks, containing the heraldic achievement of Robert, 2nd Earl Grosvenor on a slightly convex matted ground. The other side is engraved in Roman and Old English lettering, 'CHESTER / Races, / 1815', within

a matching cast and applied oval of husks. It is engraved in the same lettering to either side:

'This CUP was Purchased / with SEVENTY POUNDS won by / Sir JOHN GREY EGERTON'S / HORSE Oulton and paid by / The RIGHT HONORABLE / EARL GROSVENOR in / MONEY instead of a GOLD CUP / annually given by himself / & his ANCESTORS / since the year 1744, / but this year Omitted.'[2]

The upper edge of the cup has a cast and applied frieze of oak branches and acorns on a matted ground between bands of braiding. Each handle has cast decoration on a matted ground, with vine branches on the two curved sections and an oval patera of acanthus leaves on the straight section between. The lower part of the handle has a cast and applied stiff leaf with a palmette terminal. The raised, domed lid has an applied bezel and rim, and rises to a chased calyx of matted alternating stiff and acanthus leaves. The cast finial is in the form of a naturalistic wheat sheaf, a feature common to the arms of both the City of Chester and the Grosvenor family.

Tushingham (p.114) records the race on Thursday 4 May 1815:

'A Cup, value 70l. the gift of the Right Hon. Earl Grosvenor. - The best of heats.

Sir J.G. Egerton's ro c Oulton, 4 yrs   1   1
Lord Stafford's b c Bay Trentham, 4 yrs   2   dr
Eleven were drawn.
2 to 1 on the winner. A fine race.'

Sir John Grey-Egerton's winning horse was named after

his country seat, Oulton Park, and the same horse won the Gold Cup again the following year.[3]

Contrary to Tushingham's statement, the inscription on the cup makes it clear that Sir John Grey-Egerton won a cash prize of £70 presented by the 2nd Earl Grosvenor. Having won the Gold Cup the previous year (no.96), Sir John commissioned a matching cup from the same maker. This would have cost £70, and was almost certainly supplied through George Lowe I of Chester.

The only obvious difference between the two cups is the replacement of the frieze of Greek key pattern (which also appears on the 1808 and 1812 Gold Cups) with one of oak branches and acorns (which also appears on the 1819 cup), a motif with specifically British rather than purely Classical connotations.[4] This change was presumably sanctioned if not requested by Sir John, and probably reflects the heightened mood of patriotism both before and after the Battle of Waterloo, which took place on 18 June 1815, less than seven weeks after the race. Although otherwise appearing to match the 1814 Gold Cup, different castings were used for the heraldic medallion, the oval of husks, the handles and finial.

For biographical notes on the 2nd Earl Grosvenor, Sir John Grey-Egerton and William Bateman I see no.96.

PROVENANCE: Commissioned by Sir John Grey-Egerton, 8th Baronet, of Oulton Park, Cheshire, in 1815; By descent to Sir Philip Grey-Egerton, 12th Baronet;[5] Lowe & Sons, Chester, 1980; Purchased with grant aid from the V&A Purchase Grant Fund, National Art Collections Fund, Grosvenor Museum Society, and others as no.96 1981.25.2

EXHIBITED: Manchester 1983, no.78; London 1984, S.5.

PUBLISHED: 'Trophies for Grosvenor Museum', *Country Life*, 23 April 1981, p.1101, illustrated; NACF Report 1981, no.2914, illustrated; Moore 1982, illustrated; Bevan, illustrated p.176; Schroder 1992, fig.2; Callaghan, illustrated p.33.

NOTES:

1. Re-gilded by Lowe's before purchased by Museum (Nicholas Moore, fax, 19 August 1999).
2. The Gold Cup had, in fact, been given since 1741 (Cheny 1741, p.13).
3. *The Racing Calendar*, 1816.
4. Oak leaves appear, for example, on a gold military presentation cup of 1806 by Digby Scott & Benjamin Smith II (Schroder 1988 I, no.92).
5. Recorded in Oulton Park Plate List in 1935 (Cheshire Record Office, DEO 112). Although not recorded in the Oulton Inventory of 1953 (Sir John Grey Egerton, letter, 5 August 1999), it seems unlikely to have parted company with the 1814 cup (which was sold by the 14th Baronet between 1953 and 1962).

CHESHIRE CHURCH PLATE

St Michael's Church, Chester

St Michael's Church stands on the corner of Bridge Street and Pepper Street. It was rebuilt after a fire in 1180, but the oldest part of the present church is the chancel roof, dating from 1496. The building was enlarged in 1678 and the west tower, beneath which passes Bridge Street Row East, was rebuilt in 1710. The church was largely rebuilt by James Harrison in 1849-50. Following the church's redundancy in 1972, St Michael's plate became the responsibility of the Chester Team Parish. The building was purchased by Chester City Council and re-opened in 1975 as the Chester Heritage Centre, Britain's first architectural heritage centre. Remodelled in 1991, its displays explore the development of Chester's unique townscape.[1]

For other silver from St Michael's see:
no.1. Communion Cup, William Mutton of Chester, c.1570;
no.12. Communion Cup and Standing Paten, Richard Richardson I, Chester, 1723-4;
no.13. Plate Paten, Richard Richardson I, Chester, 1724-5.

The Grosvenor Museum also holds these pieces from St Michael's:
Pair of Pewter Plate Patens, Thomas Forde of Whitehaven, c.1683-4;
Silver-Plated Trowel, P.G. Shaw, c.1849.

NOTE:
1. Boughton 1997, no.57; Richards, p.117.

98

98 SILVER-GILT STANDING CUP / COMMUNION CUP

Edward South, London, 1635-6
Four marks below rim (maker's mark Jackson p.116). Lion passant inside foot
Height 22 cm. (8.65 in.)
Weight 346 g. (12.2 oz.), scratch weight 11=7=0

Sterling silver, regilded in 1902.[1] The angled foot-ring, die-struck with a band of alternate long and short lobes, is soldered to a concave vertical strip. The high trumpet-shaped foot is raised and flat-chased with six lobes between narrow bands of scales. Both motifs are outlined with a matted border, pointed to the lobes, whilst the scales terminate in flame-like features. A cast floral disc is soldered to the top of the foot and supports the cast elements of the stem,

comprising a sphere on an inverted dome between spindles. A thin plate supports the semi-ovoid bowl, decorated with flat-chasing on a matted ground. The lower half of the bowl repeats the decorative motifs of the foot, although with eight lobes. Unrelated to this eight-part division, the bowl's upper half carries a broad six-part band of strapwork and stylised foliage, with alternating lozenges and circles, one of which contains a blank escutcheon. The rim is pricked in script: 'The Gift of Mrs Dulcibella Harpur to the Parish of St. Michaell in Chester 1680'.

The stem has been altered, and its original form may have been similar to London-made steeple cups of the 1610s and '20s.[2] They suggest that the St Michael's cup has lost the shoulder at the top of the foot and a band beneath the surviving floral disc, a corresponding disc and band between the stem and the bowl, and three scroll brackets joining the spherical knop to the upper disc. Even closer to the St Michael's cup, because their stems lack brackets, are cups of 1599[3] and 1635.[4] The shape of the knop is consistent with these early 17th-century examples, although one might expect it to bear some engraving. If there were brackets, they were probably removed when it became a communion cup in 1680 and the stem was altered or remade, in a form close to that on a communion cup of *c*.1664 by Charles Shelley,[5] creating an unencumbered knop easier for the celebrant to use when administering the sacrament. T. Stanley Ball cast some doubt on the date of the pricked inscription but it is probably authentic, since pricking was used in the 17th century for dates and initials and the script is stylistically consistent with the date.[6]

The relative technical simplicity of flat-chasing was cheaper than sophisticated cast or engraved decoration, and its use here is typical of plate made for the middle range of the market rather than for the aristocracy.[7] The cup's decoration employs motifs which, by 1635, were distinctly outmoded for a London goldsmith, and the lack of any relationship between the two halves of the bowl reinforces the cup's unsophisticated character. The design on the foot and lower bowl was in use from at least the 1560s to the 1610s,[8] whilst flat-chased strapwork broadly comparable to that on the upper bowl was popular in the 1590s and 1600s.[9]

Cups in early Stuart England were almost always gilded. They were the most highly favoured form of gift as well as having the practical function of drinking vessels, often to be passed around and the contents shared between three or four guests. Originally, the example from St Michael's was probably a steeple cup, a form much favoured by the bourgeoisie and gentry, having a domed cover surmounted by an obelisk finial.[10] The St Michael's cup is closest in profile to steeple cups of the 1590s to 1610s, having a semi-ovoid bowl with a plain lip.[11] In the 1610s the lip becomes everted or moulded,[12] and in the 1620s the sides of the bowl become more upright.[13] Thus, in both form and decoration the St Michael's cup is stylistically closer to *c*.1600-20 than to 1635.

The churchwardens' accounts for St Michael's record on 16 April 1680 the gift 'of Mrs Dulsabellah Harper widdow to Henry Harper of this citty Gent one Gilt Bowle waighing Elleaven ounces and seaven pounds',[14] thereby confirming that the cup came to the church gilded but without a cover. Dulcibella's first husband, Richard Bavand, gentleman, died in 1640; he left her 'all my plate', which may well have included this cup, made just four or five years earlier. Later in 1640 she married her second husband, Henry Harpur, a glover who became a freeman of Chester in 1666. Dulcibella died in 1686, leaving £5 to the poor of St Michael's and various

bequests including sums of money totalling £162, plate and gold, a diamond ring, a pair of organs and a pair of virginals.[15]

About fifty steeple cups are preserved in English churches, many of them having been presented after 1660 once the form had fallen from fashion. As Philippa Glanville has noted, 'their height and elaborate (although repetitive) chased ornament made them handsome if unwieldy additions to the splendour of the altar.'[16] The gift of secular plate for ecclesiastical use was not at all uncommon: the other example in the Grosvenor Museum is a waiter of 1764 presented to Stoak Church in 1772 as a paten (no.104). Elsewhere in Chester, standing cups of 1633 and 1641 became communion cups at St John the Baptist in 1674 and at the chapel of St John-without-the-Northgate in 1717.[17]

The maker's mark on the St Michael's cup is ES in a dotted circle, recorded by Jackson (p.116) on a communion flagon of 1633 and a covered porringer of 1652. Gerald Taylor identified the maker as Edward South.[18] He was apprenticed to the plateworker Thomas Francis in 1624, became free in 1632, and was a 'poor man' by 1659. His mark is also found on a remarkable silver-mounted ivory cup and cover of 1633, a flat-chased standing dish of 1649 and a plain inkstand of 1652.[19]

PROVENANCE: Possibly bequeathed by Richard Bavand to his widow, later Mrs. Dulcibella Harpur, 1640; Presented by Mrs. Dulcibella Harpur to St Michael's Church, Chester, 1680; Transferred to Chester Team Parish, 1972; Purchased with grant aid from the MGC/V&A Purchase Grant Fund, National Heritage Memorial Fund, Pilgrim Trust, Duke of Westminster, Mary Newboult Bequest, Grosvenor Museum Society 1988.36

EXHIBITED: Chester 1951, no.17, pl.V.

PUBLISHED: Ball 1907, pp.69-70 no.II, illustrated frontispiece; Ridgway 1968, p.28; Pevsner & Hubbard, p.152; Richards, p.120 (b); Boughton 1992 I.

NOTES:

1. A metal plaque on the cup's baize-lined wooden box is inscribed: 'THIS CHALICE WAS REGILT / 1902. / A.RADFORD.L.L.M.VICAR / A.PARKES. / A.G.CUFFE. / CHURCHWARDENS.' Arthur Radford was vicar 1893-1903 (Richards, p.120). He presumably paid for this work, since it is not recorded in the churchwardens' accounts (Cheshire Record Office, P65/8/6). Although the box is otherwise unlabelled the work may well have been carried out by Lowe & Sons, whose shop is a short walk from the church up Bridge Street Row East, and who undertook a small job for St Michael's the following year (the wardens' accounts record 3s. paid on 31 July 1903).

2. For example, those of 1613 and 1618 by maker CB (Schroder 1988 I, fig.28 & no.17), of 1625 by maker TF and of 1627 by maker F (Glanville 1990, nos.23-4).

3. Maker's mark a squirrel with a nut (Glanville 1990, fig.143). Originally a steeple cup, this was given to St Mary Abbot's, Kensington: if it originally had brackets, they were probably removed when the cup was presented to the church.

4. Maker's mark RC (Oman 1970, pl.1B). This covered cup, without strapwork, also lacks the floral discs.

5. Oman 1957, pl.86. In 1907 Ball (p.69) believed that the knop had 'recently been added': this seems unlikely, but further work on the stem could have been done in 1902 before the cup's regilding, perhaps in an attempt to rectify earlier damage.

6. Ball 1907, p.69; Newman, p.249.

7. Schroder 1988 I, p.78.

8. Examples include: a covered cup of 1561, maker's mark probably a cup (Schroder 1988 I, fig.19); a covered tazza of 1584, maker's mark IG (Schroder 1988 I, fig.23); a ewer of 1586, maker's mark an escallop (Glanville 1990, fig.179); a covered cup of 1590, maker's mark RW (Hackenbroch, no.4); a covered cup of 1592, maker's mark HL (Clayton 1985 I, fig.184); a standing cup of 1604, maker's mark MW (Glanville 1990, no.16); wine cups of 1605 and 1607, both maker's mark AB (Brett, nos.404, 406); a pair of candlesticks of c.1610, maker's mark P (Schroder 1988 I, fig.26); a steeple cup of 1613, maker's mark TC (Clayton 1985 II, frontispiece); and a ewer of 1618 by Thomas Flint (Glanville 1990, no.102). These are usually embossed rather than flat-chased, generally appear on the foot and/or lower bowl and, whilst varying in their degree of similarity to the St Michael's cup, are essentially the same motif.

9. Examples include: a double salt of 1594, maker's mark NR (Glanville 1990, no.92); a covered cup of 1594, maker's mark a heart over two clubs in a saltaire (Clayton 1985 I, pl.31); a double salt of 1599 (Clayton 1985 II, p.35 no.3); a pair of 1602 tankards, maker's mark IB (Schroder 1988 I, no.14); a pair of 1602 livery pots, maker's mark TE (Sotheby's, London, 11 February 1999, lot 64); and a tankard of 1604, maker's mark IB (Clayton 1985 II, p.35 no.4).

10. Glanville 1990, pp.243-4, 252; Newman, p.300.

11. Examples include: a cup of 1599, originally with a steeple cover, maker's mark a squirrel with a nut (Glanville 1990, fig.143); and steeple cups of 1599 and 1617 (Newman, pp.68, 43).

12. Examples include cups of 1611, maker's mark AB (Clayton 1985 I, fig.186); and of 1613 and 1618, both maker's mark CB (Schroder 1988 I, fig.28 & no.17).

13. Examples include cups of 1625, maker's mark TF; of 1627, maker's mark F; and of 1629, maker's mark RB (Glanville 1990, nos.23-4 & fig.144).

14. Cheshire Record Office, P65/8/2. The records of plate handed over to new churchwardens describe it, for example, as 'one gilt Cup' (1683) or 'one communion Cup gilt' (1696).

15. Bennett 1906, p.152; Ball 1907, p.70; Richard Bavand's will (Cheshire Record Office, WS 1640); Dulcibella Harpur's will (Cheshire Record Office, WS 1686); Gerrard Barnes, report of 12 January 2000 and letter of 10 March 2000.

16. Glanville 1990, p.252.

17. Ball 1907, pp.40, 114.

18. Gerald Taylor, letter, 21 March 1986.

19. Clayton 1985 II, p.55 fig.2; Glanville 1990, no.79; Clayton 1985 II, p.61 no.13.

99 PAIR OF FLAGONS

Seth Lofthouse, London, 1701-2

Four marks on cover (maker's mark Grimwade no.1945). Four marks on body near rim (maker's mark struck twice on flagon 2). Maker's mark on handle. Leopard's head beneath foot-ring
Height to thumbpiece: (1) 36 cm. (14.2 in.); (2) 35.5 cm. (14 in.)
Weight: (1) 2,000 g. (70.55 oz.); (2) 1,991 g. (70.2 oz.)

See Colour Plate VI

Britannia standard silver. Each flagon's skirted foot is raised and has two pairs of parallel lines at its lower edge, the outer pair being more deeply incised. An applied moulding at the foot's upper edge marks its junction with the body of the flagon. The plain, slightly tapering cylindrical body is raised, with an inset circular base and a separate deep moulding at the rim. The scroll handle is of D-section, with a rounded underside soldered to a straight outer edge. The handle tapers to its lower junction with the body before widening to a five-sided heel, beneath which is a large air hole. A three-part hinge, with a cast pendant drop and bifurcated scroll thumbpiece, joins the handle to the cover. (The hinge of flagon 2 has 20th-century steel nuts and a brass threaded bar.) The low domed cover is raised from a setting-out point. It has a deep bezel, moulded on its outer face, and an applied rim. The body is engraved opposite the handle with an armorial and inscription.

Each flagon is engraved in script beneath the armorial: 'This Flagon with one more being in wt: 128 oz = 10 dwt is the / Gift of Mr: Sam: Edwards late of the City of / Chester Gold Smith to the Parrish of St: Michaels / For the Use of ye: Holy Communion 1702'. Samuel Edwardes, the fourth generation of a family of Chester goldsmiths, was the son of Peter Edwardes I and younger brother of Peter Edwardes II (see no.4). He became a freeman in 1694 and a member of the Chester Goldsmiths' Company in 1696, serving the company as warden from 1697 until his death in 1702. He was active for only a few years, and none of his work is known to survive.[1]

By his will of 1702 be bequeathed to the family church of St Michael's, where he wished to be buried, 50s. for the poor of the parish and 'the summe of forty pounds to buy a silver flaggon for the Administring the blessed sacrament'. This was enough money to buy two flagons, which were purchased through his brother Thomas, who was in London.[2] The churchwardens' accounts record: 'Received ye 2d June 1702 of Mr Thomas Edwards by the hand of Mr Henry Birkenhead

99

Two Large Silver Flaggons of the value of forty pounds & upwards being a Legacy left by his Bro Mr Saml Edwards for ye use of ye Sacrament'.[3] They were supplied with leather cases and replaced two pewter flagons.[4]

Each flagon is engraved with an heraldic achievement within Baroque mantling. The arms—a butterfly paleways wings extended between three roses in centre chief a ducal coronet—are those of Madocks of Vron Yv and Glanywern, North Wales. However, the Madocks arms do not have this crest—a butterfly within a wreath springing from a ducal coronet—or the motto DVW AC FYDD MAVR (God and great faith). The same arms appeared on the memorial to Samuel's grandfather Griffith Edwardes II (d.1637) formerly in St Michael's and, although the family was probably not entitled to these arms, they demonstrate the Edwardes' pride in their Welsh ancestry.[5]

The armorial engraving is of very high quality, and is remarkably close in both style and execution to that on a tobacco box lid of 1687-90 (no.4) by Samuel's elder brother Peter Edwardes II. He had engraved some of the plates for *The Academy of Armory* by Randle Holme III, published in 1688.[6] Elements of the armorials on the flagons relate closely to plates in the book, which contains an almost identical butterfly, a slightly reduced version of the wreath and a similar ducal coronet.[7] Since Peter was an accomplished engraver, although by 1702 no longer active as a goldsmith, it would have been natural for him to undertake the work of engraving these flagons with the arms used by his family and the inscription recording his brother's bequest to St Michael's, where Peter had been churchwarden in 1695-7. It therefore seems highly likely, on both stylistic and circumstantial evidence, that Peter Edwardes II engraved both the box lid and the flagons.

In many parishes in the late 17th and 18th centuries Holy Communion was celebrated only four times a year, and such a special event drew a large congregation, expecting to take a mouthful rather than a sip of wine. This practice required the presence of one or two large flagons containing consecrated wine with which to replenish the communion cup. Because the wine was consecrated in the flagons it was thought that they should be made of silver rather than base metal, but silver flagons were too expensive for many parishes, who therefore used pewter ones and, as at St Michael's, depended upon the generosity of local patrons to provide silver replacements.[8]

Very often made in pairs, such vessels were known as 'pots' in Elizabethan times, but the term 'flagon' appears to have become generally accepted by *c.*1640.[9] The flagons from St Michael's, with their cylindrical bodies and rounded lids, exemplify the commonest type of flagon throughout the 17th and 18th centuries.[10] These flagons were equally popular for secular purposes during the first half of the 17th century, but their long-term liturgical use conformed to the 1603 canon (repeated in post-Restoration visitations) on the provision of worthy vessels to contain communion wine.[11]

Seth Lofthouse, probably from the Leeds area of the West Riding of Yorkshire, was apprenticed to the London goldsmith William Wakefield in 1676, but his freedom is not documented. He is recorded as a plateworker in 1697, entered his mark as a largeworker in 1699, and had died by 1727. Although most of his work appears to have been fairly simple conservative hollow wares, he also had a significant sideline in church plate.[12] Elsewhere in the Chester diocese he made a standing paten in 1700 for Holmes Chapel and an alms dish in 1705 for Bowdon.[13]

PROVENANCE: St Michael's Church, Chester, 1702 (Purchased with bequest from Samuel Edwardes); Transferred to Chester Team Parish, 1972; Purchased with grant aid from the MGC/V&A Purchase Grant Fund, National Heritage Memorial Fund, National Art Collections Fund, Pilgrim Trust, Duke of Westminster, Mary Newboult Bequest, Grosvenor Museum Society 1988.37.1,2

EXHIBITED: Chester 1951, no.35; London V&A 1989 (one only).

PUBLISHED: Ball 1907, pp.70-1 no.III, one illustrated opposite p.70; Ball 1932, p.294; *The Cheshire Sheaf*, 3rd series, vol.20, no.6538, 23 January 1935; Ridgway 1968, p.115; Pevsner & Hubbard, p.152; Richards, p.120 (c); NACF Review 1989, no.3432 (10-11), one illustrated; Boughton 1992 I; Schroder 1992, p.36.

NOTES:

1. Ridgway 1968, p.137. The spoon attributed to him in Ridgway 1968, p.138, is now attributed to Ellen Dare of Taunton (Ridgway 1996, p.183).
2. Ridgway 1968, p.138.
3. Cheshire Record Office, P65/8/2.
4. The leather cases are recorded in the lists of plate handed over to new churchwardens, beginning on 15 April 1703, when the inventory included 'two Large silver flagons with Leather Cases being the Gift of Mr Samle Edwards'. The pewter flagons, recorded in these plate lists between at least 1683-1723, were not disposed of immediately. (Cheshire Record Office, P65/8/2 & 3.)
5. Gayle Glyn, report, 22 March 1991; Ridgway 1968, pp.37, 137.

6. The pictorial title page is signed by Peter Edwardes I, but only six of the book's many plates are signed, two by Peter Edwardes II (Book I, p.41 and Book III, p.284, the latter dated 1674), and the rest by three other engravers.
7. All from unsigned plates: butterfly (Book II, p.169 no.63); wreath (Book II, p.469 no.52); ducal coronet (Book III, p.2 no.11).
8. Cooper 1997, p.11; Emmerson 1991, pp.11, 13; Oman 1957, pp.144-5; Schroder 1988 I, p.84.
9. Glanville 1990, p.267; Oman 1957, p.219 n.3; Newman, p.136.
10. Oman 1957, pp.221, 223. Of those illustrated by Oman, the closest to the St Michael's flagons is one of 1636: maker's mark PG with a rose, at SS Anne and Agnes, London (Oman 1957, pl.111b).
11. Glanville 1990, p.267.
12. Grimwade, pp.584-5; Lomax, pp.10-11. Much of his plate was for West Riding churches (James Lomax, note, 22 October 1999). A 1701 flagon from Rowley (in the East Riding) is in the York Minster Treasury.
13. Canon Ridgway, letter, 18 November 1999; Richards, pp.67, 188.

St Olave's Church, Chester

St Olave's Church, on the east side of Lower Bridge Street, is a small sandstone building with a bellcote at its west end. St Olave was King Olaf of Norway, who helped establish Norwegian Christianity before his death in 1030. The church was founded later in the 11th century, possibly to serve a small community of traders from the Norse settlement of Dublin. The church and its parish were always the smallest and poorest in Chester, and in 1839 the church was closed and the parish united with St Michael's (see no.98), to which the plate was also transferred. In 1858-9 James Harrison restored the building as the parochial Sunday School and, after later use as an adult education centre and an exhibition venue, the building reopened as the Chester Community Church in 1998.[1]

NOTE:

1. Boughton 1997, no.59; Ormerod, I, p.345.

100 EWER/FLAGON

Humphrey Payne, London, 1728-9

Four marks near rim (maker's mark variant of Grimwade no.1061)
Height 27.4 cm. (10.8 in.)
Weight 1,208 g. (42.6 oz.)

See Colour Plate VI

Sterling silver. The low, spreading stepped foot is raised and has an applied outer edge. The pear-shaped body of the jug is raised and applied with a narrow seamed moulding at its junction with the foot

100

and a deeper moulding at its rim. The pouring lip is cast, with a shaped rim, an applied band and a drop pendant. The scroll handle is of D-section, with a rounded underside soldered to a straight outer edge. The handle tapers to a triangular heel, with a circular air hole beneath, and there is an oval plate at its lower junction with the jug. The body is engraved in script and Roman lettering beneath the spout: 'The Gift of / MRS. ELIZABETH BOOTH / Daughter of NATHANIEL / BOOTH of Mottram Andrew / in the County of Chester Esq. / to St Olaves Church in / Chester 1728'.

Elizabeth Booth was born in 1656, the daughter of Nathaniel Booth (1627-92) of Mottram St Andrew near Macclesfield. He was the fourth son of

William Booth of Dunham Massey, brother of the 1st Baron Delamere and heir to Sir Thomas Brereton of Honford.[1] Although unmarried, Elizabeth Booth used the courtesy title of Mrs.[2] In 1715 she built Park House in Lower Bridge Street, Chester. She left over £6,000 on her death in 1736, and her bequests included £10 per annum to the minister of St Olave's, £20 'to be laid out for the improvement of it', and £10 to the poor of the parish. Her memorial in Hawarden church, Flintshire, records that she was 'universally beneficent and universally beloved'.[3]

In 1722 Bishop Gastrell observed that St Olave's 'is not fit for any public service, nor is any performed beside baptism and burial', but in 1726 the perpetual curacy was augmented by Queen Anne's Bounty,[4] and the gift of this ewer in 1728 may be seen as symbolising a temporary revival in the church's fortunes.

This is the only surviving item of plate from St Olave's. It replaced an earlier flagon, probably of pewter, since the churchwardens' accounts for St Martin's record in 1733, 'Pd to Churchwardens of St Olaves for a flagging and salver 10/-'.[5]

In the current nomenclature of church plate a flagon contains wine and a ewer holds water, but in the terminology for secular silver a flagon has a hinged lid and the vessel from St Olave's would be called a ewer.[6] Both T. Stanley Ball (1907) and Charles Oman (1957) use the term flagon for all wine containers, regardless of their form, and that convention is recognised here.

The earliest surviving communion flagon, made for Wells Cathedral in 1572, has a pear-shaped body, and bulbous-bodied flagons competed in one form or another right down to the 19th century with the cylindrical-bodied type. Jug-shaped flagons with a spout were made in the late 17th century, and during the first half of the 18th century some new forms of bulbous flagons appeared, either variations of the contemporary wine jug or resembling hot-water jugs.[7] The vessel from St Olave's is quite different from the only ewer-shaped flagon illustrated by Oman,[8] but the body and foot are fairly close to a lidded flagon of 1730 by Gabriel Sleath.[9] The ewer-shaped flagon without a lid is remarkably well-represented in Chester: the cathedral has a silver-gilt pair of 1662 by the London maker RN; St John's has a pair of 1729 by William Darker of London;[10] and Humphrey Payne made one for St Oswald's in 1725 (discussed below).

Humphrey Payne was apprenticed to Roger Grange in 1694 and turned over to Thomas Parr. In 1701 he became free and entered his first mark as a largeworker. He was elected to the Livery in 1708 and to the Court of Assistants in 1734. He served as warden 1747-9 and died in 1751.[11]

Humphrey Payne was a well-known maker of ecclesiastical silver. He made the largest set of 18th-century church plate in Chester, commissioned for St Oswald's in 1725, comprising two communion cups, two standing patens, ewer and alms dish.[12] This set almost certainly led to the commission of a very similar ewer for St Olave's three years later. Elsewhere in the Chester diocese he made a flagon in 1707 for Wrenbury, a standing paten in 1716 for Bunbury, and a communion cup, standing paten and alms dish in 1718 for Brereton.[13] He also provided plate for 15 churches in the adjacent diocese of St Asaph between 1706 and c.1738.[14] His secular work included a tankard commissioned in 1725 for the Chester civic plate, and a pair of

covered jugs made in 1749, which are similar to the St Olave's ewer but with a moulding around the body and a lid.[15]

PROVENANCE: Presented by Mrs. Elizabeth Booth to St Olave's Church, Chester, 1728; Transferred to St Michael's Church, Chester, 1839; Transferred to Chester Team Parish, 1972; Purchased with grant aid from the MGC/V&A Purchase Grant Fund, National Heritage Memorial Fund, National Art Collections Fund, Pilgrim Trust, Duke of Westminster, Mary Newboult Bequest, Grosvenor Museum Society 1988.40

PUBLISHED: Ball 1907, pp.73-5 no.VII; Pevsner & Hubbard, p.152; Richards, pp.120 (g), 843; NACF Review 1989, no.3432 (15); Boughton 1992 I.

NOTES:

1. The 1st Baron Delamere's grandson was George Booth, 2nd Earl of Warrington, one of the most extravagant patrons of English 18th-century goldsmiths, a significant proportion of whose massive collection remains at Dunham Massey.

2. Her unmarried cousin Elizabeth, daughter of Sir John Booth, was known as Madam Elizabeth Booth (Ball 1907, p.58).

3. Ball 1907, pp.73-5; Ormerod, I, p.525; Ormerod, III, p.641; Hanshall, p.233; Cheshire Record Office, P64/1/1 and WS 1736; Gerrard Barnes, report, 12 January 2000.

4. Hanshall, p.232.

5. Information from manuscript by Canon Ridgway.

6. Emmerson 1991, p.30; Newman, pp.136, 127.

7. Oman 1957, pp.219-20, 223; Clayton 1985 I, p.189.

8. William Cripps, 1756, at Stoke Climsland, Cornwall (Oman 1957, pl.120a).

9. At St George, Bloomsbury (Oman 1957, pl.118b).

10. Ball 1907, pp.20-1, illustrated opposite p.19, and pp.47-8.

11. Grimwade, p.616.

12. Now at St Thomas's (Ball 1907, pp.135-7). The St Oswald's ewer, which is slightly larger than that from St Olave's, differs in having a less spreading foot, a cast double-scroll handle, and the rim moulding continued across the lip, which has an applied moulded band but a straight rim.

13. Canon Ridgway, letter, 18 November 1999; Richards, p.372; Pevsner & Hubbard, p.120; Chester 1951 exhibition catalogue, no.39.

14. Ridgway 1997, pp.275-6.

15. Clayton 1985 II, p.151 fig.2.

St Bridget's Church, Chester

Reputedly founded by King Offa of Mercia in the 8th century, St Bridget's is first certainly recorded in 1200. The church originally stood on the corner of White Friars and Bridge Street, opposite St Michael's. It was rebuilt in the mid-17th century and re-cased with stone in 1785. The medieval church was demolished in 1829 to make way for Grosvenor Street and a new church, designed by William Cole junior, was built in 1827-8 on the corner of Nicholas Street and Grosvenor Street. This elegant Neo-Classical building, harmonising with Thomas Harrison's nearby Castle, had Greek Doric pilasters supporting a pediment at the west end and a cupola with Ionic columns above. In 1891 St Mary-on-the-Hill became the parish church for St Bridget's, which was demolished the following year. The plate from St Bridget's was transferred to St Mary-on-the-Hill, and following the redundancy of that church in 1972 became the responsibility of the Chester Team Parish.[1]

For other silver from St Bridget's see:
no.11. Communion Cup, Richard Richardson I, Chester, 1718-19.

The Grosvenor Museum also holds another piece from St Bridget's:
Sheffield Plate Flagon, late 18th/early 19th century.

NOTE:

1. Boughton 1997, nos.53-4; Ormerod, I, p.341.

101 SILVER-GILT FLAGON

Hugh Roberts, London, 1697

Four marks on body near rim and inside lid (maker's mark Grimwade no. 2382)
Height 35.6 cm. (14 in.)
Weight 2,343 g. (82.65 oz.)

See Colour Plate VI

Britannia standard silver: the exterior of the flagon and the interior of the lid gilt, but the interior of the body and beneath the foot ungilded. The skirted foot is raised and has an applied outer edge. The convex lower portion of the foot is chased with spiral gadrooning, repaired internally with soldered strips of silver. An applied moulding at the foot's upper edge marks its junction with the body of the flagon. The slightly tapering cylindrical body is raised, with an inset circular base and a deep moulding applied to the rim. The scroll handle is of D-section, with a rounded underside soldered to a straight outer edge in two parts, the lower part scrolling back at the mid-point of the handle. The handle tapers to its lower junction with the body before widening to a triangular heel, beneath which is a circular air hole. A five-part hinge, with a cast triple pendant drop and bifurcated scroll thumbpiece, joins the handle to the cover. The low stepped and domed cover is raised and chased with a deep band of spiral gadrooning. The rim is moulded, with an applied bezel inside. The flagon is engraved in Roman lettering and script beneath the foot: 'St. Bridget's, Chester. / Chas. Price / Saml. Nickson / Church Wardens, / 1810.'

The gilding is almost certainly original. That inside the lid is in the best condition, but the colour is consistent throughout the flagon. Since gilding was expensive, it was only applied where it would show. Late 17th-century silver-gilt church plate is most commonly found in royal and episcopal chapels and in cathedrals, but gilt flagons are not particularly rare in parish churches. The chased gadrooning is unusual, since the only decoration on most contemporary flagons was engraved.[1] Also unusual is the scroll at the mid-point of the handle.[2] The marks are notably crisp, since all four punches had been newly cut for the introduction of Britannia silver. The date letter A, which appears on this flagon and the patens (no.102), was only used between 27 March and 28 May 1697.[3]

For the bequest by Mrs. Hannah Swan see no.102. The inscription, added in 1810, presumably records a repair, probably that to the gadrooning of the foot as described above.[4]

Hugh Roberts was apprenticed to Augustine Dudley in 1672 and became free in 1679. He entered his mark as a largeworker, probably in 1697, was elected to the Court of Assistants in 1704, and is recorded up to 1714. Hugh Roberts almost certainly came from Eglwyseg in Denbighshire, 18 miles south-west of Chester, and through his local connections supplied the plate for St Bridget's in 1697 and very similar flagons the following year to the churches at Wrexham in Denbighshire and Llanasa in Flintshire.[5] Elsewhere in the Chester diocese he made a standing paten in 1692 for Birkenhead Priory.[6]

PROVENANCE: St Bridget's Church, Chester, 1697 (Purchased with bequest from Mrs. Hannah Swan); Transferred to St Mary-on-the-Hill, Chester, 1891; Transferred to Chester Team Parish, 1972; Purchased with grant aid from the MGC/V&A Purchase Grant Fund, National Heritage Memorial Fund, National Art Collections Fund, Pilgrim Trust, Duke of Westminster, Mary Newboult Bequest, Grosvenor Museum Society 1988.29

EXHIBITED: Royal Archaeological Institute (after 1866).[7]

PUBLISHED: Earwaker, p.23; Ball 1907, pp.80-1 no.I; Ridgway 1968, p.114; Pevsner & Hubbard, p.151; Richards, p.116 (a); NACF Review 1989, no.3432 (1), illustrated; Boughton 1992 I.

NOTES:

1. Oman 1957, p.221.
2. This feature is seen on a silver-gilt tankard of 1690 by John Jackson (Truman, no.42). The alternate fluting and gadrooning on this tankard, and the boss on its lid, are even closer to the two flagons of 1698 by Hugh Roberts discussed below.
3. Jackson, p.54.
4. The churchwardens' accounts for 1803-10 are unfortunately

101

missing. The wardens were Charles Price, a carpenter who became free in 1778 and Samuel Nickson, a cabinetmaker and upholsterer who became free in 1802 (Bennett 1908, pp.379, 421).

5. Grimwade, p.642; Moore 1999, p.255. The flagons at Wrexham and Llanasa (Ridgway 1997, pp.114, 263-4, pl.47-8, 142) are identical to each other but more richly decorated than the Chester one, replacing the gadrooning with alternate fluting and gadrooning, and adding a boss of alternate fluting and gadrooning surrounded by punched decoration on the lid, chased acanthus on the thumbpiece and a row of graded beads on the handle.

6. Canon Ridgway, letter, 18 November 1999.

7. A paper label inside the lid is printed 'Royal Archaeological Institute' with '36' added by hand. The Archaeological Institute

acquired the prefix 'Royal' in 1866. The location and date of the exhibition are unknown.

102 PAIR OF PLATE PATENS

Hugh Roberts, London, 1697

Four marks on border (maker's mark Grimwade no.2382)
Diameter: each 24.4 cm. (9.6 in.)
Weight: (1) 457 g. (16.1 oz.); (2) 454 g. (16 oz.)

Britannia standard silver. Each circular paten has a setting-out point and is raised from a single sheet, having a shallow well and a wide border with a moulded

102

rim. Each is engraved in script around the border: 'This and such an other with a guilt Flaggon Cup and Couer are the gift of Mrs Hannah Swan to St Bridgets parish.'

Mrs. Hannah Swan was the widow of the Rev. Thomas Swan (died 1685), rector of St Bridget's,[1] whom she had married in the church in 1663. She was buried in St Bridget's on 12 February 1697, and in her will bequeathed £50 to buy plate for the church: '£30 for a flaggon, £10 for a guilded cupp and £10 for two plates for the Communion Table which plate should be bought within 6 months after my decease and should be and remain for the use of the Parish Church for ever'.[2] The gilt cup and cover referred to in the inscription were probably also made by Hugh Roberts. They may have been superseded by the communion cup acquired in 1720 (no.11), and they do not appear in the 1888 inventory of St Bridget's plate.[3]

PROVENANCE: St Bridget's Church, Chester, 1697 (Purchased with bequest from Mrs. Hannah Swan); Transferred to St Mary-on-the-Hill, Chester, 1891; Transferred to Chester Team Parish, 1972; Purchased with grant aid from the MGC/V&A Purchase Grant Fund, National Heritage Memorial Fund, National Art Collections Fund, Pilgrim Trust, Duke of Westminster, Mary Newboult Bequest, Grosvenor Museum Society 1988.30.1,2

PUBLISHED: Earwaker, p.23; Ball 1907, p.81 nos.II-III; Ridgway 1968, p.114; Pevsner & Hubbard, p.151; Richards, p.116 (a); NACF Review 1989, no.3432 (2-3); Boughton 1992 I.

NOTES:

1. Thomas Swan is recorded as rector between 1663 and 1672, but was probably not the incumbent at the time of his death.
2. Ball 1907, p.81; Earwaker, p.23 n.3; Cheshire Record Office, P15/1/1 and WS 1696; Gerrard Barnes, report of 12 January 2000 and letter of 19 January 2000. The St Michael's flagons (no.99), which were also purchased with a bequest, are likewise inscribed as a 'gift'.
3. Cheshire Record Office, P15/19/1.

St Martin's Church, Chester

The medieval parish of St Martin was one of the smallest in Chester. The church stood on the corner of White Friars and Nicholas Street. Dating from the 13th century, it had become ruinous by 1721, and was then rebuilt in brick with stone dressings. In 1842 the parish of St Martin was united with that of St Bridget, and the plate was transferred to St Bridget's (see no.101). The church was used for Welsh services, and in 1964 the building was bought by Chester City Council and demolished to make way for the inner ring road.[1]

The Grosvenor Museum also holds another piece from St Martin's:
Sheffield Plate Flagon, c.1828.

NOTE:

1. Boughton 1997, no.55.

103 PARCEL-GILT COMMUNION CUP

Peter, Ann & William Bateman, London, 1804-5

Five marks beneath foot (maker's mark
Grimwade no.2141)
Height 15.3 cm. (6 in.)
Weight 204 g. (7.2 oz.)

Sterling silver with gilt interior. The raised trumpet-shaped foot has an applied vertical foot-ring. The foot-ring is reeded, as are the lower and upper edges of the foot, which supports the raised semi-ovoid shaped cup. The side of the cup is engraved in Roman lettering and script: 'St. MARTIN'S. / Thos. Armitstead /

RECTOR. / Thos. Jones / Saml. Bennett / Church-wardens, / 1805.'[1]

This is one of a pair of identical cups from St Martin's: the other one was lent by the Chester Team Parish to the Bishop of Birkenhead in 1973. A standing paten of 1805 by Peter & William Bateman, with a very similar inscription, was given to the new parish of St Luke, Huntington, Chester in 1985.[2]

The cup's very simple Neo-Classical shape is like a domestic goblet. It was sometimes used for communion cups in the late 18th and early 19th centuries,[3] until replaced from the 1840s by the revival of medieval styles.

Ann Bateman, née Dowling, was born in 1748. In 1769 she married the silversmith Jonathan Bateman, son of Hester Bateman (see no.94). On his death in 1791 she entered in partnership with her brother-in-law Peter Bateman, and her son William joined the partnership in 1800. She retired in 1805 and died before 1813.[4] For Peter and William Bateman see no.96.

Cups with gilt interiors, identical in form to that from St Martin's, had been made by the Batemans for more than twenty years: examples include a pair of 1783 by Hester Bateman (with beading instead of reeding) and a single, more elaborately decorated cup of 1799 by Peter & Ann Bateman.[5] Peter, Ann & William Bateman supplied communion cups to three churches in the adjacent diocese of St Asaph: those of 1800 at Aberhafesp and of 1802 (presented 1818) at Berriew are similar in form.[6] The other Chester church plate by the Batemans was supplied by William Bateman I, and comprises two communion cups of 1821 at Christ Church and a communion cup of 1830 at St Paul's, Boughton.[7] Elsewhere in the Chester diocese Peter & Ann Bateman made two flagons of 1795 at Malpas, a ewer at Dodleston, a salver at Marple, two communion cups at Wistaston and one at Calveley, while Peter & William Bateman later supplied a standing paten at Dodleston and a flagon at Marple.[8]

PROVENANCE: St Martin's Church, Chester, 1805; Transferred to St Bridget's Church, Chester, 1842; Transferred to St Mary-on-the-Hill, Chester, 1891;[9] Transferred to Chester Team Parish, 1972; Purchased with grant aid from the MGC/V&A Purchase Grant Fund, National Heritage Memorial Fund, Pilgrim Trust, Duke of Westminster, Mary Newboult Bequest, Grosvenor Museum Society 1988.32

PUBLISHED: Ball 1907, pp.120-1 no.II; Boughton 1992 I.

NOTES:

1. The Rev. Thomas Armitstead was rector of St Martin's 1795-1806 (Ormerod, I, p.333). Samuel Bennett, a wine merchant, became free in 1791, sheriff in 1798-9 and mayor in 1812-13 (Bennett 1908, p.408; Hanshall, pp.179-80). There were several freemen called Thomas Jones in 1805.

2. Ball 1907, pp.120-1. The churchwardens' accounts for 1790-1815 are unfortunately missing: the two cups and paten were probably purchased by the wardens, but they may have been presented by the rector.

3. Examples of goblet-shaped communion cups in the adjacent diocese of St Asaph include Matthew Boulton & James Fothergill of Birmingham, 1775, at Ysceifiog and the London makers Charles Aldridge & Henry Green, 1775, at Ruabon; Charles Wright, 1776, at Llangwyfan; Thomas Wallis & Jonathan Hayne, 1810, at St Mary, Welshpool; and an unknown maker, 1812, at Gwyddelwern (Ridgway 1997, pls.148, 127, 81, 133, 32).

4. Grimwade, p.433.

5. Shure, pls.XLV, LXXIII(b).

6. Ridgway 1997, pp.32-3, 36.

7. Ball 1907, pp.126-7, 142.

8. Canon Ridgway, letter, 18 November 1999; Pevsner & Hubbard, p.274.

9. The 'Inventory of the Plate … belonging to St Bridget's Church' (Cheshire Record Office, P15/19/1), records the St Martin's plate as being at St Bridget's in 1888; in 'Small box at Rectory for use at St Martin's' in 1923; and 'At St Martin's 1947'.

St Lawrence's Church, Stoak

Stoak is situated five miles north-east of Chester. St Lawrence's occupies the site of a Saxon chapel, and a substantial building was recorded in the 14th century. The church was largely rebuilt by George Edgecumbe in 1827, but the 14th-century chancel and Tudor nave roof were incorporated. It was restored again in 1911-12. Since 1972 St Lawrence's has formed part of the Ellesmere Port Team Ministry.[1]

For other silver from St Lawrence's see: no.2. Communion Cup, William Mutton of Chester, c.1570-8, and Paten Cover, remade 1804-5.

NOTE:

1. Pevsner & Hubbard, p.338; Richards, pp.305-9, 430-2.

104 WAITER/PATEN

Richard Rugg, London, 1764-5

Four marks beneath waiter (maker's mark Grimwade no.2420)
Diameter 18.2 cm. (7.15 in.)
Weight 289 g. (10.2 oz.)

Sterling silver. The circular waiter is raised, supported on three cast scroll feet with gadrooned pads, and has a cast and applied gadrooned rim. The centre is engraved with the sacred monogram, cross and nails within a glory. The underside is engraved in script: 'The Gift of Mr. Grace of Whitby to the Church of Stoake 1772'.

This piece was originally made as a waiter for use by servants waiting at table, especially in bringing glasses of wine to the table from the sideboard, and for use at the tea table. In modern usage the term waiter is applied to those which measure between 15 and 25cm. in diameter.[1] This waiter was presented to the church in 1772 for use as a paten, and presumably replaced the Elizabethan paten-cover (no.2). Larger patens became necessary when the use of household bread replaced wafers for the Holy Communion,[2] and the Stoak paten shows knife scratches made when cutting up the bread.

The donor, John Grace of Whitby Hall, owned land in the township of Whitby in the parish of Stoak, and part of Ellesmere Port was later built on the family's

land. Born *c.*1706, he died in 1780 and was buried at Stoak.[3] The Stoak churchwardens' accounts unfortunately record only expenditure, and do not therefore mention John Grace's donation.

Richard Rugg was apprenticed to James Gould in 1738 and became free in 1746. He entered his first mark as a largeworker in 1754, was recorded as a plateworker in 1773, and entered his second mark as such in 1775.[4] Elsewhere in the Chester diocese he made an alms dish in 1766 for Great Budworth and two standing patens for Tarvin.[5] The simplicity of the Stoak waiter contrasts with the elaborate Chinoiserie decoration on a 1766 salver by Richard Rugg, which combines a pierced rim with flat-chasing and engraving.[6]

PROVENANCE: Presented by John Grace to St Lawrence's Church, Stoak, 1772; Purchased with grant aid from the MGC/V&A Purchase Grant Fund, Pilgrim Trust 1995.87

EXHIBITED: Chester 1979, Silver no.11.

PUBLISHED: Richards 1973, p.307; Thomas, p.19; Boughton 1992 I.

NOTES:

1. Lomax, p.64; Newman, p.345.
2. Clayton 1985 I, p.270.
3. Aspinall & Hudson, pp.6, 12, 91; Gerrard Barnes, report, 12 January 2000.
4. Grimwade, p.648.
5. Richards, p.174; Canon Ridgway, letter, 18 November 1999.
6. Grimwade 1974, fig.19A.

105 EWER/FLAGON

John Dare, London, 1771-2

Four marks beneath ewer (maker's mark Grimwade no.1244)
Height to thumbpiece 23 cm. (9.05 in.)
Weight 696 g. (24.55 oz.)

Sterling silver. The high, stepped foot is raised, with a cast and applied angled foot-ring having alternately wide and narrow reeding. The vase-shaped body is raised in two sections soldered together, the convex lower part chased with gadrooning and the concave upper part plain. The leaf-capped double-scroll handle is of D-section, with a rounded underside soldered to a straight outer edge. It has a reinforcement at the junction of the curves and a shield-shaped heel piece with an air hole beneath. The front has been cut out beneath the rim for the shaped pouring lip, which is applied with 16 graded beads. The body is engraved beneath the lip with the sacred monogram, cross and nails within a glory. The underside of the foot-ring is engraved in script: 'The Gift of Mr. Grace of Whitby to the Church of Stoake 1772'.

The vase-shaped body was a popular form for Neo-Classical jugs in the 1770s, such as those of 1775

105

by John Carter, 1777 by Nicholas Dumee and 1778 by Charles Wright.[1] Apart from the basic shape, however, these examples are not otherwise comparable with the Stoak ewer, although the decoration on the body of a 1785 cream jug by Robert Hennell is fairly close.[2]

In contrast to the modernity of the shape, the applied graded beads on the lip revive a late 17th century motif, which is discussed in the entry on Ralph Walley's jug of 1690-2 (no.8). In the 1780s applied strands of smaller graded beads appear on the spouts of coffee pots by Hester Bateman.[3]

Despite its similarity to secular pieces, there can be little doubt that the Stoak ewer was made for church use, on both functional grounds—since its lip is better suited to the pouring of wine than many flagons, which often have no lip or spout—and stylistic evidence—with the revival of the archaic motif of beading. Charles Oman observed that the piece of church plate 'which the goldsmiths found most susceptible to classicizing was the flagon', which they 'changed into finely proportioned ewers', but the example he illustrates has a lid.[4]

John Dare became free in 1770 and entered a mark in 1773. Since he was free in 1770 he may have entered a largeworker's mark in the missing register.[5]

He was almost certainly the maker of a 1772 cream jug,[6] the lower part of whose vase-shaped body is gadrooned like the Stoak ewer, although it is otherwise closer to the jugs discussed above. John Dare was probably also the maker of a 1772 baluster coffee pot,[7] the shape of whose foot and wooden handle is broadly similar to the ewer.

PROVENANCE: Presented by John Grace to St Lawrence's Church, Stoak, 1772; Purchased with grant aid from the MGC/V&A Purchase Grant Fund, Pilgrim Trust 1995.88

PUBLISHED: Richards 1973, p.307; Thomas, p.19; Boughton 1992 I.

NOTES:

1. Oman 1965, fig.161; Rowe 1965, figs.24B, 86.
2. Oman 1965, fig.168.
3. Shure, pls.III, IV, VI; Asprey's 1994, nos.52, 56.
4. 1791 by Edward Fennell (Oman 1957, p.224, pl.121a).
5. Grimwade, p.484.
6. London, maker's mark ID (Wark, no.170).
7. Attributed to John Deacon (J.H. Bourdon-Smith, Catalogue No.37, Autumn 1994, p.28).

CHESHIRE SILVER

106 THE DELAMERE HORN

Silver-gilt mouthpiece: possibly William Mutton of Chester, c.1561-6
Two silver mounts: Herbert Charles Lambert, London, 1905-6

Mouthpiece unmarked
Two other mounts: four marks (makers' mark Culme nos.7425-30)
Length 16.5 cm. (6.5 in.), diameter of bell 5.6 cm. (2.2 in.)
Weight (including band and tassel) 250 g. (8.8 oz.)

The Delamere Horn is a polished black semicircular horn. The silver-gilt mouthpiece is engraved with a deep band of diagonally-hatched scrolling arabesques between hatched borders, below which are applied two narrow notched mouldings. Its lower edge is shaped to clasp the horn with a row of engraved triangles and is secured with a single pin. The other two mounts are of sterling silver. That nearer the mouthpiece is of unequal width, fitting the curve of the horn, and is engraved with a deep band of hatched scrolling arabesques between hatched borders flanked by applied narrow notched mouldings. It is edged with rows of engraved triangles and is secured to the horn with a single pin (now missing). The mount at the bell end has a broad everted rim extending 1.9 cm. beyond the horn. Its outer face is engraved with a narrow band of hatched scrolling arabesques flanked by applied narrow notched mouldings. The lower edge is shaped to clasp the horn with a row of engraved triangles and is secured with three pins. A fringed tassel and band, tablet woven in green silk and silver-gilt, are attached to the silver suspension loops on the mounts.[1]

The Delamere Forest and the Chief Forester

The forests of Delamere and Mondrem are not mentioned by name in the Domesday Book of 1086, but there are references to places in the earl of Chester's forest which lay within the later bounds of Delamere. The earliest contemporary evidence for Delamere seems to be a charter of c.1153-81 from Earl Hugh II, while clear indications of the existence of Mondrem do not occur until the later 13th century. The forests lay in central Cheshire between the rivers Gowy in the west, Weaver in the east, Mersey in the north and an unnamed tributary of the Weaver to the south. In 1353 Richard Done claimed that the hereditary chief forestership of Delamere and Mondrem, which he then held, had been granted by

Earl Ranulph I to Ranulph de Kingsley, to be held in grand serjeantry with a horn as the title to office.[2] According to George Ormerod, 'Cheshire tradition asserts that the antient foresters were bound to use this horn, and attend in their office with two white greyhounds, whenever the earl was disposed to honour the forest of Delamere with his presence in the chace.'[3] Ranulph I was earl from 1120-8/9, and the creation of the chief forestership is traditionally given as c.1123.[4] Some two years earlier the same earl had created the office of chief forester of Wirral, likewise held by a horn, which is discussed below.

By 1353 the chief forester had a staff of eight under-foresters and two grooms. It is not clear whether there were deer in Mondrem in the Middle Ages, but there are references to both red and fallow deer in Delamere from the 13th century. In addition to the game, the woodland was important for timber, and Delamere in particular was a source of oaks. The forest region contracted during the later Middle Ages and from c.1600 the remainder, which almost entirely excluded the old forest of Mondrem, was usually referred to as Delamere.[5]

The last royal hunt in Delamere took place in August 1617 when James I stayed at the nearby Vale Royal Abbey. John Done of Utkinton (1577-1629), 19th Chief Forester, ordered the royal sport 'so wisely and contentedly', according to the annalist William Webb, that the king knighted him in his home at Utkinton.[6] There are two oil paintings of Sir John,[7] showing him dressed in green with the horn hanging from his waist and a staff in his hand, the pictures inscribed 'Domis Delameri Damaeque Dominator' (Lord of Delamere and Master of the Deer).

In 1626 Sir John Done had a staff of ten keepers and two woodwards, and his profits of office were worth £88 16s. 6d. Between 60 and 80 deer were killed annually, and the following year there were 320 deer in two of the keepers' walks. 8,346 acres of Delamere were uninclosed and belonged to the king out of a total of 12,672, and there were about 2,200 oaks. The deer were destroyed during the Civil War and were never replaced. Delamere was disafforested by an Act of Parliament in 1812, and the surviving Delamere Forest is today merely a fragment.[8]

Charter Horns and the Cheshire Forest Horns

Horns have been used as symbols of power since the days of the Old Testament, and this tradition continued in medieval England. As the gift of a horn was the giving away of a symbol of power so tenure by horn came into existence, the horn taking the place and having the force of a written charter, from which they are known as charter horns.[9] Before the Norman conquest the custom was for the lord of the land to bestow his own drinking horn, a valuable and cherished possession. This soon gave way to horns that were often merely ornamental, but they remained a valuable possession and a number still survive.[10]

Delamere and Mondrem were two of the four forests in Cheshire, along with Wirral and Macclesfield. According to later tradition, the forest of Wirral was created c.1121 when Earl Ranulph I of Chester appointed Alan Sylvester hereditary chief forester of Wirral, to be held by the tenure of blowing a horn, or causing it to be blown, at the Gloverstone (an area adjacent to Chester Castle) on the morning of every fair day, to indicate that the tolls payable on all goods bought or sold in the city during the fair belonged to the earl and his tenants there. The original charter (possibly dating from 1129-39) records only the grant of the manors of Storeton and Puddington, making no reference to the forest, the forestorship or the horn, and the earliest record of the forest seems to be a charter dating from 1194-1208. Wirral was disafforested in 1376, but the horn and its rights passed to the Stanleys of Hooton Hall, who continued as titular foresters as late as 1512. The yellow to light brown cow or ox horn, with black or blue spots or flakes, has a silver-gilt mouthpiece and an inscribed 19th-century silver plate.[11]

The earliest reference to the forest of Macclesfield is in a charter dating from 1153-60, by which Earl Hugh II of Chester appointed Richard Davenport supreme forester of the forests of Leek and Macclesfield. Leek, in Staffordshire, was detached in the 13th century, and Macclesfield forest effectively came to an end in 1684. The Davenports did not describe themselves as foresters until 1596, but their right is mentioned as late as c.1745. By the late 13th century there were eight hereditary sub-foresterships, one of which was held by the Downes of Sutton Downes and Taxal. About 1720 Reginald Downes, the then owner, claimed that he held his land by the blast of a horn on Midsummer Day, but no special horn seems to have existed.[12]

The Medieval and Tudor Delamere Horn

According to Ormerod the horn, which he described as 'that of a foreign animal', was said to be the one originally conferred by Earl Ranulph I.[13] The horn is most probably that of a female European bison (*Bison bonasus*), and it could indeed date from the early 12th century. The bison probably lived in the forests of Germany at this time,[14] and the largest community of foreign traders in 12th century London was German, particularly from the Rhineland. Since their trade included goods from Regensburg, a bison's horn from the forested heartland of eastern Germany could have

reached England via this route. However, horns were not among the principal commodities imported from Germany, and a bison's horn would have been a rare and exotic curiosity. An alternative route might be the Baltic trade, which included goods from Poland and Russia, through the Danish merchants who were also active in London at this time.[15]

Stylistically, the engraved band of diagonally-hatched scrolling arabesques suggests a date for the mouthpiece within the period c.1540-80.[16] Since it is unmarked it is more likely to have been made in the provinces rather than London and, if so, it is presumably by a Chester goldsmith. The most likely candidate is William Mutton, who was active from 1555-84. Although only one piece of his marked secular plate survives (a spoon, no.3), his communion cup for St Michael's (no.1), with its engraved arabesques and gilding, shows that he was technically capable of making the mouthpiece of the Delamere Horn. It may have been made for Sir John Done of Utkinton (c.1502-61), 16th Chief Forester from 1516. However, it is more likely to have been commissioned by his distant cousin Ralph Done junior of Flaxyards (c.1532-91), between 1561 when he inherited the chief forestership and 1566 when he granted it for life to four Cheshire gentlemen.[17]

The horn is shown hanging from a green tassel in the portraits of Sir John Done mentioned above. A woodcut, based on a drawing provided by the chief forester, was published by Ormerod in 1819: this depicts what is very probably the present band and tassel, as well as the mounts which Ormerod described as 'three hoops of gold'.[18] A photograph of the horn immediately before its Edwardian restoration clearly depicts the present band and tassel, in a condition only slightly less worn than today.[19] They may very well date from c.1561-6 along with the mouthpiece, since the style and colour are consistent with a 16th-century date, and the small-scale luxury weave of the band is of a type produced in England at this time.[20]

The Edwardian Restoration

It is believed that during the 19th century the horn was missing, but was subsequently discovered in a cottage on the Arderne estate. Its condition at this time is illustrated in the photograph mentioned above, which shows the horn with the present mouthpiece, band and tassel, but without the other two mounts. There was apparently no sign of these mounts having been on the horn, and a lack of secure attachment may well have contributed to their loss in the 19th century.[21] The Delamere Horn was discussed at some length in a lecture given by Joseph Bridge to the Chester and North Wales Archaeological and Historic Society on 16 February 1904. The horn was at this time owned by George Baillie-Hamilton-Arden, K.T., 11th Earl of Haddington and 31st Chief Forester of

Delamere, who had inherited the chief forestership from his wife in 1889. Lord Haddington was a member of the Chester Archaeological Society, and allowed the horn to be examined by the lecturer when preparing his text and photographed for its subsequent publication.

This lecture was undoubtedly the catalyst for the horn's restoration, when the two missing mounts were replaced. They date between 29 May 1905, when the London date letter for 1905-6 began, and 29 August 1905, when the maker registered a different mark.[22] The restoration drew on the woodcut in Ormerod mentioned above, which showed that the central mount was nearer the mouthpiece and of unequal width, and illustrated the form of the suspension loops for the

band. The Edwardian mounts replicate the notched mouldings and engraved triangles of the Elizabethan mouthpiece, whilst successfully adapting the engraved arabesques (with horizontal rather than diagonal hatching) to the varying widths of the mounts. The new mounts are not gilded (a fact which is only apparent upon fairly close inspection), and this was presumably deliberate, being perhaps intended as a subtle indication of their lesser historical status.

The mounts were made by Herbert Charles Lambert. He was the grandson of Francis Lambert, who in 1803 had founded the family firm of jewellers and retail silversmiths, which was known as Lambert & Rawlings c.1820-61 and then as Lambert & Co. Herbert Charles and his brother Ernest Dechement (sons of

Francis Lambert junior) continued the business after the death of their uncle George Lambert in 1901. Ernest died in 1912, and in 1916 the business was absorbed by Harman & Co. Ltd., which became Harman & Lambert (and closed c.1970). Herbert died in 1924. From at least 1829 the Lambert firm had sold both genuine antique plate and new silver, including much in the styles of English and Continental pieces of the previous three centuries, making it a natural choice for Lord Haddington when he wanted Tudor-style mounts.[23]

It was presumably in 1905 that an elaborately carved oak panel was made for the horn to hang on in Lord Haddington's Cheshire home, Arderne Hall near Tarporley.[24]

PROVENANCE: Ranulph de Kingsley, 1st Chief Forester, c.1123; By descent to Henry de Donne, Lord of Utkynton, 6th Chief Forester, in the right of his wife, Joan de Kingsley, great-great-granddaughter of the 1st Chief Forester, c.1244; By descent through 14 generations of the Donne family to Mary Crewe, née Done, 22nd Chief Forester, 1639; By descent to her daughter Elizabeth Knightley, née Crewe, 24th Chief Forester, 1711; Richard Arderne of Harden, 25th Chief Forester, great-grandson of the 19th Chief Forester, 1715; By descent to Helen Catherine Baillie-Hamilton, née Warrender, Baroness Binning and Byres, later Countess of Haddington, 30th Chief Forester, great-granddaughter of the 26th Chief Forester, 1857; By descent to her granddaughter The Lady Helen O'Brien, O.B.E., née Baillie-Hamilton, 34th Chief Forester, 1957; Her son Desmond Barnaby O'Brien, 35th Chief Forester, 1959;[25] The Trustees of D.B. O'Brien Deceased, 1969; Purchased in 1983 by private treaty through Christie's, London, with grant aid from the V&A Purchase Grant Fund, Beecroft Bequest, Grosvenor Museum Society 1984.2

EXHIBITED: Chester 1979 I, no.13; London BL 1989.

PUBLISHED: Ormerod, II, p.112, illustrated with wood-cut; Bridge, pp.107-8, illustrated frontispiece; *Cheshire Life*, October 1936, illustrated p.8; Fergusson 1968, illustrated; *The Wirral Society Annual Report & Accounts 1973/74*, illustrated on front cover; Thomas, p.16; Harris 1979 I, illustrated opposite p.33; Latham, p.22.

NOTES:

1. Linda Woolley, letter of 18 August 1999 and examination on 26 October 1999.
2. Harris 1979 I, p.172, maps pp.168, 173; Bridge, pp.104-5. In grand serjeantry a man holds his lands from the king by such services as he ought to do in person to the monarch, such as carrying his banner or acting as butler: the service has to be personal and unique (Bridge, p.105 n.28).
3. Ormerod, II, p.112.

4. Fergusson 1968.
5. Harris 1979 I, pp.172, 175-6; see p.174 for a full list of the chief forester's perquisites in 1353, which remained little altered in 1626.
6. Hughes 1966, p.28.
7. The prime version descended to the Latham family through one of his daughters and is now on long-term loan to the Grosvenor Museum. A copy, dated 1619, belonged to the Earl of Haddington at Arderne Hall (Bridge, illustrated opposite p.107) and was acquired with the horn by the museum.
8. Harris 1979 I, pp.174-6, 178.
9. Bridge, pp.86, 88, 91. Documented examples of charter horns connected with forestry and hunting in medieval England include: Northamptonshire, 1165; Lambourn, Berkshire; Wychwode Forest, Oxfordshire, 1229; Sherwood Forest, Nottinghamshire; Brimmesfield, Gloucestershire (Bridge, pp.88-90).
10. Bridge, pp.88, 91. Bridge describes eight surviving medieval charter horns: the Pusey Horn (pp.92-3; illustrated Oman 1967, fig.10), a silver-mounted ox horn; the Borstal Horn (pp.93-4), an ox horn with silver-gilt mounts, by which the custody of Bernwood Forest in Buckinghamshire was held; the Tutbury Horn (pp.95-7, illustrated opposite p.95), a white horn with silver-gilt mounts and a black silk belt; the Hungerford Horn (pp.97-101), a brass bugle horn; the Bruce Horn (pp.118-19), an ivory horn with enamelled silver-gilt mounts and a green worsted belt, associated with the hereditary bailiffs and keepers of Savernake Forest; the Ulphus Horn of York Minster (pp.119-21, illustrated opposite p.119), part of an elephant tusk with carving and silver mounts; the Ripon Horn (pp.121-2, illustrated opposite p.121), an ox horn covered in purple velvet with silver mounts and a belt; and the Bradford Horn (pp.124-8), a horn with silver mounts of 1812.
11. Bridge, pp.101-4; Stewart-Brown, pp.109-11, illustrated opposite p.107; Harris 1979 I, pp.167, 184-5. The Wirral Horn is now owned by the Dowager Countess of Cromer.
12. Bridge, pp.109-10; Harris 1979 I, pp.178-9, 184.
13. Ormerod, II, p.112.
14. Richard C. Sabin, letter of 24 September 1999 and examination on 26 October 1999.
15. John Clark, letter, 29 November 1999; Brooke & Keir, pp.266-7.
16. Oman 1978, pp.33-7.
17. Fergusson 1968; Ormerod, II, p.249. On 10 October 1566 Ralph Done granted for life 'the Master Forestorship ballywicke or keeping of the forest of Mara [an alternative name for Delamere] with appurts., with all fees and commodities pertaining' (Cheshire Record Office, DAR/A/3/8).
18. Ormerod, II, p.112: it is clearly inaccurate in omitting the engraving on the mouthpiece and in showing a different style of serated edge where it clasps the horn.
19. Bridge, frontispiece.
20. Linda Woolley, letter, 18 August 1999. They are also stylistically close to the green sash and tassel, interwoven with gold and silver, in a painting of c.1604 depicting 'Henry, Prince of Wales with Robert Devereux, 3rd Earl of Essex in the hunting field' by Robert Peake the Elder (c.1551-1619) in the Royal

Collection (illustrated Evans, no.1). Both boys have polished black horns with engraved gilt mounts very similar to the Delamere Horn.

21. Fergusson 1968; Bridge, pp.107-8.

22. Jackson, p.41; Culme, II, p.141.

23. Culme, I, pp.281-3.

24. Parcel-gilt and inscribed 'The Ancient Horn of Delamere Forest', the panel is carved with a huntsman and hound, acorns and thistles, and the earl's arms. Its central portion is illustrated in Fergusson 1968. The panel was acquired with the horn by the museum. For Arderne Hall, demolished in 1958, see de Figueiredo & Treuherz, pl.142.

25. For the complete list of Chief Foresters see Fergusson 1968.

107 THE ARDERNE TANKARD

Maker's mark WC, London, 1669-70

Four marks on body near rim and on lid (maker's mark WC over a scallop shell between two pellets in a shield)
Height 18.9 cm. (7.45 in.)
Weight 1,201 g. (42.35 oz.)

Sterling silver. The raised cylindrical tankard, with an inset circular base, has applied horizontal mouldings at the base and rim, and a rope-moulding at about one-quarter of its height. The slightly domed raised cover has a flat top and an applied bezel and rim. The three feet and the hinged thumbpiece are in the form of cast lions couchant, each resting its forepaw on a flattened ball. The cast scroll handle, in the Auricular style, is in the form of a dolphin.

The front is engraved with the arms of Arderne, within a leafy cartouche, for Sir John Arderne of Harden and Alvanley, Cheshire. He was born at Utkinton in 1630, the son of Ralph Arderne and Eleanor, daughter and co-heiress of Sir John Done of Utkinton. His succeeded his father to the Harden and Alvanley estates in 1651, and in 1654 married Mary, daughter of Thomas Legh of Lyme, by whom he had five sons and four daughters. He was knighted in 1660 and served as Sheriff of Cheshire in 1666. He died in 1702 and was buried at Stockport.[1]

There are two other examples of London tankards with cast lion feet and thumbpieces and dolphin handles. The closest, with much crisper casting, is the Glyn tankard of 1676 by Arthur Manwaring.[2] A silver-gilt tankard of 1668, maker's mark IN,[3] is very similar, but the casting is inferior and the body lacks horizontal mouldings. These dolphin handles and lion feet illustrate the general availability of castings.[4] A silver-gilt tankard of 1661, maker's mark DR,[5] has lions like the Arderne tankard but the handle, instead of a dolphin, is of the Hanseatic type discussed below.

A few other English tankards have cast lion feet and thumbpieces but plain handles. These include one by Thomas Jenkins, London, 1668;[6] a pair of parcel-gilt tankards, one each by John Plummer and Marmaduke Best, York, 1673;[7] one by maker RG, 1674;[8] and one by maker WS, 1676.[9] Later examples include a gilt tankard by Samuel Margas, London, 1713, with four lion feet,[10] and the heavily ornamented Cumberland tankard by Gabriel Sleath, London, 1746.[11] Cast lions couchant also form the finial and three feet of a covered cup of *c.*1675 by maker IH.[12] The use of cast lions for the feet and thumbpieces of tankards is also found in Scandinavian silver.[13]

The handles of tankards were usually hollow, but the grandest were solid cast and very rare.[14] The clearest example of a cast dolphin handle is on a 1671 tankard by Thomas Jenkins, which also has a cast lion thumbpiece and rope mouldings but no feet.[15] An example of lesser quality is on Thomas Jenkin's Kyrle tankard of 1669, which has cast lion feet and rope mouldings but a hedgehog thumbpiece.[16] These cast dolphin handles are in the Auricular style, whose leading exponent, Christian van Vianen, had worked in England in the 1630s and '40s and again *c.*1660-6.[17] In 1650 Christian van Vianen had published seven designs for ewers with dolphin handles in *Modelles Artificiels de divers vaisseaux d'argent*,[18] and surviving Dutch ewers with dolphin handles include two by Joannes Lutma of Amsterdam, 1647 and 1655, and one by Michiel de Bruyn of Utrecht, 1652.[19] A handle close to that of the Arderne tankard is found on a lidded ewer 'made in the second half of the 17th century by a probably English imitator of Christiaen van Vianen', mark IC with pellet above and fleur-de-lys below.[20] Dolphins were a recurrent motif in Auricular silver, and elements of this style sometimes appear in Restoration silver.[21] A later variant is the double-headed dolphin handle on a cordial pot, maker's mark FSS, *c.*1690, which also has three dolphin feet and a dolphin-headed spout.[22] An even later descendent of the Auricular dolphin handle is seen in the rising scroll handle of a silver-gilt ewer of 1744 by George Wickes.[23]

One of the manifestations of the Auricular style in Germany was the cast Hanseatic handles on tankards from Hamburg, of which an example is the parcel-gilt tankard of *c.*1660 in the Shrewsbury Civic Plate.[24] The form was introduced to England by Jacob Bodendick of Limburg and is seen, for example, on three of his London-made tankards of 1664-74.[25] Hanseatic handles also occur on three tankards of 1671, each of which has three cast eagle or hawk feet and a matching thumbpiece, plus rope mouldings: the Dodding tankard, maker's mark IH, and a pair of tankards by Thomas Jenkins.[26] The lower part of the Hanseatic handle is sometimes very similar to the dolphin handle, but the upper part is composed of abstract gristle with a projecting horn or knob. Whilst presumably sharing the

107

same origin, they had developed into two distinct forms, both of which were used by Thomas Jenkins in 1671.

The maker's mark WC over a scallop shell between two pellets is unrecorded by Jackson but appears on a snuffers and tray, London, 1670.[27] Gerald Taylor has also noted this mark on an undated communion cup in Southwark Cathedral. Yvonne Hackenbroch identified the maker as 'William Commyns?', but he was made free in 1611 and is therefore an unlikely candidate. Working from Gerald Taylor's research

notes on 17th-century makers' marks, David Beasley has identified several possible names—William Carter, William Cooke, William Cowland, William Crane, William Cuthbert—all working around 1669-71 but with no further evidence to link any of them with this particular mark.[28]

PROVENANCE: Sir John Arderne of Harden and Alvanley, Cheshire; His daughter Anne Arderne (1667-1729), who married John Shallcross (1662-1733) of Shallcross,

107

Derbyshire, in 1686; Their daughter Margaret Shallcross
(1690-1772), who married Richard Fitzherbert (d.1746)
of Somersal Herbert, Derbyshire, in 1718; By descent
to Nicholas Fitzherbert; Phillips, London, 11 October
1985, lot 186 (unsold); Purchased through Phillips with
grant aid from the MGC/V&A Purchase Grant Fund,
National Art Collections Fund, Duke of Westminster,
Grosvenor Museum Society, Lloyds Bank, Lowe & Sons,
Boodle & Dunthorne and other donations 1986.43

PUBLISHED: *The Antique Dealer and Collectors Guide*,
March 1986, p.72, illustrated; NACF Review 1987,
no.3257, illustrated.

NOTES:

1. Ormerod, I, p.74; Ormerod, II, p.86.
2. National Museum and Gallery Cardiff.
3. Untermyer Collection, Metropolitan Museum of Art, New York (Hackenbroch, no.25).
4. Oliver Fairclough, letter, 2 November 1994.
5. Draper's Company, London (Oman 1970, pl.28B).
6. Sotheby's, 17 November 1937, lot 44; identified as Thomas Jenkins in Grimwade & Banister, p.174.
7. York Civic Plate (Goldsmiths' Hall 1952 II, pl.XXIV).
8. Archibald A. Hutchinson Collection, Fogg Art Museum, Cambridge, Mass.
9. Christie's, 14 July 1965, lot 132. For a Victorian reproduction of this type of tankard see Sotheby's, London, 26 November 1992, lot 212, Crespel & Parker overstruck by Frazer & Haws, London, 1873.
10. Ironmongers' Company, London (Goldsmiths' Hall 1951 II, pl.LXII).
11. Clayton 1985 II, p.172, no.3.
12. Phillips, London, 17 July 1998, lot 156.

13. Examples include a Danish tankard dated 1696 (Lightbown, p.42), and a Norwegian tankard of *c*.1710 (Brett, no.1960).

14. Clayton 1985 II, pp.64, 81.

15. Clayton 1985 II, p.81 fig.14.

16. Balliol College, Oxford (Grimwade & Banister, fig.4).

17. Schroder 1988 II, p.303; Fleming & Honour, p.860.

18. Van Vianen, pls.6, 11, 14, 19, 26, 32, 43.

19. Frederiks 1952, pp.223, 228, 275.

20. Frederiks 1961, pl.118.

21. Fleming & Honour, p.52; Schroder 1988 II, p.114.

22. Clayton 1985 II, p.84 fig.2.

23. Schroder 1994, no.15.

24. Goldsmiths' Hall 1952 II, pl.XXV.

25. Schroder 1988 II, p.116; Brett, nos.447-9.

26. Clayton 1985 I, fig.602; Schroder 1988 II, p.118.

27. Untermyer Collection, Metropolitan Museum of Art, New York (Hackenbroch, no.150).

28. David Beasley, letter, 15 December 1995.

108 THE CHESTER PALATINATE SEAL MATRICES

John Roos, 1706

Unmarked

Diameter 10.5 cm. (4.1 in.), width across lugs 14.25 cm. (5.6 in.)

Weight: obverse matrix 408 g. (14.4 oz.), reverse matrix 546 g. (19.2 oz.)

The metal is below sterling standard (866/1000 silver). Both matrices are circular, with deeply cut faces. The obverse has two eared rings to receive the two lugs of the reverse. The exterior of the obverse matrix is engraved with the double cipher of Queen Anne, AR in ornamental script interwoven and reversed beneath a crown.

The obverse matrix bears the figure of Queen Anne, crowned, robed and bearing an unsheathed sword, riding side-saddle on a pacing horse with tasselled breastband and saddle-cloth. Beside her is a shield with three wheatsheaves—the arms of the County Palatine of Chester—in a cartouche. In the distant landscape is the town of Flint with its castle and ships on the sea. Around the edge of the image is inscribed in Roman lettering: SIGILL.ANNAE.DEI.GRATIA.MAG.BRITAN.FRAN. ET.HIB.REGINAE.FIDEI.DEFENS
(The Seal of Anne, by the Grace of God, of Great Britain, France and Ireland, Queen, Defender of the Faith).

The reverse matrix bears the shield with three wheatsheaves in a strapwork cartouche beneath an earl's coronet. Beneath it stand two dragons, back to back, each bearing a single ostrich feather. Around the edge of the image is inscribed in Roman lettering: COMITATVS.PALATINI.SVI.CESTRIAE.ET.FLINT. AN. 1706
([The Seal] of Her County Palatine of Chester and Flint 1706).

The Design

Wax originals and casts of seals of the County Palatine of Chester survive for thirteen reigns from Richard II to Queen Anne. Throughout this period the design consistently shows the sovereign riding a horse on the obverse, and a shield of arms on the reverse. The arms are successively those of England and Edward the Confessor, England and Chester, and Chester alone (from the 1616 seal of Charles, Prince of Wales onwards). The arms are almost always flanked by ostrich feathers, and from Henry VIII onwards these are supported by dragons.[1]

The large shield on the reverse of the 1706 matrices has a strapwork surround, and the cartouche enclosing the small shield on the obverse has a hint of the Auricular style. Such archaicisms are not entirely surprising, given the continuity of seal designs. In contrast, the engraved cipher on the exterior seems entirely contemporary for 1706.[2]

Charles II's Exchequer Seal for the County Palatine of Chester, dated 1660,[3] is very similar to the 1706 seal which presumably replaced it. They have virtually identical inscriptions. The obverse differs in showing the king in armour on a galloping horse, the landscape background has a town (presumably Chester) backed by hills, and the small shield is in a similar Auricular cartouche. The only difference on the reverse is the omission of the strapwork cartouche.

The Maker

The 1706 Chester matrices were made by John Roos, or Ross, engraver of the royal seals of England from 1704 until his death in 1720.[4] They are the only known surviving examples of his work. The accounts of the Royal Mint transcribe a bill submitted to the Lord High Treasurer of Great Britain from 'John Roos, Her Majestys Chief Engraver'.[5] He charged £60 'For a large Double Seale for the County Palatine of Chester and Flint', plus £7 19s. 5d. 'For Silver weighing 30oz. 17dwt. at 5s. 2d. per ounce' and £2 'For a Shagreen case to keep the Seale in'. John Roos's bill totalled £642 10s. 11d. for four silver double seals, eight steel seals and six steel signets. Like the Chester ones, the engraving of the double seals in silver for the Court of Exchequer and the Court of Common Pleas cost £60, but the Great Seal of Great Britain cost £200.

The Use of Seal Matrices

The most important seal matrices were made of silver, each half deeply cut with a reverse image. The two halves were filled with softened wax, then pressed together on to a silk ribbon which was attached to a formal document, positive images of the obverse and reverse appearing on the resulting hardened wax seal.

It was required by law that all seals of royal authority should be broken and defaced in order to prevent

fraud, either upon the death of the sovereign or when there was a change of seal. However, the 1706 Chester matrices were not defaced, presumably because they were rendered invalid with the abolition of the palatinate, rather than replaced with new matrices for a continuing institution.[6] They are the only known surviving Chester palatinate seal matrices.

After defacement, seal matrices were given as a perquisite to the holder of the office, and the silver was generally used to make seal ware, usually a cup or salver. The best known seal ware was made from the Great Seal, the principal seal of the sovereign, which was acquired by the Lord Chancellor. Comparable seal ware was sometimes made from the obsolete seals of the Chancellor of the Exchequer or other state officials.

The only known example of Chester seal ware is a salver of 1721 by Paul de Lamerie.[7] This was made from the matrices of the Judicial Seal of 1708 for the Counties of Denbigh, Montgomery and Flint, and is engraved with both faces of the seal. The matrices had been kept by Sir Joseph Jekyll (1663-1738), Chief Justice of the County Palatine of Chester 1697-1717 (a post responsible for these counties since 1542).

The County Palatine of Chester

The earldom of Chester was founded c.1070 by William the Conqueror, and under Earl Ranulph III

(1181-1232) the foundations were laid for what later became known as the palatinate. The earldom was united to the Crown after the death of the last Norman earl in 1237, and since 1301 'earl of Chester' has been one of the titles of the monarch's eldest son.[8]

The term 'count of the palace' was first used, unofficially, in the later 13th century to describe the powers of the earls of Chester, who governed the county and administered justice with a large degree of independence from control by the king, whilst acknowledging him as their superior. The phrase 'county palatine' emerged in the later 14th century, becoming commonly used in relation to Cheshire in the 15th century. The county palatine was largely run from Chester Castle and had its own law courts and system of financial administration. The quasi-independent powers of the palatinate were abolished by Henry VIII, the administration of the law being all that was left of the ancient prerogatives.[9]

By 1706, two of the most important palatinate institutions—the Court of Great Sessions and the Exchequer—still flourished, although other institutions of county government (such as Quarter Sessions) now overlapped to some extent. Both the Court of Great Sessions and the Exchequer were abolished by Act of Parliament in 1830, which marked the effective end of the palatinate.

108

The Exchequer of the County Palatine

The office of chamberlain of Chester went back to before 1237, and by the early 14th century the chamberlain had become the leading financial administrator of the palatinate, which comprised Flintshire as well as Cheshire. In the later 14th century the chamberlain superseded the justiciar to become the head of the local administration, as principal officer of the Exchequer of Chester, an office which combined the functions of a revenue department and a secretariat. The chamberlain had custody of the seal of the Exchequer (first referred to in the 1340s) and was responsible for making out and sealing writs, charters and letters patent.[10]

In 1543 the Exchequer became responsible for issuing original writs for the counties of Cheshire and Flintshire, which initiated actions in the Court of Great Sessions, and henceforth seals include references to the County Palatine of Chester and Flint. The seals are dated from 1603 onwards.[11]

After the Restoration the office of chamberlain was entirely honorific, being held, for example, from 1702-36 by James Stanley, 10th Earl of Derby (1664-1736). Sessions were usually held twice a year by the vice-chamberlain, an office which had risen in prominence since the mid-16th century. At other times business was managed by the clerk or baron of the Exchequer or his deputy. He was responsible for the other aspect of the Exchequer's functions, as the office from which writs and letters patent of the palatinate were issued.[12]

The seal matrices of 1706 remained in use until the abolition of the palatinate in 1830:[13] the seal appears, for example, on a document of 1821.[14] The Exchequer records were placed under the charge of the Master of the Rolls in 1838, at which time they were in the custody of Philip Humberston, Seal Keeper of the Chester Exchequer. The records were transferred to the Public Record Office in 1854, but the seal matrices were retained by Philip Humberston.[15]

PROVENANCE: Made in 1706 for the Exchequer of the County Palatine of Chester, where used until 1830; Philip Humberston, Seal Keeper of the Chester Exchequer, a partner in the firm of Chester solicitors whose successors sold them at Phillips, Chester, 2 November 1994, lot 63; Private collector; Purchased with grant aid from the Heritage Lottery Fund, National Art Collections Fund, Grosvenor Museum Society 1997.65.1,2

PUBLISHED: Falkiner, illustrated; Boughton 1995, illustrated; NACF Review 1996, no.4276, illustrated.

NOTES:
1. Birch, pp.49, 52; Jenkinson, p.333.
2. It is reminiscent of designs in *A New Book of Cyphers* by Benjamin Rhodes, published in 1723 but stylistically very much like those

which he had been using at the end of the 17th century (Oman 1978, pl.99, p.85).

3. Cust, pls.3-4.

4. Hocking, p.279; Forrer, p.210.

5. Public Record Office, MINT 1/7, pp.85-7. The bill was passed by the Treasury to the Royal Mint on 2 March 1707.

6. Some other matrices also survive intact, such as a William IV seal of 1831 (Brett, no.1236).

7. Clayton 1985 II, p.103.

8. Taylor 1910, pp.20-2, 25; Paul Booth, letters, 18 March 1998 and 6 July 1999.

9. Black, p.187; Taylor 1910, p.32; Paul Booth, letters, 18 March 1998 and 6 July 1999.

10. Harris 1979 I, pp.9, 18, 19, 38, 40, 96; Paul Booth, letter, 6 July 1999.

11. Harris 1979 I, pp.35, 58, 97.

12. Harris 1979 I, pp.38, 58.

13. Harris 1979 I, p.97.

14. Cheshire Record Office, DTW/Acc.2406 Box 7.

15. Black, p.188; Harris 1979 I, p.60.

109 THE TOM RANCE TEA POT

Solomon Hougham, London, 1801-2

Five marks beneath base (maker's mark
Grimwade no.2536). Lion passant inside cover
Length 27.9 cm. (11 in.), height to top of
handle 17.3 cm. (6.8 in.)
Weight 489 g. (17.25 oz.)

Sterling silver with handle and finial of stained holly (*Ilex aquifolium*).[1] The pot has an oval profile with slightly bellied sides. It is made of sheet silver seamed under the spout, the seam partly covered with a shaped applied plate. The base of the pot is a separate sheet let in. The wood handle has a scroll thumbpiece (one-third broken off), and is connected to two pinned sockets with reeded mouldings. It is on axis with the curving spout, which is seamed and has a beak-shaped aperture. There is a jagged line of solder across the lower portion of the spout, indicating a repair. The domed hinged cover has an oval wood and silver finial attached by a threaded screw and nut. The sides of the pot have plain horizontal ribbed mouldings top and bottom. The body and cover are decorated with borders of bright-cut engraving. Both sides have a matching bright-cut angular cartouche, one of which is engraved in ornamental and plain Roman lettering: 'TOM RANCE

109

/ From / EARL GROSVENOR / 1866.' A small number '10' is stamped on the underside.

Tom Rance was born in 1803. After serving Baron Rothschild as a pad groom, he was brought to Cheshire by Lord Delamere of Vale Royal Abbey, and was engaged by Sir Harry Mainwaring of Peover Hall as 1st Whipper In to the Cheshire Hounds. He held this post from 1830 to 1862, serving eight masters and seven huntsmen. He had lost an eye in a shooting accident at the age of twelve, and it was only due to failing sight that he retired. His genial tone and polite manner made him popular with everyone in the hunting field, and on his retirement the hunt raised £500 for his benefit. He died at Oakmere in 1875 and was buried at Whitegate.[2]

He was immortalised in a verse from the poem 'Farmer Dobbin: A day wi' the Cheshur fox dugs' by Rowland Egerton-Warburton of Arley Hall:

Tom Rance has got a single oie, wurth many another's two,
He held his cap abuv his yed to show he'd had a view;
Tom's voice was loik th'owd raven's when he skroik'd out "Tally-ho"!
For when the fox had seen Tom's feace he thoght it toim to go.[3]

Egerton-Warburton wrote of him: 'In the station of life in which he was placed, no one ever did his duty better. I have seen him ride the most unmanageable horses with rare nerve and temper, still keeping his one eye open to detect, and his handy lash ready to reach any riotous hound. Many a time in the course of a run I have been beholden to him for his active assistance under a difficulty ... If after charging a fence you found yourself on the other side planted in a pit (a mischance by no means unfrequent in Cheshire), Tom Rance was always at hand to pull your horse out, or if discomforted by the loss of a stirrup leather, Tom was promptly at your side to touch his cap and proffer you one of his own.'[4]

This tea pot was presented to Tom Rance by Earl Grosvenor. Hugh Lupus (1825-99), son of Richard, 2nd Marquess of Westminster, was styled Earl Grosvenor from 1845-69 and was M.P. for Chester from 1847-69. In 1852 he married Constance (1834-80), daughter of the 2nd Duke of Sutherland. They leased Calveley Hall, from where they hunted with the Cheshire Hounds. Earl Grosvenor was Master of the Cheshire Hounds from 1858-66, which cost him between £2,500 and £3,000 a year: Tom Rance's wage was £80 per annum. He relinquished the mastership as an economy measure, but continued to hunt with the Cheshire Hounds until past the age of seventy. He succeeded his father as 3rd Marquess of Westminster and inherited Eaton Hall in 1869, and was created a Knight of the Garter in 1870 and Duke of Westminster in 1874. In 1882 he married his second wife Katherine (1857-1941), daughter of the 2nd Baron Chesham.

He was Honorary Colonel of the Cheshire Yeomanry, a Privy Councillor from 1880, Master of the Horse 1880-5, A.D.C. to the Queen 1881-99 and Lord Lieutenant of Cheshire 1883-99 and of the County of London 1889-99.[5]

Solomon Hougham became free in 1786 and was elected to the Livery in 1791. He was in partnership with his brother Charles 1790-3 and entered his first mark as a plateworker in 1793. He was in partnership with his former apprentices Solomon Royes and John East Dix 1817-8 and died between 1818 and 1822.[6] A very similar tea pot of 1801 by Solomon Hougham forms part of a tea service (with a teapot stand, sugar bowl and cream jug), and is also inscribed for a presentation.[7]

PROVENANCE: Presented by Earl Grosvenor (later 3rd Marquess and 1st Duke of Westminster) to Tom Rance, 1866; By descent to his great-great-granddaughter Miss Audrey Grimsditch, Northwich, Cheshire; Purchased with grant aid from the Grosvenor Museum Society 1984.15

PUBLISHED: Fergusson 1993, p.186.

NOTES:

1. Wood identified by Graham Usher, 13 November 1999.
2. Gordon Fergusson, typescript note, September 1991.
3. Fergusson 1993, p.416; for portraits of Tom Rance see pp.124, 135, 187.
4. Gordon Fergusson, typescript note, November 1984.
5. Complete Peerage, vol.12, part II, pp.540-1; Huxley, pp.68, 73-4, 128; Fergusson 1993, p.183.
6. Grimwade, p.552; Lomax, p.112.
7. Christie's, London, 25 November 1992, lot 44.

110 THE JOSEPH RAYNER STEPHENS CUP

William Bateman I, London, 1821-2

Five marks near rim (maker's mark Grimwade no.3037)
Height 20.2 cm. (7.95 in.)
Weight 539 g. (19 oz.)

Sterling silver. The vertical foot-ring supports a raised convex section, which in turn supports the raised trumpet-shaped foot. The foot-ring is reeded, as are the lower and upper edges of the foot. The raised semi-ovoid shaped cup has a plain applied moulding at the rim.

The front of the cup is engraved with the monogram JRS in ornamental script beneath the Stephens crest of a demi-eagle displayed,[1] enclosed within a laurel wreath. Below this is engraved in Old English, script, Roman and block lettering: 'To the Reverend Joseph Rayner Stephens, / Who, for maintaining, in perilous times, the / CAUSE OF THE POOR, / SUFFERED EIGHTEEN MONTHS IMPRISONMENT IN CHESTER CASTLE; / THIS CUP / (with the accompanying Tea Service / TO / Mrs. Stephens) / was presented by admiring and devoted Friends / AT STALYBRIDGE.' The reverse is engraved in Old English, script and Roman lettering: 'George Garside AND Abel Williamson, / unsolicited, took upon themselves, on behalf of this DEFENDER of the POOR, / the responsibility of an / unconstitutionally HEAVY BAIL, which terminated / on the day of / THIS PRESENTATION. / Feby, 10th, 1846.'

Joseph Rayner Stephens (1805-79) was the son of John Stephens, a Methodist preacher, by his wife Rebecca Eliza Rayner. He became a Methodist preacher in 1825, worked at Stockholm, and was ordained as a Wesleyan minister in 1829. His Wesleyan career ended in 1834, when he resigned under suspension for attending disestablishment meetings at Ashton-under-Lyne in Lancashire. He had joined the movement for improving the conditions of factory labour, and thought establishment checked the popular sympathies of the clergy. He zealously supported the People's Charter of 8 May 1838 after which Chartism, a working class movement for Parliamentary reform, was named. Stephens was regarded as one of the 'physical force chartists' and hailed as 'the tribune of the poor', but although he repudiated even the name of 'chartist' and maintained that his views were 'strictly constitutional', the impassioned language of his powerful oratory suggested otherwise.[2]

On 27 December 1838 Stephens was arrested at Ashton-under-Lyne on the charge of 'attending an unlawful meeting at Hyde' in Cheshire. He was tried at Chester Castle on 15 August 1839, the attorney-general prosecuting and Stephens defending himself. He was sentenced to find sureties for good behaviour for five years after suffering imprisonment for 18 months. He wrote that his confinement in Chester Castle was made 'as little irksome and unpleasant as possible,' adding, 'To a man who has slept soundly with a sod for his bed, and a portmanteau for his pillow, within a stone's throw of the North Cape, and who has made himself quite at home among Laplanders and Russians, there is nothing so very, very frightful in a moderately good gaol, as gaol's now go.'[3] He was presented with this cup at the end of his five years' bail.

In 1840 Stephens settled at Ashton-under-Lyne, where he preached at a chapel which he owned. In 1852 he moved to Stalybridge in Cheshire, and preached until 1875 at a rented chapel. He took part in various local agitations, retaining his power and popularity as a speaker, but took no lead in politics and claimed to stand aloof from parties. He had married his first wife Elizabeth Henwood in 1835 and, following her death in 1852, married Susanna Shaw in 1857.[4]

For a note on the maker, William Bateman I, see no.96.

PROVENANCE: Presented to the Rev. Joseph Rayner
Stephens, 1846; By descent to Lady Unwin, Hampstead,
London; Presented by Sir Stanley and Lady Unwin
through the National Art Collections Fund 1963.61

EXHIBITED: Chester 1980; London 1984, S.6.

PUBLISHED: NACF Report 1963, no.2142; Thomas,
p.15; Boughton 1992 I.

NOTES:

1. Fairbairn, p.451, pl.22 (cr.11).
2. Dictionary of National Biography, vol.54, p.178.
3. DNB, vol.54, p.178. For fuller details see Edwards. For the
    gaol at Chester Castle see Boughton 1997, no.116.
4. DNB, vol.54, pp.178-9.

THE ORMONDE SILVER

The house of Butler, one of Ireland's greatest noble families, was established by Theobald FitzWalter, who accompanied Henry II into Ireland. In 1177 he was created Hereditary Chief Butler of Ireland, with the status of a baron: the original meaning of butler was an officer of high rank who had charge of the wine for the royal table. His son Theobald first assumed the name of Le Botiler or Butler in 1221. Theobald, 4th Butler (c.1242-85) was granted the *prisage*, a tax levied on wines imported into Ireland, by Edward I. James, 7th Butler, was created Earl of Ormonde in 1328, and in 1391 James, 3rd Earl of Ormonde, purchased Kilkenny Castle, which remained the family's principal residence until 1935. Piers, 8th Earl of Ormonde, was created Earl of Ossory in 1527, and his son James, 9th Earl of Ormonde, was created Viscount Thurles in 1535. James, 12th Earl of Ormonde, was created Marquess of Ormonde in 1642, Baron Butler of Llanthony in 1660, Duke of Ormonde in the Irish peerage in 1661, and Duke of Ormonde in the English peerage in 1682. His grandson James, 2nd Duke of Ormonde, was attainted in 1715 for his Jacobite sympathies and all his English honours were forfeited. His brother Charles succeeded him in 1745 as *de jure* [by right] 3rd Duke of Ormonde but did not assume the honours, and on his death in 1758 the marquessate and dukedom became extinct. He was succeeded by John Butler of Kilcash (a descendant of Walter, 11th Earl of Ormonde) as *de jure* 15th Earl of Ormonde, Earl of Ossory and Viscount Thurles in the Irish peerage, but did not assume the honours. His cousin Walter, *de jure* 16th Earl of Ormonde, was the earliest owner of silver in this collection.[1]

The Ormonde collection of gold, silver-gilt and silver was accepted in lieu of estate duty by H.M. Treasury in 1980 from the estate of James Arthur Norman Butler, C.V.O., M.C., 6th Marquess of Ormonde (1893-1971), and was allocated in 1982 to the Grosvenor Museum, Chester; Birmingham Museum and Art Gallery; the Bowes Museum, Barnard Castle; Doncaster Museum and Art Gallery; the Fitzwilliam Museum, Cambridge; the Royal Pavilion, Brighton; the Ulster Museum, Belfast; and the Victoria and Albert Museum, London.

The three manuscript sources for this silver are among the Ormonde Papers in the National Library of Ireland, Dublin.
Ormonde Accounts, MS 11,059.
'List of Plate in Kilkenny Castle / Novr. 1839 & 27th Decr. 1848', MS 23,809; referred to here as 1839/48 Ormonde List.

R.&S. Garrard & Co., 'Inventory of Plate / The Most Honourable / The Marquess of Ormonde', 1904, MS 23,523; referred to here as 1904 Ormonde Inventory.

Owners of the Ormonde Silver

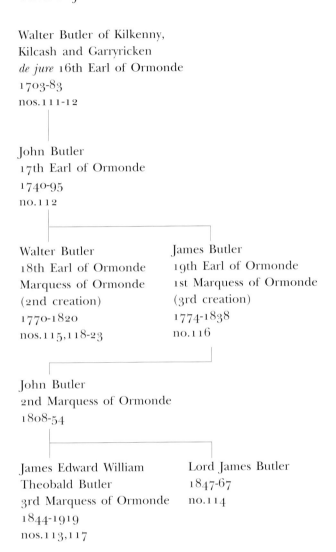

Walter Butler of Kilkenny,
Kilcash and Garryricken
de jure 16th Earl of Ormonde
1703-83
nos.111-12

John Butler
17th Earl of Ormonde
1740-95
no.112

Walter Butler
18th Earl of Ormonde
Marquess of Ormonde
(2nd creation)
1770-1820
nos.115,118-23

James Butler
19th Earl of Ormonde
1st Marquess of Ormonde
(3rd creation)
1774-1838
no.116

John Butler
2nd Marquess of Ormonde
1808-54

James Edward William
Theobald Butler
3rd Marquess of Ormonde
1844-1919
nos.113,117

Lord James Butler
1847-67
no.114

NOTE:
1. Burke's Peerage, pp.1871-3; Debrett's Peerage, pp.948-9.

111 PAIR OF TABLE CANDLESTICKS

William Abdy I, London, 1770-1

Four marks on side of each base (maker's mark variant, with notches at top and bottom of frame, of Grimwade no.3001). Lion passant and maker's mark on nozzles
Height: (1) without nozzle 32.8 cm. (12.9 in.), with nozzle 33.8 cm. (13.3 in.); (2) without nozzle 33 cm. (13 in.), with nozzle 34.1 cm. (13.4 in.)
Weight: (1) without nozzle 1630 g. (57.5 oz.), nozzle 52 g. (1.8 oz.); (2) without nozzle 1186 g. (41.8 oz.), nozzle 54 g. (1.9 oz.)

Sterling silver. The shaped quatrefoil bases with domed centres are raised and chased. They are filled with wood and pitch, and (1) retains its green baize. The borders are scrolled, and the four sections of each base are divided by knurled ribs, between which festoons of flowers and foliage alternate with a wicker basket of flowers and foliage on one face and a Rococo cartouche on the other. From each base rises an inverted baluster stem of square section, raised, chased and filled, with a cast knop below and above. Knurled ribs decorate the corners of the stems, with a single flower and foliage at the top of each face. The cast square-section vase-shaped sockets have similar decoration. The detachable nozzles, with seamed cylindrical bezels, have wide quatrefoil drip-pans, each chased with four knurled ribs and scrolled rims.

The bases are engraved in Roman lettering 'No 1 19=13' (1) and 'No 4 18 19' (2): the other candlesticks from this set of four are now in the Bowes Museum. They are described in the 1904 Ormonde Inventory as '4 - 13½ inch shaped column Table Candlesticks ornamented with flowers on round shaped bases with flowers and baskets of flowers in spaces. AD 1770'.

Engraved on each drip-pan and in the cartouche on each base is the Butler crest, probably for Walter, *de jure* 16th Earl of Ormonde. The engraving on these candlesticks is contemporary with the pieces themselves, and there is no coronet because all titles were forfeited until 1791.[1]

Walter Butler of Kilkenny, Kilcash and Garryricken, *de jure* 16th Earl of Ormonde, Earl of Ossory and Viscount Thurles, Chief Butler of Ireland (1703-83) was the son of John Butler of Garryricken. In 1732 he married Eleanor (1711-93), daughter of Nicholas Morres of Seapark Court, co. Dublin and Lateragh, co. Tipperary. In 1766 he succeeded his cousin to the family estates and *de jure* to the honours, which he did not assume. His youngest daughter, Lady Eleanor Butler, and her friend Sarah Ponsonby were the celebrated 'Ladies of Llangollen', where they lived in seclusion for some fifty years.[2]

Table candlesticks are discussed at no.46. Very close to Abdy's candlesticks is a pair of 1765, maker's mark LH.[3] They are slightly smaller and differ in having feet

to the base and flaring drip-pans. Nevertheless, they clearly share the same design source as Abdy's candlesticks, if not themselves forming his model.

The decoration of Abdy's candlesticks still follows the flowing curves of the Rococo, but in its late, symmetrical form. A slightly earlier set of four table candlesticks from the Ormonde collection, by Francis Butty and Nicholas Dumee, 1767, is now divided between Birmingham Museum and Art Gallery and the Victoria and Albert Museum. Like William Abdy's set, they are decorated with flowers and foliage, but they are more fully Rococo in their undulating asymmetry, having domed hexafoil bases and vase-shaped sockets with swirling flutes and twisting triangular baluster stems. The collection also included four 1772 'Corinthian column Table Candlesticks with rams heads and festoons on square bead bases'.[4] Thus the three sets of table candlesticks acquired by the 16th Earl of Ormonde between 1767 and 1772 illustrate the transition from Rococo to Neo-Classicism.

William Abdy I became free in 1752 and was elected to the Livery in 1763. He entered his first mark as a smallworker in 1763, and was recorded as a haft and hiltmaker and goldsmith. He was recorded again as a haftmaker in 1773, entered his seventh mark as a plateworker in 1784, and died in 1790.[5]

PROVENANCE: Presumably purchased by Walter, *de jure* 16th Earl of Ormonde; By descent to the 6th Marquess of Ormonde; Accepted in lieu of estate duty by H.M. Treasury and allocated to the Grosvenor Museum 1982.98.1,2

NOTES:
1. Gale Glynn, report, 22 March 1991.
2. Complete Peerage, vol.10, p.163.
3. Clayton 1985 II, p.196 fig.1.
4. 1904 Ormonde Inventory: unlocated.
5. Grimwade, p.419.

112 FIFTEEN TABLE KNIVES

Dru Drury II of London, c.1780-91

Two marks only on side of each handle near blade: maker's mark (Grimwade no.458) and lion passant on opposite sides
Length: (1) 26 cm. (10.2 in.), (2) 27.3 cm. (10.8 in.), (3) 26.3 cm. (10.35 in.), (4) 26.1 cm. (10.3 in.), (5) 26.2 cm. (10.3 in.), (6) 26.4 cm. (10.4 in.), (7) 26.2 cm. (10.3 in.), (8) 25.8 cm. (10.1 in.), (9) 26.3 cm. (10.35 in.), (10) 27.5 cm. (10.8 in.), (11) 27.2 cm. (10.7 in.), (12) 26cm. (10.2 in.), (13) 25.8 cm. (10.15 in.), (14) 26.3 cm. (10.35 in.), (15) handle only 10.3 cm. (4 in.)
Weight: (1) 127 g. (4.5 oz.), (2) 131 g. (4.6 oz.), (3) 128 g. (4.5 oz.), (4) 125 g. (4.4 oz.),

(5) 129 g. (4.55 oz.), (6) 120 g. (4.2 oz.), (7) 125 g. (4.4 oz.), (8,9) 124 g. (4.4 oz.), (10) 122 g. (4.3 oz.), (11) 130 g. (4.6 oz.), (12) 135 g. (4.8 oz.), (13) 126 g. (4.4 oz.), (14) 116 g. (4.1 oz.), (15) 56 g. (2 oz.)

Sterling silver handles with steel blades. The pistol handles with shell butts have four faces divided by ribs, the two broader faces rounded, the two narrower ones flatter. Each handle was struck in two halves and soldered together. The remains of the resin or shellac filling are visible in the handle (15) minus its blade. Three blades (2, 10 and 11) are longer and more pointed than the rest: they seem to have been reground and may originally have been the same shape. The knives are in poor condition.

As Ian Pickford has explained, 'up to the end of the eighteenth century the hafts of knives were usually only partially marked. Two marks (usually the maker's mark and one hallmark to indicate the standard) are normally found struck on the part of the haft nearest to the blade'.[1] No cutler's marks are visible on the steel blades, so these may not be original.

Molly Pearce has suggested, on stylistic grounds, that these knives probably date from the 1780s.[2] Engraved on one of the narrower faces of each handle

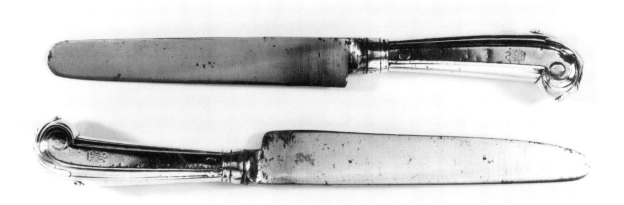

is the Butler crest for Walter, *de jure* 16th Earl of Ormonde, or for John, 17th Earl of Ormonde. There is no coronet above the crest because all titles were forfeited until 1791: this provides an upper date limit for the knives.

John (1740-95) was the only son of Walter, *de jure* 16th Earl of Ormonde (see no.111). In 1769 he married Lady Susan Frances Elizabeth (1754-1830), daughter and sole heiress of John, Earl Wandesford. He was M.P. for Gowran 1776-83 and for Kilkenny city 1783-91. In 1783 he succeeded his father to the family estates and *de jure* to the honours, and in 1791 his right to the peerages as 17th Earl of Ormonde, Earl of Ossory and Viscount Thurles, Chief Butler of Ireland, was acknowledged in the Irish House of Lords. He was Custos Rotulorum of co. Kilkenny from 1793 until his death at Kilkenny Castle.[3]

The 1904 Ormonde Inventory lists '15 Pistol handle' table knives plus '36 Rosette pattern', '93 Fancy thread and shell' and '1 Straight threaded' table knives.

Dru Drury II was born in 1725 and was apprenticed to his father Dru Drury I in 1739. He became free in 1746 and was elected to the Livery in 1751. He presumably worked with his father until the latter's death *c.*1766, and then entered his mark as a small-worker in 1767. Both father and son were specialists in knife-hafts and hilts. He was declared bankrupt in 1777 and 1786. The business was known as Drury Drury & Son from 1781-93. He had apparently retired by 1794, and by 1796 the business was run by his son William Drury. He died in 1804.[4]

Drury made the knife-hafts but purchased the blades from a cutler, as he did from Mr. Trickett Snr. of Sheffield in 1768 and from James Woolhouse of Sheffield in 1769. An indication of Drury's prices is provided by a letter to Charles Kandler, for whom 'ye blades & 3 pronged forks to 24 hafts that weighed 31 oz. 9 d.' cost 20 shillings in 1762. Lord Ormonde may have purchased these knives from the goldsmith John Locker of Dublin, whom Drury supplied with sets of knives described as 'shell haft'.[5]

PROVENANCE: Purchased by Walter, *de jure* 16th Earl of Ormonde or John, 17th Earl of Ormonde (possibly from John Locker of Dublin); By descent to the 6th Marquess of Ormonde; Accepted in lieu of estate duty by H.M. Treasury and allocated to the Grosvenor Museum 1982.102.1-15

NOTES:

1. Pickford, p.49.
2. Molly Pearce, letter, 8 July 1994.
3. Complete Peerage, vol.10, pp.163-4.
4. Grimwade, pp.495-7.
5. Grimwade, p.496.

The photograph shows (1) over (11)

113 SILVER-GILT SALVER (ROYAL CHRISTENING GIFT)

Robert Jones I, London, 1780-1; re-fashioned c.1844
Four marks beneath base near rim (maker's mark Grimwade no.2347)
Diameter 40.2 cm. (15.8 in.)
Weight 1,530 g. (53.95 oz.)

Sterling silver, gilt. The shaped circular salver is raised and is supported on four cast claw and ball feet. The cast and chased rim of scrolls, shells and foliage was either remade or, more probably, added *c.*1844. The elaborate flat-chased inner border of flowers, foliage, scrolls and trelliswork on a matted ground in the Rococo Revival style was also added *c.*1844. The salver was gilded after the centre was engraved in Roman, block, script and Old English lettering: 'PRESENTED / BY / Her Majesty / The Queen Adelaide / TO / HER GODSON / JAMES EDWARD WILLIAM THEOBALD / EARL OF OSSORY / Monday the 11th. of November, / 1844.'

James Edward William Theobald was the eldest son of John, 2nd Marquess of Ormonde (1808-54) by his wife Frances Jane (1817-1903), daughter of General the Hon.

Sir Edward Paget, G.C.B. He was born on 5 October 1844 at Kilkenny Castle, and was styled Earl of Ossory until his accession to the marquessate in 1854.[1] For his later life see no.117.

His mother was a Lady of the Bedchamber 1844-9 to the Queen Dowager Adelaide. Amelia Adelaide Louisa Theresa Caroline (1792-1849) was the eldest child of George, Duke of Saxe-Coburg Meiningen by his wife Louisa, daughter of Christian Albert, Prince of Hohenlohe-Langenburg. In 1818 she married Prince William, Duke of Clarence (1765-1837), the third son of King George III. She bore him two daughters, both of whom died in infancy. She became queen on the accession of her husband as William IV in 1830, and was crowned the following year. Her supposed interference in politics made her very unpopular in the early 1830s, but she later became highly esteemed for her blameless life and charitable munificence. William IV died in 1837 and was succeeded by his niece Victoria, the Queen Dowager thereafter living as an invalid at

Marlborough House and Bushey Park.[2] Queen Adelaide was a generous royal godmother: in 1844, the same year as her gift to the Earl of Ossory, she presented a pair of silver-gilt ewers and basins, likewise in the Rococo Revival style, to two other godchildren.[3]

The scroll and shell rim, used on trays, waiters and salvers, was particularly fashionable from the late 1740s to the end of the 1750s.[4] A late example of its use is on a salver of 1771 by Ebenezer Coker,[5] but this essentially Rococo form would have been outmoded by the time Robert Jones I made his salver in 1780, and the shell and scroll rim more probably dates from the salver's re-fashioning c.1844. Eighteenth century examples usually lack the foliage to the outer edge and the texture to the shells,[6] but these features are seen on a salver of 1824 by Paul Storr,[7] dating from the early years of the Rococo Revival in England. Flat-chased inner borders of shells, trelliswork and foliage were popular from the mid-1730s until the 1760s,[8] and were a favourite feature of Rococo Revival salvers. The Rococo Revival is discussed at no.88.

The re-fashioning of this salver could have been specially commissioned by Queen Adelaide in 1844 to form her christening gift, or it could have been purchased from stock, having already been re-decorated and the centre left blank for an armorial or inscription.[9] In addition to their functional uses (see no.116), salvers had also been used from c.1660 as presentation objects for display on the sideboard, and as such they soon became ideal vehicles for virtuoso engraving:[10] the Ormonde salver exemplifies the 19th-century continuation of this tradition.

This piece is presumably the '1 Gold Trea [sic] - Lord Ossory' and/or the 'Gold Salver of Lord Ossory' in the 1839/48 Ormonde List. It is described in the 1904 Ormonde Inventory as 'A 15 inch flat chased round Waiter with chased shell and scroll border. AD 1820 [sic]. Presented by Her Majesty Queen Adelaide'. As these entries show, the terms waiter, salver and tray were used inconsistently. According to a recent definition a waiter has a diameter of 15-25 cm., a salver is 25-55 cm., and a tray is 50-70 cm. with handles.[11]

The apprenticeship and freedom of Robert Jones I are unrecorded. He entered his first mark as a plateworker in 1774, his second mark in partnership with John Scofield (noted for his elegant design and impeccable craftsmanship) in 1776, and his third mark alone in 1778. He had probably died by 1783. The mark of his widow, Elizabeth Jones, is found almost exclusively on salvers and waiters, so these had presumably formed a major part of Robert Jones I's work.[12]

PROVENANCE: Presented by Queen Adelaide to James, Earl of Ossory, later 3rd Marquess of Ormonde, 1844; By descent to the 6th Marquess of Ormonde; Accepted in lieu of estate duty by H.M. Treasury and allocated to the Grosvenor Museum 1982.92

NOTES:

1. Complete Peerage, vol.10, pp.166-7.
2. Dictionary of National Biography, vol.1, pp.136-7.
3. By Richard Sawyer, Dublin, 1829-30: now at Belton House, Lincolnshire (James Lomax, note, 22 October 1999; Andrew Barber, letter, 7 December 1999).
4. Newman, p.278; Grimwade 1974, p.39.
5. Davis, no.138.
6. e.g. London-made salvers of 1749 by John Tuite (Wark, no.264) and of 1752 by James Morrison (Grimwade 1974, pl.18C), and waiters of 1763 by Ebenezer Coker and of 1768 by John Carter (Lomax, nos.55, 57).
7. Sotheby's, London, 1 November 1990, lot 338.
8. Grimwade 1974, pp.38-9, pl.19A.
9. The Royal Archives can find nothing relating to this salver in Queen Adelaide's private bills between July 1844 and June 1845 (Pamela Clark, letter, 30 July 1999).
10. Lomax, p.64.
11. Newman, pp.345, 273, 332.
12. Grimwade, pp.563-4, 653.

114 SILVER-GILT TWO-HANDLED CUP (CHRISTENING CUP)

Michael Homer, Dublin, 1784-5; re-fashioned c.1847

Three marks below rim: maker's mark (Jackson p.636), Hibernia, crowned harp
Height 13.8 cm. (5.4 in.), width across handles 16.7 cm. (6.6 in.)
Weight 433 g. (15.3 oz.)

Sterling silver, gilt. The spreading, stepped circular foot and low stem are raised. They support the raised, inverted bell-shaped cup, which has an everted rim and an applied horizontal moulding (originally plain) around the body. The two cast leaf-capped double-scroll handles have small lozenge-shaped panels at their lower junction with the bowl. The cup was re-fashioned c.1847 in the Rococo Revival style, with a chased and matted band on the foot, the rib around the body reworked into beading, and the body chased with flowers and scrolls on a matted ground (virtually identical both sides). The cup was gilded after the engraving of the Butler crest in two cartouches on the upper part of the body, and the inscription toward the base in Old English, block and Roman lettering: 'The Lord James Hubert Henry Thomas Butler / from his Godfather / THOMAS FORTESCUE / October 1847'.

Lord James Butler (1847-67) was the second son of John, 2nd Marquess of Ormonde (1808-54). He became a cornet in the 9th (The Queen's Royal) Lancers in 1866.[1]

His godfather Thomas Fortescue (1784-1872) was the son of Gerald Fortescue by his wife Elizabeth, daughter of John Tew. In India he acted as secretary to his Irish cousin Henry Wellesley (later 1st Baron Cowley), lieutenant-governor of the newly ceded province of Oude, 1801-3, and on the capture of Delhi in 1803 was appointed civil commissioner there. He married Louisa Margaret, daughter of Thomas Russell, in 1859.[2]

Michael McAleer dates the cup to 1784-5, since this was the only year in which the mark of the crowned harp has five strings.[3]

This type of two-handled cup was made in Dublin from c.1720 and remained much the same throughout the 18th century: a cup of 1739 by William Williamson has a slightly lower stem than the Ormonde cup, and a pair of 1788 by Matthew West have higher stems.[4] The robust style of this cup in its original form contrasts with the delicate Neo-Classical decoration on other pieces by Michael Homer, such as a cream jug of 1786 and a salver of 1788.[5]

Many pieces of Irish silver have been re-chased, and the Rococo Revival style reached a high standard of virtuosity in the hands of the Dublin goldsmiths, who employed freelance chasers for the more

elaborate pieces.[6] Comparable examples include a Dublin two-handled cup of 1725 with Victorian chasing, and a two-handled cup of 1775 with 1820s decoration.[7]

It seems likely that the Rococo Revival decoration on this cup was executed in Dublin, and the date letter was presumably lost at this time. The cup was probably purchased from stock, already re-decorated, to form a christening gift in 1847 since, although the cartouches were clearly intended for armorials or short inscriptions, the long inscription is fitted on toward the base rather than forming an integrated part of the design.

This cup appears as an addition in the 1839/48 Ormonde List as '1 Gold Cup—Lord Hubert', and in the 1904 Ormonde Inventory as 'A Small chased two handle Cup ... Dublin'.

Michael Homer had work assayed at Dublin in 1752-3: this may be a misreading of the mark for William Homer, who had plate assayed in 1754-8. Michael Homer registered with the Dublin Goldsmiths'

Company in 1784, had work assayed in 1785-8, and was prosecuted for tax evasion in 1795.[8]

PROVENANCE: Presented by Thomas Fortescue to Lord James Butler, 1847; By descent to the 6th Marquess of Ormonde; Accepted in lieu of estate duty by H.M. Treasury and allocated to the Grosvenor Museum 1982.91

NOTES:

1. Complete Peerage, vol.10, p.166.
2. Dictionary of National Biography, vol.20, p.48.
3. Michael McAleer, telephone conversation, 10 June 1994.
4. Bennett 1972 I, figs.29, 30.
5. Ticher, fig.47; Bennett 1972 I, fig.22.
6. Newman, p.178; Lomax, p.147.
7. Bennett 1972 I, fig.30; Bennett 1984, fig.79.
8. Jackson, pp.636, 692, 701; Bennett 1972 I, pp.219, 310; Ticher, fig.47.

115 SAUCEPAN

Robert Sharp, London, 1800-1

Five marks beneath base (maker's mark Grimwade no.2436)
Length across handle 25.3 cm. (9.95 in.)
Weight 383 g. (13.5 oz.)

Sterling silver with handle of stained holly (*Ilex aquifolium*).[1] The bulbous body is raised, with a flat, circular base and an everted rim. The beak-shaped pouring lip is cast and applied. At a right-angle to the lip is an uplifted baluster handle of turned wood, pinned to a long, tapering silver ferrule with a narrow double moulding at the handle end and a circular reinforcing plate at its junction with the bowl. The body has been repaired between the lip and the handle.

The saucepan is engraved opposite the handle with the Butler crest, enclosed within the Order of St Patrick and surmounted by a marquess's coronet, presumably for Walter, 18th Earl of Ormonde, created Marquess of Ormonde in 1816. The crest appears to be contemporary with the saucepan, but possibly the order and certainly the coronet were added in or after 1816.[2]

Walter (1770-1820) was the eldest son of John, 17th Earl of Ormonde (see no.112). He was M.P. for co. Kilkenny 1790-5, when he succeeded his father as 18th Earl of Ormonde, Earl of Ossory and Viscount Thurles, Chief Butler of Ireland. He was Custos Rotulorum and Governor of co. Kilkenny 1796-1820. He became a Privy Councillor in 1797, a Knight of St Patrick in 1798, and was created Baron Butler of Llanthony in 1801. In 1805 he married Anna Maria Catherine (1789-1817), only daughter and sole heiress of Job Hart Price-Clarke of Sutton Hall, Derbyshire. His Irish estates were said to be worth £22,000 per annum in 1799, and in 1811 he was granted £216,000 by Parliament as compensation for the resumption by the Crown of the hereditary prisage of wines. He was a companion of the Prince Regent, whom he followed in acquiring silver by Robert Sharp, Paul Storr, William Pitts and Benjamin Smith. He was a Lord of the Bedchamber 1812-13, and in 1816 was created Marquess of Ormonde (the second creation). He died without issue, and the marquessate and barony became extinct.[3]

This may be the '1 Silver Saucepan old' in the 1839/48 Ormonde List, and it is described in the 1904 Ormonde Inventory as 1 Plain Saucepan 'smaller no cover. AD 1800'.

Robert Sharp was apprenticed to Gawen Nash in 1747 and turned over the same day to Thomas Gladwin. He became free in 1757 and was elected to the Livery in 1771. He entered his first mark in partnership with Daniel Smith, apparently by 1763, and they are recorded as plateworkers in 1773. Sharp and Smith were in partnership with Richard Carter 1778-80, and without him 1780-8. Sharp worked alone from 1788 and died in 1803. His firm supplied plate to Parker & Wakelin, and they almost certainly later supplied Wakelin & Taylor and Jefferys, Jones & Gilbert (Royal Goldsmiths from 1784), and probably much of the plate for Carlton House.[4]

Robert Sharp and his partners produced magnificent race cups in the Adam taste, candelabra in the French Neo-Classical style, and much dinner plate.[5] This simple saucepan is therefore an unusually modest example of Sharp's work.

PROVENANCE: Presumably purchased by Walter, 18th Earl of Ormonde, later Marquess of Ormonde (possibly from Jefferys, Jones & Gilbert); By descent to the 6th Marquess of Ormonde; Accepted in lieu of estate duty by H.M. Treasury and allocated to the Grosvenor Museum 1982.100

NOTES:
1. Wood identified by Graham Usher, 13 November 1999.
2. Gale Glynn, report, 22 March 1991.
3. Complete Peerage, vol.10, pp.164-5.
4. Grimwade, p.655.
5. Grimwade, p.655.

115

116 THREE SALVERS

Ashforth, Ellis & Co., Sheffield, 1802-3

Each: five marks beneath base near rim
(maker's mark Jackson p.441, colon between G:A)
Length: (1,2) 35.4 cm. (13.9 in.), (3) 23.1 cm. (9.1 in.)
Weight: (1) 807g. (28.45 oz.), (2) 824g. (29.05oz.), (3) 307 g. (10.8 oz.)

Sterling silver. The oval salvers are raised and have cast and applied gadrooned borders. Each is supported on four cast and applied bracket feet with reeded borders. All are dented, and the engraving on (3) is badly worn.

They are described in the 1904 Ormonde Inventory as '2 14 inch oval gadrooned Waiters on 4 feet, engraved Arms in centre. Sheffield Hall AD 1802. 2 9¼ inch do; to match. Sheffield Hall AD 1802.' The second smaller salver is now unlocated.

The centre of each salver is engraved with the Butler arms, crest and motto, differenced with a crescent for Lord James Butler (1774-1838), second son of John, 17th Earl of Ormonde (see no. 112). He was M.P. for Kilkenny city 1796, and for co. Kilkenny 1796-1800 and 1801-20. In 1807 he married Grace Louisa (1779-1860), second daughter of the Rt. Hon. John Staples. In 1820 he succeeded his brother Walter, Marquess of Ormonde (see no.115) as 19th Earl of Ormonde, Earl of Ossory and Viscount Thurles, Chief Butler of Ireland. In 1821 he was created Baron Ormonde of Llanthony, a Knight of St Patrick, and officiated as Chief Butler of Ireland at the Coronation of George IV: the gold covered cup of 1821 by Philip Rundell, presented to him at the Coronation, is now in the Victoria and Albert Museum.[1] In 1825 he was created Marquess of Ormonde (the third creation). He was Vice-Admiral of Leinster, Lord Lieutenant and Custos Rotulorum of co. Kilkenny 1831-8, Militia A.D.C. to the King (extra) 1832-7 and to the Queen 1837-8.[2]

In addition to the use of salvers for display on the sideboard (see no.113), there were two other uses for salvers and waiters in the 18th-century dining room, as explained by James Lomax.[3] 'First, they were used for waiting at table by the servants, especially in bringing glasses of wine to the table from the sideboard since contemporary etiquette forbad the placing of drinking glasses on the table itself.' Secondly, 'they were used on the table at the dessert course as raised dishes for holding fruits, sweetmeats and syllabub glasses'. Trays, salvers and waiters were also used at the tea table, particularly to support tea kettles. Later, letters, visiting cards, newspapers, etc., were placed on a salver for formal presentation by a servant.

Ashforth, Ellis & Co. was founded in Sheffield c.1770. The main partners were George Ashforth and Samuel Ellis, a cutler turned die sinker. They made Old Sheffield Plate, silver and cutlery. Before the Sheffield Assay Office opened in 1773 they sent their silver to London to be hallmarked. Like most firms of platers, they maintained a branch in London, and they also had one in Paris in connection with Wedgwood's showroom. In 1792 George Ashforth settled in London, and the firm closed in 1811.[4]

PROVENANCE: Purchased by Lord James Butler, later 19th Earl and 1st Marquess of Ormonde; By descent to the 6th Marquess of Ormonde; Accepted in lieu of estate duty by H.M. Treasury and allocated to the Grosvenor Museum 1982.99.1-3

NOTES:
1. Jones 1907, pl.XXXV.
2. Complete Peerage, vol.10, p.165.
3. Lomax, p.64.
4. Molly Pearce, letter, 3 September 1993.

117 SILVER-GILT CUP AND COVER ON STAND (WEDDING GIFT)

Cup: no maker's mark, London, 1803-4
Cover: probably Thomas Edwards, London, 1825-6
Stand: Stephen Smith & Son, London, 1875-6

(1) Cup

Four marks on foot: lion passant, leopard's head, date letter, duty mark. Lion passant on each of four wing-nuts which fasten foot to base. Base unmarked
Height 36.5 cm. (14.4 in.), width across handles 29.1 cm. (11.45 in.)
Weight apx. 5,815 g. (205.1 oz.)

(2) Cover

Three marks inside: lion passant, date letter, maker's mark (worn TE in rectangular cut-corner punch, see Grimwade no.2745 note)
Height to Neptune's head 13.2 cm. (5.2 in.), diameter 25.8 cm. (10.15 in.)
Weight 840 g. (29.6 oz.)

(3) Stand

Five marks on each plaque (maker's mark Culme nos.13532-3)
Height of stand 23.9 cm. (9.4 in.), width of principal plaque 17.4 cm. (6.85 in.)

All sterling silver, gilt. The cup's square base, chased with scalework, supports a further shaped square scroll base. The raised circular foot is chased with *rocaille*, and the short stem has a cast knop of lobes. The raised *kalyx krater* shaped cup has a cast and applied band of trailing vine leaves and bunches of grapes, and the wide everted rim is cast and chased in imitation of sea foam. The two cast handles are formed as classical helmeted ships' figureheads. The raised domed cover is chased to match the cup's rim, although the tooling is clearly by a different hand. It is surmounted by a detachable cast standing figure of Neptune with a dolphin, his trident made separately.

The square stand is of ebonised mahogany (*Swietenia macrophylla*).[1] It bears three cast plaques of the badge of the 1st Life Guards: a number 1 above the double cipher LG in ornamental script interwoven and reversed, enclosed within the Garter, with a crown above and a scroll inscribed 'PENINSULA WATERLOO' in Roman lettering below. The principal plaque, with a shaped and chased Rococo Revival scroll-work border, is engraved in ornamental Roman lettering: 'PRESENTED TO / JAMES, THIRD MARQUIS OF ORMONDE; / LATE CAPTAIN FIRST LIFE GUARDS, / ON HIS MARRIAGE. / BY HIS BROTHER OFFICERS SERVING IN THE REGIMENT, / FEBRUARY, - 1876.' The smooth parts of all three pieces are frosted, and the whole was electro-gilded in 1875-6 by Stephen Smith & Son.

It is described in the 1904 Ormonde Inventory as 'A vase shape Cup with Roman figure head handles ornamented with vine leaves round body with shaped scroll base on a lower square base and figure of Neptune on cover. on mounted wood base. Officers Wedding Present 1876. dates various.'

James, 3rd Marquess of Ormonde, 21st Earl of Ormonde, Earl of Ossory, Viscount Thurles and Baron Ormonde of Llanthony, Chief Butler of Ireland (1844-1919) succeeded his father in 1854. For his early life see no.113. He became a cornet and sub-lieutenant in the 1st Regiment of Life Guards in 1863, lieutenant in 1866, captain in 1868, and retired in 1873. He was Colonel of the Royal East Kent Mounted Rifles and Honorary Colonel of the 4th Battalion the Royal Irish Regiment. He became a Knight of St Patrick in 1868, and was Lord Lieutenant and Custos Rotulorum of co. Kilkenny 1878-1919. He was Vice-Admiral of Leinster, Honorary Captain of the Royal Naval Reserve, Commodore of the Royal Yacht Squadron and of the Royal Irish Yacht Club. He became a member of the Privy Council of Ireland in 1902, and was a Knight of the Order of the Crown of Prussia. On 2 February 1876 he married Lady Elizabeth Harriet Grosvenor (1856-1928), eldest daughter of Hugh Lupus, 1st Duke of Westminster, at Aldford on the Duke's Cheshire estate. They had two daughters, Beatrice Elizabeth (1876-1952) and Constance Mary (1879-1949). He died at Kilkenny Castle.[2]

Another wedding gift is now in the Victoria and Albert Museum. It is a silver-gilt model of a prowling fox by Robert Garrard, London, 1876-7, on an oval ebony plinth with an applied plaque engraved '1876 to James Marquis of Ormonde on his marriage from his hunting friends in the County of Kilkenny'.

The cup was originally a wine cooler, for holding iced water and lumps of ice to chill a bottle of wine. It would have been called an ice-pail or ice-bucket, the term wine cooler being used from the 1840s. It is shaped like an ancient Greek *kalyx krater*, which was also the form of the celebrated Medici Vase, popular at this time following its publication in G.B. Piranesi's *Vasi* (1778) and C.H. Tatham's *Etchings of Ancient Ornamental Architecture* (1799). Appropriately, this form was much used for wine coolers during the early 19th century, since in ancient Greek pottery the krater was used for mixing wine and water. This is further reflected in the decoration, the vine symbolising wine, and the sea foam and ships' figureheads referring to water. The cup is also an early example of the revival of foamwork, which is more often found from c.1810.[3]

Vessels very close to the Ormonde cup, lacking only the base and having twisted vine handles in place of the figureheads, were made by Edward I, Edward II, John & William Barnard. Examples include a covered cup of 1829 with its pair made by Hamilton & Co. of

117

Calcutta *c*.1830-3, and a pair of wine coolers dating from 1837.[4] A pair of 1844 wine coolers by Benjamin Smith III, represent a later development of the Ormonde cup.[5] Formed as *kalyx kraters*, their wide everted rims are similarly cast and chased to imitate sea foam, but the rims undulate more markedly and have applied bunches of grapes.

The addition of the cover in 1825-6 produced an ensemble similar to the slightly later Weymouth Regatta Cup of 1827, a silver-gilt covered wine cooler by Rebecca Emes & Edward Barnard.[6] Although both vessels were still capable of functioning as wine coolers, the covers made them more suitable for use as display pieces. The finial on the cover of the Weymouth

Regatta Cup is a standing sailor beside an anchor. The Ormonde cup is surmounted by a figure of Neptune, echoing the watery theme of the sea foam and the classical allusions of the ships' figureheads.

A seated figure of Neptune surmounts Paul Crespin's centrepiece of 1741 made for Frederick, Prince of Wales, and two copies were made in 1780 by Robert Hennell. Rundell, Bridge & Rundell added an elaborate base *c*.1826, and their designers were certainly inspired by the marine ornament on such pieces of old royal plate.[7] Two examples of covered cups with seated Neptune finials, both symbolically appropriate, are Paul Storr's 1799 Battle of the Nile Cup and a yachting cup of 1830 by Jonathan Hayne.[8]

Thomas Edwards may have been apprenticed to John Robins in 1789, but his freedom is unrecorded. He entered his first mark as a plateworker in 1816 and his last mark in 1840.[9]

Stephen Smith I was born in 1822, the son of Benjamin Smith III. The latter had been taken into partnership by his father Benjamin Smith II (see no.122) in 1816, and had run the firm from 1818 until his death in 1850. The business was continued by Stephen Smith I, in partnership with William Nicholson 1851-64, then with his son Stephen Smith II (born 1846) trading as Stephen Smith & Son, manufacturing silversmiths and electroplaters, from 1865. They supplied silver to other retailers, as well as retailing other manufacturers' work. The firm was purchased in 1886 by the manufacturing and retail silversmiths and electroplaters Mappin & Webb (which had been founded in 1859 and is now a subsidiary of Sears Holdings Ltd.). Stephen Smith I became prime warden of the Goldsmiths' Company in 1885 and died in 1890.[10]

The firm, under earlier partnerships, had produced presentation plate, including a testimonial presented to Garibaldi in 1861 by his Jamaican admirers.[11] The Ormonde cup and cover on stand illustrates Stephen Smith & Son's continuing involvement in the supply of presentation plate.[12]

PROVENANCE: Presented by the officers of the 1st Regiment of Life Guards to James, 3rd Marquess of Ormonde, 1876; By descent to the 6th Marquess of Ormonde; Accepted in lieu of estate duty by H.M. Treasury and allocated to the Grosvenor Museum 1982.90.1-3

NOTES:

1. Wood identified by Graham Usher, 13 November 1999.
2. Complete Peerage, vol.10, pp.166-7; Burke's Peerage, p.1874.
3. Newman, p.362; Lomax, p.25; Glanville 1987, p.119.
4. Fallon; Crighton, p.49.
5. Bury, p.82.
6. Oman 1965, fig.210.
7. Newman, p.222; Snodin 1984, p.114; Queen's Gallery 1991, p.124.
8. Penzer 1971, p.107; Lomax, no.18.
9. Grimwade, p.502; Culme, I, p.138.
10. Culme, I, pp.308, 424.
11. Culme, I, p.424.
12. As does an 1868 racing trophy illustrated in Bury, p.85.

118 VEGETABLE DISH AND COVER

Paul Storr, London, 1807-8

(1) Dish
Five marks on outside beneath rim (maker's mark Grimwade no. 2235)
Length 34.5 cm. (13.6 in.), height 5.8 cm. (2.3 in.)
Weight 1,398 g. (49.3 oz.)

(2) Cover
Three marks beneath top: maker's mark, lion passant, date letter. Finial unmarked
Length 29.7 cm. (11.7 in.), height 16.8 cm. (6.6 in.)
Weight 1,177 g. (41.5 oz.)

(3) Two-Part Divider
Four marks on divider: lion passant, date letter, duty mark, maker's mark
Length 28.8 cm. (11.3 in.)
Weight 437 g. (15.4 oz.)

(4) Three-Part Divider
Four marks as (3)
Length 28.9 cm. (11.4 in.)
Weight 487 g. (17.2 oz.)

See Colour Plate VIII

All sterling silver. The raised oval dish has an applied deep bezel and a cast shell, foliage and gadroon border with a gallery. The raised high-domed cover is chased with a gadrooned band above an applied rim. It is surmounted by an applied oval plate bordered by applied beading, with four pierced steam-escape holes beneath. The cast finial, attached by a silver screw, is in the form of the Butler crest, a falcon rising from a plume of five ostrich feathers within a ducal coronet. The detachable dividers have central ring handles.

The pieces are inscribed with number 2 on the gallery of the dish, 2 on the rim of the cover, 12 beneath the handle, and 1 on the rims of the dividers. Described in the 1904 Ormonde Inventory as '2 Oval Vegetable dishes to match with dome covers and divisions and crest handles and silver two handle warmers on 4 feet', the second dish was sold at Phillips c.1932.

The cover is engraved twice with the Butler arms within the Order of St Patrick, with supporters, motto and marquess's coronet for Walter, Marquess of Ormonde (see no.115). The Butler crest surmounted by a marquess's coronet is engraved twice inside the dish and once on each divider. The armorial engravings were added after the creation of the marquessate in 1816.

A pair of circular covered vegetable dishes of 1808 by Paul Storr, *en suite* with that at Chester, is now in the Bowes Museum. They are presumably from the set of '4 Round Entree dishes to match with dome covers and crest handles and plated warmers' in the 1904 Ormonde Inventory, marked '2 Phillips' in a later hand. They retain their Old Sheffield Plate two-handled stands, which include a section for hot sand or water to keep the food warm, and have four feet to protect the table from the heat.[1] The dish at Chester is now missing its stand. According to the 1904 Ormonde Inventory there were also '2 Oval part fluted gadroon Soup tureens and covers and linings with crest buttons on oval stands with leafage ends and on 4 claw feet'

(unlocated), and '2 do; to match (smaller)' (marked 'Phillips' in a later hand), all by Paul Storr 1808.[2] Also by Paul Storr are four incurving rectangular entree dishes and covers, 1808 (the covers, 1807), now divided between the Royal Pavilion and the Victoria and Albert Museum. They are *en suite* with the dish at Chester, having shell, foliage and gadroon borders, and covers with beaded bands and Butler crest finials; they likewise originally had plated warmers (according to the 1904 Ormonde Inventory) but these are now missing.

Further pieces continue the motif of Butler crest finials. Four 1808 Paul Storr sauce tureens and covers (from a set of eight according to the 1904 Ormonde Inventory), the tureens more richly decorated but the covers having beaded bands and Butler crest finials, are now in the Victoria and Albert Museum. According to the 1904 Ormonde Inventory the Dinner Service (see no.122) also included the following unlocated pieces with crest handles: two 20 ¼ inch and two 15 inch dish covers by Benjamin Smith 1808, and four pincushion entree dishes with covers by Paul Storr 1807. Again by Paul Storr, with Butler crest finials, are a four-light candelabrum of 1810 in the Bowes Museum and a pair of three-light candelabra of 1811 in the Victoria and Albert Museum.[3]

The shell, foliage and gadroon motif, used on the border of the dish, was popular among several Regency goldsmiths.[4] It was earlier used by Paul Storr on the four incurving rectangular entree dishes of 1806 presented to Rear-Admiral Sir Samuel Hood.[5] These entree dishes also have oval beaded bands with cast crest finials, as do the *en suite* tureen and four sauce-boats.

Paul Storr was born in 1771, the son of Thomas Storr of Westminster, silver-chaser. He was apprenticed *c.*1785 to Andrew Fogelberg. He entered his first mark as a plateworker in partnership with William Frisbee in 1792 and his second mark alone in 1793. He was the leading Regency goldsmith, working in collaboration with the firm of Rundell, Bridge & Rundell 1807-19, and with the retailer John Mortimer 1822-38. He retired in 1838 and died in 1844.[6]

The only bill from Rundell, Bridge & Rundell to survive in the Ormonde Accounts is for 17 April 1804 - 14 February 1806 totalling £2,440 4s. 9d., although none of the silver itemised here can be identified in the surviving collection.

Other silver by Paul Storr in the Ormonde collection included:
a pair of trays, 1808 (Bowes Museum and Royal Pavilion)
a cruet frame, 1808 (Bowes Museum)
a pair of wine coolers, 1808 (Fitzwilliam Museum)
a tankard, 1809 (Birmingham Museum and Art Gallery)
a pair of sauce tureens and covers, 1809 (Birmingham Museum and Art Gallery)

119

twelve salts, 1809 (Bowes Museum and Royal Pavilion) [see no.121]
four wine coolers and stands, 1809 [liners 1808] (Royal Pavilion and Victoria and Albert Museum)
a pair of dessert stands, 1810 (Royal Pavilion)
a six-light candelabrum centrepiece, 1810 (Royal Pavilion)
a pair of trays, 1811 (Bowes Museum)
For Paul Storr tea silver see nos.119 and 123.

PROVENANCE: Purchased by Walter, 18th Earl of Ormonde, later Marquess of Ormonde (presumably from Rundell, Bridge & Rundell); By descent to the 6th Marquess of Ormonde; Accepted in lieu of estate duty by H.M. Treasury and allocated to the Grosvenor Museum 1982.101.1-4

NOTES:

1. Coutts 1994 I, fig.11.
2. Two of these tureens were sold at Christie's, New York: a large one on 21 October 1993, lot 455, and a smaller one on 18 April 1989, lot 428.
3. These candelabra are *en suite* with eight table candlesticks of 1811, divided between the Bowes Museum and the Victoria and Albert Museum.
4. Lomax, p.78.
5. Penzer 1971, p.121.
6. Grimwade, p.672; Lomax, p.76.

119 PARCEL-GILT CREAM EWER

Paul Storr, London, 1808-9

Five marks on foot-ring (Grimwade no.2235)
Length 18.5 cm. (7.3 in.), height 10.3 cm. (4.05 in.)
Weight 482 g. (17 oz.)

See Colour Plate VIII

Sterling silver with gilt interior. The raised, spreading circular foot is chased with a band of gadrooning. It supports the raised, compressed circular vase-shaped body, whose lower section is chased with gadrooning. The broad convex shoulder is applied, with cast gadrooning at its outer edge and a cast egg and dart rim, which continues across the lip. The wide pouring lip is applied on axis with the cast bifurcated serpent handle.

One side of the body is engraved with the arms of Butler within the Order of St Patrick, *en accole* with the arms of Butler within an oak leaf wreath with those of Price-Clarke in pretence. The arms, with supporters, motto and helmet, are displayed within a mantle surmounted by a marquess's coronet. The other side of the body is engraved with the crest surmounted by a marquess's coronet with ermine mantling. The engraving probably dates from between January 1816, when Walter Butler (see no.115) was created Marquess of Ormonde, and 19 December 1817, when his wife Anna Maria Catherine, née Price-Clarke, died.

This ewer is one of a pair; the other is now in the Bowes Museum. They are presumably the '2 Cream Ewers' in the 1839/48 Ormonde List, and are described in the 1904 Ormonde Inventory as '2 Part fluted Cream ewers with serpent handles to match. AD 1808. Paul Storr.' For the use and terminology of such vessels in the 18th century see no.23, and for the other Paul Storr tea silver in the Ormonde collection see no.123.

The double serpent handle, which had been a feature of Neo-Classical silver in the 1770s,[1] was a favourite Storr motif. Norman Penzer illustrates six examples between 1802 and 1818, ranging from a simple handle, like the Ormonde one, on an 1810 cream ewer to the excess of four writhing serpents on a set of 1815 salts.[2] Eleven of the 18 tea services listed by Penzer had serpent handles,[3] as did the tea urn, hot water jugs and sugar basins in Storr's Ormonde tea silver (see no.123). These appear to have influenced Robert Garrard, who used bifurcated serpent handles on a pair of 1853 tea pots for the Ormondes.[4] Eighteenth-century variants of the single serpent handle on milk and cream jugs include a large curved serpent,[5] a writhing serpent,[6] and a serpent entwining the handle.[7]

PROVENANCE: Purchased by Walter, 18th Earl of Ormonde, later Marquess of Ormonde (presumably from Rundell, Bridge & Rundell); By descent to the 6th Marquess of Ormonde; Accepted in lieu of estate duty by H.M. Treasury and allocated to the Grosvenor Museum 1982.94

NOTES:

1. Rowe 1965, p.41.
2. Penzer 1971, pp.143, 195.
3. Penzer 1971, pp.268-9, 280.

4. 1904 Ormonde Inventory; one now in the Victoria and Albert Museum.
5. e.g. jugs of 1719 by David Willaume I and of 1780 by Andrew Fogelberg & Stephen Gilbert (Wees, no.253; Wark, no.176).
6. e.g. jugs of c.1745 by Eliza Godfrey and of 1766 by Charles Clark (Brett, no.930; Wark, no.166).
7. e.g. jugs of c.1740-50 by Charles Frederick Kandler I and of 1756 by Peter Werritzer (Wark, no.144; Grimwade, pl.65A).

120 PAIR OF SALVERS

John Crouch II, London, 1808-9

Five marks beneath base (maker's mark Grimwade no.1791)

Diameter 26.9 cm. (10.6 in.)

Weight: (1) 857 g. (30.2 oz.), (2) 833 g. (29.4 oz.)

Sterling silver. The shaped octagonal salvers have circular depressions and cast gadroon, anthemion and shell borders. Each rests on three cast anthemion feet with gadrooned edges.

The centre of each salver is engraved with the arms of Butler, *en accole* with the arms of Butler with those of Price-Clarke in pretence, displayed within a mantle surmounted by a marquess's coronet, as on no.119, for Walter, Marquess of Ormonde (see no. 115). The engraving probably dates between January 1816 and December 1817.

These salvers come from a set of four; the others are now in the Bowes Museum. They are possibly the '4 Round Waiters' in the 1839/48 Ormonde List, and are described in the 1904 Ormonde Inventory as '4 10 inch gadroon and shell octagonal Waiters on 3 feet. AD 1808.'

John Crouch II was apprenticed to his father John Crouch I in 1790 and became free in 1797. He entered

121

his first mark in 1799 as junior partner with Thomas Hannam (with whom John Crouch I had been in partnership 1766-93). He entered his second mark alone in 1808, presumably on Hannam's death or retirement. He was elected to the Livery in 1829 and died in 1837.[1]

Thomas Hannam's partnerships with John Crouch I and II 'appear to have had a virtual monopoly in the trade as makers of fine quality salvers and waiters'.[2] The Ormonde salvers date from John Crouch II's first year working alone.

PROVENANCE: Purchased by Walter, 18th Earl of Ormonde, later Marquess of Ormonde; By descent to the 6th Marquess of Ormonde; Accepted in lieu of estate duty by H.M. Treasury and allocated to the Grosvenor Museum 1982.95.1,2

NOTES:

1. Grimwade, pp.480-1.
2. Grimwade, p.533.

121 FOUR PARCEL-GILT SALTS

William Pitts, London, 1808-9

Five marks beneath base (maker's mark Grimwade no.3263)

(1) Diameter 11.1 cm. (4.4 in.), height 5.8 cm. (2.3 in.), weight 391 g. (13.8 oz.)
(2) Diameter 11.2 cm. (4.4 in.), height 6 cm. (2.35 in.), weight 415 g. (14.6 oz.)
(3) Diameter 11.3 cm. (4.45 in.), height 5.9 cm. (2.3 in.), weight 406 g. (14.3 oz.)
(4) Diameter 11.5 cm. (4.5 in.), height 5.9 cm. (2.3 in.), weight 377 g. (13.3 oz.)

Sterling silver with gilt interiors. The compressed circular bulbous bodies are raised, with cast everted gadrooned rims. Each salt stands on four cast lion mask and paw feet, with separately cast and applied floral festoons between.

Each is engraved once below a festoon with the Butler crest, within the Order of St Patrick and surmounted by a marquess's coronet, for Walter, Marquess of Ormonde (see no.115). The engraving was added after the creation of the marquessate in 1816.

The basic type, known as a 'cauldron' salt, was a Huguenot introduction of the 1730s.[1] Examples by Paul de Lamerie, almost identical to those by William Pitts, include a 1733 set of four.[2] Variants by Paul de Lamerie, but with faun and satyr masks on hoof feet, include a 1731 set of four with festoons of flowers and fruit,[3] and a 1746 set of six in the Thanet dinner service with festoons of grapes and vine leaves.[4] As Susan Hare has explained, 'such was the influence of Paul de Lamerie that reproductions of his work have been made almost ever since and the salt with floral festoons, generally with lion mask and paw feet, has been among the most copied'.[5] Many dozens of these salts were produced by Paul Storr's workshop, including eight silver-gilt examples of 1814 at Goldsmiths' Hall.

The Ormonde Accounts record that on 15 October 1804 the 18th Earl of Ormonde purchased from Rundell, Bridge & Rundell '8 salts with lions feet, gilt inside, 40 oz £39 4s 9d / each engraved twice with crest and coronet 16s'. Whilst giving an interesting indication of prices, these items are now unlocated, but a set of 12 salts by Paul Storr, 1809, does survive, divided between the Bowes Museum and the Royal Pavilion. Similar to but more elaborate than the Grosvenor Museum's, these are of silver-gilt with cut-glass liners, and have three lion mask and paw feet between floral festoons with shell and gadroon rims. A pair of plain circular salts from the Ormonde collection, each on three hoof feet, maker's mark IS, London, 1736, is now in the Victoria and Albert Museum. The 1904 Ormonde Inventory also lists '10 Round festooned Salt Cellars on 3 lion mask feet and gadroon border. AD 1808' (probably those at Chester, although the number of feet differ), and '6 Round fluted Salt Cellars. Dublin AD 1807. West' (unlocated).

The term salt-cellar is derived from *saliere*, the French for salt-box, and was used from *c.*1820. Each bowl holds salt for individual use at the dinner table. The gilded interiors protect the silver against corrosion by damp salt.[6]

William Pitts was born *c.*1755, apprenticed to his father Thomas Pitts I in 1769, and became free in 1784. He entered his first mark as a plateworker in 1781, and was in partnership with Joseph Preedy 1791-8. He supplied silver to Rundell, Bridge & Rundell, and executed the chasing on several of their important pieces. He was active up to 1822.[7]

Like his father, William Pitts made epergnes and dessert-baskets and stands. In the Regency period he turned to the production of ornate cast candelabra in the Rococo Revival style,[8] of which a pair of 1822 candlesticks provide an outstanding example,[9] and in both style and technique the Ormonde salts clearly belong to this later phase. Other silver by William Pitts in the Ormonde collection included a pair of 1809 rose-water dishes (Bowes Museum) and an 1809 sideboard dish (Royal Pavilion).

PROVENANCE: Presumably purchased by Walter, 18th Earl of Ormonde, later Marquess of Ormonde (possibly from Rundell, Bridge & Rundell); By descent to the 6th Marquess of Ormonde; Accepted in lieu of estate duty by H.M. Treasury and allocated to the Grosvenor Museum 1982.97.1-4

NOTES:

1. Hare, p.122.
2. Christie's, London, 25 November 1992, lot 81.
3. Hare, p.107.
4. Sotheby's, London, 22 November 1984, lot 60.
5. Hare, p.107.
6. Newman, pp.272-3.
7. Bury, p.80; Grimwade, p.626; Lomax, pp.22-4.
8. Grimwade, p.626.
9. J.H. Bourdon-Smith Ltd., Catalogue No.39, Autumn 1997, p.48.

122 TWENTY-FOUR PIECE DINNER SERVICE

Benjamin Smith II, London, 1808-9
Two pieces by Benjamin Smith II & James Smith III, London, 1809-10

(1-10, 13-20) Five marks beneath rim (maker's mark Grimwade no. 229)
(11, 12) Five marks beneath rim (makers' mark Grimwade no.238)
(21-4) Five marks on exterior near rim (maker's mark Grimwade no. 229)

(1-4) Four circular second-course dishes
Diameter: (1-3) 32.4 cm. (12.75 in.), (4) 32.5 cm. (12.8 in.)
Weight: (1) 1,075 g. (37.9 oz.), (2) 1,084 g. (38.2 oz.), (3) 1,083 g. (38.2 oz.), (4) 1,057g. (37.3 oz.)

(5, 6) Pair of oval meat dishes
Length: (5) 60 cm. (23.6 in.), (6) 59.9 cm. (23.6 in.)
Weight: (5) apx. 4,840 g. (170.7 oz.), (6) apx. 4,950 g. (174.6 oz.)

(7, 8) Pair of oval meat dishes
Length: (7) 54 cm. (21.25 in.), (8) 53.9 cm. (21.2 in.)
Weight: (7) apx. 3,425 g. (120.8 oz.), (8) apx. 3,375 g. (119.05 oz.)

(9, 10) Pair of oval meat dishes
Length: (9) 52 cm. (20.5 in.), (10) 51.8 cm. (20.4 in.)
Weight: (9) 2,975 g. (104.95 oz.), (10) 2,963 g. (104.5 oz.)

(11, 12) Pair of oval meat dishes
Benjamin Smith II & James Smith III
Length: (11) 48.5 cm. (19.1 in.), (12) 48.2 cm. (19 in.)
Weight: (11) 2,622 g. (92.5 oz.), (12) 2,649 g. (93.45 oz.)

(13-16) Four oval meat dishes
Length: (13, 14) 45.7 cm. (18 in.), (15, 16) 45.5 cm. (17.9 in.)
Weight: (13) 2,083 g. (73.8 oz.), (14) 2,067 g. (72.9 oz.), (15) 2,134 g. (75.3 oz.), (16) 2,141 g. (75.5 oz.)

(17-20) Four oval meat dishes
Length: (17-20) 40.4 cm. (15.9 in.)
Weight: (17) 1,614 g. (56.9 oz.), (18) 1,593 g. (56.2 oz.), (19) 1,502 g. (53 oz.), (20) 1,472 g. (51.9 oz.)

(21-4) Four octagonal entree dishes
Height: (21, 23) 5.7 cm. (2.25 in.), (22) 5.4 cm. (2.1 in.), (24) 5.6 cm. (2.2 in.)
Length: (21, 24) 33.7 cm. (13.25 in.), (22) 33.8 cm. (13.3 in.), (23) 33.9 cm. (13.35 in.)
Weight: (21) 1,419 g. (50.05 oz.), (22) 1,393 g. (49.1 oz.), (23) 1,454 g. (51.3 oz.), (24) 1,489 g. (52.5 oz.)

Sterling silver. The four shaped circular second-course dishes and the 16 shaped oval meat dishes have broad rims with cast gadroon and shell borders. The four raised octagonal entree dishes with upcurved walls have cast gadroon and shell borders with galleries but without covers; the galleries are inscribed with numbers 1 to 4.

The many scratches from serving utensils show why the engraving was confined to the rims. The rims are engraved, once on the second-course dishes and twice on the meat dishes, with the arms of Butler, *en accole* with the arms of Butler with those of Price-Clarke in pretence, displayed within a mantle surmounted by a marquess's coronet, as on no.119. The exterior of each entree dish is engraved twice with the Butler crest surmounted by a marquess's coronet. The armorials are for Walter, Marquess of Ormonde (see no.115). The engraving on the second-course and meat dishes probably dates from between January 1816 and December 1817 (see no.119). The marquess's coronets on the entree dishes were added in or after 1816.

Walter, Marquess of Ormonde, acquired the full range of silver required for dining *à la francaise*. This fashion had begun at the court of Louis XIV, became standard throughout rich European homes by the mid-18th century, and by the mid-19th century was succeeded by the fashion for serving dinner dish-by-dish in the modern manner *à la russe*. When dining *à la francaise*, the different foods of each course were laid out symmetrically, often in groups of four, and symmetry was maintained because the dishes of each course were cleared and replaced four at a time. The food was kept

warm by means of covers or underdishes of hot water, and the guests helped themselves to whatever was in front of them.

Table plans showing the layout of both courses for dining *à la francaise* are illustrated in a number of publications, including Elizabeth Raffald's *The Experienced English Housekeeper* (1786).[1] In Britain, the first course frequently began with thick and thin soup in a pair of tureens at opposite ends of the table. The soup was followed by a substantial roast joint, served on the meat dishes. This was accompanied by vegetables in the vegetable dishes (e.g. no.118) and by *entrees*, meat side dishes, served in the entree dishes. The second course comprised dishes of fowl and game at opposite ends of the table, accompanied by *entremets*, side dishes of vegetables in sauce and cooked puddings, served in the second-course dishes. The last course, the dessert, comprised fresh and preserved fruit, jams and ice cream.[2]

The decoration of gadroon and shell borders on dinner services was long-established, having been used, for example, by Paul de Lamerie on a 1741 meat dish in the Brooklyn Museum.[3] As Norman Penzer has explained, 'the usual pattern preferred by Storr for plates and dishes, of which he was an extensive maker,

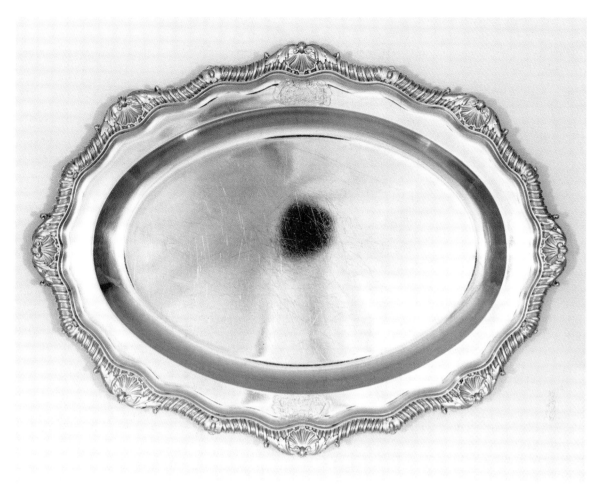

was perfectly plain with a simple shell and gadroon border. The Worshipful Company of Goldsmiths possesses 107 dinner plates of 1809-11 and eighteen soup plates of 1810 of this type ... The largest number of Storr plates with gadroon and shell borders, however, is that in the Royal Collection. It totals 409.'[4]

The service at Chester corresponds to the following entries in the 1904 Ormonde Inventory:

4 12.5 inch Second course Dishes to match. 1808. Benjamin Smith

2 23.5 inch shaped shell & gadroon Meat dishes. 1808. Paul Storr

2 21.5 inch shaped do; do; 1808. Paul Storr

2 20.5 inch do; do; do; 1808. Paul Storr

2 19 inch do; do; do; 1809. Paul Storr

4 18 inch do; do; do; 1808. Paul Storr

4 16 inch do; do; do; 1808. Paul Storr

4 13 inch Octagonal Entree dishes to match. 1808. Benjamin Smith

Entree dishes were often supplied with covers,[5] but these four had none by 1904.

The two oval and four circular vegetable dishes, four oval soup tureens, four rectangular entree dishes, eight sauce tureens and four pincushion entree dishes by Paul Storr, and the four dish covers by Benjamin Smith, are discussed at no.118. As listed in the 1904 Ormonde Inventory, the Dinner Service also included the following unlocated pieces:

1 27 inch shell and gadroon border Venison dish with plated warmer. 1807. Benjamin Smith. ['Phillips' in later hand]

2 19 inch plain Mazareens. 1808. Benjamin Smith.

1 15 inch do; do; 1801. Paul Storr.

24 Soup plates to match. 17 1808. 7 1809. Paul Storr. ['missing. WF.' in later hand]

4 Pincushion Entree dishes, no covers. 1808. Paul Storr. ['Phillips' in later hand]

Benjamin Smith II was born at Birmingham in 1764. He and his brother James Smith III were in partnership with Matthew Boulton of Birmingham 1791-1800. Benjamin then set up his workshop at Greenwich. He was in partnership with Digby Scott 1801/2-7; worked alone 1807-9; in partnership with his brother James 1809-12; alone 1812-16; in partnership with his son Benjamin Smith III 1816-18; and died in 1823. His firm was, together with Paul Storr (see no.118), manufacturing almost entirely for Rundell & Bridge, who may have supported his move to London.[6] For the subsequent history of the firm see Stephen Smith & Son (no.117).

James Smith III appears to have remained with Matthew Boulton, after Benjamin Smith II's move to London, until he entered in partnership with Benjamin 1809-12.[7]

Other silver by Benjamin Smith in the Ormonde collection included:

122

a cigar lighter, 1807 (Victoria and Albert Museum)
eight wine coasters, 1807 and 1808 (Bowes Museum and Royal Pavilion)
a pair of four-light candelabra, 1807 and 1808 (Royal Pavilion)
four sugar vases and covers, 1808 (Bowes Museum)
nine wine labels, 1808 (Royal Pavilion)
a pair of salvers, 1808 (Royal Pavilion)
nine wine labels, 1809 (Bowes Museum)
a pair of trays, 1804 and 1809 (Royal Pavilion)
a dessert service (four circular dishes, four kidney-shaped dishes, and a pair of oval dishes), 1810 (Bowes Museum and Royal Pavilion)

PROVENANCE: Purchased by Walter, 18th Earl of Ormonde, later Marquess of Ormonde (presumably from Rundell, Bridge & Rundell); By descent to the 6th Marquess of Ormonde; Accepted in lieu of estate duty by H.M. Treasury and allocated to the Grosvenor Museum 1982.93.1-24

NOTES:
1. Coutts 1994 II, figs.10-11.
2. Coutts 1994 I, pp.30-1; Coutts 1994 II, pp.186-90, 193.

3. Lomax, p.94.
4. Penzer 1971, p.170.
5. Newman, p.125.
6. Grimwade, pp.661-2; Culme, I, p.424; Lomax, p.108.
7. Grimwade, p.664.

123 TEA POT

Paul Storr, London, 1813-4

Five marks on body behind handle (maker's mark Grimwade no.2235). Three marks on base of handle: maker's mark, duty mark, lion passant. Lion passant and date letter inside cover
Length 27.5 cm. (10.8 in.), height 15.1 cm. (5.95 in.)
Weight 952 g. (33.6 oz.)

See Colour Plate VIII
Sterling silver with ivory finial and insulation fillets. The raised, spreading circular foot is chased with a band of gadrooning. It supports the compressed circular vase-shaped body, whose lower section is raised and joined to the cylindrical central section with an applied horizontal moulding. The upper

196

section is chased with a band of gadrooning on the shoulder, within which rises a deep convex collar with a cast gadrooned rim. The raised and slightly domed cover is attached to the body by a five-part flush hinge. The gadrooned ivory finial has a silver cap attached by a threaded screw and silver wing nut. The curving spout, with a heart-shaped aperture, is raised in two sections and soldered together. The body of the teapot beneath the spout is perforated to form a strainer. The cast loop handle, on axis with the spout, has a scrolled thumbpiece and is connected to two sockets by ivory insulation fillets, each with four pins.

The side of the body is engraved with the Butler crest, within the Order of St Patrick surmounted by an earl's coronet, for Walter, 18th Earl of Ormonde (see no.115). The engraving was executed before the creation of the marquessate in 1816.

This tea pot was one of a pair; the other is now in the Bowes Museum. They are presumably the '2 Best Tea Pots' in the 1839/48 Ormonde List, and are described in the 1904 Ormonde Inventory as '2 Plain round Tea pots with gadroon border and fluted band. AD 1813. Paul Storr.'

In addition to the pair of cream ewers (see no.119), the 1904 Ormonde Inventory lists the following Paul Storr tea silver (now mostly unlocated):
A plain round tea kettle with gadroon rim with stand and lamp. 1813. (Victoria and Albert Museum)
An oval part fluted Tea urn with stand and lamp, and serpent handle and lion mask tap. 1808.
A part fluted Hot water Jug with serpent handle and round gadroon and shell stand on tripod base and ring handles. 1808.
A Hot water Jug with Grecian bound [sic] round body and ivory and silver serpent handle on collet foot with round Grecian stand and lamp on 4 claw feet. 1814.
2 Part fluted round Sugar basins with serpent handles to match. 1808.
A plain Coffee pot with gadroon border and round gadroon stand and lamp on 3 feet. 1813. (Victoria and Albert Museum)
2 Oblong gadroon Bread Baskets with leaf and shell ends and swing handles on collet feet. 1808. (one in Victoria and Albert Museum)
A large plain Etruscan shape Water Jug with lift off cover and mask on back of body. 1812.

The Ormonde tea kettle and coffee pot have gadrooned ivory finials and insulation fillets like the tea pots. The tea pot from another service of 1810 by Paul Storr has a gadrooned foot and rim like the Ormonde ones, with an identical cover and ivory finial, but the body is a plain compressed sphere and its spout is formed as a Roman lamp.[1]

PROVENANCE: Purchased by Walter, 18th Earl of Ormonde, later Marquess of Ormonde (presumably from Rundell, Bridge & Rundell); By descent to the 6th Marquess of Ormonde; Accepted in lieu of estate duty by H.M. Treasury and allocated to the Grosvenor Museum 1982.96

NOTE:
1. Penzer 1971, p.143.

APPENDIX

London

124

124 SUGAR BASKET

Solomon Hougham, London, 1799-1800

Five marks beneath foot (maker's mark
Grimwade no.2536)
Length 15.7 cm. (6.2 in.)
Weight 225 g. (7.9 oz.)

Sterling silver. The side of the body is engraved within
a cartouche with the crest of a demi wolf rampant
holding in its paws a quatrefoil, rose or flower. The
crest is possibly that of Cooke, Goodenough or
O'Crean.[1]

PROVENANCE: Miss M.C. Singlehurst, Hooton, Cheshire;
Bequeathed 1970.105

EXHIBITED: Chester 1979 I, no.1 (as Samuel Hennell).

PUBLISHED: Thomas, p.21 (as Samuel Hennell).

NOTE:
1. Gale Glynn, report, 22 March 1991.

125

125 SALT SPOON

Duncan Urquhart & Naphtali Hart,
London, 1805-6

Four marks on back of stem near top: maker's
mark (Grimwade no.510), lion passant, date
letter, sovereign's head
Length 11 cm. (4.3 in.)
Weight 11 g. (0.4 oz.)

Sterling silver. The front of the stem is engraved with
the same crest as no.124.

PROVENANCE: Miss M.C. Singlehurst, Hooton, Cheshire;
Bequeathed 1970.110

PUBLISHED: Thomas, p.21.

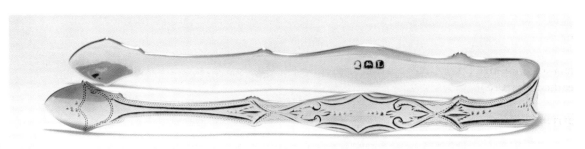

126

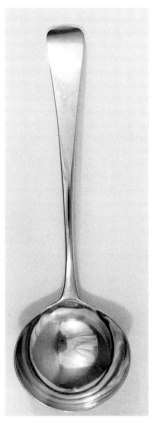

127   128   129

126 SUGAR TONGS

Peter & William Bateman, London, 1806-7

Four marks inside arms: maker's mark
(Grimwade no.2143) on one side; sovereign's
head, lion passant, date letter on other side
Length 14.5 cm. (5.7 in.)
Weight 35 g. (1.2 oz.)

Sterling silver. The outer curve of the handle is engraved with the initials M.D.

PROVENANCE: Miss Amy Smith (died 1955); Chester City
Treasurer (appointed Receiver); Transferred to Museum
1980.33.9

127 SAUCE LADLE

Thomas Wallis II, London, 1808-9

Five marks on back of stem near top (maker's
mark Grimwade no.2975)
Length 17.4 cm. (6.85 in.)
Weight 44 g. (1.55 oz.)

Sterling silver.

PROVENANCE: Miss M.C. Singlehurst, Hooton, Cheshire;
Bequeathed 1970.107

EXHIBITED: Chester 1979 I, no.17.

PUBLISHED: Thomas, p.21.

128 SALT SPOON

Attributed to Robert Rutland, London, 1809-10

Four marks on back of stem at top: lion passant,
date letter, sovereign's head, maker's mark R_
Length 9.9 cm. (3.9 in.)
Weight 9 g. (0.3 oz.)

Sterling silver. Although its second letter is illegible,
the maker's mark is probably that of the spoonmaker
Robert Rutland (Grimwade no.2425). The front of
the stem is engraved with the same crest as no.124.

PROVENANCE: Miss M.C. Singlehurst, Hooton, Cheshire;
Bequeathed 1970.111

PUBLISHED: Thomas, p.21.

129 PAIR OF SALT SPOONS

Solomon Hougham, London, 1812-13

Four marks on back of each stem at top:
maker's mark (Grimwade no.2536), lion
passant, date letter, sovereign's head
Length: both 9.7 cm. (3.8 in.)
Weight: (1) 8 g. (0.3 oz.), (2) 7 g. (0.25 oz.)

Sterling silver. The front of each stem is engraved with
the same crest as no.124.

PROVENANCE: Miss M.C. Singlehurst, Hooton, Cheshire;
Bequeathed 1970.109.1,2

PUBLISHED: Thomas, p.21.

130

130 CRUET FRAME, CRUETS AND CASTERS

Abstainando King, London, 1826-7

Five marks on side of stand (maker's mark Grimwade no.49). Four marks on divider beneath handle and on lid of pepper caster: sovereign's head, lion passant, date letter, maker's mark. Maker's mark and sovereign's head on lid of salt caster

Height: cruet stand (1) 20.2 cm. (7.95 in.); cruet bottles (2) 15.5 cm. (6.1 in.), (3) 14.3 cm. (5.6 in.), (4) 13 cm. (5.1 in.); salt caster (5) 12.4 cm. (4.9 in.); pepper caster (6) 11.9 cm. (4.7 in.)
Weight: stand alone 329 g. (11.6 oz.), total weight 1,262 g. (44.5 oz.)

Cruet stand of sterling silver with base of mahogany (*Swietenia macrophylla*);[1] three cruet bottles of cut glass with glass stoppers; salt and pepper casters of cut glass with sterling silver lids. The side of the stand is engraved within a cartouche with the crest of a falcon standing on a hawk's lure, a crest used by four different families.[2]

PROVENANCE: Miss L.L. Drumm; Bequeathed to Chester Record Office, 1966; Transferred to Museum 1970.44.1-6

PUBLISHED: Thomas, p.20.

NOTES:

1. Wood identified by Graham Usher, 13 November 1999.
2. The crest is that of Barker of Over and Vale Royal, Cheshire; Hewitt, London; Magill, Ireland; or Soame, London and Suffolk (Gale Glynn, report, 22 March 1991).

131

132

131 FIVE TEA SPOONS

William Bateman I, London, 1832-3

Five marks on back of each stem at top
(maker's mark Grimwade no.3038)
Length: (2,3) 13.7 cm. (5.4 in.), (4,5) 13.6 cm.
(5.35 in.), (6) 13.1 cm. (5.15 in.)
Weight: (2) 17 g. (0.6 oz.), (3) 15 g. (0.5 oz.),
(4) 18 g. (0.6 oz.), (5) 16 g. (0.55 oz), (6)
14 g. (0.5 oz.)

Sterling silver. The front of each stem is engraved with
the initials JP.

PROVENANCE: Miss Amy Smith (died 1955); Chester
City Treasurer (appointed Receiver); Transferred to
Museum 1980.33.2-6

132 TEA SPOON

Unknown maker, London, 1835-6

Five marks on back of stem near bowl (maker's
mark illegible)
Length 14.3 cm. (5.6 in.)
Weight 28 g. (1 oz.)

Sterling silver. The front of the stem is engraved with
the letter G.

PROVENANCE: Miss E.M. Sutcliffe, Hebden Bridge, West
Yorkshire; Presented 1962.78.1

PUBLISHED: Thomas, p.20.

133

134

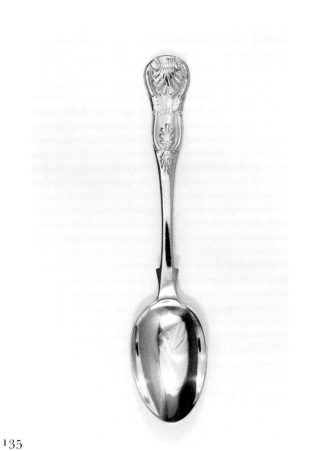

135

136

133 NAPKIN RING

Unknown maker, London, 1881-2

Five marks on side (maker's mark illegible)
Diameter 4.4 cm. (1.7 in.)
Weight 32 g. (1.1 oz.)

Sterling silver. The interior is engraved with the inscription: 'Anna Skelton / to her dear little Godchild / Ida Mary Bullows. / April 11th 1893'.

PROVENANCE: Presented by Anna Skelton to Ida Mary Bullows, 1893; Miss L.L. Drumm; Bequeathed to Chester Record Office, 1966; Transferred to Museum 1970.46.1

PUBLISHED: Thomas, p.20.

134 WORK BOX

Frederick Bradford McCrea, London, 1889-90

Five marks near foot (maker's mark Culme no.3779)
Length 19.3 cm. (7.6 in.)
Weight 715 g. (25.2 oz.)

Sterling silver casing over wooden body covered with green velvet and lined with green silk.

PROVENANCE: Mrs. E.D. Norman, Great Barrow, Chester; Presented 1977.165

135 TEA SPOON

James Wakely & Frank Clarke Wheeler, London, 1890-1

Four marks on back of stem near top (maker's mark Culme nos.10478-93)
Length 14.2 cm. (5.6 in.)
Weight 27 g. (0.95 oz.)

Sterling silver. The front of the stem is engraved with the initials AC.

PROVENANCE: Miss E.M. Sutcliffe, Hebden Bridge, West Yorkshire; Presented 1962.78.2

PUBLISHED: Thomas, p.20.

136 TWO-HANDLED CUP

Mappin & Webb Ltd., London, 1905-6

Four marks on side (makers' mark Culme nos.11274-6)
Height 13.9 cm. (5.5 in.)
Weight 116 g. (4.1 oz.)

Sterling silver. The side is engraved with the inscription: 'R.M.C. SPORTS 1906 / 2 Miles Race / 3rd Prize / T.B.S. Marshall'.

PROVENANCE: T.B.S. Marshall, 1906; By descent to Miss M. Marshall, Ringwood, Hampshire; Presented via Cheshire Record Office 1971.99.4

PUBLISHED: Thomas, p.20.

Birmingham

137 CHILD'S KNIFE & FORK

Joseph Willmore, Birmingham, 1805-6

Five marks on blade of knife (maker's mark Jackson, p.355). Three marks on shank of fork: sovereign's head, lion passant, maker's mark
Length: knife (1) 13.4 cm. (5.3 in.), fork (2) 12.3 cm, (4.8 in,), case (3) 14.8 cm. (5.8 in.)
Weight: (1) 13 g. (0.45 oz.), (2) 12 g. (0.4 oz.)

Sterling silver with ivory handles, in what is very probably their original red leather case. Each handle is engraved MCS, the initials of the donor's grandmother.

PROVENANCE: Miss M.C. Singlehurst, Hooton, Cheshire; Bequeathed 1970.114.1-3

EXHIBITED: Chester 1979 I, no.17.

PUBLISHED: Thomas, p.21.

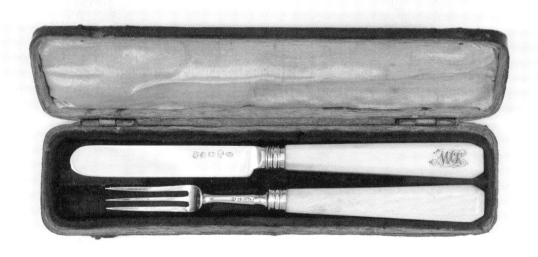

137

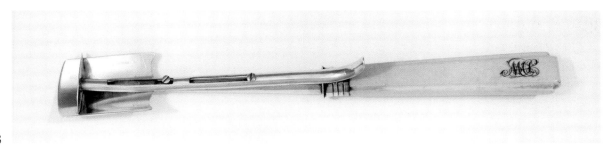

138

139

139

138 CHEESE SCOOP

George Bragg & Thomas Crockett, Birmingham, 1811-12

Five marks on back of blade (maker's mark
Jones 1981, p.326)
Length 22.2 cm. (8.7 in.)
Weight 51 g. (1.8 oz.)

Sterling silver with ivory handle. The handle is engraved with the same initials as no.137.

PROVENANCE: Miss M.C. Singlehurst, Hooton, Cheshire;
Bequeathed 1970.106

EXHIBITED: Chester 1979 I, no.18.

PUBLISHED: Thomas, p.21.

140

139 HIP FLASK

John Linegar, Birmingham, 1874-5

Three marks on front: sovereign's head, maker's mark JL,[1] lion passant. Three marks on back: anchor, maker's mark, date letter. Three marks on cover: maker's mark, sovereign's head, date letter
Length 12.7 cm. (5 in.)
Weight 103 g. (3.6 oz.)

Sterling silver with screw cover. The front is engraved with the arms, crest and motto of Marshall, and the back with the arms, crest and motto of Stapleton or Stapylton beneath the inscription 'H.S. MARSHALL, 22ND REGT'.[2]

PROVENANCE: H.S. Marshall; By descent to Miss M. Marshall, Ringwood, Hampshire; Presented via Cheshire Record Office 1971.99.8

PUBLISHED: Thomas, p.22.

NOTES:

1. Identified by Phyllis Benedikz, letter, 11 November 1993.
2. Gale Glynn, report, 22 March 1991.

140 PEPPER CASTER

E.S. Barnsley & Co. Ltd., Birmingham, 1886-7

Four marks on side of body: makers' mark (Jones 1981, p.334 1st mark), anchor, lion passant, date letter. Lion passant and date letter on bezel of cover
Height 7.5 cm. (2.95 in.)
Weight 29 g. (1 oz.)

Sterling silver with detachable cover.

PROVENANCE: Miss L.L. Drumm; Bequeathed to Chester Record Office, 1966; Transferred to Museum 1970.48.1

PUBLISHED: Thomas, p.21.

141 CHAMBER CANDLESTICK

George Charlton Wildman of Wolverhampton, hallmarked Birmingham, 1901-2

Four marks on drip-pan of candlestick (maker's mark GCW).[1] Lion passant and date letter on nozzle and extinguisher. Lion passant on ring linking chain to handle
Width across handle 8.8 cm. (3.5 in.)
Weight 89 g. (3.1 oz.)

Sterling silver, with detachable nozzle and extinguisher on chain.

PROVENANCE: Miss L.L. Drumm; Bequeathed to Chester Record Office, 1966; Transferred to Museum 1970.47

EXHIBITED: Chester 1973, p.54 no.20; Chester 1979 I, no.5.

PUBLISHED: Thomas, p.20.

NOTE:

1. Identified by Phyllis Benedikz, letter, 22 July 1993.

141

142

142 STANDING CUP

William Bruford & Son, Birmingham, 1914-15
Four marks on side of cup (makers' mark Culme
no.14461)
Height 12.3 cm. (4.8 in.)
Weight 129 g. (4.55 oz.)

Sterling silver. The side of the cup is angraved with
the inscription: 'TENNIS DOUBLES / 1919. / PRE-
SENTED BY THE / KADUNA GAMES CLUB.'

PROVENANCE: Presented by the Kaduna Games Club;
Marshall family of Northwich, Cheshire; By descent to
Miss M. Marshall, Ringwood, Hampshire; Presented via
Cheshire Record Office 1971.99.3

PUBLISHED: Thomas, p.22.

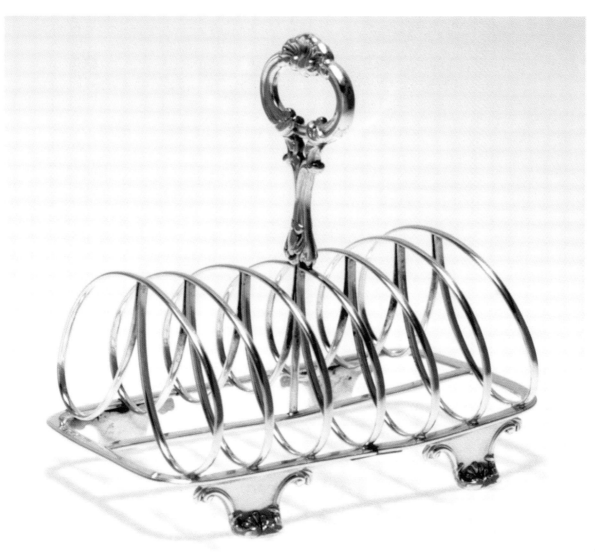

143 TOAST RACK

Hawkesworth, Eyre & Co., Sheffield, 1837-8

Four marks on base: date letter and crown contained
in one stamp, makers' mark (Jackson, p.445), lion
passant, sovereign's head
Length 16.2 cm. (6.4 in.)
Weight 295 g. (10.4 oz.)

Sterling silver.

PROVENANCE: Miss M.C. Singlehurst, Hooton, Cheshire;
Bequeathed 1970.104.

EXHIBITED: Chester 1973, p.53 no.11.

PUBLISHED: Thomas, p.21.

144

145

146

144 SALT CELLAR

Lee & Wigfull, Sheffield, 1862-3
Four marks on side: makers' mark (Jackson, p.446),
crown, lion passant, date letter
Length 6.9 cm. (2.7 in.)
Weight 43 g. (1.52 oz.)

Sterling silver.

PROVENANCE: Miss L.L. Drumm; Bequeathed to Chester Record Office, 1966; Transferred to Museum 1970.48.2

PUBLISHED: Thomas, p.21.

145 NAPKIN RING

John Round & Son Ltd., Sheffield, 1912-13
Four marks on back (makers' mark Jackson, p.446)
Width 4.9 cm. (1.9 in.)
Weight 24 g. (0.85 oz.)

Sterling silver. The front of the ring is engraved with the initials CGM.

PROVENANCE: Miss L.L. Drumm; Bequeathed to Chester Record Office, 1966; Transferred to Museum 1970.46.2

PUBLISHED: Thomas, p.20.

Newcastle

146 SAUCE LADLE

Christian Ker Reid I, Newcastle, c.1800-4
Four marks on back of stem at top: sovereign's head, lion passant, three castles, maker's mark (Jackson, p.503)
Length 13.2 cm. (5.2 in.)
Weight 23 g. (0.8 oz.)

Sterling silver. The ladle probably dates from *c.*1800-4, since this was the only period in which these four marks were used in the forms found here.[1]

PROVENANCE: Miss M.C. Singlehurst, Hooton, Cheshire; Bequeathed 1970.108

PUBLISHED: Thomas, p.21.

NOTE:

1. Identified as sauce ladle by Ian Pickford (telephone conversation, 3 February 2000). Dating confirmed by Dr. Margaret Gill (letter, 9 September 1993).

147

147 SMALL SERVING FORK

Joseph M. Latimer of Carlisle, hallmarked Newcastle, 1838-9
Six marks on back of stem at top (maker's mark Jackson, p.505)
Length 13.7 cm. (5.4 in.)
Weight 23 g. (0.8 oz.)

Sterling silver.[1]

PROVENANCE: Miss M.C. Singlehurst, Hooton, Cheshire; Bequeathed 1970.112

PUBLISHED: Thomas, p.21.

NOTE:

1. Identified as small serving fork by Ian Pickford (telephone conversation, 3 February 2000).

148

149

Edinburgh

148 TWO TABLE SPOONS

John McKay, Edinburgh, 1823-4 and 1824-5

Five marks on back of each stem near top (maker's mark, Jackson p.552)
Length: (1) 22.1 cm. (8.7 in.), (2) 22 cm. (8.65 in.)
Weight: (1) 81 g. (2.85 oz.), (2) 82 g. (2.9 oz.)

Sterling silver. The front of each stem is engraved with the initials AC.

PROVENANCE: Miss E.M. Sutcliffe, Hebden Bridge, West Yorkshire; Presented 1962.77.1,2

PUBLISHED: Thomas, p.20.

Wincanton

149 DESSERT SPOON

Attributed to Charles Lewis of Wincanton, c.1719-33

Maker's mark CL struck three times along back of stem
Length 17 cm. (6.7 in.)
Weight 47 g. (1.65 oz.)

Silver. Nicholas Moore attributed the spoon to Charles Lewis of Wincanton in Somerset, who was active from 1719-33. Timothy Kent has tentatively agreed that Lewis may perhaps be an attribution for this spoon.[1]

PROVENANCE: Sotheby's, Chester, 2 May 1984, lot 1159 (part); Purchased 1984.28

NOTE:
1. Timothy Kent, letter, 29 August 1993.

BIBLIOGRAPHY

Aspinall & Hudson. Peter J. Aspinall & Daphne M. Hudson, *Ellesmere Port: The Making of an Industrial Borough* (Ellesmere Port), 1982.

Asprey 1994. Asprey, *Silver from a Golden Age 1640-1840: A Private Collection* (London), 1994.

Ball 1905. T. Stanley Ball, 'Chester Civic Plate and Regalia', *The Chester Courant*, 15 weekly articles, 18 January - 26 April 1905.

Ball 1907. T. Stanley Ball, *Church Plate of the City of Chester* (London & Manchester), 1907 [originally published in *The Chester Courant*, 12 weekly articles, 26 October 1904 - 11 January 1905].

Ball 1914. T. Stanley Ball, 'Ancient Chester Goldsmiths and their Work', *Transactions of the Antiquarian Society of Lancashire and Cheshire*, vol.32, 1914, pp.179-200.

Ball 1932. Stanley Ball, 'Ancient Chester Goldsmiths and their Work', *The Connoisseur*, May 1932, pp.291-301.

Ball 1961. Berenice Ball, 'Whistles with Coral and Bells', *The Magazine Antiques*, December 1961, pp.552-5.

Banister 1962. Judith Banister, 'Last of the Chester Silver', *Antique Dealer and Collectors Guide*, September 1962, pp.38-40.

Banister 1967. Judith Banister, 'Sixty Glorious Years of Silver Tea Caddies', *Antique Dealer and Collectors Guide*, April 1967, pp.44-8.

Banister 1973. Judith Banister, 'Silver at the Chester Festival', *Country Life*, 28 June 1973, pp.1876-7.

Barrett 1981 I. G.N. Barrett, *et al, Norwich Silver in the Collection of Norwich Castle Museum* (Norwich), 1981.

Barrett 1981 II. Geoffrey N. Barrett, *Norwich Silver and its Marks 1565-1702: The Goldsmiths of Norwich 1141-1750* (Norwich), 1981.

Bennett 1906. J.H.E. Bennett, *The Rolls of the Freemen of the City of Chester, Part I, 1392-1700* (Lancashire & Cheshire Record Society), 1906.

Bennett 1908. J.H.E. Bennett, *The Rolls of the Freemen of the City of Chester, Part II, 1700-1805* (Lancashire & Cheshire Record Society), 1908.

Bennett 1972 I. Douglas Bennett, *Irish Georgian Silver* (London), 1972.

Bennett 1972 II. Ian Bennett, 'Silver - the prospects are bright', *Art & Antiques Weekly*, 22 July 1972, pp.27-35.

Bennett 1984. Douglas Bennett, *Collecting Irish Silver 1637-1900* (London), 1984.

Bevan. R.M. Bevan, *The Roodee: 450 years of racing in Chester* (Northwich), 1989.

Birch. W. de G. Birch, *Catalogue of Seals in the British Museum*, vol.2 (London), 1892.

Bishop & Roscoe. Philippa Bishop & Barley Roscoe, *Holburne of Menstrie Museum and Crafts Study Centre, Bath: A Guide to the Collections* (Bath), 1980.

Black. W.H. Black, 'On the Records of the County Palatine of Chester', *Journal of the British Archaeological Association*, vol.5, 1850, pp.187-95.

Blair. Claude Blair, ed., *The History of Silver* (London), 1987.

Boughton 1992 I. Peter Boughton, 'Church Plate in Chester's New Silver Gallery', *Ecclesiological Society Newsletter*, September 1992.

Boughton 1992 II. Peter Boughton, 'Ducal Art: A Study of Changing Tastes', *The Art Quarterly of the National Art Collections Fund*, Winter 1992, pp.39-41.

Boughton 1992 III. Peter Boughton, 'Victorian Silver at the Grosvenor Museum's New Silver Gallery', *Victorian Society Manchester Group Newsletter*, Autumn 1992, pp.15-16.

Boughton 1993. Peter Boughton, 'Chester's New Silver Gallery', *The Silver Society Journal*, Autumn 1993, pp.145-6.

Boughton 1995. Peter Boughton, 'A pair of silver seal matrices for the County Palatine of Chester', *The Silver Society Journal*, Autumn 1995, pp.409-11.

Boughton 1997. Peter Boughton, *Picturesque Chester: The City in Art* (Chichester), 1997.

Boutell. Charles Boutell, *English Heraldry* (London), 1899.

Bradbury. Frederick Bradbury, *History of Old Sheffield Plate* (Sheffield), 1968.

Brett. Vanessa Brett, *The Sotheby's Directory of Silver 1600-1940* (London), 1986.

Bridge. Joseph C. Bridge, 'Horns', *Journal of the Chester and North Wales Archaeological and Historic Society*, new series, vol.11, 1905, pp.85-166.

Brooke & Keir. Christopher N.L. Brooke & Gillian Keir, *London, 800-1216: The Shaping of a City* (London), 1975.

Brown. William Brown, *A History of the Municipal Charities of Chester from 1837 to 1875* (Chester), 1875.

Burke's General Armoury (London), 1884.

Burke's Landed Gentry. Sir Bernard Burke, *A Genealogical and Heraldic History of the Landed Gentry of Great Britain & Ireland*, vol.2 (London), 1894.

Burke's Peerage. Peter Townend, ed., *Burke's Peerage, Baronetage & Knightage* (London), 1963.

Bury. Shirley Bury, 'The Lengthening Shadow of Rundell's: Part 1: Rundell's and their Silversmiths', *The Connoisseur*, February 1966, pp.79-85.

Callaghan. Sarah Callaghan, 'The Goldsmiths of Chester', *Goldsmiths' Review 1992/93*, pp.28-33.

Calloway. Stephen Calloway, *Baroque Baroque: The Culture of Excess* (London), 1994.

Chaffers. William Chaffers, *Hall Marks on Gold and Silver Plate*, 1st ed. (London), 1863 [10th ed., 1969].

Chapel & Gere. Jeannie Chapel & Charlotte Gere, *The Fine and Decorative Art Collections of Britain and Ireland* (London), 1985.

Cheny. John Cheny, *An Historical List of all Horse-Matches Run, and of all plates and prizes run for in England and Wales* (London) annual volumes 1728-35, 1738-41, 1743-50.

Clayton 1985 I. Michael Clayton, *The Collector's Dictionary of the Silver and Gold of Great Britain and North America* (Woodbridge), 1985.

Clayton 1985 II. Michael Clayton, *Christie's Pictorial History of English and American Silver* (Oxford), 1985.

Clifford. Helen Clifford, ed., *Sporting Glory: The Courage Exhibition of National Trophies at the Victoria and Albert Museum* (London), 1992.

Complete Peerage. G.E.C. [George Edward Cokayne], *The Complete Peerage*.
Vol.6, edited by H.A. Doubleday, Duncan Warrand & Lord Howard de Walden (London), 1926.
Vol. 10, edited by H.A. Doubleday, Geoffrey H. White & Lord Howard de Walden (London), 1945.
Vol.12, part 2, edited by Geoffrey H. White & R.S. Lea (London), 1959.

Cooper 1984. Walter G. Cooper, *The Ancient Order of Foresters Friendly Society 1834-1984* (Southampton), 1984.

Cooper 1997. Trevor Cooper, 'A Parish Church Service in 1717', *Ecclesiology Today*, April 1997, pp.11-13.

Coutts 1994 I. Howard Coutts, 'The Dinner Service', *Antique Dealer and Collectors Guide*, July 1994, pp.28-31.

Coutts 1994 II. Howard Coutts, 'Formal Dining in Europe', *The Magazine Antiques*, August 1994, pp.186-97.

Crighton. R.A. Crighton, *Cambridge Plate* (Cambridge), 1975.

Cripps. Wilfred Joseph Cripps, *Old English Plate, Ecclesiastical, Decorative, and Domestic; Its Makers and Marks*, 1st ed. (London), 1878 [8th ed., 1903; 11th ed., 1926].

Culme. John Culme, *The Directory of Gold & Silversmiths, Jewellers & Allied Traders 1838-1914*, two vols. (Woodbridge), 1987.

Culme 1977. John Culme, *Nineteenth-Century Silver* (Feltham), 1977.

Cust. Sir Edward Cust, 'An Investigation into the Right of the County Palatine of Chester to bear a Coat of Arms', *Transactions of the Historic Society of Lancashire and Cheshire*, vol.2, 1849, pp.9-18.

Davidson. Paul Davidson, 'Tea Caddies', *Antique Collecting*, July/August 1999, pp.34-5.

Davis. John D. Davis, *English Silver at Williamsburg* (Williamsburg), 1976.

Debrett's Peerage. Charles Kidd & David Williamson, ed., *Debrett's Peerage and Baronetage 1990* (London), 1990.

de Figueiredo & Treuherz. Peter de Figueiredo & Julian Treuherz, *Cheshire Country Houses* (Chichester), 1988.

Dictionary of National Biography.
Vol.1, edited by Leslie Stephen (London), 1885.
Vol.20, edited by Leslie Stephen (London), 1889.
Vol.24, edited by Leslie Stephen & Sidney Lee (London), 1890.
Vol.54, edited by Sidney Lee (London), 1898.

Dowler. Graham Dowler, *Gloucestershire Clock and Watch Makers* (Chichester), 1984.

Dutton. Hugh T. Dutton, *Chester Town Hall and its Treasures* (Chester), 1928.

Earwaker. J.P. Earwaker, *The History of the Church and Parish of St Mary-on-the-Hill, Chester* (London), 1898.

Edwards. Michael S. Edwards, *Purge This Realm: A Life of Joseph Rayner Stephens* (London), 1994.

Egerton. Judy Egerton, *George Stubbs 1724-1806* (London), 1984.

Einberg. Elizabeth Einberg, *Manners and Morals: Hogarth and British Painting 1700-1760* (London), 1987.

Emmerson 1984. Robin Emmerson, *The Norwich Regalia and Civic Plate* (Norwich), 1984.

Emmerson 1991. Robin Emmerson, *Church Plate* (London), 1991.

Evans. Mark Evans, ed., *Princes as Patrons: The art collections of the Princes of Wales from the Renaissance to the present day* (London), 1998.

Evans & Fairclough. Mark Evans & Oliver Fairclough, *The National Museum of Wales: A Companion Guide to the National Art Gallery* (Cardiff), 1993.

Fairbairn. James Fairbairn, revised by Laurence Butters, *Fairbairn's Crests of the Families of Great Britain & Ireland* (London), 1989.

Falkiner. Richard Falkiner, 'Collector may grant museum his £21,000 seal of approval', *Antiques Trade Gazette*, 3 December 1994, p.30.

Fallon. John Fallon, 'Two covered cups with stands', *The Silver Society Journal*, Autumn 1998, p.117.

Fergusson 1968. J.G. Fergusson, 'Roll of the Hereditary Chief Foresters, Master Foresters, Masters of the Game and Bowbearers-in-Chief of the Forests of Mara and Mondrem (Delamere Forest)', *The Cheshire Sheaf*, 4th series, no.136, 21 June 1968.

Fergusson 1993. Gordon Fergusson, *The Green Collars:*

The Tarporley Hunt Club and Cheshire Hunting History (London), 1993.

Fleming & Honour. John Fleming & Hugh Honour, *The Penguin Dictionary of Decorative Arts* (London), 1989.

Forrer. L. Forrer, *Biographical Dictionary of Medallists*, vol.5 (London), 1912.

Forrest. Herbert Edward Forrest, *Old Shropshire Houses and their Owners* (Shrewsbury), 1924.

Fothringham. Henry Fothringham, 'Silver appearing before the Reviewing Committee on the Export of Works of Art from 1953 to 1993', *The Silver Society Journal*, Winter 1994, pp.302-22.

Fraser. Flora Fraser, *Beloved Emma: The Life of Emma, Lady Hamilton* (London), 1986.

Fredericks 1952. J.W. Fredericks, *Dutch Silver*, vol.1 (The Hague), 1952.

Fredericks 1961. J.W. Fredericks, *Dutch Silver*, vol.4 (The Hague), 1961.

Friel. Paddy Friel, *Kilkenny Castle* (Dublin), n.d. [pre-1994].

Garner. Philippe Garner, ed., *Phaidon Encyclopedia of Decorative Arts 1890-1940* (Oxford), 1978.

Gilbert. Christopher Gilbert, *et al*, *Country House Lighting 1660-1890* (Leeds), 1992.

Gilchrist & Inglis. James Gilchrist & Brand Inglis, *Lynn Silver* (King's Lynn), 1972.

Gill. Margaret A.V. Gill, *A Directory of Newcastle Goldsmiths* (Newcastle upon Tyne), 1980.

Glanville 1987. Philippa Glanville, *Silver in England* (London), 1987.

Glanville 1990. Philippa Glanville, *Silver in Tudor and Early Stuart England: A Social History and Catalogue of the National Collection 1480-1660* (London), 1990.

Glynne. Gale Glynn, 'Some tontines commemorated on English plate', *The Silver Society Journal*, Autumn 1996, pp.445-61.

Goldsmiths' Hall 1951 I. Goldsmiths' Hall, *Catalogue of the Exhibition of the Historic Plate of the City of London* (London), 1951.

Goldsmiths' Hall 1951 II. Goldsmiths' Hall, *The Historic*

Plate of the City of London: Illustrations of some of the exhibits (London), 1951.

Goldsmiths' Hall 1952 I. Goldsmiths' Hall, *Corporation Plate of England and Wales: Catalogue of the Exhibits* (London), 1952.

Goldsmiths' Hall 1952 II. Goldsmiths' Hall, *Corporation Plate of England and Wales: Illustrations of some of the exhibits* (London), 1952.

Grimwade. Arthur G. Grimwade, *London Goldsmiths 1697-1837: Their Marks and Lives* (London), 1976.

Grimwade 1951 II. A.G. Grimwade, 'A New List of Old English Gold Plate: Part II: 1700-1750', *The Connoisseur*, August 1951, pp.10-16.

Grimwade 1951 III. A.G. Grimwade, 'A New List of Old English Gold Plate: Part III: 1750-1830', *The Connoisseur*, October 1951, pp.83-9.

Grimwade 1974. Arthur Grimwade, *Rococo Silver 1727-1765* (London), 1974.

Grimwade 1999. Arthur G. Grimwade, 'Silver Scrapings: Life at Christie's', *Goldsmiths' Review 1998/99*, pp.30-3.

Grimwade & Banister. Arthur Grimwade & Judith Banister, 'Thomas Jenkins unveiled: A leading Caroline Goldsmith', *The Connoisseur*, July 1977, pp.173-81.

Groombridge. Margaret J. Groombridge, *Guide to the Charters, Plate and Insignia of the City of Chester* (Chester), n.d. [1950].

Hackenbroch. Yvonne Hackenbroch, *English and other Silver in the Irwin Untermyer Collection* (London), 1963.

Hall. James Hall, *Dictionary of Subjects and Symbols in Art* (London), 1985.

Hanshall. J.H. Hanshall, *The History of the County Palatine of Chester* (Chester), 1823.

Harbison. Peter Harbison, Homan Potterton & Jeanne Sheehy, *Irish Art and Architecture from Prehistory to the Present* (London), 1993.

Hare. Susan Hare, ed., *Paul de Lamerie: The Work of England's Master Silversmith (1688-1751)* (London), 1990.

Harris 1979 I. B.E. Harris, ed., *The Victoria History of the County of Chester*, vol.2 (Oxford), 1979.

Harris 1979 II. Brian Harris, *Chester* (Edinburgh), 1979.

Hocking. William John Hocking, *Catalogue of the Museum of the Royal Mint*, vol.2 (London), 1910.

Hogben. Carol Hogben, *et al*, *British Art and Design 1900-1960* (London), 1984.

Holland. Margaret Holland, *The Illustrated Guide to Silver* (London), 1985.

Holme. Randle Holme III, *The Academy of Armory, or, A Storehouse of Armory and Blazon* (Chester), 1688.

Honour. Hugh Honour, 'Silver Reflections of Cathay: Part II', *The Magazine Antiques*, March 1962, pp.306-10.

Hubbard & Shippobottom. Edward Hubbard & Michael Shippobottom, *A Guide to Port Sunlight Village* (Liverpool), 1988.

Hughes 1966. Hubert Hughes, *Cheshire and its Welsh Border* (London), 1966.

Hughes 1990. Eleanor Hughes, *Silver for Collectors* (London), 1990.

Huxley. Gervas Huxley, *Victorian Duke: The Life of Hugh Lupus Grosvenor, First Duke of Westminster* (London), 1967.

Hyman. John A. Hyman, 'Skewers at Colonial Willamsburg', *The Silver Society Journal*, Autumn 1996, pp.508-13.

Impey. Oliver Impey, *Chinoiserie: The Impact of Oriental Styles on Western Art and Decoration* (London), 1977.

Jackson. Ian Pickford, ed., *Jackson's Silver & Gold Marks of England, Scotland & Ireland* (Woodbridge), 1989.

Jackson 1905. Charles James Jackson, *English Goldsmiths and their Marks*, 1st ed. (London), 1905.

Jackson 1921. Sir Charles James Jackson, *English Goldsmiths and their Marks*, 2nd ed. (London), 1921.

Jenkins & Sloan. Ian Jenkins & Kim Sloan, *Vases and Volcanoes: Sir William Hamilton and his Collection* (London), 1996.

Jenkinson. Hilary Jenkinson, 'The Great Seal of England: Deputed or Departmental Seals', *Archaeologia*, vol.85, 1936, pp.293-340.

Jervis 1983. Simon Jervis, *High Victorian Design* (Woodbridge), 1983.

Jervis 1984. Simon Jervis, *The Penguin Dictionary of Design and Designers* (Harmondsworth), 1984.

Jervis 1987. Simon Jervis, *Art and Design in Europe and America 1800-1900* (London), 1987.

Jewitt & Hope. Llewellyn Jewitt & W.H. St. John Hope, *The Corporation Plate and Insignia of Office of the Cities and Towns of England and Wales*, vol.1 (London), 1895.

Jones 1907. E. Alfred Jones, *Old English Gold Plate* (London), 1907.

Jones 1935. E. Alfred Jones, 'The Plate at Wynnstay of Sir Watkin Williams-Wynn, Bart.', *The Connoisseur*, July 1935, pp.12-17.

Jones 1981. Kenneth Crisp Jones, ed., *The Silversmiths of Birmingham and their Marks 1750-1980* (London), 1981.

Kennett. Annette M. Kennett, ed., *Georgian Chester: Aspects of Chester's History from 1660 to 1837* (Chester), 1987.

Kent. Timothy Kent, *West Country Silver Spoons and their Makers 1550-1750* (London), 1992.

Kevill-Davies. Sally Kevill-Davies, 'Sauceboat for the Gosling!', *Antique Collecting*, December 1992/January 1993, p.33.

Kremlin. Sotheby's, *English Silver Treasures from the Kremlin: A Loan Exhibition* (London), 1991.

Langley. Batty & Thomas Langley, *Gothic Architecture, Improved by Rules and Proportions* (London), 1742.

Latham. Frank A. Latham, ed., *Delamere: The History of a Cheshire Parish* (Whitchurch), 1991.

Lever. Christopher Lever, '400 Years of Chester Goldsmiths', *Country Life*, 4 July 1974, pp.40-1.

Lewis & Harrison. Marilyn Lewis & Simon Harrison, *From Moot Hall to Town Hall: 750 Years of Local Government in Chester* (Chester), n.d. [1988/9].

Lightbown. R.W. Lightbown, *Victoria and Albert Museum: Catalogue of Scandinavian and Baltic Silver* (London), 1975.

Lincoln. William A. Lincoln, *World Woods in Colour* (Hertford), 1991.

Lloyd. J.Y.W. Lloyd, *The History of the Princes, the Lords Marcher, and the Ancient Nobility of Powys Fadog*, vol.5 (London), 1885.

Lomax. James Lomax, *British Silver at Temple Newsam and Lotherton Hall: A Catalogue of the Leeds Collection* (Leeds), 1992.

McCausland. Hugh McCausland, *Snuff and Snuff-Boxes* (London), 1951.

Moore 1979. C.N. Moore, *Silver of the City of Chester* (Chester), 1979.

Moore 1982. C.N. Moore, 'The Chester Race Trophies', *Cheshire Life*, May 1982, p.58.

Moore 1984 I. C.N. Moore, *Chester Silver* (Chester), 1984.

Moore 1984 II. C.N. Moore, 'The Regional Styles and the Development of Silver Trefid Spoons', *Antique Collecting*, November 1984, pp.44-7.

Moore 1985 I. C.N. Moore, 'Collecting Liverpool Silver', *The Antique Dealer and Collectors Guide*, February 1985, pp.54-6.

Moore 1985 II. C.N. Moore, 'The Stylistic Development of English Provincial Silver Tankards 1640-1810', *Antique Collecting*, June 1985, pp.32-7.

Moore 1985 III. C.N. Moore, 'Chester Silver of the Georgian Period', *The Antique Dealer and Collectors Guide*, September 1985, pp.70-3.

Moore 1986. Charles Nicholas Moore, 'Silver from the City of Chester', *The Magazine Antiques*, June 1986, pp.1292-9.

Moore 1987. C.N. Moore, 'Cups for Many Purposes', *The Antique Dealer and Collectors Guide*, July 1987, pp.60-3.

Moore 1999. Nicholas Moore, 'Review of Maurice H. Ridgway, Church Plate of the St. Asaph Diocese', *Flintshire Historical Society Journal*, vol.35, 1999, pp.250-5.

Morgan 1852. Octavius Morgan, 'On the Assay Marks on Gold and Silver Plate', *The Archaeological Journal*, vol.9, 1852, pp.125-40.

Morgan 1853. Octavius Morgan, 'Table of the Annual Assay Office Letters', *The Archaeological Journal*, vol.10, 1853, pp.33-43.

Muller. Hannelore Muller, *The Thyssen-Bornemisza Collection: European Silver* (London), 1986.

NACF Report. *National Art-Collections Fund Report*, annual volumes until 1981.

NACF Review. *National Art-Collections Fund Review*, annual volumes from 1983.

Newman. Harold Newman, *An Illustrated Dictionary of Silverware* (London), 1987.

Oman 1957. Charles Oman, *English Church Plate 597-1830* (London), 1957.

Oman 1965. Charles Oman, *Victoria and Albert Museum: English Silversmiths' Work, Civil and Domestic: An Introduction* (London), 1965.

Oman 1967. Charles Oman, *English Domestic Silver* (London), 1967.

Oman 1970. Charles Oman, *Caroline Silver 1625-1688* (London), 1970.

Oman 1978. Charles Oman, *English Engraved Silver 1150 to 1900* (London), 1978.

Ormerod. George Ormerod, revised by Thomas Helsby, *The History of the County Palatine and the City of Chester*, three vols. (London), 1882.

Parkinson. Michael Parkinson, *Catalogue of Silver from the Assheton Bennett Collection* (Manchester), 1965.

Penzer 1971. N.M. Penzer, *Paul Storr 1771-1844 Silversmith and Goldsmith* (London), 1971.

Penzer 1974. N.M. Penzer, *The Book of the Wine-Label* (London), 1974.

Pevsner & Hubbard. Nikolaus Pevsner & Edward Hubbard, *Cheshire* (Harmondsworth), 1971.

Pickford. Ian Pickford, *Silver Flatware: English, Irish and Scottish 1660-1980* (Woodbridge), 1983.

Piranesi. Giovanni Battista Piranesi, *Vasi, candelabri, cippi, sarcofagi, tripodi, lucerne ed ornamenti antichi* (Rome), 1778.

Pond. John Pond, *The Sporting Kalendar: Containing a distinct account of what plates and matches have been run for* (London), annual volumes 1751-7.

Queen's Gallery 1988. The Queen's Gallery, *Treasures from the Royal Collection* (London), 1988.

Queen's Gallery 1991. The Queen's Gallery, *Carlton House: The Past Glories of George IV's Palace* (London), 1991.

The Racing Calendar, published annually (London): by Edward & James Weatherby, 1794-1830; by Edward &

Charles Weatherby, 1831-5; by Edward, Charles & James Weatherby, 1836-9; by Charles & James Weatherby, 1840-58.

Raffald. Elizabeth Raffald, *The Experienced English Housekeeper* (London), 1786.

Ransome-Wallis. Rosemary Ransome-Wallis, *Matthew Boulton and the Toymakers: Silver from the Birmingham Assay Office* (London), 1982.

Rhodes. Benjamin Rhodes, *A New Book of Cyphers* (London), n.d. [1723].

Richards. Raymond Richards, *Old Cheshire Churches* (Manchester), 1973.

Ridgway 1968. Maurice H. Ridgway, *Chester Goldsmiths from early times to 1726* (Altrincham), 1968 [published simultaneously as *Journal of the Chester and North Wales Architectural, Archaeological and Historic Society*, vol.53].

Ridgway 1973. Maurice H. Ridgway, *Some Chester Goldsmiths and their marks* (Chester), 1973.

Ridgway 1976. Maurice H. Ridgway, 'Chester Silver', *Antique Finder*, January 1976, pp.18-21.

Ridgway 1977. Maurice H. Ridgway, 'Church Plate of the Diocese of Chester: Part One', *Journal of the Chester Archaeological Society*, vol.60, 1977, pp.129-46.

Ridgway 1978. M.H. Ridgway, 'Church Plate of the Diocese of Chester: Part Two', *Journal of the Chester Archaeological Society*, vol.61, 1978, pp.79-95.

Ridgway 1980. M.H. Ridgway, 'The Early Plate of Chester Cathedral', *Journal of the Chester Archaeological Society*, vol.63, 1980, pp.95-108.

Ridgway 1985. Maurice H. Ridgway, *Chester Silver 1727-1837* (Chichester), 1985.

Ridgway 1989. Maurice H. Ridgway, 'Chester and Associated Towns', in Ian Pickford, ed., *Jackson's Silver & Gold Marks of England, Scotland & Ireland* (Woodbridge), 1989, pp.377-424.

Ridgway 1993 I. Maurice H. Ridgway, 'Chester Spoonmakers (6): William Mutton and J. Lindley', *The Finial*, February 1993, pp.21-4.

Ridgway 1993 II. Maurice H. Ridgway, 'Chester Assayed Silver Coffin Plates from Mold', *Archaeologia Cambrensis*, vol.142, 1993, pp.330-9.

Ridgway 1996. Maurice H. Ridgway, *Chester Silver 1837-*

1962, with special reference to the Chester Duty Books 1784-1840 (Denbigh), 1996.

Ridgway 1997. Maurice H. Ridgway, *Church Plate of the St. Asaph Diocese* (Denbigh), 1997.

Rowe 1957. Robert Rowe, *Silver in the Manchester City Art Galleries* (Manchester), 1957.

Rowe 1965. Robert Rowe, *Adam Silver 1765-1795* (London), 1965.

Rudoe. Judy Rudoe, *Decorative Arts 1850-1950: A Catalogue of the British Museum Collection* (London), 1994.

Ryskamp. Charles Ryskamp, *et al*, *Paintings from The Frick Collection* (New York), 1990.

Savage. George Savage, *Dictionary of 19th Century Antiques and later objets d'art* (London), 1978.

Schroder 1988 I. Timothy B. Schroder, *The Gilbert Collection of Gold and Silver* (Los Angeles), 1988.

Schroder 1988 II. Timothy Schroder, *The National Trust Book of English Domestic Silver 1500-1900* (London), 1988.

Schroder 1992. Timothy Schroder, 'No Finer Provincial Provenance', *Country Life*, 24/31 December 1992, pp.36-7.

Schroder 1994. Timothy Schroder, *Silver at Partridge: Recent Acquisitions* (London), 1994.

Sheehy. Jeanne Sheehy, *The Rediscovery of Ireland's Past: The Celtic Revival 1830-1930* (London), 1980.

Shrigley. Ruth Shrigley, ed., *Inspired by Design: The Arts and Crafts Collection of The Manchester Metropolitan University* (Manchester), 1994.

Shure. David S. Shure, *Hester Bateman: Queen of English Silversmiths* (London), 1959.

Simon. Jacob Simon, *The Art of the Picture Frame: Artists, Patrons and the Framing of Portraits in Britain* (London), 1996.

Simpson. Frank Simpson, *A History of the Church of St Peter in Chester* (Chester), 1909.

Snodin 1974. Michael Snodin, *English Silver Spoons* (London), 1974.

Snodin 1984. Michael Snodin, ed., *Rococo: Art and Design in Hogarth's England* (London), 1984.

Stewart-Brown. R. Stewart-Brown, 'The Charter and Horn of the Master-Forester of Wirral', *Transactions of the Historic Society of Lancashire and Cheshire*, vol.87, 1935, pp.97-112.

Tatham. Charles Heathcote Tatham, *Etchings of Ancient Ornamental Architecture drawn from the Originals in Rome and other parts of Italy during the years 1794, 1795 and 1796* (London), 1799.

Taylor 1910. Henry Taylor, 'The County Palatine of Chester: its place in history', in E. Barber & P.H. Ditchfield, eds., *Memorials of Old Cheshire* (London), 1910, pp.19-32.

Taylor 1956. Gerald Taylor, *Silver* (Harmondsworth), 1956.

Thomas. Graham A. Thomas, *Grosvenor Museum Information Sheet 4: Silver* (Chester), n.d. [1977].

Ticher. Kurt Ticher, *Irish Silver in the Rococo Period* (Shannon), 1972.

Treuherz. Julian Treuherz, ed., *Sporting Art from the Manchester City Art Galleries* (Chester), 1984.

Truman. Charles Truman, *The Glory of the Goldsmith: Magnificent Gold and Silver from the Al-Tajir Collection* (London), 1989.

Trusler. John Trusler, *The Works of William Hogarth in a Series of Engravings*, vol.2 (London), n.d. [1833].

Tushingham. J. Tushingham, *A List of Chester Races, from the Year 1758, to 1815* (Chester), n.d. [c.1815].

Van Vianen. Christian van Vianen, *Modelles Artificiels de divers vaisseaux d'argent* (The Hague), 1892 [reprint of 1650 original].

Wainwright. Clive & Jane Wainwright, 'Letter from London', *The Magazine Antiques*, May 1983, pp.976-86.

Walton 1989. Rachel Walton, *Chester Silver* (unpublished B.A. thesis, Middlesex Polytechnic), 1989.

Walton 1998. Rachel Walton, 'The Spirit of Chester Bowl', *Brilliance* [Magazine of Waltons the Jewellers (Chester) Ltd.], 1998, p.36.

Wark. Robert R. Wark, *British Silver in the Huntington Collection* (San Marino, California), 1978.

Warner. Christopher Warner, 'From members' collections: Highlights of an exhibition of sixty tumbler cups at Lotherton Hall', *The Silver Society Journal*, Autumn 1999, pp.254-5.

Wees. Beth Carver Wees, *English, Irish & Scottish Silver atthe Sterling and Francine Clark Art Institute* (New York), 1997.

Whinney. Margaret Whinney, revised by John Physick, *Sculpture in Britain 1530-1830* (London), 1988.

Wills. Geoffrey Wills, *Silver for Pleasure and Investment* (London), 1969.

Wivell. Abraham Wivell, *An Inquiry into the History, Authenticity and Characteristics of the Shakespeare Portraits* (London), 1827.

Woodward. Donald Woodward, 'The port of Chester in context 1500-1800', in Peter Carrington, ed., *'Where Deva spreads her wizard stream': Trade and the Port of Chester* (Chester), 1996, pp.61-5.

EXHIBITIONS

Chester 1951. *Festival Exhibition of Ecclesiastical and Secular Silver*, County Hall, Chester, 19 May - 29 September 1951 [catalogue by Charles Brocklehurst].

Chester 1973 I. *Exhibition of Antique Silver*, Lowe & Sons, Chester, 15 May - 14 July 1973 [no catalogue].

Chester 1973 II. *Silver on View at the Grosvenor Museum: An exhibition of silver for the Chester Festival 1973*, Grosvenor Museum, Chester, 23 June - 31 July 1973 [catalogue by Margaret Buchanan].

Chester 1979 I. *A Chester Celebration: An Exhibition of Paintings, Ceramics and Silver*, Grosvenor Museum, Chester, 23 May - 24 September 1979 [catalogue by Janet Goose].

Chester 1979 II. *Silver of the City of Chester*, Chester Town Hall, 15-29 September 1979 [booklet by C.N. Moore does not list exhibits].

Chester 1980. *Chester Assayed Silver*, Lowe & Sons, Chester, 2-15 October 1980 [no catalogue].

Chester 1982. *Richard Richardson Silver*, Mappin & Webb, Chester, 21-27 June 1982 [no catalogue].

Chester 1984. *Chester Silver: A loan exhibition of Chester hallmarked silver, with related documents and manuscripts from the Chester Goldsmiths Company, dating from the end of the 15th century to the closure of the Assay Office in 1962*,

Sotheby's, Chester, 26 July - 11 August 1984 [catalogue by C.N. Moore].

London 1952. *Corporation Plate of England and Wales*, Goldsmiths' Hall, London, 1952 [catalogue by J.F. Hayward].

London 1966. *Oar Maces of Admiralty*, National Maritime Museum, London, 1966 [catalogue].

London 1978. *Touching Gold and Silver: 500 Years of Hallmarks*, Goldsmiths' Hall, London, 7-30 November 1978 [catalogue by Susan Hare].

London 1984. *National Art Collections Fund* display, Fine Art and Antiques Fair, Olympia, London, 1-9 June 1984 [leaflet].

London BL 1989. *Particular Places: English Local History and the Victoria County History*, British Library galleries, British Museum, London, 20 April - 17 September 1989 [no catalogue].

London V&A 1989. *Object of the Month* display, Victoria and Albert Museum, London, 1-31 August 1989 [no catalogue].

Manchester 1983. *Eighty Years On: Treasures from Galleries in the North-West acquired with the help of the NACF 1903-1983*, Manchester City Art Gallery, 15 April - 28 May 1983 [catalogue].

CONCORDANCE
OF ACCESSION AND CATALOGUE NUMBERS

Accession No.	Catalogue No.
1952.103	6
1962.77	148
1962.78.1	132
1962.78.2	135
1963.61	110
1970.44	130
1970.46.1	133
1970.46.2	145
1970.47	141
1970.48.1	140
1970.48.2	144
1970.104	143
1970.105	124
1970.106	138
1970.107	127
1970.108	146
1970.109	129
1970.110	125
1970.111	128
1970.112	147
1970.114	137
1971.99.3	142
1971.99.4	136
1971.99.8	139
1972.163	8
1973.25	33
1974.77	93
1974.131	65
1975.92	85
1977.15	7
1977.165	134
1978.91	15
1978.96	95
1979.82	24
1979.83	47
1979.96	10
1980.33.2-6	131
1980.33.7,8	35
1980.33.9	126
1980.48	22
1980.58	67
1980.75	79
1980.82	49
1980.95	29
1981.25.1	96
1981.25.2	97
1981.33	62
1981.36	75
1981.37	70
1981.38	57
1981.89	18
1981.102	66
1982.55	63
1982.75.1,2	64
1982.75.3	54
1982.76	28
1982.88	38
1982.89	83
1982.90	117
1982.91	114
1982.92	113
1982.93	122
1982.94	119
1982.95	120
1982.96	123
1982.97	121
1982.98	111
1982.99	116
1982.100	115
1982.101	118
1982.102	112
1983.48	41
1983.63	60
1983.71	91
1983.77	34
1983.78	80
1984.1	89
1984.2	106
1984.15	109
1984.23	5
1984.24	32
1984.25	19
1984.26	20
1984.27	14
1984.28	149
1984.51	58
1984.52	51
1984.53	81
1984.54	73
1985.82	90
1985.83	92
1985.100	39
1985.101	31
1985.102	21
1985.125	88
1985.126	36
1986.43	107
1986.113	3
1986.167	82
1986.170	27
1987.41	25
1987.44	59
1988.29	101
1988.30	102
1988.31	11
1988.32	103
1988.35	1
1988.36	98
1988.37	99
1988.38	12
1988.39	13
1988.40	100
1988.44	16
1988.45	17
1988.46	23
1988.47	30
1988.48	45
1988.49	44
1988.50	37
1988.51	40
1988.52	42
1988.53	43
1988.54	84
1988.55	76
1988.56	52
1988.57	77
1988.58	50
1988.59	55
1988.60	56
1988.61	61
1988.62	69
1988.63	68
1988.64	71
1988.65	72
1989.127	26
1990.5	53
1991.98	48
1991.99	86
1991.233	87
1992.33	74
1994.19	9
1994.23	78
1995.86	2
1995.87	104
1995.88	105
1995.89	46
1996.550	4
1997.65	108
1998.15	94

INDEX OF GOLDSMITHS

Numbers refer to catalogue entries

INDEX OF OBJECT TYPES

Numbers refer to catalogue entries

INDEX OF PROVENANCE

Owners, dealers, auction houses and purchase funds

Numbers refer to catalogue entries